BORIS SUCHKOV

A HISTORY OF REALISM

PROGRESS   PUBLISHERS
MOSCOW

Translated from the Russian

Designed by G. Dauman

Б. СУЧКОВ.

ИСТОРИЧЕСКИЕ СУДЬБЫ РЕАЛИЗМА

На английском языке

First printing 1973

Printed in the Union of Soviet Socialist Republics

CONTENTS

REALISM AND REALITY

The creative process in art, that most important of man's intellectual activities, involves thinking in terms of images. It is in the very nature of our perception that these images are engendered in the artist's mind by the outside world.

Even where the artist contrives something which he feels to be beyond the pale of verisimilitude, he is really doing no more than reorganising and reproducing in a new form the component parts of that whole which we call reality.

When Hieronymus Bosch painted his *Temptation of St. Anthony*, in depicting the monsters pouring up from hell to assail the ascetic in his cell he made use of the materials which reality offered in such abundance. Despite their weird appearance, the devils and fiends testing the patience and faith of the hermit were in fact made of perfectly normal stuff. Bosch merely combined in them the visible elements of natural beings and man-made things which he saw around him every day. He simply altered their natural proportions, put parts of living organisms in the strangest combinations, joining everyday objects like pots and pans, knives and helmets, to insects' tails and feelers, giving animals spiders' and grasshoppers' bodies, and clothed these monsters in armour, endowing these creations of his wild fancy with human emotions, making fiends from hell behave like malicious practical jokers.

Thus, while his pictures at first strike one as being apparently at variance with everyday experience, they in fact fit perfectly naturally into the system of everyday values and concepts of his age.

Callot's fantastic pictures or Goya's *Caprichos*, works which the artist consciously and deliberately freed from a superficial resemblance to reality, were nonetheless based on elements of intellectual, emotional and visual impressions objectively engendered by reality.

Even when primitive man tried to give the fruit of his imagination the attributes of godliness and express his understanding and concept of a deity with the means of art, he could not, in clothing the creation of his fantasy in flesh, go beyond the limits of this earth. The attentive gaze will recognise proto-elements of real concepts of the world reflected in the human mind in the idols and totems of primitive peoples, the monstrous, cruel gods of bygone civilisations, and ritual symbols and masks. Moreover, even such an "abstract" form of art as ornament is based on a composition of geometric shapes reflecting the objective relationship of things, or conventionalised animals and plants, or a combination of both.

It is interesting to note that the theoreticians of abstract art Winthrop Sargeant, Andrew C. Ritchie and Reginald H. Wilenski, and the father of abstract painting Vassili Kandinsky before them, tried to justify this trend in modern art by maintaining that the abstract artist's canvas reflects the latest discoveries in nuclear physics, thereby penetrating the very essence of the universe. Thus, these convinced opponents of reality were nonetheless forced to invoke reality in support of their aesthetic theories, for nuclear physics and transformation of energy are every bit as real as trees and fruit, mountains and buildings, people and flowers, and everything else that has always been depicted by genuine painters, on whom the champions of abstract art pour such vehement scorn, accusing them of blind empiricism. This appeal to the microcosm, to reality which is invisible but perceptible to the human mind, is of course pure humbug. There is no connection at all between an arbitrary application of colour purporting to represent the processes going on in the world of elementary particles, and genuine reality. But the nature of the arguments used by the supporters of abstract art to justify their theories is worth noting: struggling against reality, they capitulate to it.

Art is not concerned purely with representing apparent reality. A work of art is not intended to be taken as a *likeness* of reality. Art's creations differ greatly from objects of the external world, for as well as absorbing impressions and concepts deriving from reality, it reflects too man's inner world, his experience, his personality and his attitude to the world around him. As a special form of spiritual and intellectual activity, and a powerful expression of man's creative powers, art, while ultimately deriving from reality, is to a certain extent independent of it. Goethe had the tremendous perspicacity to point out this rich and complex dialectical relationship between reality and art. Polemicising with Diderot, who reduced the purpose of art to straightforward representation of natural phenomena, Goethe wrote:

"Art does not try to compete with nature in all its breadth and depth, but keeps on the surface of natural phenomena. Nevertheless, art has its own depth, its own strength. It captures the supreme aspects of these superficial phenomena, disclosing what is regular in them—the rational perfection of proportions, the acme of beauty, the virtue of meaning and noble passions.

"We see nature as acting on its own account; the artist acts as a man—on man's account. From what nature offers us, we take into our lives only a small amount, that which is worth desiring, and gives pleasure; what the artist offers man should be entirely accessible and pleasing to the senses, should all give pleasure and have an appeasing effect, should all give food for the spirit, should all educate and ennoble; and the artist is grateful to nature that produced him, and in this way brings back to her a kind of second nature, nature born of the feelings and thoughts, nature perfected by man.

"But if all is to be thus, the genius, the artist by vocation, should act according to laws and rules prescribed by nature herself, laws that do not contradict her, that represent his greatest wealth, for it is with their help that he learns to master and employ both the wealth of his talent and the great riches of nature."[1]

Reality is the basis of any image. This is natural, for art is a kind of special language mankind has been talking since ancient times, and just as a word cannot exist without a corresponding concept, so real art cannot deprive an image of its content, that is, of its relationship to what exists objectively, either in the realm of nature or in the realm of human thought and feeling, which is as much a part of reality as the material world.

Art has been man's faithful companion throughout history, developing and improving together with the development and improvement of the human mind. This is why art could never be an amusement to fill the hours of idleness, a source of carefree pleasure, or a means of satisfying purely aesthetic demands. The dual function of art —cognitive and aesthetic, the two being united and inseparable—was there right from the start, from the moment art emerged.

The earliest extant examples of cave paintings, hunting scenes executed with remarkable accuracy and expression, combined both these aspects of art. In creating these works, the primitive artists must have abandoned themselves to the joyous power and enchantment of line and colour, transferring onto the hard unyielding granite the images and impressions overflowing their souls. Presumably these unknown artists were not the only ones who were moved by their creations. We can assume that their hairy fellow-tribesmen also derived pleasure from the sparkle of art in the prehistoric tribal gloom. The cave paintings were also a part of a magic ritual connected with work, sympathetic magic—a plea to the dark, threatening forces of earth and sky that influenced the life of the tribe. George Thomson, a modern expert on prehistoric culture, writes: "The Australians are in the habit of decorating rocks and caves with figures of men and animals. . . .

"The human figures are of both sexes, the females with exaggerated sex marks. The animals and plants, so far as

---

[1] Johann Wolfgang von Goethe, "Diderots Versuch über die Malerei" in Sämmtliche Werke, Bd. 34, Leipzig, S. 100-01.

they have been identified, are all edible species—kangaroos, lizards, nalgo fruits. . . .

"For the interpretation of these designs we can appeal to the natives themselves, who still use them for ceremonial purposes. At the opening of the breeding season the pictures are repainted or touched up in order to bring rain or to propagate the species represented. Abundance of kangaroos and nalgo fruits is thus ensured, and women are made prolific."[1] Referring to a number of features common to Bushman art and the upper paleolithic cave paintings in France and Spain, Thomson goes on to say: "The resemblance is so close that some authorities regard them as the work of the same people. . . . All archaeologists are now agreed that the primary intention of these paintings was magical."[2] On the subject of the genesis of art he makes the following emphatic statement: "Art grows out of ritual. Stated in general terms, that is a proposition no serious student would deny."[3]

Thus, at the dawn of history, when the human mind was first becoming aware of artistic images, we find social experience having a say in the matter. The primitive artist's desire to express his impressions of life goes hand in hand with an attempt to understand and explain life.

This invaluable feature of art, present from the very start, is what makes art a great chronicle, a history of the human race told in words, marble or paint by countless volunteer historians, who captured the events and the spirit of bygone civilisations far more fully than the old sheets of parchment that bear the laws and instructions of rulers, or the silent remains of material culture which the archaeologists and historiographers interpret for us.

We can still understand the thoughts and feelings of the citizens of a Greek polis or of Rome, thanks to Aeschylus' tragedies, Aristophanes' merciless satire, and Catullus' moving lyrics. The feather grass steppes of the Don country have flowered and withered countless times, and the bones of Russians, Polovtsi and Khazars have long since

---

[1] George Thomson, *Studies in Ancient Greek Society. The Prehistoric Aegean*, London, 1954, pp. 53-54.
[2] Ibid., pp. 54-55.
[3] Ibid., p. 463.

turned to dust, yet the voices of the Russian warriors who scooped up the clear waters of the Don in their helmets still ring in our hearts, preserved for posterity by the unknown author of *The Lay of Igor's Host*. The violent political passions the Italian towns seethed with at the time when medieval Europe has discovered the timeless cultural heritage of a small people who had lived on the southern tip of the Balkan peninsula are brought to us by the *terza rima* of Dante's *Divine Comedy*, and Michelangelo's *Last Judgement*.

Throughout their existence, art and literature have registered with the sensitivity of a barometer all the changes in the course of mankind's stormy development. The collapse of the humanistic ideals of the Renaissance, which were trampled underfoot with the emergence of bourgeois social relations, was reflected in Shakespeare's later tragedies, in the wise sorrow of *Don Quixote*, and the gnomic philosophy of Calderon's tragedy *La Vida Es Sueño*, which sounded the death knell for the vital, optimistic world of Renaissance culture. Swift's black satire and the tragic motives that burst into the bright ethereal element of Mozart's symphonies are like a prelude to the nineteenth century, that "age of iron" with its greatly intensified social contradictions.

The picture of the world that works of art and literature present is not a slavish copy of reality, and has retained the colours and smells of the world for the simple reason that art has at all times dealt with the essential aspects of nature and human life. Every genuine work of art must have a message; this is the very foundation and vital element for its existence. Art cannot help but submit to the great discipline of reality, but this does not mean that art has always and at all times been realist.

Realism as a creative method is an historical phenomenon that arose at a certain stage in human intellectual development, at the time when people began to feel pressing need to understand the nature and direction of social development, when people began to realise, at first vaguely, then more clearly, that human actions and feelings do not derive from wild passions or a divine design, but are determined by real, or more precisely, material causes.

Tre realist method arose in art and literature when the members of society were faced with the task of apprehending those hidden underlying forces which determine the working of the mechanism of social relations.

There are traits of reality in the writings of the Ancients, in Gothic, Baroque and Rococo art, or in the works of the classicist writers, but the study of the life of society and individuals in all their complex relationships only came with realism. The works of the early realists already give us a true picture of the life of society, of the interests and demands that occupied the minds of people of various social groups and classes in the past. They show us the development of man's social awareness, and how people living in a society based on private ownership came into conflict with that anti-human social order. Between them, the realist writers produced an epic of the modern age. In many cases unwittingly, merely by their sober objective portrayal of the life they saw, they condemned the evils of the irrational civilisation of property owners.

Realism began its road in the realm of everyday life. Depiction of the life man sees around him is to be found in the facetiae, the fabliaux and the *Schwänke*, and later in the picaresque novel, born of the ferment of popular uprisings, peasant rebellions and bloody religious wars in the sixteenth and seventeenth centuries. However, this was not realism in the strict sense of the word, but rather a prelude to realism.

But theoretical philosophic thought too, wrestling with problems of existence on the threshold of the modern age, and struggling to free itself of the spiritual concepts that theology and scholasticism had deeply implanted in people's minds, was only beginning to approach an understanding of the world as a material entity.

Descartes with his idea of the indivisibility of existence and thought, and Francis Bacon, who drew attention to the importance of experience in taking cognizance of the world, revolutionised scientific thought, opening the way for its penetration into the nature of things.

Despite the originality and shrewdness of their conjectures, they were still largely dependent on the level scientific thought had reached in their age. The transcendental dualism and mechanistic approach inherent in his views of the living world prevented Descartes from producing a dialectical picture of reality. Yet by raising the question of the indivisibility of existence and thought he encouraged the investigation of their relationship. His elder contemporary Bacon had the genius to grasp the chief requirement of the thought of the new age—the need for *analytic* investigation of reality.

In *Letters on the Study of Nature*, Alexander Herzen wrote that the basic principle of Bacon's philosophy is that "he starts from the particular, from experiment, from the observation of phenomena and arrives at a generalisation, at a collation of all that has been thus acquired. For Bacon experience is not a passive perception of the external world with its attending circumstances. Quite the contrary, it is the conscious interaction of thought and things external, their joint activity, which, while developing, Bacon keeps in curb, neither allowing thought to make conclusions to which it is not yet entitled, nor allowing experience to remain a mechanical accumulation of facts 'undigested by thought'. The greater and richer the sum total of observations, the more inalienable is the right to deduce from them the general rules by means of induction. But as he discovers them Bacon, ever doubting and cautious, demands another plunge into the stream of phenomena, in search of a generalisation or a qualification.

"Before Bacon, experiment was an accident, it was used as a basis even more rarely than was tradition, let alone intellectual speculation. Bacon turned it into an essential, primary factor of knowledge, which subsequently accompanied the entire development of knowledge, which presupposed constant verification, and, by its irrefutable precision and its concrete universality, acted as a curb on the inclination of abstract minds to rise into the rarefied atmosphere of metaphysical generalities. Bacon believed as much in the mind as in nature but his confidence was greatest when they were at one because he foresaw their unity. He demanded that the mind, leaning on experience, should progress hand in hand with nature, that nature should guide the mind as its pupil until it was in a condition to lead nature towards complete elucidation in thought.

"That was new, extremely new and grand...."[1]

Investigation of the external world took many courses. Philosophy absorbed more and more of the knowledge accumulated by the natural sciences, which were gradually preparing for the great Industrial Revolution. Meanwhile, as bourgeois relations developed and class antagonisms became more acute, the tendency towards analysis of reality grew stronger in art and literature too, and this naturally above all meant analysis of the human environment.

Analysis, one of the essential features of realism, began to develop in the art of the Renaissance, which saw so many various styles, with the Gothic forms existing side by side with the genre novel and anecdote, represented by the works of Poggio Bracciolini and Masuccio di Salerno, where the medieval *conte de geste* was transformed into the witty comic verse of Pulci or the heroic gallantry of Ariosto's *Orlando Furioso*, where the subjectivism of the neo-Platonists, mannerism and the baroque spirit gradually replaced the pure poetic tradition descending from Petrarch.

The analytic approach is already present in the works of the major writers of the Renaissance period—Rabelais, Cervantes and Shakespeare. The Rabelaisan novel, which had close affinities with folk literature and myth and disregards external, rationalistic logic in the narration, solved an important new aesthetic problem of the time. The characters in *Gargantua and Pantagruel*, despite all exaggeration and extraordinary situations, were inherently true to life. The novel undoubtedly contains the seeds of the analytic approach, deeply planted in a bed of mythology, it is true, but nonetheless sufficient to enable the writer to capture the social features of the papacy, scholasticism, feudal statecraft and morality and, most important of all, features of the new man, providing an early glimpse of the bourgeois in the making. One of the

---

[1] A. Herzen, *Selected Philosophical Works*, Moscow, 1956, pp. 265-66.

main characters, Panurge, who said he knew many ways of getting rich, among which the most honest was daylight robbery, for all his charm represents a destructive element, and personifies the new social forces that were gradually maturing within the feudal system. The Renaissance humanist ideal of utopia, the abbey of Thelema, is quite incompatible with panurgianism, with real human relations, which were not developing as Rabelais and other humanists hoped. The presence of this conflict in the novel shows that Rabelais sensed the fundamental contradiction in social life, without being aware of either its true nature or its scale. However, the very fact that he revealed this conflict was an important step towards realism.

Fifty years later this same conflict was to underlie *Don Quixote*, a work which absorbed elements from many different genres of the day, from galant-pastoral prose and ironically revalued poetics of the *conte de geste* to the tale of manners (*mœurs*). Despite the fact that during his wanderings over many a stony, sun-baked road, Don Quixote meets a whole host of people from practically every level of society, and his excursions take him into country inns and duke's palaces, the novel does not give a complete picture of Spain at that time. As regards the details it gives us of everyday life and morals, it is of considerably less interest than the anonymous work on the travels of the roguish Lazarillo de Tormes. Yet it towers above the literature of the time by virtue of its literary merits and universality, its conflict reflecting the tragic gap between man's noble aspirations for goodness and justice and life as it really is.

The analytic tendency is more manifest in Cervantes' novel than in Rabelais', although convention and the fantastic element still play a big role in it. Cervantes' analysis of society is much more accurate than that of his predecessor. He analyses human relations more fully, and penetrates more deeply into root causes of the discrepancy between humanist ideals and reality. This is because in examining the essence of the contradictions of his age he resorted to the wisdom of the people, poeticised in the person of Sancho Panza. If Rabelais sincerely believed that harmony could be achieved in life and Thelema's utopia could be attained the wisdom of *Don Quixote* lies elsewhere, in the way Cervantes, while glorifying good, destroys the illusion of its triumph being possible in existing conditions.

At the dawn of the modern age people had already acquired considerable experience of life in society based on private ownership. The feudal lords who oppressed the serfs had themselves bowed to absolute monarchy. The wealth collected in the royal treasuries was slowly but surely drained into the coffers of the bankers and usurers.

The Fuggers had no less influence in state affairs than many a crowned head of Europe, and the bourgeoisie waged a fierce, relentless struggle with the nobility for a place in the sun. Crowds of adventurers set out across the wide, unchartered oceans in search of El Dorado, for gold had become the measure of virtue and order, freedom and happiness. As Shakespeare wrote in "Timon of Athens":

> Gold? yellow, glittering, precious gold? ...
> Thus much of this will make black, white; foul, fair;
> Wrong, right; base, noble; old, young; valiant, coward. ...

Within the moss-grown walls of the towns, where craftsmen still produced works of exquisite beauty, the low, stuffy buildings of the manufactories sprang up, crowding out their workshops. Material inequality divided people. Egoistic passions and ideas, the thirst for wealth became part of their flesh and blood, the determinant factor of their social psychology.

The collapse of patriarchal morals and their adaptation to the new historical conditions accompanied the strengthening of those organic, permanent features of private ownership society which derived from its class structure. Michelangelo, in words of great power expressed the mood of the foremost thinkers of the age, who sensed the eventual triumph of the bourgeois order.

> Oh! In this evil, shameful age, to live not
> Nor to feel is a most enviable lot,
> To sleep 't were best, and to be like unto a stone.

Just as science was bringing mankind greater knowledge of the laws of nature, so nascent realist art and literature, by investigating man's spiritual and social life, his actions, thoughts and feelings, was beginning to shed light on the nature of historical progress. Shakespeare's multi-level depiction of life was based on analysis of the real essence of social relations. With Shakespeare the same conflict that is central to the works of Rabelais and Cervantes lost its conventional and fantastic colouring and acquired a concrete historical form, without, however, losing its universality in the process, for Shakespeare was a thinker and artist of genius who generalised the essential and permanent features of the social outlook of people in private ownership society. This is indeed the main reason why his works have stood the test of time.

However, even Shakespeare's view of the world is not entirely free of mystical, fantastic concepts. Deep as he penetrated the human soul, Shakespeare nonetheless subscribed to many of the illusions prevalent in his day and age. His art is syncretic, with realistic and non-realistic elements interwoven. But dominant with him are a realistic portrayal of characters and a truthful, authentic depiction of the environment that engenders the moral conflicts which beset his heroes and, most important of all, a realistic approach to the relationship between man and society. The tragic situations in which his heroes find themselves owe nothing to fatalism or irrational predetermination: they are always determined by material causes and first and foremost by the conditions of life itself. The fate of Romeo and Juliet, Hamlet's spiritual drama, Timon's discord with the world, Lear's or Othello's loss of faith in mankind, are all the result of objective contradictions in life itself. Life is the source of the tragedy.

In describing his heroes' sufferings and inner emotional conflicts and analysing their thoughts and passions, Shakespeare saw through it all the free play of material interests, perverting people's natures and shattering the humanist belief that the chaos of life could be brought to a state of harmony. Michelangelo's bitter invective against his age was undoubtedly something Shakespeare understood only too well. But Shakespeare did not simply understand the drama of the time which was so "out of joint": by going to the very wellsprings of human feelings, thoughts and actions, he showed that the absence of harmony derived from the structure of society itself. If his heart went out to Prospero, in his mind he understood only too well that Shylock could quite possibly be the man of the future. In order to portray society as a theatre of war between conflicting material interests, Shakespeare had to initiate an analytic study of society, which he did, thereby laying the cornerstone of realism.

After Shakespeare the tendency towards analytic study of social life gradually gained ground in art and literature, despite the fact that there were whole periods where other, non-realistic, trends held the field—baroque, mannerism and classicism. This tendency corresponded to the spirit of the times. When John Locke proved that there are no inborn ideas in the human mind, received from some external, superior power, he forced social thought to investigate man's environment, which is the original motive force determining his way of thinking and conditioning his actions. Locke saw man's environment first and foremost as the sphere of his social practice, which it was essential that he should know, since otherwise he would be powerless in the face of unknown forces influencing his life. Art's investigation of human activity in the broadest sense finally resulted in realism acquiring clear, distinctive features and emerging as a creative method.

In the eighteenth century, in the period leading up to the French Revolution, which brought about the final collapse of the economic and ideological structure of feudalism, realism took a great step forward, from the depiction of everyday life and manners to depiction of social existence.

The works of the early realist writers, great and small— writers like Richardson, Defoe, Smollett, Fielding, Swift Steele, Diderot, Goethe, Lessing, Mercier and Marivaux, and many, many others—enable us to determine the essential characteristic feature of the new method, the fundamental distinction between it and all other literary movements.

The essence of realism was *social analysis*, the study and depiction of the life of man in society, of social relations, the relationship between the individual and society, and the structure of society itself.

Realism took the content of all art and literature— depiction of the world and human thoughts and feelings— and made it a principle, thereby rising above the flat copying of reality and subjective presentation of human nature as a playground of unbridled passions. Realism does not arbitrarily isolate man from the social environment in which he lives and acts, but instead sets out to perceive and portray the dialectic of social relationships with their real contradictions. Just as spectral analysis enables the physicist to discover the secrets of the movement of matter, so social analysis, the essence of realism, enables the writer or artist to discern life's essential features and approach an understanding of its laws. The more closely the realist scrutinises reality and investigates the connections between the events his work describes, the more full-blooded and convincing his reproduction of reality is, for he has not only perceived it emotionally, but has interpreted it and generalised it as well.

The realist writer discerns the general pattern of the movements and counter-movements of various social forces behind individual events and phenomena. Thus realism depends on the writer's cognition of reality. As Schiller once put it: "In order to seize the fleeting phenomenon, one must chain it with the bonds of a law, dismember the beautiful body into concepts and preserve its living spirit in the spare verbal framework." The intellectual element that permeates realist works requires that the writer has a definite unequivocal view of life, for generalisation of life and people as they really are is impossible if the writer offers a surrogate for reality or treats the sense and substance of the events and phenomena he is examining in an arbitrary, subjective manner. If the social analysis of the environment in which the characters act is to be realistic, the writer must see and portray reality in its determinant, typical, manifestations, which are objectively present in the sphere of human social relations, refracted through the prism of individual characterisations. Engels insisted that this was a major requirement of the realist method.

The realist principle of typification involves the tracing of the causality that exists in the world of social phenomena. Since it is human life and the life of society that form the subject matter of a work, the hero's inner world, and the sum of his individual traits which we call character are examined and described by the realist writer as the product of numerous, but typical circumstances, which are in a causal relationship with the personal destiny of the hero. Thus, the typical character is a kind of derivative of social forces. The typical character of the hero accumulates and combines the main determinant features of the environment of which he is a product, and it is through him and his personal fortunes that the features of that environment are revealed.

We do not find this typification of characters in non-realist works. Thus, Racine, a master of character portrayal, was a classicist, like Molière, in his aesthetic views and creative method. But Molière's classicism had strong connections with the popular element, and his characters have concrete historical features explained by a certain degree of social analysis. His characters are exaggerated almost to the point of caricature and lack the depth to be fully realistic. They are one-sided, dominated by a single passion—for example, avarice in the case of Harpagon, and hypocrisy in the case of Tartuffe. These characters are one-sided because Molière was guided by the rationalist aesthetics and philosophy which underlay classicism. Nevertheless, his characters, which have since become proverbial, have something that Racine's characters lack. This "something" is the result of a definite attempt to comprehend such universal qualities as avarice and hypocrisy in the context of the contemporary social scene. That is why Molière, although a classicist, is to be regarded as a precursor of realism in modern French literature.

The student of Port-Royal, on the other hand, concentrated on analysing human feelings and passions. Neither Phèdra nor Hermione, Roxana, Iphigenie, or indeed any other of Racine's characters, rich and full as they are, become types. His men and women are detached and isolated from society, from the rough, cruel life of French society in the period of absolutism. In the words of the eminent Soviet literary historian V. Grib "Molière's works reflected the major conflicts and problems of the seventeenth century. Corneille and Racine grasped the psychological results of the great social problems of their age. From Racine it is impossible to tell what these problems were in the actual historical reality, or what was the real stuff of life that went into the making of his theatre."[1] Naturally the characters in Racine's tragedies, and the passions that torment their souls were the product of his age. But in Racine's portrayal their feelings seem somehow purified, ennobled, and to a large extent abstracted from life. They are purged of the authentic stuff of life, and thus, despite the verisimilitude of characters and events, his plays are essentially non-realist.

Racine's plays are literary masterpieces. Keeping within the bounds of classicism and making good use of the means it put at his disposal, Racine created works of great inner harmony and beauty, which depict human relationships ruled by passions, and the contradictions and conflicts of the moral world of the individual. There is nothing irregular about this, for aesthetic effect can be produced in literature by a variety of means, which is the secret of its capacity to develop, and of the simultaneous existence of various trends and movements, each with different aesthetic principles, different ideological and aesthetic approaches to the perception and description of reality.

The existence side by side of various trends and movements naturally results in antagonism and struggle between them, and, of course, in many cases, mutual influence. Behind the diversity of aesthetic principles underlying various literary movements (and often within the framework of a given movement) lies the dialectic of social contradictions, the diversity of social aspirations finding their aesthetic expression in art. The history of art and literature is by no means a calm idyll: there is a fierce clash of tastes, views and aesthetic concepts running throughout its course.

---

[1] V. Grib, *Selected Works*, Russ. ed., Goslitizdat, Moscow, 1958, p. 357.

Laying the foundations of realist aesthetics, which rejects both naturalist copying of reality and abstract generalisations of phenomena of life, Lessing made great efforts in both his *Laocoon* and *Die Hamburgische Dramaturgie* to prove that the content and form of classicist works were lifeless, that the passions were presented in a stilted manner, that the style was rhetorical, and the social ideals were unproductive.

"Racine speaks the language of the feelings. Of course, if we accept that proposition then there is nothing too elevated for him. But I don't know where and when feelings speak in such a language. This is a second-hand portrayal of feelings, but never or only very rarely vital, immediate, uncoloured movements of the spirit, seeking for words and finding them."[1] Thus, Herder defended the principles of realist art. And despite their sharply polemical nature these words of the great democrat and thinker are based on weighty historical reasons and not subjective bias.

The romanticists of the early nineteenth century, although making a tremendous contribution to world literature, did not create a single typical character. In Byron's poems with their violent social protest, the hero is an embodiment of the writer's emotions and political views rather than a character in the real sense of the word, that is in his own right. Typical features in the hero's character only begin to emerge with Beppo, that is, in the hero of the poem that marked Byron's transition from romanticism to realism.

Neither the French nor the German romanticists produced anything comparable to the whole gallery of typical characters we find in the works of the realist writers, whose epic novels contain a deep and penetrating analysis of the social milieu, of the typical conditions that determine their heroes' fortunes. However, the romanticists did perceive and present certain features and contradictions of bourgeois society of which the realist writers were not immediately aware. Without the contribution of the

---

[1] J. Herder, "Shakespeare", in: *Von deutscher Art und Kunst*, Hamburg, 1773, S. 73-74.

romanticists before them, the realists would never have been able to make such advances in the investigation of the living history of their age.

While realism as a distinct creative method that made possible analysis of social environment and the causal relationships present there made for an objective portrayal of reality, each realist writer had his own highly individual view of the world. His view of events and his understanding of life and history reflect his attitude to the contemporary social struggle in which he inevitably participates.

A work that portrays reality is bound to reflect too the writer's personal outlook, and the writer is never an impartial chronicler of his time but always champions the ideas which in his opinion embody the wisdom of his age. Naturally, the writer's subjective understanding of history by no means always corresponds to its objective substance.

However, by investigating the development of ever-changing reality and analysing social relationships, the realist writers produced an authentic picture of contemporary personal and social life, since the underlying principle of the realist method, active cognition, brought important new achievements. The realists were able to portray the essential conflicts of their age which conditioned the inner world of their heroes, their way of thinking and behaving, and to see the sources of social evil that were having such a destructive effect on the human personality. Hence the humanistic perception of reality characteristic of the realists who made a social analysis of life in their time in accordance with an individual philosophy of life.

This distinctive feature of pre-socialist realism was already apparent in the earlier stages of the emergence of the method in the period of the French and English bourgeois revolutions.

The banner of the eighteenth century was bourgeois progress, which was out to destroy the moral and economic structure of the feudal system. The main historical task of the age was the transformation of society. The ideas of civic liberty were blowing in the wind, and they were great ideas, heralding a new stage in the development of human society.

Until the nascent bourgeois society had revealed its contradictions, it was hailed by philosophers and writers connected with the democratic movement of the age as an ideal and perfect form of civilisation, assuring harmony of individual interests. The idea of free or "natural" man came to the fore, man independent of the absolutist morality and the hierarchical and seigniorial concept of duty towards feudal power, towards the political and moral props of the moribund feudal order.

"Natural" man was free from the dogmas of absolutism propagated by classicism. He was regarded by the ideologists of the third estate as being naturally endowed with such new virtues as honesty, enterprise, and persistence. They were considered his inner essence and not introduced from outside, not, that is, implanted in him by the ethics of feudalism.

Fielding's boisterous heroes, with their tremendous *joie de vivre*, and the sober, practical Robinson Crusoe, were highly charged with historical optimism. Tom Jones behaves as his nature dictates, and if his nature sometimes lets him down, causing him to behave thoughtlessly or wrongly on occasion, no doubt is cast on his intrinsic virtue: he is simply revealing human nature as it is.

When Robinson Crusoe is left alone to battle with the elements and creates a whole civilisation on his island— helped, to be sure, by the previous collective experience of mankind—his essential "natural" self remains intact and emerges triumphant from the hardest trials.

With their active, independent characters possessed of tremendous drive and tenacity, the early realists reflected in their works the chief feature of their age—the emergence of a new man, fundamentally different from the refined hero of classicism. The creation of the hero of the new age was a great triumph of realism, a triumph indeed that only the realists could have achieved, concerned as they were with the investigation and analysis of social environment.

However, while the early realists achieved undeniable successes in the portrayal of new characters, their depiction of environment was in many ways empirical. They did not spiritualise the surrounding world, which for them was not the independent aesthetic object it is for modern realism. Their prose was precise and businesslike, and they often presented situations, without subtle shades and details. Robinson Crusoe's tale of life on his island is more a sober factual account of a business trip than a literary description of the colourful world. This sober, factual, businesslike approach also characterised the prose of Smollett and Swift, and in the case of the latter became an original stylistic device, perfectly in accord with the aesthetic tastes of the time.

Empiricism is the most significant feature of the early realist descriptions of environment. It is to be seen also in the presentation of the psychology of the heroes, who are revealed through their actions rather than in the sphere of the innermost workings of their minds and hearts. The reader was expected to divine the hero's inner life from his actions, for it was not so much personal as universal traits that were stressed in the character's psychology. The characters' spiritual life had not yet been submitted to deep, let alone many-sided, analysis in the realist prose of the eighteenth century. This sphere of personal life was not to be investigated until the nineteenth century.

In early realism empiricism in the portrayal of reality went hand in hand with a pronounced tendency to idealise the hero. This at first sight rather strange contradiction arose from the concept of freedom upheld by realism, which was based on Enlightenment philosophy and ethics.

Rousseau's words "Man is born free, yet everywhere he is in chains" rang out as a tocsin in the middle of the century. This powerful formula proclaiming freedom to be the natural right of natural man expressed the very essence of the age, and was born of the revolutionary ferment sweeping Europe on the eve of the French Revolution. It demanded emancipation from the suffocating fundamental spiritual principles of feudalism that were bringing people so much misery, and recognised the need to change the structure of society. The ideologists of the third estate did not regard the practical aspect of the matter as presenting much of a problem. It all seemed perfectly simple: free man from his chains and he would become for ever more the free citizen of a harmonious society, since considered from the point of view of abstract law all men were equal at birth.

In actual fact, however, man was obviously not free from birth, or indeed even before his birth. Rousseau overlooked the simple fact that the infant letting out its first cry in a lowly peasant hovel was not free since he inevitably inherited not only his parents' appearance but also their material condition. The child born in the nobleman's castle or in the house of a respectable merchant was incomparably freer from the start.

Man was not born free, since the society in which he lived and which had existed before him preserved material inequality and therefore could not possess the quality of genuine freedom.

The bourgeoisie sought *its own* freedom for *itself*, and when it finally won it, defined it in the codes which became the holy of holies of bourgeois democracy. Article Six of the French Constitution of 1793 produced by the bourgeois revolution gave a classical definition of freedom as understood by the third estate that had acquired power. "Freedom is the right of man to do anything which does not prejudice the rights of another." In Article Sixteen this moralising thesis received unambiguous sociological substantiation. "Natural" man was allowed to "use and dispose of his possessions and income as he thought fit". Thus, the freedom of man to do whatever was not prejudicial to the interests of another, the ethical ideal so triumphantly proclaimed in the Convention, legalised an illusory freedom, for it affirmed the inviolability of the principle of private property, the fundamental principle of a society based on exploitation. In this way the man was in fact standing aloof from society, and by implication gaining the right to wage war on his neighbour and the whole of society, for what he "thought fit" was bound to conflict with what other members of society "thought fit".

The complex casuistry of the bourgeois ideal of freedom was revealed magnificently by Marx. Contrasting true freedom with the concept of the citizen's social obligations as embodied in the 1793 Constitution, he wrote: ". . . So the right to freedom is not based on human unity, but, on the contrary, on human isolation. It is the *right* to this isolation, the right of the *limited* individual." He goes on: "The right of a man to private property is therefore the right to use his possessions and dispose of them as he pleases *(à son gré)* irrespective of other people; it is the right to selfishness."[1]

Thus the rights of natural, that is, "free" man, supposedly granted him by nature, were now peremptorily placed within the iron framework of the law, which for the protection of its precepts from those who might wish to introduce real freedom *for all*, and not only for the man of property, resorted to instruments like the guillotine (in the case of the more progressive French bourgeois) or the gallows (preferred by the more conservative English bourgeois).

The guillotine was what awaited the Babouvists, the members of the Conspiracy of Equals who proclaimed true freedom for all and championed the idea of communist organisation of social relations. The French bourgeoisie saw a more fearsome enemy in Gracchus Babeuf than in all the emigrés in Koblenz put together.

The law of the victorious bourgeoisie also made short work of the second part of Rousseau's classic formula. The chains of feudalism were indeed removed, but "natural" man suddenly found to his amazement and horror that he was now wearing handcuffs, admittedly of far more subtle workmanship than the rough, primitive chains the serf blacksmith had forged in the baron's smithy.

The relentless logic of history removed the mask from "natural" man to reveal an ennobled, idealised, enterprising bourgeois, a slave of his selfish *personal interests*.

This then was the real dialectic of the development of bourgeois class society, which appeared in the realm of ideology and social consciousness in the form of an antinomy between the ideal of "natural" man as it appeared to the revolutionary thinkers of the Enlightenment, and the practical implementation of this ideal.

The real bourgeois was engaged in speculation, organising financial deals, lending money on interest to the reckless, spendthrift aristocracy who lived with no thought for

---

[1] K. Marx, F. Engels, *Werke*, Bd. 1, S. 364.

the morrow. He took over their estates, built roads and ships which he sent off to mysterious distant lands and whose cargoes of gold, copra, and silks gave off a heady aroma that turned the head of the respectable *pater familias*, encouraging him to undertake risky enterprises. The real bourgeois soon grasped the possibilities machines offered compared to human hands, and organised factories, learning to turn the sweat of the workers into hard cash.

The antinomy between the social ideal of freedom and reality was a puzzle for many of the realist writers, since, reflecting the mood of the democratic plebeian masses, they sincerely wished to see the new society a harmonious one. Although they were bourgeois thinkers with the limitations that implies, they nevertheless presented in their works the sharp social contrasts of the age and many imperfections of the social order, thereby leaving invaluable testimonies.

But the early realists were inclined to ascribe the imperfections of social organisation to the imperfection of human nature, the natural qualities of which needed to be corrected, polished and educated in the spirit of reason. Their natural tendency to idealise the hero reflected the objective revolutionary impulse of the age and the faith and hope of the popular masses, whose beliefs were formulated by realist art, that emancipation from feudal institutions could free people wholly and completely.

The tendency to idealise the hero was also an expression of the didactic aims of the progressive ideology which produced the *Encyclopédie*, Holbach's *Système de la nature* and the pedagogical utopia of *Emile* in the hope that if the views and opinions that prevailed in society could be changed, then society itself would be changed as a result and would acquire the harmony and justice it was so lacking. If, as the Enlighteners believed, inculcating rational notions in people's minds could transform heterogeneous egoistic interests and instincts that still guided human actions into some organic harmonious whole, then art and literature with their power to influence through live images could contribute to such education of society. That is why in the works of the eighteenth century realists we find a certain amount of didacticism and a strong moralising element. This applies not only to the more obvious examples, like Voltaire's *Candide,* where the moral of reason was contrasted with the unreason of the ruling morality of society. There is also a strong didactical element woven into the fabric of such genre works as Defoe's *Moll Flanders,* or Fielding's *Jonathan Wild,* as well as in Richardson's novels. Even in Beaumarchais' plays, which bubble with plebeian revolutionary *joie de vivre* and extol the skill and cunning, energy and practicality of the third estate, the feudal morality was condemned from the standpoint of the morality of the revolutionary bourgeoisie.

In early realism moralising went hand in hand with criticism of the social morals. This was perfectly natural, for the feudal world and the feudal consciousness reflecting the decline of the old order was least of all concerned with preserving and strengthening moral principles. While pathetic imitators of the great dramatists of the eighteenth century were attempting to uphold the idea of aristocratic hegemony with a stream of precious, bombastic, insufferably pompous tragedies, elevating the wretched passions of the decayed nobility, the rest of aristocratic literature was characterised by a spirit of vulgarised Epicureanism and frivolity. The feudal world was nearing its end in an atmosphere far from solemn. The pleasures of the flesh replaced the strict concepts of morality which were the backbone of Cornelian tragedy. The aristocracy hid their own corruption and spiritual bankruptcy behind a façade of refinement, under powder and beauty spots, ruches and farthingales. Frivolous verse, salon comedies with ambiguous situations bordering on the indecent mocked the principles which the bourgeoisie held sacred and inviolable, such as family life, the home, marital fidelity, thrift and economy, respect for one's elders, and so on and so forth.

In its criticism of the feudal-aristocratic morality, revolutionary-democratic literature did not limit itself to exposing the ethical foundations of the old society. Diderot's *Le Neveau de Rameau,* Schiller's *Kabale und Liebe,* the novels of Godwin and Crébillon (fils) and the articles and satires of Steele, all revealed the imperfections of the existing social order through criticism of morals.

But while early realism had some great achievements to its credit as regards condemnation of the old order and its essential moralising and idealising tendency found support in the revolutionary ferment of the age, while attitudes of social protest inspired the works of the great writers and thinkers of the eighteenth century, associating them with the social struggle of the masses, the emergent bourgeois literature proper reflected the antinomy between the social ideal of freedom and its practical realisation with almost documentary accuracy. Side by side with the epic of the new age, the novel, developed the drama, gradually ousting both "high" tragedy and comedy, which had been the dominant genres of the earlier part of the century, answering as they did to the demands of feudal society. The drama, or as it was then called "comédie larmoyante" or "middle-class tragedy" bore distinct marks of its bourgeois origins.

The realist basis of the new drama lay in its accurate, authentic portrayal of bourgeois life, and the vicissitudes of the struggle of the third estate for a place in the sun, at a time when power and the commanding heights were still in the hands of the privileged classes. Its normal theme and conflict was portrayal of the clash between a bourgeois and feudal society, and the literary presentation of this conflict required investigation and analysis of environment. The realistic nature of the main conflict in the bourgeois drama was matched by accuracy in the presentation of details of everyday life, the way of life of the bourgeois family and social environment. However, the "comédie larmoyante" was still marked by rationalism, rather "stock" heroes with a tendency to philosophise and embark on rather obvious, long-winded moralising. The founders of the moralising drama—Lillo, Destouches, Niveau de la Chausse, and even Diderot and Lessing—did not succeed in overcoming the natural prosaic nature of the "natural man", that is the bourgeois, despite their deliberate exaggeration of his positive qualities. The aesthetic contradictions of bourgeois drama were ideological contradictions, for the aim its creators had set themselves, that of poeticising the private man, was impossible. The real hero of the "comédie larmoyante" was not a suitable object for poeticisation. His practical activities were based on self-interest, and his true face was far removed from the ideal figure the creators of the bourgeois drama saw in their mind's eye. As realists, keen observers of reality, they could not help discerning the negative aspects of their bourgeois heroes, their egoism, callousness and narrow-mindedness. But since bourgeois development had not yet revealed its main imperfections, its essentially inhuman, dehumanising nature, the negative features of the heroes of the middle-class drama were generally attributed, in accordance with the prevailing attitudes of the day, to the imperfections of human nature, which could be overcome and put right with time.

However, time was to destroy and refute this illusion typical of early realism. The historical process was not only marked by the collapse of feudal ties and the growth of revolutionary protest from the oppressed masses, but also by the establishment of bourgeois social relations. The new features of life forced people to give serious consideration to questions such as: Could not the new conditions be the cause of imperfections and weaknesses in human nature? Could human failings be in fact overcome by educational and pedagogical measures, which according to the ideas of the revolutionary Enlighteners should work without fail, yet in practice showed purely marginal success when they did not fail altogether?

The antinomy between man's spiritual and social development, reflecting objective social contradictions and felt by all the major thinkers and writers of the time, demanded clarification and explanation. If human nature is imperfect and not very susceptible to influence by enlightening reason, then there was clearly a need for further investigation of human nature itself and human psychology. The crisis in the concept of modern man as "natural" man resulting from bourgeois development which instilled views and habits contradictory to the ideal norms of civic and human virtue formulated by the morality of the Enlightenment, produced a psychological trend in realist prose, first apparent in the works of Prévost, Sterne, Goethe in his *Werther* period, and later Choderlos de Laclos. These writers examined aspects of the human soul that the novel of the Enlightenment had failed to notice or deliberately ignored.

Lawrence Sterne perceived and revealed the true complexity of the human heart. No one had ever before submitted to such close scrutiny the movements of the human soul. Like painstaking natural scientist he examined the human heart through a magnifying glass and saw not only its bright aspects, but also the contradictions for which it was difficult to find a rational explanation. A strange melancholy pervades his works. His characters' inner world is an eminently healthy one. There is nothing pathological about them, no deviations from normality. Yet all of them—and especially the narrator—lack the self-confidence of a Tom Jones or a Peregrine Pickle, who are never at a loss and sail blithely through life's most complicated situations. For them life is an open book, which they read without fear, taking the caprices of fortune and the numerous ups and downs of life in their stride.

Sterne's heroes found things far less clear and simple than did the heroes of the Enlightenment novels. The simplest impending action involved much thought and hesitation. While Fielding and Smollett's heroes went out and grappled boldly with the world, striding cheerfully and confidently along the highways of England, popping into inns and squires' halls, joking with buxom serving wenches, coming to blows with hotheads, crossing the Channel and finding their way into the dens of vice of the French capital to fight their way through rows and brawls with the same tireless energy as back at home, Sterne's rather eccentric heroes were confined to the world of their own Ego and a small circle of friends, and they are clearly baffled by life.

Like other representatives of the psychological trend in the 18th century novel, Sterne was aware of the complexity of the ties between man and his social environment, and felt that this environment, reality, which history formed not according to the laws of the philosophy and morality of the Enlightenment, but according to laws of its own, was far more complex than it appeared to the exponents of the rationalist realism of the Enlightenment. Nevertheless, Sterne's character portrayal has much in common with that of his contemporaries. While making an accurate analysis of his heroes' feelings, he singled out their dominant characteristic presenting it in ingenious interplay with other, less important, features. What distinguished Sterne from his contemporaries was not so much the original composition of *Tristram Shandy*, or the melancholia which gave such a unique charm to his prose, as what was new in his understanding of the relationship between the personal and the social in life. While Condorcet denied any contradiction between man's personal and social interests and saw a guarantee of progress in their supposed harmony, thereby ignoring the absence of class harmony and failing to realise that any attempt to identify essentially different interests could only mean unbridled freedom of personal interests, Sterne showed the divorce between the individual and society. Sterne's nervous irony might soften and blur the painfulness of this divorce, glossing over its causes, but his heroes were confined to their own little world simply because they saw the outside world as an unfavourable sphere of activity.

Goethe laid bare the inevitability and social roots of this divorce between the personal and the social most clearly in his *Leiden des jungen Werthers*, in which he presents man's spiritual life and emotional world with incomparable lyricism combined with analytic acumen.

That universal genius Goethe recognised the strength of the realist method relatively early on. Discovering for himself (and thereby for literature as a whole) the possibilities the new method offered, the young writer turned first and foremost to the lesson of Shakespeare. A revival of interest in the great English dramatist was characteristic of the eighteenth century as a whole. But the young Goethe grasped better than any other of Shakespeare's admirers and followers the essential feature of his art by virtue of which he can be considered the founder of realism.

Goethe's speech "Zum Shakespeare Tag", made shortly before he began work on his tragedy *Götz von Berlichingen*—one of the finest works of eighteenth century realism which owed a great deal to Shakespeare's histories—con-

tained a precise formulation of the basic tenet of realism.
Goethe pointed out that Shakespeare's tragedies "revolve
around a hidden point ... where all that is original in our
Ego and the bold freedom of our will clash with the inexorable course of the whole"[1]. The natural laws of "the
inexorable course of the whole", that is, the course and
development of social relations, could naturally only be
shown by realism, capable of analysing phenomena and investigating their causes and effects. Goethe realised that a
man's personality and individual psychology could not be
understood and explained unless the complex underlying
secrets of "the inexorable course of the whole" were first
discovered.

When l'abbé Prévost created the baffling Manon Lescaut,
although a subtle psychologist and perspicacious observer
of manners, he found himself at a loss to explain the
inner contradictions of his heroine, who combined apparently irreconcilable qualities: fidelity in love and extreme inconstancy, great purity of soul and levity bordering on immorality in her actions, generosity and meanness,
frivolity and a serious nature, and so on and so forth.
L'abbé Prévost is like an alchemist of old mixing different
substances he imagines to be incompoundable in his flask
and to his great surprise finding they have produced a
totally unexpected and hitherto unknown compound. The
new conditions had not only changed the social relations
in a class society, but had shaped a new psychology, the
peculiarities of which amazed l'abbé Prévost.

Goethe pondered much on the essence and final aim of
"the inexorable course of the whole" throughout his long
life. In *Werther* he boldly lifted the lid off the mysterious
world of human feelings and related the sphere of the emotions to the reality of the external world. His novel quite
stunned his contemporaries, and this was not only because
the power of love—usually put on the pedestal of tragedy,
or larded with sentimentality, or simplified and shown as
"the pale fire of desire"—at last acquired the poetry of
simplicity and naturalness, and was allowed into the sphere

---

[1] J. W. Goethe, "Zum Shakespeare Tag" in: *Von deutscher Art und
Kunst*, Hamburg, 1773, S. 146.

of everyday life. Along with a lyrical portrayal of complex human feelings, there are strong notes of condemnation of tyranny, and even more important, the novel lays bare the antinomy between a man's longing for freedom and the impossibility of achieving it. This fateful antinomy that racked the young Werther's soul was a burning issue of the time. However, while revealing the new reality, penetrating and investigating so many aspects of it, subjecting the principles of feudalism, its morality and ethics, to merciless criticism, and not stopping short of criticism of the negative aspects of the developing bourgeois society, the eighteenth century realists showed themselves unable to offer any solutions to the basic conflict of the age. Indeed, in accordance with changes in social consciousness and under pressure from other literary methods a transformation of realism began.

The revolutionary democratic social thought of the eighteenth century and the emergent bourgeois ideology sensed the approach of revolution whose fiery breath was searing the whole continent, and were each fighting for their own understanding and practical realisation of human freedom. The material and spiritual conditions for a revolution had already matured, and like any other revolution it was attracting many minds and striking fear into the hearts of those who were against any change in the existing order. Like any bourgeois revolution it contained an inalienable contradiction: while declaring freedom it affirmed a new form of exploitation. The storming of the Bastille and the subsequent events of the French Revolution, which became more and more fierce as the revolutionary crisis deepened, while inspiring revolutionary democratic thought, modified the social, and hence the aesthetic, aims of democratic art and literature, which did not rise enough to become truly revolutionary. As Marx wrote in his article "Moralising Criticism and Criticising Morality": "The reign of terror in France could ... only serve to wipe away as if by magic all the feudal ruins of France with blows of its fearful hammer. The bourgeoisie with their cowardly caution would never have managed to do the job over decades even. The bloody actions of the people, therefore, merely cleared the way for the bourgooisie."[1] If the revolutionary democratic art and literature of the time (Forster, Schubart, Joseph Chénier, Radishchev, the painter David and the composer Gossec and so on) were inspired by the ideas of the Revolution, undismayed by what was called its "excesses", democratic, not to mention bourgeois, art and literature, although also seething with civic ideas and sentiments, and considering man's emancipation from the burden of feudal relations an historical necessity, displayed "cowardly caution".

The character of the development of thought at the end of the 18th century was determined by the fact that the Enlightenment outlook called to life by the ripening revolutionary situation was unable to rid itself of its inner contradictions. For both the ideologists of the third estate and revolutionary democrats expressing the true interests of the oppressed masses, the root causes of the historical process and its real prospects remained a mystery. Nor was realism in a position to bring them to light, for its strength and weakness lay in social analysis of reality, which was constantly changing and fraught with completely new unforeseen tendencies and features of development.

Describing the theoretical achievements of social thought in the eighteenth century in generalising on the practical experience and demands of the bourgeoisie, Engels wrote in his *Outlines of a Critique of Political Economy:*

"The eighteenth century, the century of revolution, also revolutionised economics. But just as all the revolutions of this century were one-sided and bogged down in antitheses—just as abstract materialism was set in opposition to abstract spiritualism, the republic to monarchy, the social contract to divine right—likewise the economic revolution did not get beyond antithesis. The premises remained everywhere in force: materialism did not contend with the Christian contempt for and humiliation of Man, and merely posited Nature instead of the Christian God as the Absolute facing Man. In politics no one dreamt of examining the premises of the State as such. It did not occur to economics to question *the validity of*

---

[1] K. Marx, F. Engels, *Werke*, Bd. 4, S. 339.

private property. Therefore, the new economics was only half an advance. It was obliged to betray and to disavow its own premises, to have recourse to sophistry and hypocrisy so as to cover up the contradictions in which it became entangled, so as to reach the conclusions to which it was driven not by its premises but by the humane spirit of the century.... All was pure splendour and magnificence—yet the premises reasserted themselves soon enough, and in contrast to this sham philanthropy produced the Malthusian population theory—the crudest, most barbarous theory that ever existed, a system of despair which struck down all those beautiful phrases about love of neighbour and world citizenship. The premises begot and reared the factory-system and modern slavery, which yields nothing in inhumanity and cruelty to ancient slavery. Modern economics—the system of free trade based on Adam Smith's *Wealth of Nations*—reveals itself to be that same hypocrisy, inconsistency and immorality which now confront free humanity in every sphere."[1] This analysis of the contradictions inherent in eighteenth century social thought also explains why realism was unable to meet the requirements of the age, not having "gone beyond antithesis", and being gradually ousted by a new type of classicism, which represented an attempt by art and literature to solve the fundamental contradictions developing in life. Fundamentally different from the old Cornelian variety of classicism, the new trend did, however, have one feature in common with it, and that was its civic spirit.

Classicism as a literary method arose in the period when the countries of Europe were consolidating as nation states, when centralised power was suppressing feudal liberties (which was of unquestionable benefit to the bourgeoisie). Therefore, the essential ideology of classicism was founded on the civic principle, on the absolutisation of *monarchic duty*, which was placed above personal interests. In the age of the bourgeois revolution, classicism again shaped and expressed civic passions and sentiments, civic aware-

---

[1] K. Marx, *Economic and Philosophical Manuscripts of 1844*, Moscow, pp. 177-78.

ness, but it now absolutised the concept of *public duty.* The Jacobins, the most consistent revolutionaries, were also the most consistent classicists, which is only natural, since for them the question of civic duty and public-spiritedness was literally a matter of life and death. Through classicism the democratic and bourgeois consciousness also affirmed their understanding of man's duty to society in the new conditions created by the revolutionary crisis.

Lessing, Diderot, and even Rousseau, were favourably disposed towards revolutionary classicism because of its social content, for the revolutionary democrats drew a sharp distinction between social interests (essentially, those of the whole people) and arbitrary, selfish, personal interests. The moderate bourgeois ideology of the third estate, on the other hand, characterised, to use Marx's term, by "cowardly caution", regarded classicism first and foremost as a means of compromise with reality, although the theoreticians of bourgeois classicism also insisted on the principle of freedom as the natural precondition for human progress. Winckelmann, who did so much to promote the study of the art of antiquity, declared in his *Geschichte der Kunst des Altertums,* an important landmark in the development of eighteenth century social thought, "calm is the quality most characteristic of beauty",[1] thereby expressing through aesthetic theory the political demands of the moderate bourgeoisie and formulating the programme for the development of the new art.

Winckelmann did not wish to relate the new art directly to the social struggle. "The mind of a rational being", he wrote, "has an innate longing to transcend matter into the realm of abstract ideas".[2] This definition can be said to characterise German ideology as a whole with its aptitude for accomplishing universal historical revolutions in the realm of pure thought. It clearly reveals the inability of the burghers of Germany (and not only Germany) to go very far in criticism of reality by real, practical, as opposed to theoretical, methods. In the years when Win-

---

[1] J. Winckelmann, *Geschichte der Kunst des Altertums,* Weimar, 1964, S. 144.

[2] Ibid., S. 135.

ckelmann formulated the aesthetico-political credo of bourgeois classicism, the "rational being", far from aspiring to the "realm of thought" was trying in the most insistent manner to introduce the rational demands of ideology into everyday life. Basically, Winckelmann was reconciling himself to reality, sanctifying his conciliation with refined aestheticism imbued with the spirit of antiquity.

For all their important differences, the various classicist trends in eighteenth century literature all arose for perfectly logical reasons, as reflections of changes in social consciousness. The logic of the emergence of classicist tendencies is to be seen especially clearly in the spiritual evolution of Goethe and Schiller whose works represent the consummation of the aesthetic and social quests of eighteenth century literature considered as an independent stage in the development of world literature.

Both Goethe and his younger contemporary, the initiators and finest representatives of eighteenth century realism, had a rare awareness of the historical essence of their time. Both deliberately and warrantably went over to new creative positions, realising that the existing realist means, based as they were on insufficient comprehension of the laws of social development, did not allow of solving the riddles that arose with the emergence of bourgeois social relations. In turning to classicism and attempting to revive the noble, harmonious spirit of the art of antiquity, with its perfect form and great sense of artistic proportion, Schiller and Goethe were basically resolving the same humanistic problems as they had posed in their pre-classicist works.

Unlike Jacobin classicism, which supported the idea of revolution all the way, the classicism of Goethe and Schiller proceeded from rejection of terror as a method of implanting the new social relations. But if their classicism had been simply a reaction to the events of the Revolution, it would have degenerated into an effete philistine apology for reality or pure formalism manipulating motives borrowed from classical antiquity, and essentially eclectic and sterile. As it was, their classicism was based on the consequences of the revolutionary changes which had failed to usher in an era of genuine human happiness. Naturally, *Götz von Berlichingen* and *Werther*, *Die Räuber* and *Kabale und Liebe*, despite their powerful protest against the abnormalities of social relations, also contained doubts as to the possibility of their transformation by revolution. The world order that was established following the victory of the French Revolution, and especially after Thermidor, far from removing the inherent contradictions of class society, tended to exacerbate them. In regarding beautiful—and hence moral—art based on perfect classical models as a means for educating man and destroying the egoism and disharmony in his soul, Goethe and Schiller were essentially continuing to uphold the ideals of the Enlightenment, displaying wise humanistic faith in the idea of the perfectability of human nature and society. Their classicism, unlike Winckelmann's, did not represent a compromise. Characterised by the *universalisation of moral, humanitarian duty*, it represented rather an attempt to resolve by new means the new ethical and social problems that the course of historical progress had posed, and it arose on the basis of the achievements of realism. Although late eighteenth century literature was marked by a retreat from realism and the birth of pre-romantic and romantic trends, these new trends were unable to develop without taking into account the achievements of realism.

Goethe and Schiller were aware of the fruitlessness and futility of the bourgeois individualist cult of self-will preached by the Sturm und Drang school. They found equally unacceptable the attempts to find new ways of reflecting reality made by their pre-romanticist and romanticist contemporaries, who began to perceive life as a fabric of interwoven illusions, left the world of reality for the world of fancy, or proposed, like Novalis in his treatise *Die Christenheit oder Europa*, the restoration of the old order destroyed by history. The time was not yet ripe for revolutionary romanticism to take the stage.

At the turn of the century, the literature which reflected the results of the revolutionary crisis, like philosophical thought, was making a serious attempt to perceive and comprehend what had happened, and raise, on the ruins of shattered hopes and illusions, a new outlook, a new understanding of nature, society and human consciousness.

While bourgeois economists were busy justifying strictly bourgeois progress, substantiating its inevitability with frank delight, while German idealist philosophers and Natural philosophers were concentrating all their efforts on criticising the mechanistic materialism of the Enlightenment, while nascent romanticism, painfully aware of the growing discord between the individual and society, was unable to shed any light on the origins of this discord, in the midst of this very confused period a new idea was emerging that was to revolutionise thought— *the idea of development.* At the turn of the century, the basic group of questions of outlook later to be formulated by Hegel in his *Die Phänomenologie des Geistes* (substantiation of dialectics, definition of the law of the negation of a negation, and a constant attention to history) was already taking shape. New theories developed at this point, new social theories suggesting an unexpected solution to the apparently insoluble question of human freedom, with which the thinkers of the Enlightenment had wrestled in vain, theories proceeding from rejection of *capitalist* private-ownership relations and seeming to confirm by the very fact of their existence the correctness of Hegel's law of the negation of a negation. Out of the ruins of the feudal system, out of the scaffolding of the capitalist system, utopian *socialism* arose, attempting to apply the idea of development to history, seeking a logic in its flux.

In his *Théorie des quatre mouvements,* which appeared the year after *La phénoménologie de l'esprit,* Fourier wisely pointed out the need of the new age for a new spiritual synthesis based on other ideological and social foundations than the democratic ideology of the Enlightenment, not to mention strictly bourgeois political economy and philosophy. "After the disaster of 1793, all illusions were shattered; the political and moral sciences were in disgrace and all faith in them had been irretrievably lost. Henceforth it was to be foreseen that happiness was not to be expected from any acquired knowledge, that social welfare must be sought in some new science, and new paths laid for the political spirit; for it was clear that neither the philosophers nor their rivals knew the cures for social sufferings and that under cover of the dogmas of both, the most terrible ills, including poverty, would continue forever."[1] This need for synthesis and generalisation of the social experience acquired during and after the bourgeois revolution was also felt by Hegel, who raised the edifice of an encyclopaedic philosophical system, and by Saint-Simon with his idea for a new encyclopaedia, and also by the circumscribed, pedantic, bourgeois thinker Auguste Comte, who emasculated the revolutionary and socialist substance of Saint-Simon, borrowing only the rationalist-positivist aspect of his theory.

The need to acquire an understanding of the new social reality that was taking shape naturally produced a heightened interest in history, which was to characterise the intellectual life of the early nineteenth century.

Such geniuses as Goethe and Schiller also turned their attention to history and tried to understand the lessons of the French Revolution through its events and consequences. Schiller, who had made an extensive study of the past as an historian, and was the author of works on the Netherlands Revolt, the Thirty Years War and the political struggle in France in the reign of Henry IV, all written by an artist rather than a scholar, realised that the hidden mainspring of human passions and actions lay in material interests, or in other words adopted a realist approach in his analysis of events. The realist view of life, which enabled Schiller to rise above the theories and principles of classicism, is already to be seen in *Kabale und Liebe.* In his later dramas, in the *Wallenstein* trilogy and *Mary Stuart,* and especially *Wilhelm Tell,* it is the principle underlying the whole action. Schiller did not merely turn to history in search of subjects and great figures for the purpose of drama and tragedy. He regarded history as the struggle of various moral principles,

---

[1] Ch. Fourier, *Œuvres Complètes,* T. 1, "Théorie des quatre mouvements", Troisième edition, Paris, 1846, pp. 2-3.

and it was this study of history that brought him round to the belief in the idea of rule by the people in his later years although he had previously rejected the Jacobin method of transforming society.

Features of utopianism were also clearly manifest in his outlook, for the objective basis of historical changes remained a mystery to him, a mystery that was to be solved in the near future by social thought, art and literature, once the contradictions of the capitalist system had become apparent.

Both in his *Briefe über die ästhetische Erzeihung*, where he expresses great hopes in the power of art to change man and hence society, and in his later tragedies, Schiller adhered to the aesthetic canon of his classicism, exaggerating the power of man's intrinsic moral essence and devoting considerably less attention to study and analysis of the real underlying factors of the historical process. Hence the frequent irruptions of fatality into his heroes' fortunes, this really being none other than disguised historical necessity and conditionality which the author failed to perceive (viz., *Wallenstein*). His portrayal of personal passions, thoughts and feelings pushed into the background the environment in which the character moved and acted, the "Falstaffian background" which could have imparted realistic completeness to the whole structure of his tragedies. Schiller often abandoned objectivity, making his hero the carrier of and voice for his own ideas, resorting to exalted and somewhat abstract rhetoric. All these features of Schiller's drama have a logical historical explanation, and bear witness to the fact that he was constantly developing as an artist, doing his utmost to embody in artistic images the new reality, which could only be apprehended and presented in word form by realism, and on no account by that revived classicism to which the poet so frequently declared allegiance. Nevertheless, Schiller's later plays do comprise tremendous love of man, magnificent characters, a remarkably full and accurate presentation of the characters' inner worlds, and quite extraordinarily intense and authentic conflicts. Most important of all, Schiller had come to realise that the practical result of the French Revolution, the new order that was establishing itself in place of the old world destroyed by the revolution, was not the end product of social development, and that history was a process in the course of which old ways of life and social forms that pass away are replaced by new ones. The idea of rule by the people which Schiller reached in *Wilhelm Tell*, after overcoming his bourgeois fears of popular revolt, shows that he realised that only the future would be able to resolve the apparently indissoluble contradictions of his age.

If Schiller turned to history in order to comprehend the meaning of the social revolution he was witnessing, Goethe's works and spiritual evolution reflected the essence of the age somewhat more indirectly. In his treatise *Über naive und sentimentalische Dichtung* Schiller made a very shrewd assessment of the main feature of Goethe's original genius, expressed in his spontaneously realist and powerful perception of life. Goethe strongly disapproved of various forms of subjectivism in art and philosophy, and often openly expressed his contempt for it. He valued the objectivity of the world and nature over and above all else, and constantly felt the living pulse of existence: he preferred the Spinozan brand of determinism to the painful attempts of contemporary Naturphilosophie to derive laws of nature, exclusive to nature, from human thought. Goethe considered *development* to be a natural feature of nature and extended this concept to history, frequently employing and adapting the views expressed by Herder in his *Ideen zur Philosophie der Geschichte*.

Versuch, die Metamorphose der Pflanzen zu erklären, which like the works of Geoffroy Saint-Hilaire, anticipated the idea of evolution, and *Faust*, that bold, triumphant hymn to creative, constructive, searching human thought, are pervaded with the idea of development, the idea of the incessant movement of life, constantly in the making, continuously changing.

Goethe always saw man as a child of ever-changing, flowing nature, a leaf on the evergreen tree of eternity. Faust, while evoking the spirit of the Earth and recognising its power, at the same time feels himself a part of the Universe, to the understanding of which he devoted all the powers of his mind.

But if the objectivity of nature and its laws was obvious to Goethe and he was able to grasp the concrete features of the evolution of the living being (suffice it to remember his discovery of the intermaxillary bone); if we can agree with the Russian poet who wrote: "The book of the stars was clear to him and the salt wave spoke with him", the idea of development which was such an organic part of Goethe's *Weltanschauung* never acquired true realist concreticity in his later works when applied to the social sphere, the domain of living history. Following in Herder's footsteps and accepting that history, like nature, conformed to certain reasonable laws, Goethe was unable to discover the forces that determine human social relations. Time put fetters even on his indomitable mind.

Despite the fundamental differences between the two great writers, there is a definite similarity in their approach to the presentation of history, to be attributed to the identical social conditions in which their art matured. The fate of the gloomy, ambitious Wallenstein marching inevitably towards his doom, has its counterpart in Egmont who throws himself with equal passion and delight into sensual pleasures and social struggle. Portraying Egmont as an active participant in the national liberation movement, Goethe focussed his attention on the idealistic political blindness of his hero, his inevitable progress towards the executioner's block, rather than on the struggle between real social forces, which is relegated to the background. This was no accident: Goethe substituted analysis of the spiritual world of his tragic hero for the dialectic of historical contradictions of a class origin which determined the behaviour of Egmont as an historical figure, and thus the fatality, the predetermination of his fate expresses, just as in the case of Schiller's trilogy, the poet's ignorance of the nature of historical necessity.

Goethe, like Schiller, did not welcome the French Revolution and offered in contrast to the fierce political passions raging in France the orderly, limited and moderate bourgeois existence extolled and idealised in sweet hexameters in *Hermann und Dorothea*. Yet, again like Schiller, he understood perfectly well that the results of the revolution did not represent the final stage in the historical development of mankind.

In his latter years, Goethe followed closely the successes and advances of contemporary social, political and aesthetic thought. In the new period that followed the Revolution of 1789, a period full of events of tremendous scale and importance, Goethe could observe much that was unknown to the 18th century, and utopian elements begin to feature more and more distinctly in his outlook and literary works.

The idea of education as a means of creating first a harmonious individual and later a harmonious society, was characteristic of Weimar classicism too, and forms the core of *Wilhelm Meister*. But the new age had introduced new elements into the positive programme for perfecting social relations expounded in the novel. The theme of part two, *Wilhelm Meisters Wanderjahre*, shows a marked similarity to the practical ideas for reorganising society propagated by Fourier and Saint-Simon. Goethe's ideas were particularly akin to the ideas that received this final expression in Saint-Simon's treatise *Opinions littéraires, philosophiques et industrielles*, containing the famous epigraph: "The Golden Age which blind tradition has hitherto placed in the past is yet to come".

Saint-Simon wrote: "The nineteenth century philosophers should now be proceeding with their task which is very different from that performed by the philosophers of the 18th century.

"The nineteenth century philosophers should unite to demonstrate fully and comprehensively that at the present state of knowledge and civilisation only industrial and scientific principles can serve as the foundation for social organisation, or rather to show that at the present state of knowledge and civilisation society can be organised in such a way as to tend directly towards an improvement of its moral and physical welfare.

"The philosophers of the 18th century created Encyclopaedia to refute the theological and feudal system. The philosophers of the 19th century should in their turn produce their Encyclopaedia to establish the industrial and scientific system.

"All the ideas there should be submitted to analysis in order to prove that the *common weal* will be the necessary result of the influence exercised by scientific and industrial principles in place of that which had been exercised on society up to now by feudal and theological principles."[1]

In *Wilhelm Meisters Wanderjahre*, Goethe, foreseeing the gigantic role industry would come to play in the life of mankind, accorded a great deal of space to reflections on the organisation of industry on a kind of communal basis. He attached equally great importance to collective labour in working the land, made the property of all. For Goethe labour was inseparable from the problem of education, preparing man for socially useful activity. "The Province of Pedagogy", that social and pedagogical utopia, like the whole system of organisation of life described in the novel, served one end—the future, the affirmation and propagation of a more rational system of social relations than that which had resulted from the Revolution.

The philosophy of *Faust* also has a utopian element. The spiritual pivot of the tragedy is undoubtedly the scene of the atonement, the scene of Faust's victory over Mephistopheles, when Faust's bold desire for knowledge turns to the good of others, when, having completed the course of his earthly existence and experienced all human joys and sorrows, he undertakes the re-creation of a whole land and in labour in the name of human happiness and freedom finds happiness for himself and the summit of his desires. Surely Goethe never attained such supreme, stirring tragedy as in this scene where the wild joy and elation of man the creator, at having discovered the meaning of life in fruitful activity, is clouded by the clanging of spades, and the dull sound of earth slipping into the grave Mephistopheles' faithful servants, the Lemurs, are digging for him. The historical optimism in Faust's last monologue, when he says:

> Only he deserveth life and liberty
> Who every day goes out to fight for them

---

[1] Saint-Simon, *Opinions littéraires, philosophiques et industrielles*, Paris, 1825, pp. 83-84.

remove the gloomy tragic atmosphere of the scene, but not the real difficulty of achieving the ideal of freedom which Goethe extols in *Faust*.

Accepting the idea of development as historically legitimate and inevitable, the great poet understood that the tremendous social progress the Revolution had ushered in would not be consummated, for the Revolution had also called forth forces arresting mankind's advance towards rational social relations. Goethe saw that egoism and individualistic desires were eating away the humanistic ideal of the common weal and preventing it from taking root in the soil of life, which had been ploughed by the Revolution and well watered with human blood in the European wars that followed. But he did not reveal the root causes of social egoism, nor the motive forces of the historical process, and thus his social views, while evolving towards utopian socialism by no means always concurred with it in everything.

Fourier and Saint-Simon applied the idea of development to history and came to the conclusion that the motive force in the historical process was the *class struggle*. Despite his interest in his theory of new Christianity, towards the end of his life Saint-Simon had begun to speak in the name of "the lower class", the force which had formed in the depths of bourgeois society, in the name, that is, of the proletariat. The social organisation which in his opinion would replace the egoistic civilisation which had grown up on the ruins of the feudal system, should promote "the growth of welfare of the proletarians"[1]. Like Fourier and Robert Owen, Saint-Simon still had illusions about the ways and means of reorganising society, but he already spoke with complete conviction of the ability of the proletariat to take part in the government and organisation of the "system of social welfare", thereby demonstrating remarkable historical perspicacity and prescience. The combination of the idea of development with the theory of class struggle, and the discovery of the laws of history governing social relations led to the emergence of scientific socialism, which brought about a major revolu-

---

[1] Ibid., pp. 158-59.

tion in human thought and social life. But this discovery of universal historical importance was to be made later, and in the early years of the 19th century progressive social thought was only just beginning to come to grips with the new reality, so that it was perfectly natural that Saint-Simon, continuing the tradition of such outstanding 18th century thinkers as Morelly and Mably, and with Gracchus Babeuf as an immediate precursor, should have gone much further than Goethe in his theoretical views. The demarcation line between the democratic and humanist views of Goethe and the socialist theories of the utopists arose for the simple reason that the great poet's *Weltanschauung* was formed in a backward country with a cowardly and ready-to-compromise bourgeoisie, that displayed more than average "cowardly caution" towards the Revolution. Genius though he was, Goethe was a scion of the German middle class, and this was bound to leave its mark on his attitude to history.

The evolution of Goethe's social views in the latter part of his life entailed corresponding changes in his basic aesthetic principles. The classicist elements in his work were on the decrease and he was searching more and more purposefully for new artistic ways and means of presenting "the inexorable course of the whole". *Wilhelm Meister* had been experimental both from the point of view of its inner spiritual content and the manner in which it was expressed. Realistically reproduced pictures of life and manners alternate with romantic scenes which Goethe, despite his reserved and even critical attitude towards Romanticism, insinuated into his novel, often unwittingly, while the concluding part really represents a socio-philosophical treatise. Goethe was seeking a new literary idiom that would enable him to express the ideas he had reached and convey their objective, historical significance. But his ignorance of the causes determining the "inexorable course of the whole" prevented him from achieving their realistic embodiment.

The work that crowned Goethe's literary career, his tragedy about Doctor Faustus who sold his soul to the Devil to learn the meaning of things, and after long torments and sufferings rose from the personal, individualist search for the meaning of life to appreciation of the common good and service to one's fellow men, was syncrotic in form. The popular legend of the magician and wizard, on which the plot of the tragedy was based, introduced the historical colour of Germany's distant past, conveyed in Sachs' verse; the dramatic episode of the seduced maiden becoming a child murderer brought a powerful folklore current into the tragedy; the gloomy imagery of northern mythology is paralleled by elements from ancient mythology adapted and developed in complexity; the baroque splendour of the court scenes is combined with the strict classical severity of the Helen episode; the poetic exposition of natural science theories did not prevent the inclusion in the tragedy of the solemn liturgical finale; the allegory of the Walpurgisnacht scenes is closely interwoven with elevated symbolics, and the whole work, with its wealth and complexity of artistic elements is reminiscent as regards structure of the old mystery plays and is distantly related to the puppet theatre, that is to the folk tradition, to folk tales and legends. Goethe created a colourful, unusual, fantastic world, owing its completeness to the unity of content and manner of expression. Since the personal fate of the hero represents the fate of the whole of mankind seeking the right path in life and history, intent on discovering the secrets of the Universe, and, in Goethe's opinion, called upon to overcome the tremendous obstacles on his historical path and introduce a rational foundation to his life, Faust and his adversary Mephistopheles are symbolic. Symbolism and (often extremely nebulous) allegory also attach to other characters in the tragedy.

It is in the very nature of the artistic image to lend itself to different interpretations (including symbolic ones), for no art reflects reality with mirror-like accuracy, providing a perfectly unambiguous copy of the world of things and phenomena. Nor could it, for the human mind does not reflect objective reality like a passive mirror. There can be various principles underlying an artistic image: it can be built on associations, on similarity or comparison; it can be sharpened and made grotesque or a caricature; it can be allegorical, perfectly three-dimensional and plastic, literal and figurative, at the same time, but whatever its structure and whatever features—rationalistic or emotional—predominate, it is always based on some particular manner of apprehending reality depending on the social nature of the author's outlook.

The aesthetics of the naturalist school began to emerge in the mid-19th century at a time when profound changes were taking place in bourgeois social consciousness based on an empirical approach to reality, which the theoreticians and exponents of naturalism considered a static category *not subject to development.* Naturalism cultivates the principle of copying reality, and photographic images which cannot be generalised and made to express the essence of things. Thus the naturalist aesthetics not only impoverished art and literature but detracted from the cognitive value of the image, and hence from the cognitive value of art itself.

Unlike non-realist trends, realism makes good use of all the inherent possibilities of thinking in images that help express the substance of the apprehended object. Realism absorbs all the available principles of creating an image and reveals the qualities and features of apprehended reality. In this way the realistic image objectivises reality and is equivalent to it in its own right. Realism conveys the essence of things and not their superficial appearance as naturalism does, and its aesthetics are thus truly rich and varied. The epic fullness of Tolstoi's imagery recreating the tangible, material texture of the fabric of existence, is as typical of realism as is the controlled, rationalist intellectual imagery of Stendhal; the nervous, tense, highly emotional imagery of Dostoyevsky's novels also provided a realistic picture of the life of his age, as did the laconic, concise prose of Chekhov, with its complex overtones conveying the deeper undercurrents of events. The Russian satirist Saltykov-Shchedrin used symbolism and grotesque distortion in his scathing criticism of the social structure of Russia's capitalist-landowner society. His *History of the Town of Glupov*, although it avoids oversimplified, didactical allegory, is full of symbolism and its characters, too, are symbolic. But the symbolic presentation of the town officials, far from being at

variance with realism, flows straight from the realist tradition, for the author is embodying in these characters
typical concrete historical features of social reality. Behind the rather phantasmagorial surface of Shchedrin's
satire lay the reality of semi-feudal Russian life, the
author's vision of its future path and the impending doom
of the existing order. Shchedrin resorted to symbolism as
the best means he could find of presenting and typifying
the universal features of the social system.

The subjectivist trends that arose at the turn of this century lacked an integrated view of life and went further
than naturalism towards destroying the cognitive function
of the image. The surrealists, for example, broke the link
between the image and reality, treating the image as a
form without objective content and only using it as a
vehicle for chaotic feelings and emotions, associations and
sensations arising in the poet's soul, which is supposedly
independent of the external world and unaffected by its
logic. The theoreticians of surrealism (André Breton and
company) seem to have been unaware of the fact that
the "mysterious" soul of the poet and the emotions it expressed had absorbed the chaos of the outside world. The
symbolists, for whom the essence of reality was dark and
inscrutable, presented their perception of it by vague, in-
substantial allusions. Vyacheslav Ivanov, one of the foremost theoreticians and exponents of symbolism, defined
the nature of symbolist imagery thus: "The symbol is only
a true symbol when it is inexhaustible and infinite in its
meaning, when it utters in its secret language (hieratic
and magic) of allusion and suggestion something indelible,
that is not equivalent to external words. It is many-
faceted, polysemantic and always dark in the deepest
depth. It is an organic formation, like a crystal. It is a
certain monad and hence differs from the complex and
disparate composition of allegory, parable or simile.
Allegory is teaching; the symbol is indication."[1] Vyacheslav Ivanov and the other symbolists (Maeterlinck, Hofmannsthal and Bely) raised an impassable barrier between
literature and reality, refusing to apprehend reality and
declaring the symbol to be the only means of expressing

[1] Vyacheslav Ivanov, *From Star to Star*, 1909, p. 39 (in Russ.).

the essence of life. Adopting an intuitive outlook, they assigned to art the miserable role of diviner of the holy mysteries dispensed in the universe, by some supernatural power which they named, according to taste, personal inclination and what they had read in philosophical and theological literature, the universal spirit, or will, or the life urge, or death, or somewhat more clearly—the divine principle.

The symbolism in *Faust* was not merely the product of poetic fancy: it was the result of an incomplete apprehension of the concrete forms of the historical process, its foundations and essential root causes. Philosophical abstraction, allegory and symbol made their appearance in Goethe's tragedy where he was unable to impart real, authentic life substance to his reflections on the historical destiny of man and human society. But, like his hero, Goethe aspired to rise from ignorance to knowledge, to apprehend the meaning and goal of man's social development. Goethe, like the progressive thinkers of his day, came to the conclusion that the Golden Age lay not in the past but in the future. The noble ideal of mankind's one day achieving *earthly* happiness illuminated his last great work, in which the antinomy between the ideal of freedom and the ways it could be achieved although not solved, was at least in the process of being surmounted. This ideal was extremely potent, being deeply rooted in the soil of life, and answering the demands that history had produced in the popular masses, for whom the change in the form of exploitation that was the chief result of the bourgeois Revolution meant the beginning of a new period in the struggle for emancipation. Goethe's tragedy crowns a whole stage in the development of world art and literature, confirming that the solution of the questions the historical process had placed before social thought, questions that arose as a result of the bourgeois Revolution, must be sought in history itself.

This is indeed what happened: with the exacerbation of the contradictions of bourgeois society which came to light in the very hour of its triumph over feudalism, history became of necessity an object of cognizance and investigation for literature and art.

HISTORY AND REALISM

After the French Revolution, which had a colossal impact on all spheres of social and spiritual life in Europe, art and literature entered a new stage of development.

Revolutionary classicism, with its enthusiasm for the strict civic virtues of the ancient Romans, was exhausted as an independent school by the beginning of the 19th century, for the flame of freedom of which it was a reflection was burning low. The painter David, who had given such a touching portrayal of Marat's death agony in famous canvas, already worshipped a new deity. His paintings glorified a new Caesar: Bonaparte, on his prancing horse, pointing towards the Alpine peaks, as misty as his future; Bonaparte, in his splendid court, placing the imperial gold crown on his own head. . . .

Yet despite the crisis in revolutionary classicism, its poetics, imbued with sincere civic ardour, became an essential element in the aesthetic views of many writers who were aware that literature was capable of being an active social force and were ideologically connected with the democratic movements—writers like Byron, Béranger, the Russian Decembrist poets, and Griboyedov.

On the whole, classicism was obviously falling into decay and was ultimately doomed to extinction, for the conditions which had produced the kind of artistic thought of which it was the expression had already disappeared. The new reality could not be apprehended and presented in the classicist manner partly because its canons—the distinction between high and low style, the strict reglementation of genres, the theory of the three unities, and the formalism of classicist associations and motives—were obsolete, but especially because the very essence of classicism, whose basic feature was a conception of life as something static, prevented the works of the classicists from reflecting life's renewed, changing forms. At a time when the idea of development had penetrated the human consciousness thanks to an acceleration in the course of history, development by leaps and bounds, enabling the most progressive thinkers of the early years of the century to divine something of the nature of social ties, classicism revealed its inability to grasp their dynamics, the dynamics of social development. The classicists regarded the passions as the basis of character, considering them to be immutable, the same in all ages. Hence the way their characters were so often mere personifications of particular passions or ideas, and were devoid of real-life concreticity and unable to develop and reveal themselves. The classicists dissolved the individual in the species, depriving their characters of personality, and were therefore unable to combine the general and the particular. They abstracted their heroes from real life, so that their works acquired a general universality often bordering on the schematic. Even their best works show static composition, a tendency to posing in the characters, and a declamatory, rhetorical style, as in David's *The Oath of the Horatii*, a work which glorifies self-sacrifice. The heroes of the civic tragedy are depicted as if frozen in their spiritual élan at the moment they take their vow, and have not been very individualised by the painter. Their womenfolk stand leaning towards one another in an orderly and rather impersonal attitude of sorrow without ruffling in the slightest impeccable folds of their long garments. The whole painting is in a heavy declamatory style which presents us with the main idea but makes no attempt to go into details. The action is also weak in ·Goethe's tragedy *Iphigenie auf Tauris*, which was finished two years after David's picture, and marks the beginning of Weimar classicism. The drama in the play certainly does not derive from the action. Whereas *The Oath of the Horatii* was in praise of civic action, the necessity and indeed the inevitability of social struggle, Goethe's tragedy poeticised the moral principle as an agent of transformation, and Iphigenie's meek kindness is contrasted to Orestes's dagger. While in the painting the old man blesses his sons and hands them swords for the battle, Iphigenie takes her brother's weapon from him. This tragedy of renunciation shows Goethe's rejection of the idea of revolutionary transformation of the world.

The spirit of conciliation in *Iphigenie auf Tauris* did not lessen the moral sufferings of the heroes, but these sufferings were expressed not through the action but through elevated and somewhat impersonal rhetoric, in the cold, measured dialogues and monologues. The static inner world of this tragedy seems distilled as compared with the movement of life throbbing and seething in Goethe's realist works.

While inclining more to the elevated and the lofty, extracted from the mundane, classicism did not turn its back entirely on the everyday stuff of life. What it did do was to regard it as a "low", amusing sphere and accord it a subsidiary position in the run of aesthetic objects, thereby failing to rise from portrayal of everyday manners to portrayal of the vast canvas of human life which realism presented. Nevertheless, the question of the social foundations of progress was a major one in art, literature and social thought at the beginning of the 19th century, and by failing to investigate the practical aspects of life, failing to observe its objective movement, classicism was lagging behind the spirit of the times. Classicism gradually became the banner of the inveterate supporters of the old order, who were ready to accept anything rather than change, and it therefore incurred fierce attacks from the romanticists and the realists, who saw it as a force arresting the development of art, and an ideological weapon of reaction.

By the middle of the century classicist painting had degenerated into cold, soulless academicism, despite the fact that such talented artists as Ingres, Bryullov and Thorwaldsen continued to work in the manner. In literature classicism was represented by a host of hack imitators, and not until the latter part of the century, with the appearance of neo-classicism proclaimed and defended by Jean Moréas, Ernest Seillière and Charles Maurras in France and Paul Ernst, Wilhelm von Scholz and others in Germany, did it again come to merit attention.

The neo-classicists with their insistence on clarity and strict form as against the obscureness of symbolism were least of all concerned with questions of pure aesthetics. Their ideology was based on the Nietzschean interpretation of classical antiquity, and their works and philosophical treatises propagated the morality of the masters and the principles of the hierarchical organisation of society based on strict social discipline. They combined support of class inequality with militant nationalism, and aesthetic refinement with adoration of power and will. The product of new forms of social consciousness, and one of the currents of European decadent art and literature, neo-classicism had nothing in common with classicism apart from its name.

Romanticism played the leading role in the art of the early 19th century. "Only romantic poetry, like the epos, can be the mirror of the whole surrounding world, the reflection of the age," Schlegel wrote, and rightly to a certain extent, for it was Romanticism that first shed light on the new sentiments and outlook that were characteristic of the post-revolutionary period, and indeed on whole new aspects of reality.

Romanticism enriched world art and literature with the *sense of history*, without which the new order that replaced feudalism could not be properly comprehended. "There is no other kind of self-knowledge other than the historical," wrote Schlegel. "Nobody knows what he is unless he knows his fellow men and above all his supreme fellow man, the master of masters—the genius of the age." These words are a pretty shrewd comment on what was essentially new in the work of the romantic writers, for prior to romanticism art had not noted the changeability of history, and what preceded and prepared the present had not been regarded as essentially different from the present. Earlier art and literature on themes from the past had tended to eliminate the temporal dimension. Thus, paintings of biblical subjects showed Roman legionaries dressed as medieval mercenaries, and townsfolk dressed very much as the artist's contemporaries. As Stendhal wrote: "Our grandfathers were moved by Orestes in *Andromache* who was played in an enormous powdered wig, red stockings and shoes with fire-coloured bows."[1] This was perfectly natural, for it never even occurred to the audiences who were so delighted with plays like *Andromache* that Orestes or Achilles did not wear wigs. Neither in the Enlightenment novel nor in baroque literature, as in Lohenstein's pseudo-historical novels, was history treated as a process. It was only with the pre-romantic trends in the intellectual life of Europe at the time of the Revolution that history's movement in time began to be examined, as witnessed by the extensive study of folk art and the epic, Macpherson's interest in *The Poems of Ossian*, and the appearance of historical themes in the so-called "Gothic novel", where in actual fact historical events still played a purely decorative role.

The heightened interest in history observable in the social thought of the early 19th century was by no means due to purely intellectual causes; history itself burst into people's lives, for the new century did not descend on the world lightly as a dove but to the thunder of cannon, the beating of drums and whiffs of grape-shot. The rhythmic march of soldiers' feet shook the continent from the Pyrenees to the Volga, and the bloody fields of Austerlitz, Borodino and Waterloo marked the course of Napoleon's cruel star, its zenith and its nadir.

The invasions of the French armies led by Napoleon's marshals, bloated with victory, helped sweep away the feudal order in the countries of Europe. But the oppressive regimes they set up in the occupied territories produced a rapid growth in national consciousness among the subject peoples and encouraged the development of national liberation movements. Napoleon had a strong taste of this first in Spain and then during his fateful 1812 campaign,

---

[1] Stendhal, *Œuvres complètes*, "Racine et Shakespeare", Paris, 1954, p. 58.

when the Grande Armée was crippled by the blows inflicted on it by the Russian people and the foundations of Napoleon's Empire were so shaken as never to recover.

The national liberation movements in Europe in the first quarter of the nineteenth century were organically linked with the democratic movements trying to carry through the destruction of the bastilles of feudalism begun by the French Revolution. "Napoleon's imperialist wars continued for many years, took up a whole epoch and exhibited an extremely complex network of imperialist[1] relationships interwoven with national liberation movements. And as a result, through all this epoch, unusually rich in wars and tragedies (tragedies of whole peoples), history went forward from feudalism to 'free' capitalism."[2]

The Spanish guerrilla movement created the preconditions for the bourgeois revolution of 1820. Under pressure from the popular masses, whose mood was expressed by the Tugendbund, the frightened heads of states of the German confederation, vowed to introduce constitutional government, and only the fierce resurgence of feudal reaction following Napoleon's defeat enabled them to avoid carrying out their solemn promises. In Italy the carbonari who had headed an anti-French and anti-Austrian movement, led bourgeois revolutions in Naples and Piedmont in 1820-21. Among the officers who entered Paris with the victorious Russian armies were those who took part in the tragic Decembrist uprising on Senate Square in St. Petersburg one cold winter's day in 1825.

The restoration under the aegis of the Holy Alliance of the pre-revolutionary order affected first and foremost the political aspect of European social life. The Restoration was unable to halt the development of the new capitalist system of economic relations.

While social movements on the continent where the bourgeois transformation of society had not yet been completed were mainly bourgeois-democratic or revolutionary-democratic, in England, which was more advanced in-

---

[1] "I call here imperialism the plunder of foreign countries in general and an imperialist war the war of plunderers for the division of such booty." (Lenin's note.)

[2] V. I. Lenin, Collected Works, Vol. 27, p. 51.

dustrially and socially, another historical factor was making itself felt: the class struggles of the proletariat were beginning. "The new mode of production," wrote Engels, "was, as yet, only at the beginning of its period of ascent; as yet it was the normal, regular method of production—the only one possible under existing conditions. Nevertheless, even then it was producing crying social abuses."[1] These social evils were naturally borne by the have-not sections of the population and especially the proletariat, for the development of machine production, the vast increase in exploitation and the growth of the towns was producing fundamental changes in their patriarchal forms of labour, their way of life and thinking. At the beginning of the nineteenth century the struggle of the working class in Britain had become extremely serious, heralding the fierce class battles that were to erupt on the Continent and culminate in the revolutions of 1848. Driven to desperation by grinding poverty, the workers openly attacked the factory system and, singing hymns fell upon the machines they so loathed with heavy hammers, seeing in the machines the source of their grievances. The bourgeoisie punished the Luddites as an example, but were unable to put a stop to unrest among the workers and in 1819 resorted to arms against a peaceful meeting at St. Peter's Field near Manchester. The Peterloo massacre, as this shameful event went down in history, revealed the extreme acuteness and uncompromising nature of the major social antagonism of the new age to which all the other contradictions of capitalist society were objectively subordinate. But in the first quarter of the nineteenth century this antagonism had not yet taken its place at the centre of spiritual life and was not perceived as the basic contradiction of the age. At that time, as Marx remarked: "The class-struggle between capital and labour is forced into the background, politically by the discord between the governments and the feudal aristocracy gathered around the Holy Alliance on the one hand, and the popular masses, led by the bourgeoisie on the other."[2]

---

[1] F. Engels, *Anti-Dühring*, Moscow, 1969, pp. 309-10.
[2] K. Marx, *Capital*, Moscow, 1965, Vol. I, p. 14.

In the process of assimilating history in the making art, literature and social thought were constantly coming across new phenomena, reflecting its motion from feudalism to "free" capitalism. The Enlighteners' illusion of the possibility of social harmony following from the Revolution was shattered on contact with reality, for instead of a harmonious man capitalism produced an unharmonious man, instead of a coherent society, a divided society, instead of concord between people, their estrangement, instead of the individual living for the common good, the individual with selfish thoughts and feelings.

Social consciousness perceived the system of capitalist relations which was inexorably emerging as a sphere of elemental conflicts between heterogeneous, hostile interests, whose destructive power was not only manifesting itself in people's practical activities, but was determining man's spiritual world, mentality and character.

There was naturally nothing new about this observation. The French thinkers of the Enlightenment in their investigations into the mechanism of social relations had come to see interest as the primary motive force of human ideas and actions. Helvetius wrote in his treatise *De l'esprit* that all people are subject to their interests. Holbach in his *Le Système de la nature* maintained that personal gain and interest lie at the root of such feelings as love and hate. They were not dismayed by this observation, for, like the Russian thinker Chernyshevsky with his theory of "reasonable egoism", they believed in the essential goodness of human nature, did not consider different personal interests to be necessarily hostile, and saw no reason why they should not give way to the principle of the common good. However, the thinkers of the Enlightenment did not fully understand the social nature of personal interest and were therefore unclear as to how concern for the common weal could overcome personal interest, and this made their ideas rather utopian.

The bourgeois ideologists proper saw the struggle of interests as perfectly natural and normal. The English utilitarians with Jeremy Bentham at their head considered the concept of the common weal an empty abstraction, pure illusion. For Bentham and his followers the only reality was individual interests, which they regarded as regulating and guaranteeing just relations between people in society. Hegel, however, in his examination of legal structure of society, destroyed the liberal theory of the utilitarians that individual interests acted as regulators in human relations. In his *Philosophie des Rechts* he noted: "Individuals are in the quality of citizens ... of a state *private persons* pursuing the aim of personal interest."[1] Thus society is a battlefield of individual private interests, a struggle of all against all (here Hegel repeats Hobbes' idea), an arena where personal interest conflicts with the special interests of society, and at the same time the interests of private persons and society clash with the established order of the state. This was a pretty accurate description of the bourgeois system. It merely omitted to explain the reasons why society had become a battlefield of divergent interests, an explanation that only Marxism was to provide, by showing that interest is a consequence of the private ownership principle on which class society is based, that it is the *expression* of the *class antagonisms* inherent in such a society.

Describing the features of the new, capitalist period in the development of human society, Engels wrote: "The elevation of interest to the principle that links mankind automatically entails—as long as that interest remains directly subjective, purely egoistic—general disintegration, the concentration of individuals on themselves, isolation, and the transformation of mankind into a crowd of mutually repellent atoms. ..."[2]

The elevation of interest to the position of the principle linking mankind was the objective result of the bourgeois revolution, of bourgeois progress and the process of formation of the capitalist system of social relations. Social atomisation progressed simultaneously and its spread had a tremendous effect on intellectual life and people's social psychology in the post-revolutionary period.

---

[1] G. Hegel, *Philosophie des Rechts*, Berlin, 1840, S. 245.
[2] K. Marx, F. Engels, *Werke*, Bd. 1, S. 556.

The historical self-awareness to which the romanticists aspired could only begin with cognition of contemporary history. Romanticism observed life and saw the growth of social atomisation as an anomaly of the historical process. The romanticists had not yet seen this process to be directly dependent on the private ownership system of relations. Able to observe the results and ignorant of the causes, the romanticists sought the explanation of the important phenomenon they had observed in the features of human characters instead of in the circumstances that produced these characters.

The first works of the new school were thus basically studies of human character marked if not by exclusiveness at least by striking novelty. Through the complex fusion of religious, mystical, philosophical and mythological ideas and images of Novalis's *Heinrich von Ofterdingen*—like a carved crystal cup from which the blue flower of romanticism emanated a strange, mysterious, fairy-tale light—we can distinguish the features that relate the novel to Chateaubriand's *René*, Senancour's *Obermann*, Tieck's *William Lovel*, Nodier's *Le Peintre de Saltzbourg* and Constant's *Adolphe*. Irony and melancholia, preoccupation with their own thoughts and their own persons, and exaggerated sensibility are to a varying degree characteristic of all the early romantic heroes. Their intense feelings and dramatic approach to life represent a tremendous leap forward from the heroes of the pre-revolutionary literature, who compared to them seem embodiments of healthy spirit.

The characters of the early romantic novels were somehow completely detached from their environment, attention being focussed on the new qualities of the social psychology produced by the complex and turbulent historical situation. The romantic hero was always a solitary figure. The gloomy atmosphere of an ancient baronial castle that is René's family nest, or the deserted mountain pastures of Scotland, the sun-soaked Italian countryside, ocean storms, or the deceptive silence of the virgin forests of North America are a mere accompaniment to the spiritual moods of Chateaubriand's hero, just as the austere Alpine scenery accompanies the thoughts and feelings of Obermann. The grandiose, exalted life of nature did not leave its mark on René's soul, like it did on the moral and spiritual make up of Nathaniol Bumppo, alias Leather Stocking, who felt himself to be as much a part of nature as the rushing rivers and shining lakes of the primordial forests that were his home. But then Bumppo was the creation of James Fenimore Cooper—a realist writer.

The life of the Indian tribe among which René found refuge in his wanderings, the slave-like devotion of his redskin wife,—nothing could affect his soul, which proved impervious to all outside influences. This was not because it was forged of the strongest metal, but because it was simply unable to make contact with the world around; it was refractory to the chemistry of social ties. Between the early romantic hero and his environment stood a kind of barrier formed by his own introvert nature, his devoted attention to his own "ego", which was hostile to the world, as the world was to it. René does not only have a pessimistic view of life: he expects his own soul to be the focus of existence. His individualism and egoism are little short of self-deification, making him a distant forerunner of Byron's Manfred who demanded more of life than life could provide.

While René reflects that new feature of the age, the individual's self-centeredness, *Adolphe* examines the social and psychological results of the transformation of society into a cluster of mutually-repellent atoms that had resulted from a great schism in the human consciousness. Like Chateaubriand, Benjamin Constant merely postulates the effect of environment on the thought and actions of his heroes. In his novel which reveals such profound understanding of the secrets of the human heart, he tells how "this defiance which follows such complete confidence, forced to direct itself against a being separate from the rest of the world, extends to the whole world",[1] thereby penetrating a phenomenon that goes far beyond the bounds of the intimate drama or a love conflict. Yet in his portrayal of the separation of two hearts, of the tragic discord between two lovers who can neither be together

---

[1] B. Constant, *Adolphe*, Paris, 1965, p. 44.

nor live without each other, he merely investigated the metamorphoses of his heroes' feelings, considering that "circumstances have but little importance, it is character that is essential".[1] In this he differed from the realists whose aim it was to go deeper and more fully into circumstances and character, and examine the connection between them, revealing their mutual influence. Nevertheless, despite the poverty of its social background, Constant's novel, by continuing the psychological prose tradition of the late eighteenth century, helped pave the way for psychological realist prose.

As a romanticist, Benjamin Constant portrayed the tragic consequences of alienation without investigating its social origins, believing the causes to lie within people themselves, in their moral qualities. Hence his belief that alienation could be overcome by moral education, and his attack in *De la religion* on the views of the utilitarians and scholars of the Enlightenment (and especially Helvetius) who explained human behaviour by the motives of profit or rational interest. His view being that the ideal of a society based on these principles could only be industrial production or "unification organised like a beehive", he considered that such a society would not be stable, for the application of the principles of gain or rational interest would have dire results: "Their natural consequence is to transform every individual into his own Centre. However when each man becomes his own centre, all are isolated."[2] However, as Stendhal rightly pointed out, "the majority of Frenchmen consider that this philosophy is excellently borne out by everyday life" and Constant's attack on it merely served as a further illustration of the spread of social atomisation.

All forms of consciousness and all kinds of ideology were affected by this process. Fichte's philosophy is based on the concept of the absolute "Ego", producing or realising its activity in the empirical "Ego", that is, in the subject, the individual, whose individual "Ego" is contrasted to the empirical "non-Ego" of the world lying out-

---

[1] B. Constant, *Adolphe*, p. 182.
[2] B. Constant, *De la religion*, Bruxelles, 1824, pp. XIX, XX.

side subjective experience. It might seem as though Fichte were reducing the concept of the absolute "Ego" as a supreme active, creative force or supreme principle to the experience and scale of the individual. In actual fact though, he raised to the level of an absolute the experience of the individual, who feels himself to be an atom in the world, extends his subjective view of things to the whole universe, attempting to expand his atomic size to its scale.

The Byronic hero, a gloomy, proud dissenter, fighting a one-man battle for his own individual rights as he understood them, something of a mystery to those around him and incurring their hostility, flouting laws and the accepted moral code as being made not for him but for the "crowd", combined in his demoniac and seductive figure the features of outlook produced by the process of alienation. Byron's Giaour and Lara were strong individuals challenging society. But their struggle was individualist, and in this they differed as carriers of the new socio-psychological features of social consciousness from the rebels found in the literature of the period leading up to the French Revolution. For Prometheus, who challenged the gods for the sake of man, and in whom Goethe extolled man's eternal natural longing for freedom, the important thing was other people, for whom he made his sacrifice. Byron's heroes put their own will and desires above all else. Caleb Williams, the hero of the novel by the pre-romantic writer Godwin, is a solitary figure who rejects egoistic society with all its evils and injustices, in favour of the interests of the oppressed classes. In his critique and rejection of the system of private ownership relations, Godwin was close to the ideas of the utopian socialists. Byron's romantic heroes stood beyond the fringe of society, and only opposed it as individuals. Jean Sbogar, the noble rebel rogue in Charles Nodier's eponymous novel, is also outside society. As mysterious and enigmatic as any Byronic hero, the same strong lone rebel, he dreams of human happiness and has come, after a great deal of thought on the course of history, to the conclusion that "equality, the object of all our desires and the aim of all our revolutions, is really only possible in two states—

slavery and death".[1] This pessimistic conclusion was the result of direct experience and was confirmed by life itself. Since the development of society in the post-revolutionary period did not bring man welfare and happiness, since the inexorable laws of capitalist competition made society more and more hostile to man, it was only natural that the romanticists should be brought face to face with the question of the objective content and direction of historical progress. Romanticism did not merely reflect the changes in social consciousness that ensued from the Revolution. Registering life's mobility and changeability and the corresponding changes in the world of human feelings, romanticism was bound to turn to the study of history as a source of arguments in its attempt to define and understand the prospects of social progress, and tried to understand the past in order to divine the future.

Feudal reaction, trying to arrest the progress of society along the path of bourgeois development, also produced its theoreticians and philosophers, who sought the model for the future in the recent, absolutist past. Edmund Burke, author of *Reflections on the French Revolution* contrasted bourgeois reality with an idyllic distilled picture of the feudal world which he saw as the embodiment of order and social harmony. Bonald, Joseph de Maistre and the Swiss historian Haller, author of a lengthy work entitled *Restauration der Staatswissenschaften*, presented in most vivid and frank form the ideas propounded by the numerous champions of reaction. The most militant of them, Joseph de Maistre, whose works were boiling with the rage of the aristocrat at the insolence of the people, revolution, progress and freedom, launched furious attacks in such treatises as *Du Pape, Examen de la philosophie de Bacon*, and the semi-fictional *Les soirées de St.-Pétersbourg* on materialist philosophy and the socio-political views of the Enlightenment. Nobody, possibly with the exception of Nietzsche, was such a virulent critic of Jean-Jacques Rousseau as de Maistre.

De Maistre opposed the ideas of changing the established institutions of society by revolution with the prin-

---

[1] Charles Nodier, *Jean Sbogar*, Paris, p. 140.

ciple of absolute monarchy, sanctified by religion and the Catholic Church. If a strong force was necessary to keep the people in check, de Maistre was not averse to restoring the Inquisition as a politico-spiritual institution for the supervision of citizens' souls and social behaviour. He was equally prepared to declare force the basis of public order, and the executioner a pillar of the state, a figure worthy of great respect. But if de Maistre's theorising and Bonald's dogmatic defence of monarchy, testifying as they did to the violence of political passions, corresponded to the spiritual demands of the feudal aristocratic reaction, they were quite out of tune with the spirit of the age, for they were purely metaphysical. History was not going to be turned backwards, and its heavy step was felt in all aspects of social consciousness. Even the conservative ro-manticists—and this was one of the great paradoxes of spiritual life in the early nineteenth century—while reject-ing the new post-revolutionary reality and the emergent system of capitalist relations and polemicising with the bourgeois ideology, nevertheless turned to history, and by comparing past and present, indirectly confirmed the idea of development.

In a letter to Mehring, in which he spoke of the social views of a representative of the so-called "historical school", Engels made a remark that sums up fairly well the nature of the conservative romanticists' views on his-tory. "However the most peculiar thing is that the correct conception of history is to be found *in abstracto* among the very people who have been distorting history most *in concreto*, theoretically as well as practically."[1]

Chateaubriand, who had created René in his novel *Les Natchez* about the life of the North American Indians, tried in his vast romantic epic *Les Martyrs* to produce an all-embracing picture of the Hellenic world, the tragedy of the first Christians, the clash between the Romans and the barbarians, including in his grandiloquent, rhetorical narrative pictures throbbing with life of the everyday existence and morals of the ancient world changing under

---

[1] K. Marx and F. Engels, *Selected Correspondence*, Moscow, 1955, p. 533.

the impact of the new, Christian culture that was coming to replace it. Written to glorify Catholicism as a pillar of the old society, *Les Martyrs* is of interest not so much for its message as because of the way the idea of development, entering the aesthetic sphere, came into contact with history, which in turn became an aesthetic object.

History also became the object of study and portrayal in the works of the German conservative romanticists. The German romanticists were prompted by the demands of the national liberation struggle to accord particular attention to folklore, collecting and adapting it, seeing in it the fullest expression of the national spirit. Arnim and Brentano's *Des Knaben Wunderhorn*, and Grimms' fairy tales are evidence enough of the romanticists' great interest in folklore. It was studied along with the way of life and manners of the periods in which the popular tales and legends were set, and the romanticists' interest in baroque and Gothic art and in the literature of the Renaissance, and especially Shakespeare, was in contrast to the classicists' interest in the ancient world.

In presenting the past in their works, the romanticists portrayed the historical colour of the age in question, whether is was post-Reformation Germany as in Arnim's novel *Die Kronenwächter*, or the idealised life of the craftsmen in old Germany as described by Hoffmann. But the romanticists' interest in the past was still of a purely empirical character. While stressing the difference between the past and present and the changes that had taken place in history, they did not know what determined the motion of history, which is why they were mystified both by past and by present and gave a very approximate picture of the social conflicts of their time. This also accounts for the fact that their criticism of capitalism had a purely ethical character: condemning the egoistic features of the bourgeois outlook and bourgeois society, they railed pathetically against the power of gold and its corrupting influence. Aware that the new society was hostile to man, they ascribed a demoniac nature to the forces at work in it, unaware that the anti-human element that seemed to be superhuman and demoniac, was in fact "bourgeois society, the society of industry, of universal competition, of private interest, freely following its aims of anarchy, of self-alienated natural and spiritual individuality...."[1]

Real criticism of social contradictions appeared so irreal to the German romanticists, that they were led to distort contemporary history in presenting it *in concreto*. Their dreamer heroes perceived reality in a dual light, in both the fantastic, fairytale, and the mundane, everyday aspects. Minor bureaucrats of petty German states, narrow-minded hide-bound and pedantic, in another, romantically pretersensual sphere of their existence became good or evil masters of the elemental forces of nature. A hero longing for wealth sells his soul, receptive to passion and sympathy, to a divine spirit in return for an unfeeling heart of stone. A dead man rises from the grave and finds employment, hiding the gold he earns in his grave. A turnip is miraculously turned into a cocky little fellow with an ability to find hidden gold and treasure, who finds favour with rulers and begins to play an important role in society. All these ironic and poetic phantasmagoria only give a very approximate impression of the processes going on in the post-revolutionary world and evidence that the ideological seed-bed for the growth of non-realist aesthetic forms, including romanticism, was a failure to apprehend reality.

German romanticism was free from all revolutionary impulses and developed against a background of political compromise between the bourgeoisie and feudal reaction, recognising the changeability of social forms only indirectly. It never found the true material foundation of the historical process, which was grasped far more clearly and fully by revolutionary romanticism.

Byron's art absorbing as it did the moods and views of the European democrats who adopted revolutionary methods against the attempts of reaction to prevent the advance of the peoples towards emancipation from the vestiges of the feudal system, even in those poems where the hero never went beyond an individualistic protest, touched on the real social conflicts of his age, which reflected the clash of interests between the masses and

---

[1] Marx and Engels, *The Holy Family*, Moscow, 1956, p. 164.

feudal lords and governments united around the Holy Alliance. In examining the disposition of social forces in the period of the Napoleonic wars, Byron acquired a deeper understanding of the historical process, and gradually began to realise that since it was the popular masses, who bore the burden of progress, they were most probably the force that moved history forward.

Early on, in his *Childe Harold's Pilgrimage*, Byron had been aware of the antagonistic nature of social relations, and had stressed the difference between the interests of the people, the poor and oppressed part of the nation, and those of the rulers, who were quite indifferent to the former's needs and sufferings. This understanding, combined with political protest against the national enslavement of the peoples, with struggle for the freedom of the oppressed man, and passionate rejection of the principle of authoritarian rule, broadened the social content of his poetry, gradually enabling him to become aware of the real foundation of the historical process, and preparing his adoption of the principles of realism. This change was greatly hindered by the mood of despair and cosmic pessimism that emanated from the individualistic nature of Byron's rebellion, from awareness of the fact that a man isolated from society had not the strength to change society. Shelley gave a very accurate definition of the difference between Byron's views and his own in his dialogue poem *Julian and Maddalo,* in the passage that runs:

> . . .and I (for ever still
> Is it not wise to make the best of ill?)
> Argued against despondency, but pride
> Made my companion take the darker side.

If for Byron the future appeared shrouded in gloom, and in *Darkness* and the mystery *Heaven and Earth* he looked on suffering and mankind's struggle for freedom as futile, these moods were largely fed by the weaknesses of the revolutionary movements in the early years of the century. The Italian and French carbonari, the members of the German Tugendbund, and the Russian Decembrists—noblemen opposed to autocracy—did not see revolution as a mass popular uprising, but fondly imagined that a revolution and the abolition of absolutism could be effected through the work of secret societies, a firmly-rooted illusion shared by many later revolutionaries such as Mazzini, Blanqui and the Russian People's Will organisation. As a rule, the conspirators' struggle with the governments involved enormous sacrifices and produced scant results, for it was waged without the participation of the masses, the only force that was in fact capable of changing the existing order. Byron witnessed more than once the tragic defeat of European revolutionaries, and these failures made a profound impression on him. Like all the revolutionary romanticists of the time, Byron regarded individual action as the basic impulse in social development. Yet, while realising that bourgeois society could not satisfy man's natural aspirations for freedom, Byron was unable, as long as he adhered to the principles of romanticism, to determine what external objective principles and conditions were really capable of promoting the practical achievement of freedom. As a revolutionary he accepted the idea of development, the idea of historical change, and served it with all the power of his great talent appealing for the emancipation of mankind from all forms of bondage. At the same time, Byron lost hope in the future and saw history as an essentially tragic process, at the end of which it was not the reign of freedom that awaited man, but chaos and hopelessness. He was only to emerge from this ideological blind-alley by overcoming the romantic individualist character of his early works, and this meant beginning where the realists of the past had begun, with the study of the influence of environment and circumstances on man, the study of the objective factors that condition the life not only of the individual but of the whole of society. Hence *Beppo* and *Don Juan*, and the satires of the 'twenties like *The Age of Bronze* and *The Irish Avatar*, works which represented a revival in English literature of the dormant traditions of realism.

Shelley did not know this ideological contradiction since his poetry lent on different social forces. Shelley's poetry marked the beginning of a tradition that was to develop organically and naturally into the socialist art of our present century.

Shelley regarded himself as more than a poet: he regarded himself as a social reformer. From his observations and reflections on contemporary society he, too, came to understand its antagonistic nature. Once he had realised that the sources of this antagonism lay in material inequality, he placed his art once and for all in the service of the lower classes and his poetry began to express the social ideas the movement of the oppressed masses produced. His mind and his poetry were directed towards a tireless search for happier conditions of social, moral and political life than those which capitalism offered. The motive impelling Shelley to seek a new social ideal outside the domain of the ethics, morality and social philosophy of capitalist society was the same as that which caused Robert Owen to first undertake his social reformist activity in New Lanark and later to adhere to Communism— and that was the position of the working class in England. Capitalist• progress, connected with the growth of machine production which had given rise to the struggle of the English bourgeoisie for world hegemony, was achieved at the expense of merciless exploitation of the people and especially the proletariat, their economic enslavement and demoralisation. Shelley had been quick to observe this, and in his poetry humanistic motifs were organically interwoven with criticism, and even rejection, of bourgeois society. His early work *Declaration of Rights* was a militant propaganda work containing socialist ideas in embryo form, while in his still somewhat immature poem *Queen Mab* the idea of development is clearly applied to history, which Shelley considers as a process of human emancipation from slavery and from the sufferings and miseries which society based on private ownership inflicted on man. Historical optimism became a dominant feature of Shelley's poetry, and this was what distinguished him from his contemporary romantics for whom pessimism was characteristic, as Shelley himself noted. In the preface to *The Revolt of Islam* he wrote: "This influence has tainted the literature of the age with the hopelessness of the minds from which it flows. Metaphysics, and inquiries into moral and political science, have become little else than vain attempts to revive exploded superstitions, or sophisms like those of Mr. Malthus, calculated to lull the oppressors of mankind into a security of everlasting triumph. Our works of fiction and poetry have been overshadowed by the same infectious gloom. But mankind appears to me to be emerging from their trance. I am aware, methinks, of a slow, gradual silent change."

Shelley's optimism was not unfounded, for it did not simply spring from his hope of the people being freed by revolution but was based on his conviction that life develops according to the law of necessity.

While voluntarism was a characteristic feature of romantic art, and especially of Byron's poetry, and the romanticists saw their hero's self-will as the expression of his inner freedom and independence of any societal influence on his proud soul, Shelley had quite another view of freedom, and could say, like Leibnitz, that the crux of the matter was that people knew their aspirations, but not the external reasons for their aspirations. Thus, the child imagines it is free in desiring the milk that is its diet.

In his recognition of the power of necessity Shelley had taken the first and most important step towards understanding the objective external laws governing the development of nature and society. He naturally came to the conclusion that the laws of necessity also apply to the historical process, and that therefore the changes in social forms that occur throughout history are not fortuitous but inevitable. Thus, the French bourgeois revolution which served to destroy the old order was no sudden, spontaneous burst of political passions or God's oversight, as the reactionary ideologists supposed, but a logical stage in the progressive development of mankind. Likewise, it was also in the order of things that the social system established on the ruins of feudalism—an unjust order where self-interest reigned supreme and which was totally unable to satisfy the demands of the working masses— should be inevitably replaced by another social order, this time based on the principles of freedom and justice. This idea runs through the poem *The Revolt of Islam* and becomes a major theme in Shelley's works, making him a forerunner of socialist aesthetics. The fierce criticism of capitalist society contained in Shelley's pamphlets and poems, in his political satires and works that attack tyranny, was reinforced by the conviction of the inevitability of a change in the existing social relations and the ceaseless advance of human history towards emancipation, an idea which found its ultimate expression in *Prometheus Unbound*, undoubtedly one of the masterpieces of world poetry.

In this poem of emancipation a joyous and youthfully fresh view of the universe merged with a passionate feeling which Shelley himself defined as "a passionate desire to transform the world". The poet conjures up a world splashed by the spray of the morning sea, fanned by winds bearing on their wings the sharp heady odour of the earth, with chariots drawn by winged horses and driven by the messengers of necessity, flying over rocky mountains and fertile valleys lit by the light of the planets—a radiant world where clouds gold-tipped with sunlight float across the azure sky and god-like Oceanides, Asia, Panthea and Ione, elements in the form of wondrous beings, lament Prometheus being tormented by the furies, and greet his liberation with cries of joy. In this pristine world glistening with dew, Demogorgon, the mysterious, inescapable power of change, the principle of development and formation, that has not yet taken on a definite shape, casts down into eternal darkness Jupiter, the ruler, so that "the tyranny of heaven none may retain". The whole radiant universe, the elements and spirits, the Oceanides and the indomitable Prometheus himself receive the tyrant's fall with great jubilation. Now the ocean's "streams will flow... tracking thin path no more by blood and groans and desolation, and the mingled voice of slavery and command". A new life has begun with the victory over Jupiter and the spirit of the Hour tells of the beneficent changes that have taken place on earth, where "the man remains sceptreless, free, uncircumscribed, but man equal, unclassed ... just, gentle, wise". This hymn of triumph to freedom and social justice that crowns Shelley's works was at the same time a hymn to the ceaseless advance of man towards a harmonious society.

In *Prometheus Unbound* the idea of development found perfect poetic expression, though not in a concrete-historical form. This was perfectly natural, for the poet's awareness, like that of the founder of English utopian socialism, Robert Owen, was formed in the period when the class conflicts of the new social order were but little developed and the real root causes of the historical process were not yet clear. As Engels remarked: "To the crude conditions of capitalistic production and the crude class conditions corresponded crude theories. The solution of the social problems, which as yet lay hidden in undeveloped economic conditions, the utopians attempted to evolve out of the human brain."[1] These factors conditioned the utopian features of Shelley's outlook.

The real root causes of the historical process were only gradually discovered and revealed by realist art, literature and social thought, which undertook analytical investigation of the new order that arose after the victory of the bourgeoisie. Realism set out with new artistic means, different from those of eighteenth century realism, to study the dialectic of post-revolutionary social relations and the causes determining the movement of history, its development, and hence people's behaviour and psychology. Romanticism (that is, the first wave of romanticism, resulting from the clash of interests between the people and feudal reaction), although absorbing and expressing many of the essential contradictions of post-revolutionary social life, was prevented from doing this by the very nature of the romantic method.

Romanticism was extremely sensitive to the mobility and pulse of history and, breaking with the canons of classicism, the static form of classical works, and with the objective form of realist works, it made subjective freedom of expression its banner, regarding only the free soaring fantasy of the writer, not subject to any laws or prescriptions, as being capable of presenting the dynamics of life. Indeed, the works of the romanticists reveal a free

---

[1] F. Engels, *Anti-Dühring*, Moscow, 1969, p. 305.

treatment of composition, liberties taken with the order of narration, and a free choice of place and time for the action. The author's presence is felt throughout, and many romantic works are really protracted monologues. The feelings in romantic poetry are intensified and exaggerated, and on the whole romanticism concentrates on man's inner world, looking on life and history as the theatre in which people's passions and ideas are realised, determining, by their fortuitous play and flux, the flux of life. Novalis writes thus of the essence of romanticism as a creative method: "Absolutisation, the conferring of a universal meaning, and classification of the particular moment, and of the particular situation and so on, is the essence of any creation in romanticism." He goes on to say: "The elements of romanticism. Objects, like the sounds of the Aeolian harp, must arise suddenly, spontaneously, without revealing the instrument that has produced them." In other words, romanticism was indifferent to causal relationships between the phenomena of life. But what was it that romanticism absolutised? What exactly did it universalise?

In his *Aesthetics* Hegel expressed many opinions on romanticism that accurately define its essence (although he mistakenly applied its features, which have a strict historical place, to past ages). Having written: "Romantic art no longer has as its aim free vitality of the Being in its quiet and immersion of the soul in the corporeal; it is not interested in this life as such,"[1] he correctly notes somewhat later: "Lyricism is a kind of basic element of romantic art, the tone in which the epos and drama also speak, and which pervades, like some universal aroma of the soul, even works of the plastic arts."[2] He goes on to say that the truly romantic characters in whom "the personal attains its full significance" are "independent individuals who only reckon with themselves, and set themselves special aims which are exclusively their own aims and are dictated only by their own individuality"[3].

---

[1] Hegel, *Werke*, Bd. 10, 2 abt., Berlin, 1837, S. 134.
[2] Ibid., S. 133.
[3] Ibid., S. 197.

Thus romanticism—and this is its chief feature as a creative method—grossly inflated the individual and imparted universality to his inner world by isolating him from the objective world. Realism, on the other hand, examined life as an integral whole, within which relations and links were causally conditioned by one another. *If the realists singled out one side of life as revolutionary art did, it was simply because it expressed the dominant trend in social development or that trend which was destined to become the dominant one and subordinate to itself all other sides of life.* The romanticists universalised and inflated one aspect of reality or the human consciousness, often one that had a particular significance. Thus Constant studied and described character in its pure form, so to speak, independent of the conditions which produced it. The German romantics, such as Kleist, made their characters subordinate to the power of their feelings or passions and studied that power as completely divorced from the surrounding world. Byron gave the heroes of his romantic poems a rather one-dimensional character. Therefore romanticism did not achieve the historical self-awareness towards which it aspired, since it did not investigate the objective preconditions of human consciousness. Treating reality as a sphere for the application and struggle of subjective expressions of will, the romanticists were unable to explain what lay at the root of and conditioned the movement of different human aspirations.

Criticising subjectivism in social thought (which was also present in romanticism) Marx wrote: "Thus the conflicts of innumerable individual wills and individual actions in the domain of history produce a state of affairs entirely analogous to that prevailing in the realm of unconscious nature. The ends of the actions are intended, but the results which actually follow from these actions are not intended; or when they do seem to correspond to the end intended, they ultimately have consequences quite other than those intended. Historical events thus appear on the whole to be likewise governed by chance. But where on the surface accident holds sway, there actually it is always governed by inner, hidden laws and it is only a matter of discovering these laws."[1] This was no simple task, for nothing was enveloped in such a thick and voluminous cloak of illusions as the content of the historical process. Although history, in the words of Marx, is but the activity of man pursuing his aims, it was exceedingly difficult to perceive and comprehend the hidden inner laws that determine that activity, its motives and end results, and to free them from the numerous metaphysical layers and misconceptions. Only Marxism was to prove capable of coping with that truly titanic task. Progressive social thought prior to Marxism, and realism too, studying as it did life in all its concrete contingencies and participating in the social battles of the age—prepared the great act of cognizance by man of his historical activity and sought to disclose the nature of social relations first and foremost through the investigation of reality itself.

Social theory in apprehending and cognizing reality considered history as a process. "If we now take a glance at universal history in general, we shall see a vast picture of changes and actions, infinitely varied formations of peoples, states and individuals, continuously appearing one after the other," writes Hegel in his *Philosophie der Geschichte*. "The all-embracing idea," he continues, "the category that emerges above all in this ceaseless replacement of individuals and peoples, which exist for a while and then disappear, is *change* in general. A look at the ruins that remain from past glory moves us to take a closer look at this change in its negative aspect.... But the closest definition applicable to change is that change, which is destruction, is at the same time the emergence of new life, that death comes out of life and life out of death."[2] In regarding history from the point of view of formation and recognising the replacement of moribund social forms by new nascent ones to be an inevitable process, Hegel was essentially denying the possibility of a cessation of progress, a halt in the historical development of society.

---

[1] K. Marx and F. Engels, *Selected Works* in 3 volumes, Moscow, 1970, Vol. 3, p. 366.
[2] G. W. Hegel, *Werke*, Bd. 9, Berlin, 1840, S. 90.

Bourgeois ideology proper, as soon as it took shape, rejected outright the idea that history was a process. Arthur Schopenhauer, the father of bourgeois pessimism, considered history to be essentially the study of individuals. In his major work, *Die Welt als Wille und Vorstellung* published in 1818, he wrote: "The true philosophy of history consists in the insight that in all these endless changes and their confusion we have always before us only the same, even, unchanging nature, which to-day acts in the same way as yesterday and always; thus it ought to recognise the identical in all events, of ancient as of modern times, of the east as of the west; and, in spite of all difference of the special circumstances, of the costume and the customs, to see everywhere the same humanity. This identical element which is permanent through all change consists in the fundamental qualities of the human heart and head—many bad and few are good."[1]

Ideas such as this prepared the way for Nietzsche's theory of "eternal recurrence" and have become a basic element of the modern bourgeois consciousness, which is essentially anti-historicist.

However, Hegel, who approached history from the point of view of formation, continuous development, with its inherent contradictions, its ups and downs, its periods of progress and regression, nevertheless perceived and interpreted history as a purely logical process, not a material one. He was aware that man's ideology, way of thinking, philosophy and law, religion and art, and technical activity are always a product of his time and his time alone, that is, are conditioned by the whole historical character of a particular age. But he explained this particular character as expressing the various stages in the development of the Spirit, Reason, and did not take into account the *objective* conditions for historical changes, their material and social foundations.

It fell to realist art to fill the speculative and abstract conception of historical process with real objective content, thereby answering the most essential spiritual demands of the time. After having been largely ousted by

---

[1] A. Schopenhauer, *The World As Will and Idea*, Vol. III, Seventh Edition, London, p. 227.

non-realist currents at the end of the eighteenth and beginning of the nineteenth centuries, realism now came into its own as an instrument for cognizing life, receiving a tremendous impetus to development and improvement. Many features of the new social relations that arose with the collapse of the feudal system were perceived and depicted by realism.

Realism was reborn in the same historical soil as romanticism, and faced the same ideological task—that of presenting the real substance and direction of historical progress. Hence the similarities between realism and romanticism, the presence of romantic elements in the works of Pushkin, Balzac, Dickens, Gogol, and Stendhal, not to mention the realists of lesser stature. In describing his own *realism* in *Etudes sur M. Beyle,* Balzac was quite justified in claiming that it contained both features of "the literature of images", that is, of romanticism, and of the "literature of ideas", as he referred to realism, the exponents of which "...avoid discussion, do not like reverie and aspire to achieve tangible results"[1].

Another similarity between romanticism and realism was the fact that both movements judged capitalist reality unfavourable for the individual. But while the progressive romanticists simply made a social criticism of capitalism, the realists *added social analysis,* which brought them, in Balzac's words, very "tangible results" in revealing the social nature of the contradictions in post-revolutionary society advancing steadily towards "free" capitalism. "There are *no* 'pure' phenomena, nor can there be, either in Nature or in society," wrote Lenin, "that is what Marxist dialectics teaches us, for dialectics shows that the very concept of purity indicates a certain narrowness, a one-sidedness of human cognition, which cannot embrace an object in all its totality and complexity."[2] But the fact that the two artistic movements shared common features did not mean that the revival of realism consisted in the wholesale adoption of the ideological and aesthetic innovations of romanticism. Realism asserted itself by making use of these innova-

---

[1] Honore de Balzac, *Etudes sur M. Beyle,* Paris, 1846, p. 481.
[2] V. I. Lenin, *Collected Works,* Vol. 21, p. 236.

tions and went on to overcome *romanticism's one-sided view of life*, as evidenced by the experience of Walter Scott and Pushkin, whose works embraced the most disparate spheres of life and by various paths led literature to a single goal—the creation of *a new type of realism.*

Walter Scott went through the same stages in his creative evolution as many other romantic writers. From an early interest in gathering and studying folklore material, he went on to investigate the history of the periods in which it was produced. But unlike the other romanticists, he did not rest content with admiring the mysteries of the folk soul as revealed in ancient beliefs, songs and tales, but analysed the objective conditions, both social and spiritual, that influenced the life of the people. Child of a tempestuous and fierce age, Walter Scott combined analytic study of the past, great erudition and a vast knowledge of the life, manners and customs of the past with a keen sense of history, presenting man in his novels not simply as a member of society but as a participant in the historical process. This represented a tremendous step forward.

While in classicism there was a tendency to idealise the hero and stress his noble character to the extent even of ennobling his negative features, and while the romantic hero was an exceptional individual, in his own eyes too, his originality being the distinctive feature of romantic art, the heroes of Walter Scott's numerous novels were *ordinary people.* The romantic hero's spiritual world was fenced off from the outside world and presented as an independent sphere professedly uninfluenced by environment. The Walter Scott hero is above all an integrated character, his individual nature and spiritual world being organically linked to his environment, of which he is a part, so that he acts as *historical man,* that is, as the point of intersection of the various conflicting forces in society, as a representative of a particular social force.

This principle of character portrayal represented the triumph of realism. Walter Scott not only continued the realist tradition of the eighteenth century English novel where social environment was given considerable attention, but he enriched this tradition with the addition of a new quality, by differentiating the social substance of environment, portraying it as the theatre of clashes between conflicting *class interests* and endowing his heroes with clearly defined *class consciousness*. Freeing the narrative of the subjectivist element that was so typical of romantic literature, Walter Scott and the other great realists of the nineteenth century imparted truly epic features to the novel, enabling it to become a mirror of life.

Walter Scott's conclusion on the nature of social relations in bourgeois society was proved to be truly momentous and vital by the subsequent development of social thought. Three years after the publication of the Waverley novels, the French historian Augustin Thierry, broke away from the influence of the theories of Saint-Simon and embarked on a work on the English revolution, in which he also concluded that the class struggle is the motive force at the root of the historical process. The affirmation and development of this view in the works of Thierry and Guizot was to be greatly influenced by Walter Scott's philosophy of history as embodied in his novels.

Thierry broke with the accepted canons of historiography, asserting that it was not heroes and rulers but the common people, participants in the movement of the masses, that were the real makers of history. This too betrays the influence of Walter Scott, whose best novels presented the story of ordinary individuals against the background of important historical events that have a direct impact on their destiny, events in which the masses play an important role.

Whether he is writing of the decline of the Scottish clans or Jacobite abortive uprisings, going far back into the past as in *Rob Roy,* or the Waverley novels, or writing of his own times as in *St. Ronan's Well,* his manner of portraying his hero's psychology and behaviour is always the same. Scott is not interested in describing his hero's self-contained passions, thoughts and feelings and conveying the illusion of their free play. His novels present the struggle between various social interests, and class conflicts, the clash of socio-political forces at work in society, inevitably involving the main characters of the story, who become participants in the historical drama whether they like it or not. It is these social forces that form the hero's inner world, imparting to him unique individual qualities that are naturally and organically dependent upon the social environment that produced them.

Walter Scott adopts an *historical* approach to the portrayal of character. The Knight Templar in *Ivanhoe*, the oppressed Saxon peasants and feudal lords, think and act in accordance with the historical conditions of their age. The psychology of the sons of rebellious Scottish clans depends directly on the ties of kinship which hold them in their tight grip and force them to subordinate their own interests to the interests of the clan. Both the stern rebel Rob Roy and his fierce wife are unthinkable outside the environment which bred and educated them. The noble villain Jean Sbogar of whom his creator Nodier is so fond acts in a perfectly artificial world, appearing now amid the inhabitants of some Balkan state, now in splendid salons, and everywhere remaining the embodiment of the author's own views and not a living flesh-and-blood character. Rob Roy emanates the fresh breath of the Scottish mountains, his plaid is made by the calloused hands of women from poor Scottish crofts, his proud bearing, slyness and cunning in his dealings with strangers, his power over his fellow clansmen, indeed his whole nature and behaviour, are determined by the fact that he is a member of a mountain clan. One can only imagine Rob Roy, that bold, rough and ready Highlander, with his own personal code of honour, as he is—dressed in home-spun clothes that reek of sheepskin and night fires, and not in the cloak of the romantic hero.

The pure-hearted, quick-witted and prudent Jeanie Deans,—Scott's best portrait of a character of the people— reveals great moral fortitude and will-power and a strong sense of justice, in saving her rather flighty sister who is accused of murdering her child after being seduced and abandoned by a dissolute laird's son. Jeanie's journey to London where she manages to get an audience at court and save her innocent sister is a kind of Odyssey, which enabled Scott to present a whole historical period in English life, by making an original historical cross-section. In *The Heart of Mid-Lothian*, as in Scott's other novels, the *personal interest of the individual*—in this case Jeanie— is shown to be interwoven with the social interests of many other people, and indeed to depend on them and form an integral part of the whole system of social relations. Such a view of the interdependency and interconditionality of heterogeneous *social phenomena in a causal relationship* was a feature of realism, and it is on this that the *epic quality* of realism is based.

Balzac criticised the romanticists for neglecting to analyse the ensemble of social phenomena observable in life. In his philosophical treatise *La recherche de l'absolu* he launched a strong attack on "certain ignorant and avid people, who demand feelings without the principles that produced them, the flower without the seed that was sown and the baby without the mother's pregnancy. But can art be stronger than nature?"[1] The author of *La Comédie humaine* insisted that the events of human life, both personal and public, form an organic whole. "Wherever you begin everything is connected, everything is interwoven. The cause enables us to divine the effect, and an effect enables us to trace the cause."[2]

Causality never appears in realist literature as a mechanical succession of events, a chain with every link firmly joined to the next. This is the approach of naturalism, which attempts to present a photographic copy of reality, mixing indiscriminately essential and secondary features and often allowing the particular to obscure the general, and failing to bring to light the hidden processes of life that lie below the surface and determine its movement.

Causality in realism is expressed not only in the organic unity of the whole work and its parts, the unfortuitous nature of the details, the consistent development of the plot and the relationships between the characters, and a well-founded structure, but also, and indeed, above all, in a *historicist approach.*

Walter Scott evolved a historical approach as the result of his observation of and speculation on the development and intensification of the class struggle going on in

[1] Honore de Balzac, *Œuvres complètes*, V. 14, 2me p., p. 308.
[2] Ibid., p. 309.

English society during the writer's lifetime. Scott's works covered the long period in English history between the Glorious Revolution and his own day and age. In presenting the antagonism between the two forces of feudalism and the bourgeoisie with their class hostility, the compromises they concluded in the course of the political struggle in which the masses were involved, and in portraying the religious dissentions, conflicting philosophies of life, the clash of material interests, the division of society, and hence of the characters in his novels, into supporters of the old feudal order and supporters of the new bourgeois society, Scott was able to perceive in the mass of facts and events the major trend in social development—the formation of capitalism in England. He was a sufficiently shrewd observer of life to grasp the inevitability of the process and to see it as an historically progressive one. He also realised that the formation of capitalism affected every aspect of English life, and that therefore the personal fortunes of his heroes were dependent on this process, realised, that is, that there was a *causal relationship*. Thus, in order to understand and present the personal fortunes of his hero, the realist writer had to study the social environment in which the character lived and acted in its entirety, taking note of the general trends in its development, in order to understand and show its influence. This approach put an end to the subjectivism of the romantics' method of treating character, by which circumstances were regarded to be of slight importance, and characters were abstracted from the environment of which they were the product. When Byron ironically combined in Don Juan the character of the seducer sanctified by the old tradition of romantic exclusiveness with a realistic, authentic environment, he was producing far more than a remarkable aesthetic effect: by portraying both character and environment, Byron created a truly realist work.

Scott's historicism destroyed the romantic idea that only the exceptional individual could be the hero of a work of fiction, for he practically proved that realism could depict *both the ordinary and the exceptional* and not merely the ordinary and mundane as the romanticists asserted. Scott's heroes were ordinary people, who as a rule did not stand out in any way from the masses. But acting as they do in close connection with important historical events, in the magnetic field so to speak, of these events, in the conditions they produce, his heroes acquire *substance* for the events that affect their lives are *substantial*. Likewise, Scott portrayed important historical figures not as despotic demiurges of history but as children of their age, linked by numerous threads to the historical soil that grew them and whose minds reflected and refracted the ideas and prejudices of their day. For this reason they have a fulness and completeness which was lost by the twentieth century writers who portray historical figures as independent incisive characters determining the whole course of history.

In presenting an exceptional phenomenon or character, realism explains them, revealing *the sources of the exceptional in life itself*. Pushkin's *Captain's Daughter* is a fine example of this. There is no doubt that Pugachov is an exceptional, highly unusual individual.[1] Yet Pushkin explains the appearance of such an exceptional figure by the particular nature of the peasant war in which he plays such an important part. Since the whole psychology and class consciousness of Pugachov and his "generals" was inseparable from the social environment that produced them, from the violence and grandeur of the rebellion, the scale of the events which shook the Russian Empire to its foundations imparts scope to the character of the leader and his supporters, making them natural without reducing their significance. The perfectly ordinary squire Grinyov also acquires significance since he is bathed in the reflected glow of history and his life is drawn into the mainstream of the life of the nation.

The idea that the practical activity of perfectly ordinary people is at the same time *historical* activity gave Scott's novels an epic dimension and a democratic flavour. Although we find no direct depiction in his works of the life of the oppressed and exploited masses, and his social

---

[1] Yemelyan Pugachov, the leader of the peasant uprising in Russia in 1773-1775.—*Ed.*

views were certainly not revolutionary, his method of portraying history through the lives of ordinary people showed the way for literature to follow if it was to arrive at a broad presentation of the life of the masses, a way that it indeed followed.

But Scott's democratic outlook is not only revealed in his destruction of the view of history as being purely the domain of rulers and heroes. The French historians who discovered the laws of the class struggle in society claimed that this struggle ends with the triumph of the third estate, after which an age of general welfare ensues. Walter Scott studied the actual results of the bourgeois revolution and came to a different conclusion. In *St. Ronan's Well*, which dealt with contemporary life, he showed that bourgeois society resulting from the class struggle had a corrupting influence on human morals. The novel contains in a nutshell Scott's views on England's social development, and shows how, adopting a democratic standpoint, he changed his view of the nature of bourgeois progress, and came to regard it as *relative progress* since it had not only failed to bring people social welfare, but had revealed its essentially inhuman nature.

Scott came to understand the motive forces of social development through history, as it was history he was concerned with presenting. Pushkin solved a far more complicated aesthetic task, revealing the way these forces influenced contemporary society, *observing the influence on society of the very same factors that conditioned historical development.* Pushkin was thus concerned with portraying contemporary life, that is history in the making.

Scott's historicism arose against the background of the class struggle which was gaining momentum with the development of the Industrial Revolution in England, bringing with it all the contradictions of capitalism. Pushkin grew to spiritual maturity and came to form his historicist approach at a time when a recent peasant war that had brought to the fore the antagonism between the peasantry and the gentry was still very much in people's minds, at the time of a remarkable upsurge of the national and social consciousness of the Russian people due to the war against Napoleon, in the atmosphere of the Decembrist struggle, when the spirit of Revolution was rising in Europe, and the injustice of the social order was becoming perfectly obvious, for despotism was depriving millions of Russian peasants—the bulk of the country's working population—of the most elementary rights and freedoms.

The unbearable position of the peasantry was the most important social factor in Russian life, and just as radiation changes the structure of live tissues so this factor influenced the minds of Russian thinkers and writers, from Radishchev to Tolstoi, changing the structure of their consciousness, and compelling them to defend the interests of the downtrodden exploited peasant masses. The position of the peasantry attracted the attention of Russian social thought to the essential problems of the historical process, for the emancipation of the peasantry was ultimately associated with the establishment of Russian capitalism, and hence necessitated the adoption of attitude to capitalism as a whole and the clarifying of the prospects of social development in general.

Pushkin was not a peasant poet, but a truly national poet, yet the question of the position of the peasantry, in other words of the people, was at the centre of all his reflections on the principles of social organisation, and it was this that conditioned all those features of his work that go to make him a poet of the people. "Shall I ever see the people free" was practically the leitmotif of his work. For Pushkin the emancipation of the peasants betokened the emancipation of man and serfdom was a sign of wrongly organised society. Thus, the need to find a way of achieving the emancipation of the peasantry became for him the point of departure for *studying the nature and sources of the power some men wield over others and man's objective position in a society based on private ownership.*

Pushkin did not only achieve an encyclopaedic portrayal of Russian society. His brilliant mind grasped the results of post-revolutionary development in Europe and was quick to realise the negative effect of capitalist progress on the consciousness and morals of man. Criticism of capitalism became an important aspect of Pushkin's many-sided work.

The bourgeois ideologists inferred from the post-revolutionary development of Europe which so favoured the growth of capitalism that the main positive result of progress was that the individual was able to freely exercise his own will. The apologia for individualism was a reflection of the development of bourgeois society towards "free" capitalism and "free" competition, characteristic of pre-monopoly capitalism. It was this type of thinking that produced the apologia for bourgeois individualism in Max Stirner's *Der Einzige und sein Eigentum*. Egoism as a constructive factor, and the individual as its bearer, indeed Stirner's whole outlook fitted very easily into the general anti-revolutionary pattern of bourgeois consciousness, while retaining the *semblance of criticism of life*. Ideas such as these were blowing in the wind at that time and naturally caught the attention of writers. They became the subject of the half-serious conversations between the young people at Madame Voquet pension that had such serious consequences, hardening Rastignac's heart and arming him with indifference for his fellow men. They turned Julien Sorel's heart to stone and drove Raskolnikov to make his terrible test of the value of his own self, and they were the substance of the nihilism and seductive mixture of criticism and denial of revolution characteristic of Ivan Karamazov's views. Pushkin strongly criticised ideas exalting individualism, and showed their hostility to goodness and humaneness. He began by debunking the selfish romantic hero. *The Gypsies* represented a turn towards realism, and with such works as Byron's *Don Juan* and *The Age of Bronze* and Stendhal's essay *Racine et Shakespeare* ushered in a new period in the development of realism. *The Gypsies* contains a brilliant exposé of the features bourgeois social development had introduced into the human consciousness, and reveals that eminently sober view of life and people typical of true realism. Aleko, the hero, is an extremely self-centered individual, who is isolated from others since he only pursues his own personal interests. His rejection of civilisation à la Jean-Jacques Rousseau turns out to be an illusion, a mistaken and ineffectual way of overcoming life's contradictions, for the civilised world has set its seal on Aleko's soul forever. "For yet among you sons of nature, happiness I do not see...". For no man can be happy and free who encroaches on the freedom of others and is unable to master and overcome his own selfishness. So it was that there emerged in Pushkin's work and in world realist literature as a whole *a new type of humanism involving a search for ways and means of freeing man from all forms of social injustice.*

Aleko was given the opportunity to overcome his selfishness; the Old Gypsy indicated it to him in his tale about his acceptance of his wife's desertion. Yet Aleko answered the old man's wise humanism with the classic formula of individualism, "I'll not give up my rights", and the close knot of relationship between the characters ended in tragedy and bloodshed, in the spiritual bankruptcy of the "lone wolf" who had sought freedom only for himself. With its striking generalisation and powerful, tragic climax—"There's no escape from fateful passions and no defence from Fate"—Pushkin's poem clearly points an accusing finger at the destructive nature of the dominant outlook of contemporary society.

Condemnation of selfishness and self-will as principles conditioning the relations between people in society based on private ownership is a recurrent theme in Pushkin's works, where it gradually received more concrete historical and social expression as the poet matured spiritually, for Pushkin saw and presented social egoism not as an irrational force but as the direct product and result of a wrongly organised society. As well as studying character and passions, he at the same time investigated society, its manners and morals, its consciousness, the various ideas and moods that prevailed, its structure and social conflicts. He evaluated the development of life and history from a truly humanitarian standpoint. He showed that one of the causes of Boris Godunov's tragic end was that in gaining absolute power and satisfying his own selfish interests, he neglected the welfare of the people and flouted the unwritten laws of true humanity. "Son by marriage... of a hangman, himself in soul a hangman," he played up to the people, trying to placate them for a while in the pursuit of his own selfish interests and get them to forget the heinous crime he had committed in order to seize the throne. Boris is unable to bring the people true welfare, for his autocratic rule, *despotic by its very nature*, is based on violence and hostile to freedom.

The memory of the murdered child constantly haunts Boris, destroying all his undertakings and drawing him inexorably towards his doom. The murder of Dmitry was more than a trump in the hands of Boris's political rivals intriguing against him: in the play the image of the dead child is raised to become a symbol accusing the power of man over man, and injustice and evil in life. The question of the effectiveness of this symbol is one that has been much discussed, but it is no accident that Ivan Karamazov's powerful and shattering argument in his revolt against God and the unjust world he has created should be based on the symbol of a child's suffering. The meek defencelessness of a child in the face of the cruelty and inhumanity of life and people, like the defencelessness of the weak in general, developed as a leitmotif in Russian realist literature, with its tradition of the "little man", the underdog—from Pushkin's Yevgeny in *The Bronze Horseman*, terrorised by the great statue symbolising the power of the state, and Vyrin, the hero of *The Postmaster*, to Akaky Akakievich in Gogol's *The Greatcoat* and Makar Devushkin in Dostoyevsky's *Poor Folk*, and a whole host of other tragic figures of "little men" in Russian literature. But unlike many of his successors—Dostoyevsky for example—Pushkin, the father of Russian realism, was never to ignore the possibility of his underdog *rebelling* against the social order. The pathetic St. Petersburg clerk in *The Bronze Horseman* amid the raging elements that crush his brittle happiness dares to raise his voice against the powerful lord and master whose autocratic will was the cause of his woe. It is no accident that Pushkin studied the possibility of the "injured and insulted" man joining a peasant rebellion in *Dubrovsky*, or that in *The Captain's Daughter*, despite the many reservations, the hero's contact with the element of a peasant rebellion filled him with "exalted awe", for Pushkin had no doubts about the *law-*

fulness of a popular uprising. Thus, the main idea of *Boris Godunov*, the opposition of violence and humaneness, arose from the poet's profound awareness of the antagonism that existed between the oppressors and the oppressed.

An historical approach to the present was what determined the historicism of the tragedy, in which the conflict between two states, the struggle between different political interests around the Muscovite throne, human destinies, and the relations between government and people were presented in accordance with the spirit and meaning of history. The tragedy in *Boris Godunov* springs from Pushkin's understanding of the real underlying factors of the historical process, of the material interests which determine events. In the play Pushkin *presented the characters and the circumstances that produced them, man's environment and psychology in their unity and mutual influence*, without which realism, and especially the realist novel, could not have developed as they did.

At the time when Pushkin's contemporary Balzac was still writing amorphous works in an ultraromantic and melodramatic spirit, like *Clotilde de Lusignan, ou le beau Juif*, and Stendhal was writing travel notes and treatises on aesthetics, only just setting out to embody in the novel form the "iron laws of the real world" he had perceived (which he had not succeeded in doing in *Armance)*, when E. Bulwer-Lytton was just laying the foundations of *bourgeois realism*, and in his novels *Falkland* and *Pelham or the Adventures of a Gentleman*—as in those of his elder contemporary Jane Austen, and later in the forties, in the works of the critical-realist Brontë sisters—realism was strongly spiced with romanticism, Pushkin had already produced *Evgeni Onegin*, a novel in a new realist manner, whose canons have preserved their validity down to the present day. Despite the fact that the lesson of *Evgeni Onegin* only became part of the general heritage of European and world realist literature not directly but through the Russian realist novel when it came to occupy a dominant position in the world literary scene in the mid-nineteenth century, the genetic ties between it and the novels of other great realists are easily traced.

For a long time the European novel had preserved Lesage's system of plot development, whereby the hero meets with numerous obstacles and overcomes them. The character of the hero or the narrator are little influenced by environment, and are presented as already formed. Events succeed one another in a chain which could be made quite endless at will. It was of no basic importance what form the writer chose to tell his story, whether epistolary as Richardson or narrative: the general pattern remained the same. We find it in Fielding and Smollett. It was convenient in that it enabled the writer to draw a broad background and cram the narrative with incidents, insert little self-contained novellas and make the work entertaining. The preromantics injected a strong subjective element, and while the early realists often concentrated on portraying environment to the neglect of the characters' psychology, the pre-romantics, especially in the Gothic and romantic novel, subordinated environment to the subjective world of the feelings. But both preromantic and romantic novels are influenced by the traditional plot structure. Paradoxical though it may seem, Sterne, for example, who showed the most pronounced subjective approach, could have ended *Tristram Shandy* anywhere or added several further volumes, for the inner world of the heroes did not depend on the objective processes of the external world and the artist was little concerned with relating the events of the characters' inner lives with real external events. The same applies to the novels of Jean-Paul Richter and the early works of Victor Hugo. Walter Scott's historical sense led him to give a synthetic portrayal of environment and psychology, yet even he did not completely abandon the traditional plot scheme, something that was first achieved by Pushkin.

In *Evgeni Onegin* the psychology of the characters and the environment which formed them are presented *in organic unity* and the action is subordinated to the task of revealing individual and unique features of the characters. For the romanticist Constant circumstances were essentially unimportant: for Pushkin analysis of character was unthinkable without investigation of environment, investigation from a historical angle and a clear understanding of the social features of society. Thus, Pushkin's presentation of his characters' natures and their relationships with one another, their various conflicts, expands to embrace a picture of the life of society with all its social contradictions. The personal life of the heroes, their clashes of opinion and emotional conflicts—everything that had hitherto appeared in novels as *independent* of environment, was in Pushkin *determined* by environment and *typified*, and reflected the main features of the social structure. The mental sufferings of the heroes also reflect their specific class psychology and the basic characteristic feature of the age—its hostility to the normal, healthy, *natural* development of the personality and the baneful influence of propertied social relations on man.

Evgeni Onegin, like Pushkin's previous works, showed the spiritual bankruptcy of the self-centered, selfish hero. The poem condemned egoism as a typical feature of social relations and social consciousness, and in this sense *Evgeni Onegin* develops the humanitarian trend in Pushkin's work a stage further.

Pushkin attributed the hero's selfishness to social causes: his freedom was based on the unfreedom of others, who enabled him to lead his empty life of leisure, and since his spiritual world is immoral it follows that the social order which produced such a character is also immoral and abnormal. Pushkin's *criticism of his hero implied criticism of life's order.*

Onegin's selfishness makes him defy the norms of moral behaviour: he coldly rejects Tatiana's love, trampling her poor heart and ruining her life, dispassionately kills another man, and sails through life vainly searching for pleasure, perfectly indifferent to the fate of others, concerned only with his own self and his own selfish whims. And it was only when he fell hopelessly in love with the woman he had once spurned, when he felt the torture of repentance and was assailed with regrets in much the same way as Boris was by the "blood-stained ghost... appearing every day", only then, when he realised the baneful effects of egoism, that he began to feel his loneliness as a curse and his own self-will as a punishment. Onegin's scepticism and selfishness are in sharp contrast to Tatiana's moral integrity, her pure, firm faith in human dignity. Her conscious refusal to build her happiness on the misfortunes of others raises Tatiana above the hero and gives her self-denial the strength of a moral example. The humanitarian idea with which Pushkin imbues Tatiana makes her a perfectly enchanting and delightful character. This poor, modest provincial girl and society lady with tremendous pain locked away in her heart was the first in the gallery of fine women characters in Russian literature on which the People's Will and Bolshevik women of the future were to be brought up.

Confining the conflict to the love relationship between the hero and heroine but analysing their feelings in the wider context of society, Pushkin imbued his heroes with a tremendously rich inner life. In this *Evgeni Onegin* was vastly different from the novel of the Enlightenment and early realism. This comprehensive approach to character portrayal was soon to become a distinctive feature of realism. Stendhal, comparing the novel in his time with that of the eighteenth century could write in *Mémoires d'un touriste:* "Have you read Fielding's *Tom Jones* which has practically been forgotten nowadays? This novel occupies the same place among novels as *The Illiad* does among epic poems, and yet Fielding's characters, like Achilles or Agamemnon, now seem too primitive to us."[1] The realists freed their heroes from what Stendhal referred to as their primitiveness, and were to go on to improve the methods of psychological analysis. But it was Pushkin who laid the foundations of analytic study of the human heart in realist literature.

Pushkin studied the nature of human alienation and the causes of man's preoccupation with himself with the thoroughness of the historian and the penetration of the sociologist. Analysis of an apparently purely moral problem inevitably led him to undertake an analytic study of life, for it was there, he knew, that he would find the an-

---

[1] Stendhal, *Mémoires d'un touriste*, Tome I, Bruxelles, 1838, p. 27.

swer to the question of what was causing alienation and self-centeredness and social conflict. This fundamental problem for realism was brought into special relief in the *Little Tragedies*, and was in fact the basis of all the tragic conflicts in these plays which form a cycle by virtue of their common philosophical conception. Pushkin demonstrates exceptionally strong historical sense in the cycle. Only a writer aware that the manners and customs of society and people's social and moral conduct depend on circumstances of place and time and perfectly concrete historical conditions could have created such a set of vivid characters from various periods. The characters of the *Little Tragedies* do not only wear the costume of their age: they are also endowed with many psychological features typical of their age. At the same time they are *generalised and realistically typified* to an extent that is only equalled in Shakespeare's characters, and thereby go beyond the confining limits of historical fact. Pushkin managed to generalise in them the essential, more permanent features of human consciousness formed by the world of property relations. Following the main theme of his art, Pushkin brought his heroes—self-centered individuals—into direct conflict with humanitarian principles, with the unwritten laws of humaneness, condemning egoism as a basis for human relations. Each of the heroes of the *Little Tragedies* has his own individual type of conflict with other people and the world, and yet in a way all these conflicts have a common denominator. The gay seducer Don Juan, who regards life purely as a source of pleasure and satisfaction of his own desires, is finally crushed by his own inhuman intention to sacrifice another person's virtue, honour and life to his own transient whim; Walsingham in *The Feast During the Plague,* is assailed by a most bitter moral torment for having turned a deaf ear to the sufferings and hardships of his fellow men in this terrible time of trial and joined with his reckless friends in godless revelry. Salieri suffers a crushing defeat in his moral duel with Mozart, driven as he is to crime by his own pitifully narrow and selfish view of art. Making of art a mystery whose secrets are only revealed to the initiated few, Salieri dares to oppose his will to the great unifying and educative power of art that freely gives joy to mankind. He extinguishes Mozart's radiant genius, thereby doing a terrible violence to the creative element in man. He acts like all those who seek to extinguish reason and put a stop to its hard and utterly selfless work to free mankind from the power of prejudice, ignorance and evil. Pushkin's humanitarian idea acquires tremendous power of generalisation and great critical force.

But what was the soil in which all these human tragedies arose, what is it that feeds misanthropy and breeds disharmony in human relations? The answer to this question was provided by *The Covetous Knight,* the key work in the cycle. Here we have the world where all ideas of what is right and wrong are turned upside down, where son is advised to murder his own father, where the lascivious murderer seduces the wife of his victim, where selfless kindness produces hatred and anger, where "bloody villainy" is always ready to be called to life, where tears and sorrows evoke scorn or indifference, youth and talent are forced to sell themselves and a man's worth is judged by what he owns, where self-interest and personal gain are the guiding principles and conscience and morality go by the board—a world ruled over by an old knight-usurer, the master and slave of gold. His armour is rather too tight for him: with his understanding of the essential features of the new masters who were consolidating their position in the post-revolutionary world, Pushkin did not endow the baron with contemporary, early nineteenth century features, lest he should be at variance with the general pattern of the cycle. But despite his knightly attributes, the old baron had parallels in the realist literature of Pushkin's day. He represents very much the same as Balzac's Gobseck, in the understanding of the processes going on in life that he reflects. Gobseck serves his master gold with equally fanatical devotion, and in the same ways as the baron rejects the outward signs of wealth and power for the secret but very real power of wealth, likewise understanding that self-interest and gain are the prime movers in relations between people in the society in which he lives. Like the baron, Gobseck is a powerful, monumental character, despite his petty avariciousness. They are still *accumulating* capital, not using it to run the world. They are typical of the early period of bourgeois accumulation, and represent the first portrayals of capitalist vultures in world realist literature.

For Pushkin, as for Balzac, Stendhal, Dickens and Thackeray, the main thing in judging the nature of historical development was the question of their attitude to capitalism. In studying the effect the new social system was having on the life of society, they all sought for social forces and principles of social organisation to counter capitalism. Balzac mistakenly supposed that the unruly development and anarchy of capitalist enterprise and the corrupting influence of selfish bourgeois morality could be curbed by the strict authority of the monarchy and the Church. Dickens held that the power of moral feelings— which must be aroused in people—would be able to counter the destructive influence of capitalism on social consciousness. Pushkin, however, like Stendhal, explored the possibility of union with the revolutionary people in such works as *Dubrovsky* and *History of the Revolt of Pugachov*, and also in *Scenes from the Days of Chivalry*, whose basic idea is similar to that of Mérimée's *La Jacquerie*. Like the other great realists of the past, Pushkin looked beyond life as it was in an attempt to guess the future course of social development. *The search for a perspective arises from the very nature of realism and is its sine qua non.* When a writer analyses reality he is bound to achieve an understanding of the direction in which the world he is investigating is moving. The great realist writers of the nineteenth century embarked on their search for a perspective due to their refusal to accept the bourgeois society they lived in. Pushkin rejected capitalist progress outright, both in its "pure" American form, and in the form characteristic of Europe. "They were amazed to see democracy in its disgusting cynicism, its cruel prejudices and its unbearable tyranny," he wrote of American bourgeois democracy. "All that is noble, selfless, and elevating is crushed by egoism and a passion for contentment; the majority presumptuously oppressing society; Negro slavery amid education and freedom; genealogical persecution in a people that has no nobility; cupidity and envy on the part of the electors; temerity and servility on the part of the rulers...."[1] Stendhal criticised American democracy in almost exactly the same words in his account of the journey of a certain Captain Holly to North America. Of course, the freedom to which Pushkin and Stendhal were referring was the freedom of private enterprise proclaimed by the bourgeois revolution. These same features of American civilisation were also criticised by Dickens in his superb satire of bourgeois democracy *Martin Chuzzlewit.*

Pushkin also wrote as follows. "Read the complaints of the English factory workers, and it's enough to make your hair stand on end. What dreadful tortures and incomprehensible torments! What cold barbarity, on the one hand, what terrible poverty! You might think it were a question of building the pyramids of the pharaohs, of the Jews labouring beneath Egyptian whips. Not at all; it's merely Mr. Smith's fabrics or Mr. Jackson's needles. And note that this is not abuse, it is no crime, but is all performed strictly within the limits of the law. There seems to be no more unfortunate lot in the world than that of the English worker, but look what happens when a new machine is invented and five or six thousand people are immediately released from hard labour and deprived at the same time of their regular means of subsistence...."[2]

Engels had the following to say on the position of the English working class. "Every improvement in machinery throws workers out of employment, and the greater the advance, the more numerous the unemployed; each great improvement produces, therefore, upon a number of workers the effect of a commercial crisis, creates want, wretchedness, and crime."[3] Such were the inherent contradictions of capitalist progress which did not remain hidden from the perceptive gaze of Pushkin and the other great realists of last century. Pushkin gave a great deal of thought to these contradictions and studied the effect they had on man's moral world. Thus, in his *Queen of*

[1] A. S. Pushkin, *Collected Works* in ten volumes, Moscow, 1949, Vol. 7, p. 449 (in Russ.).

[2] Ibid., p. 290.

[3] K. Marx and F. Engels, *On Britain*, Moscow, 1962, p. 167.

Spades he was able to create a hero of the new age in whom *typical features of bourgeois consciousness* found clear *realistic expression* and were generalised. Hermann, whose actions had a single motive in his passion for enrichment was, like Rastignac and de Rubempré, the perfect individualist. His obsession with his own self and his own interests poisoned and smothered all his natural human impulses, making him completely callous, cold and calculating. Blinded by the lure of wealth he will stop at nothing—even deception and crime—to attain his lifelong aim, which he pursues with maniacal devotion. Mercilessly crushing or sweeping aside everything and everyone that stands in his way, he follows the savage side of his nature, seeing society as a battlefield and other people as either enemies or tools for the achievement of his own ends. It was no accident that the tale was given its urban setting, and the haunting image of St. Petersburg that pops up throughout gives a foretaste of the atmosphere in Gogol's *Nevsky Prospect* and of the intensely dramatic scenes of St. Petersburg life in Dostoyevsky's works, for it was in St. Petersburg that all the social contradictions of Russia were concentrated and stood out in bold relief.

Describing the features of bourgeois society, Engels remarked that they made themselves felt most strongly in the life of the big towns, the centres and strongholds of bourgeois civilisation. "And, however much one may be aware that this isolation of the individual, this narrow self-seeking is the fundamental principle of our society everywhere, it is nowhere so shamelessly barefaced, so self-conscious as just here in the crowding of the great city. The dissolution of mankind into monads, of which each one has a separate principle and a separate purpose, the world of atoms, is here carried out to its utmost extreme.

"Hence it comes, too, that the social war, the war of each against all, is here openly declared. Just as in Stirner's recent book, people regard each other only as useful objects; each exploits the other, and the end of it all is that the stronger treads the weaker under foot, and that the powerful few, the capitalists, seize everything for themselves, while to the weak many, the poor, scarcely a bare existence remains."[1] These features of bourgeois consciousness and bourgeois relations remarked upon by Engels are reflected in *The Queen of Spades*. Hermann should really have been struggling for wealth and power not in a gaming house but on the stock exchange, his whole character and outlook predisposing him for that.

In both *The Queen of Spades* and *The Covetous Knight*, where Pushkin demonstrates a perfect awareness of the processes going on in society, a deep understanding of the new social phenomena that had arisen since the revolution, and does so with consummate artistry, the emphasis is on analysis of the moral consequences of the growing influence of social egoism on man. This feature of Pushkin's method of presenting bourgeois society was conditioned by the slower rate at which capitalism was developing in Russia. While fully aware of the main trend in social development and understanding perfectly well that the bourgeoisie was bound to come out on top and feudalism was doomed, Pushkin was unable to study and investigate the formation and establishment of the new social relations with the same breadth and fulness as were other realists who actually lived under capitalism. But it was he who laid the foundations of a new type of realism, *critical in character, synthetic in the method of portraying the relationship between man and his environment, between man and society.* Pushkin portrayed his contemporaries *historically,* that is, as the product of a particular social environment, and possessing a perfectly clear-cut class consciousness that was their own, and theirs alone. Pushkin's typical method of portraying reality was *characteristic of critical realism as a whole in the classical period of its development.*

It was this method that enabled Balzac and Stendhal, Dickens and Thackeray, the Brontë sisters, Gogol, and the Russian writers of the "natural school" to reveal and analyse the contradictions inherent in the new capitalist relations that were growing up on the ruins of feudalism. As it happened, only *critical realism* proved capable of assimilating the new life, for bourgeois realism, which re-

---

[1] K. Marx and F. Engels, *On Britain*, p. 57.

garded capitalist progress as the *natural form* of social development, made no effort at all to study life in its actual movement, but substituted portrayal of the spiritual life of man isolated from society for *portrayal of the contradictions in society.* This attitude was clearly stated by a leading exponent of bourgeois realism, that talented psychologist and portrayer of morals and manners Bulwer-Lytton, who wrote in *Pelham or the Adventures of a Gentleman:* "Works which treat upon man in his relation to society, can only be strictly applicable so long as that relation to society treated upon continues. For instance, the play which satirises a particular class, however deep its reflections and accurate its knowledge upon the subject satirised, must necessarily be obsolete when the class itself has become so. ... The novel which exactly delineates the present age may seem strange and unfamiliar to the next; and thus works which treat of men relatively, and not man *in se*, must often confine their popularity to the age and even the country in which they were written. While on the other hand, the work which treats of man himself, which seizes, discovers, analyses the human mind, as it is, whether in the ancient or the modern, the savage or the European, must evidently be applicable, and consequently useful, to all times and all nations."[1] The portrayal of *"man as such" became the chief characteristic feature of bourgeois literature of the nineteenth and twentieth centuries.* Carried to its extreme, this principle of portraying man abstracted from the world of social ties lies at the roots of modern decadent literature.

Nor was romanticism able to reveal the real contradiction in the "free" capitalist system that was developing. The new features of life that lay bare the inhuman nature of bourgeois society *needed to be investigated and understood.* To the romanticists the process of bourgeois development seemed to be irrational, and extremely difficult if not impossible to understand. The conservative romanticists either adopted a position of stoical non-acceptance of life and the new society, like Alfred de Vigny, or open-

---

[1] E. Bulwer-Lytton, *Pelham or the Adventures of a Gentleman,* New York, p. 48.

ly supported feudal reaction like Arnim, Southy and so on. Those romanticists who, like Lamartine, believed in the illusions of bourgeois liberalism while being opposed to the more unpleasant aspects of bourgeois progress, were of the opinion that the new social order merely required certain minor improvements. Only the revolutionary romanticists who were to a greater or lesser extent connected with the rise of the proletarian and democratic revolutionary movement which culminated in the revolutions of 1848—people like Heinrich Heine, Freiligrath, Moreau, Barbier, Lenau, the worker poets and Chartists—revealed the contradictions of capitalist progress, though without giving a complete, integrated picture of bourgeois society. The critical realists alone were able to see and comprehend the contradictions in social development as a whole and analyse the main distinctive features of the bourgeois consciousness and social order. Critical realism flourished at a time when bourgeois society had already turned its back on the heroic days of the Jacobins and the bloody epic of the Napoleonic wars, and was consolidating its own gains and entering the stage of free competition. The bourgeoisie were fêting their freedom. The cancan replaced the Carmagnole, the bowler hat replaced the Phrygian cap, the Hussar's uniform with its colourful trimmings had given way to the practical frock-coat of the new world conqueror, the knight of debit and credit. The orators of the Convention who had shaken the world with their fiery speeches had been superceeded by parliamentary windbags. The bourgeoisie were mercilessly enforcing their rule at bayonet-point. They ruthlessly quelled the masses on the barricades during the July revolution, shed the blood of the Lyons workers who had the audacity to demand human rights for themselves, crushed the uprising of the Silesian textile workers and mobilised their forces against the Chartists, who were naive enough to believe that the democratic freedoms declared by the bourgeoisie would permit the working class to free itself from capitalist enslavement.

A spirit of research and a thirst for knowledge characterised the great realists of the nineteenth century, who in portraying and investigating life and revealing the objective contradictions of capitalism inevitably adopted a critical attitude towards bourgeois society. "The public demands beautiful pictures from us," wrote Balzac, "but where are the models for them? Your hideous clothes, your abortive revolutions, your garrulous bourgeois, your dead religion, your degenerate power, your kings without thrones, are they really so poetic as to be worth portraying? All we can do now is mock at them."[1] Balzac's novels have a strong cognitional and critical strain. He frequently interrupts the narrative to give detailed descriptions of his characters' means and interests, and their economic relations, with all the minutiae of everyday life, dress, manners, customs and habits, tastes, scientific discoveries, financial and banking operations, mortgage business, land deals, and legal business, examining juridical institutions, the relations between Church and State, inheritance laws and economic legislature, portraying fashionable salons and money-lenders' chambers, city slums and the manners and morals of rural France.

"Before writing a book, the writer must analyse the characters, immerse himself in all manners, travel round the globe, and experience all passions; or the passions, countries, manners, characters, natural phenomena and moral phenomena must all pass through his mind."[2] Balzac did his best to follow his own advice and endeavoured to examine and portray the life of the individual, the life of society, and history in synthesis. What a contrast there is between Pushkin's light, delicate prose which time seems not to have aged at all so simple and unadorned it is and so perfectly and naturally does it fit into the background of contemporary literature, and Balzac's heavy, somewhat archaic prose with its Cyclopean monumentality! Some parts of the vast incomplete edifice of *La Comédie Humaine* have become moss-grown with the passing of time, yet nonetheless, this truly titanic work still continues to exert a considerable influence on literature, partly due to its powerful characters and because it reveals the innermost passions of the scions of the bour-

---

[1] Honore de Balzac, *La peau de chagrin*, Bruxelles, 1831, Vol. I, p. 19.
[2] Ibid., p. 15.

geois world, and also because it concentrates and conveys with supreme realism the quintessence of life itself in movement, in all its fulness and intensity. Like Hermann in *The Queen of Spades*, Balzac's heroes are engaged in a crazed pursuit of their own personal interest, and have that same "monism", their inner world being entirely occupied by one all-consuming passion. All Père Goriot's other feelings were completely submerged by his paternal feeling, just as Gobseck, Nucingen, Lucien de Rubempré, du Tillet, the Cointet brothers, Gaubertin, Rigou, Père Grandet and hundreds of other characters were completely ruled by their passion for wealth. Presenting his characters' self-absorption, their total pursuit of their own private interests, often at variance with the common interest or the interests of other individuals, Balzac was revealing an objective feature of bourgeois social development—the growth and spread of *social atomisation.*

Although he viewed character as man's inner world ruled by a particular guiding passion, Balzac did not equate character with passion: for him the two were dialectically related, but not identical. The passion was the guiding motive force in a character, and could, and often did, contradict the hero's moral and mental make-up. A man's character was formed under the influence of his environment, reflecting its distinctive features and dependent on it. Thus the heroes of *La Comédie Humaine* were clear-cut individuals despite their social typification, and were neither reduced to their purely social essence or their particular overriding passion, as was the tendency in classicism, nor representative of some universal feature or trait of character, as with the romanticists.

In portraying his "monistic" characters Balzac revealed remarkable perception and discernment of life in breadth and depth, and his works contained all the minutiae of human existence. With his truly encyclopaedic knowledge of such far-ranging subjects as the art of land speculation, the way the peasants steal timber from the landowners, the value of the jewelry some Viscountess or Marchioness stricken with love and grief takes to a Parisian pawnbroker, what goes on in the stately homes tucked away in the quiet woods of St. Germain, the sordid secrets of stock exchange manoeuvres and political intrigues, Balzac studied the penetration of self-interest into all spheres of private and public life with a historian's thoroughness, and showed how this corrupted people's minds and embittered human relations. Sentiments of kinship *(Les parents pauvres)*, family relationships *(Le Père Goriot, Eugenie Grandet* and *Le Colonel Chabert)*, friendship *(Les Illusions perdues)*, love *(Interdiction, La muse du département* and *La femme de trente ans)*, honesty *(Cesar Birotteau)*, the state machine *(Les Employés, Une ténébreuse affaire)*, the press, the theatre, publishing, art and banking—everywhere self-interest and egoism reigned supreme, making life a battlefield where the weak were given no quarter, where morals and goodness were trampled underfoot or sullied. A struggle going on in society is not merely a struggle between a man and his fellows, one individual and another, and between the individual and society. In the words of Doctor Bénassis, Balzac's alter ego, this struggle is none other than the war of the poor against the rich going on in bourgeois society, "a union of the haves against the have-nots". It is also the struggle between the bourgeoisie and the nobles, between the peasants and the landowners, between the workers and the manufacturers, in short the *class struggle which lies at the root of social relations explains the mystery of the development of history and is the motor of progress.*

Balzac's analysis of society led him to the conclusion that the bourgeoisie was bound to triumph, and therefore despite his loathing for the bourgeoisie and his love for fine and noble, *aristocrats untainted by self-interest*, he was forced to portray the decline of the old society, to sing its swan-song, giving his depiction of the nobility and the aristocracy a strong critical flavour. Balzac made his bourgeois powerful figures, with tremendous will-power and boundless energy, qualities his highly idealised aristocrats seldom possessed. He saw the aristocrats antagonists as the carriers of social activity and drive, and in this respect his founders of financial dynasties anticipate the Gründers in later realist literature—old Buddenbrook, Artamonov senior, and Cowperwood, who have the same strong characters as Balzac's heroes. But while recognising the strength of the new class that had emerged victorious—and this shows his spontaneous historicism—Balzac did not consider the bourgeois system of social relations to be the summit of creation or eternal. It was his humanism, his refusal to accept the inhuman nature of capitalist civilisation that led Balzac to this conclusion. In his view capitalism was doomed to perish as surely as it was unable to secure happiness for mankind. This ethical criticism of capitalism represents both the strength and the weakness of Balzac's outlook. While correctly considering alienation, social atomisation, to be the most important result of capitalist progress, Balzac failed to see the other side of capitalism, its *unifying role*, the way the new social conditions abolished feudal separatism and increased people's dependence on one another, strengthening connections between people in the sphere of production, and that of industrial production in particular, and in commerce, creating the objective conditions in the capitalist system for the poor to unite against the rich, the oppressed against the oppressor, with a view to changing the existing social order.

Balzac was full of scorn for bourgeois democracy and bourgeois liberalism and had a pretty clear idea of the real contradictions and the negative aspects of capitalist progress. He was full of sympathy for the republicans, whom he saw as defenders of the rights and interests of the people. Yet for all this, for all the tremendous perspicacity and penetration of his analysis of bourgeois social relations and social undercurrents, the hidden processes of history, Balzac was not up to the level of the Utopian socialists whom he knew well, and with whom he polemicised, pointing out the weak points in their teaching. Balzac's failure to understand certain important aspects of life occasionally marred his work, and brought romanticist elements into play, introducing a strain of Gothic horror into his essentially realist approach, resulting in such highly improbable, fantastic and naive works as *Les Treize*. When he came to examine social questions and try and work out the ways and means of overcoming the negative results of capitalist progress, Balzac adopted a kind of conservative utopianism, suggesting that the power of the aristocracy resting upon the moral values of religion could bring social welfare without destroying the existing property relationships and merely curbing but not abolishing the principle of private ownership. This was the kind of theory expounded by Bénassis, the hero of the didactic and utopian novel *Le medecin de campagne*, a rather colourless, insipid work, only remarkable for the fact that it contains an exposé of the author's ideas concerning the reorganisation of society. The same thing happened to Balzac as happened to Gogol and Dostoyevsky. Rejecting the capitalist path of social development, while at the same time refusing to accept the idea of revolution as a method of changing the world for the better, they had to seek support in the struggle against bourgeois egoism in authoritarian power and Christian ethics. In the case of Balzac, his conservative utopianism also resulted from the fact that in studying the forces at work in the society of his day he did not take into account the people as an *independent factor, determining* the movement of history. At a time when the utopian socialists led by Saint-Simon were insisting that the "lower classes" including the proletariat were capable of managing all branches of the political and economic life of a country on their own, Balzac openly polemicised with them, maintaining the opposite. In revealing the real contradictions inherent in capitalist progress and criticising capitalism for its failure to satisfy the needs of the masses and of the individual, Balzac was clearly expressing the feelings and attitudes of the "lower classes" that were oppressed by capitalism, in other words, the views of the masses. Yet at the same time he considered that social reforms aimed at abolishing the noxious effects of the capitalist system could only be introduced *from above.*

Although witness to the 1848 Revolution, Balzac was to cling to this attitude to the end of his days. Not so Stendhal, who had no illusions about the possibility of authoritarian power resting on the aristocracy and the Church being able to iron out the contradictions in bourgeois society and abolish social egoism through the agency of Christian ethics. For him, a republican with a strong spiritual link with the democratic revolutionary movement, the Church, the aristocracy and all authoritarian power were anti-popular forces. As for the views of the ruling classes, he was firmly convinced that they could not be reformed to serve the common good by rational arguments, for they were borne of advantage. In the same way and to the same extent, the bourgeoisie who had struggled hard to gain its privileges and thought only of increasing its power and wealth, would not sacrifice their own interests to the aristocracy, let alone the masses, without a hard and bitter struggle. Thus, besides seeing the society of his day not simply as a battlefield where it was every man for himself, as also did Balzac and other critical realists, Stendhal—and in this is manifest the truly democratic nature of his outlook—was also aware that a constant struggle was being waged in society between the ruling classes, the propertied classes, and the deprived masses, and it was to the latter that he gave his wholehearted political and personal allegiance. Stendhal's heroes, unlike the characters in *La Comédie Humaine*, are either opposed to society as an alien force, like Julien Sorel, Lamiel, Valbayre or the carbonari Missirilli, or begin to sever their link with society like Olivier, Fabrice, and Lucien Leuwen. A number of Balzac's heroes struggle with society, with its laws and customs, and its oppressive forces—characters like Vautrin, Raphaël, Lucien de Rubempré, and even Rastignac. But their struggle is waged *within the system*, and the main stimulus behind their struggle is the desire to gain a good firm position in society, and if they are successful they eventually come to find society's laws quite acceptable. The escaped convict Vautrin who is an outcast from society returns to the fold and is willingly received back, becoming a pillar of the society whose laws he had formerly broken. Julien Sorel, forced to make his own way in life and win a place in the sun by his own efforts, uses the same weapon to achieve his aim as those other ambitious people whose victories and defeats are presented in *La Comédie Humaine*. Yet he never merges to become one with the ruling class in whose orbit he moves, and far from accepting their views, remains their sworn enemy until his dying day, for his plebeian origin makes him socially hostile to bourgeois society. Whereas the conflict between the heroes of *La Comédie Humaine* and society can be resolved, that between Julien Sorel or Lamiel and their social environment cannot, for it is based on class antagonism, which will last as long as the existing system of social relations persists.

Despite the fact that the range of subject matter is far narrower in Stendhal's works than in *La Comédie Humaine*, he revealed social contradictions no less vividly, and indeed far more sharply and intensely than Balzac. The reason for this is that Stendhal approached the study of society as a democratic writer for whom the fact that bourgeois society was hostile to the true interests of the people was more obvious than to Balzac, whose vision of life was somewhat blurred by the conservative aspects of his outlook.

Stendhal's works provide a particularly clear example of the analytic nature of realism. Heir to eighteenth century materialism, Stendhal saw man as combining moral, psychological and physiological principles which could be apprehended and analysed. As a child of his own age, he knew that a man's spiritual world depends on his environment and his behaviour is motivated by social, that is, material causes. Realising that in bourgeois society man became a monad shut up in himself since private interest tended to disunite people, he did not consider that interest as such had a purely egoistic character. He believed—and it was this that Stendhal regarded as the guarantee of the possibility of social improvement—that personal interest did not necessarily have to be satisfied at other people's expense: man could also satisfy his own interests and at the same time bring benefit to his fellow men and hence to society as a whole. Thus, while adhering to the views of Helvetius and Holbach, who considered personal gain to be the sole stimulus of human behaviour, Stendhal was proceeding from the humanist belief in man's creative powers, the might of his intellect and his ability to perfect himself, a belief based on his democratic convictions. He considered that the capitalist system *corrupted human nature* and the ubiquitous egoism gradually stifled human qualities opposed to self-interest. The gradual destruction of the human being by society or the shattering of his hopes of happiness was the subject which Stendhal was most concerned with.

Studying the effect of social environment on man's spiritual and moral world, Stendhal focussed his attention on portraying the psychology of his heroes as subject to the "iron laws of the real world", and indeed as a *part* of the real world. He reduced description of situation and circumstances to a minimum, transposing the action to the sphere of human relationships, making the human mind the mainspring of the drama, developing and perfecting the art of psychological analysis in critical realism.

Stendhal studied the motives of human behaviour, conditioned, directly or indirectly, by a person's own interests, and described the way man "sets out to hunt for happiness". At the same time he made a thorough analysis of man's feelings and passions. Thus while in *De l'amour* he tried to penetrate the innermost mysteries of the apparently most irrational passion by means of rational analysis, describing the *abstract feeling, divorced from environment and actual conditions,* in his later works he went beyond mechanical rationalism stemming from the philosophy of the eighteenth century and *examined the psychological and social in man in unity and synthesis.* Man and his feelings and passions was not, for Stendhal, an island washed by the waves of life. Stendhal perceived in his personality and general make-up features *typical* of the milieu, society and class to which he belonged. Signor Valenod and Monsieur de Rênal, Count Mosca and Rassi are all social types, but Stendhal reveals their typicality through the sphere of psychology, by studying their inner world which conditions their actions in the given circumstances. Since Stendhal saw character to be a dynamic synthesis of "moral habits", and these "moral habits" to be the result of the influence of the social order on the human consciousness, he naturally included in the sphere of character essential *heterogeneous* qualities. Stendhal compared the novel to a mirror placed along the highway and reflecting both the azure sky and the roadside mud. He might as well have said the same of his heroes, for they, like a mirror, reflected both the noble and base, generous altruistic and egoistic "moral habits". This is what gives Stendhal's characters their tremendous authenticity, vitality and completeness. A dynamic synthesis of various qualities, a Stendhalian hero seems to reflect in his inner life, in the inner struggle of contradictory characteristics, the objective movement and contradictions of life itself.

Julien Sorel combines vastly differing elements: vanity, cold calculation, selfishness and noble ideals, heavy, gloomy suspicion, and an open, generous nature, strict self-control and violent, unbridled passion are all mixed and fused in his nature into a mobile, dynamic whole. All these different elements of his nature intermingle, and react on one another. Stendhal examines this contradictory movement, this conflict and development of different thoughts and feelings by means of psychological analysis, and in so doing makes several important literary discoveries, like introducing to the narrative art the *inner monologue*, which enables him to penetrate with his searching, dissecting lancet further and deeper into the living flesh of the hero's heart. Equally rich in inner movements and subtle shades of feeling and thought are Stendhal's other characters—Fabrice, Gina Sanseverina, Count Mosca, the old Leuwen, and Lucien Leuwen. Yet despite the highly variegated nature of the elements that form the character's dynamic entity, the result is not a loose mixture. It is rather like a magnetic field where the movement and direction of different lines of force can be observed. Every one of Stendhal's characters has an *inner social dominant*, to which all the other elements are subordinate. For Stendhal character is the product of circumstances and social environment. The hero acts in certain given circumstances and his actions are the result of his particular character and *not accidental:* they have their own logic determined by the way the hero sets out "to hunt for happiness", dependent, that is, on how he struggles to achieve and satisfy his own particular aim or interests and how he clashes with the interests or aims of others in the process. Julien Sorel, a plebeian out to attain success and power in bourgeois society, behaves all the time, and especially when among the upper classes, as if he were behind enemy lines. *Class awareness pervades* his every thought and action. He even turns up to meet his future mistress armed to the teeth. The behaviour of Fabrice, Gina Sanseverina and Monsieur de Rênal are also conditioned by their class psychology. The banker Leuwen, a sceptical free-thinker and Epicurean, retains his essential class consciousness as a capitalist for all his broad views. He despises the common people and plays around with the values of bourgeois democracy just as he does with money on the stock exchange. In Stendhal we find *causality*—that essential feature of realism—in the form of a social, *class dominant, determining the psychology and behaviour of the characters*, which are very clearly and methodically analysed.

Stendhal makes an equally comprehensive analysis of the destructive influence of bourgeois society on the human consciousness. Julien Sorel, with his frank, open nature and heroic ideals, whose whole bold, resolute character would seem to destine him to join the struggle for social justice finds itself *on the wrong side of the barricades*, devotes his outstanding abilities to ensuring his own advancement in the upper class milieu he so hates, and makes one compromise after another with his ideals. His soul becomes corroded by social egoism, which conditions the main features of social psychology and consciousness in a propertied world. It becomes a part of his flesh and blood, making him a slave of bourgeois prejudices, an out and out individualist, guided in his behaviour by the principle: "every man for himself in this desert of selfishness called life". Julien Sorel was the first in a long line of characters in world literature of young people corrupted by capitalism. They include Greslou in Bourget's *Le Disciple*, London's Martin Eden and Eugene Witla, the hero of Dreiser's *The Genius*, and especially Raskolnikov in *Crime and Punishment*, who under the influence of the terrible and unnatural conditions prevailing in the society in which he lived evolved the supremely individualist idea that the chosen individuals had the right to sacrifice other people in the interest of achieving their own aims and purposes, the idea that lies behind the concept of the "hero and the crowd", a theme which in variations is ubiquitous in the philosophy and morality of bourgeois individualism.

Society had a similar destructive influence on Lamiel, leading her on the path of crime. The feudal-bourgeois reaction crippled the lives of Fabrice and Clélia. Bourgeois society was hostile to the people, oppressing them. It was also hostile to the individual, instilling egoism in him and *impoverishing and standardising his nature*. Stendhal often shows the flagging of energy in members of bourgeois society, the erasure and loss of true individuality. Stendhal's views were formed at the time when the class struggle between labour and capital had faded into the background and the chief conflict to be discerned was the struggle between the masses and feudal reaction, which explains why he regarded rule by the people and a republic to be the essential condition for the harmonious development of society. Later, when bourgeois democracy had *already revealed* its limitations, he was able to distinguish between it and the *principles* of popular democracy, and indeed believed in the possibility of *rule by the people* being one day achieved. He rejected the American brand of bourgeois democracy quite emphatically. Lucien Leuwen learns by experience the non-popular character of the bourgeois democracy the July Revolution ushered in. He leaves the army so as "not to have to sabre workers". But though unwilling to join the ruling classes in the impending struggle between the bourgeoisie and the proletariat which he realises is inevitable, he does not understand that the proletariat is not merely brave fellows, but an historical force coming to the fore of the social, class and political struggle. Stendhal himself did not grasp this either, any more than did the other writers of the classical period of critical realism.

The manner of character portrayal where psychology and action were interrelated, which Pushkin and Stendhal introduced to realism, co-existed with Balzac's method of concentrating mainly on the study of the social conditions determining the mentality and the "sum of moral habits" of the hero, and also with the original method Dickens affirmed. Dickens created character on the basis of *generalisation, intensification and exaggeration* (satirical or comic) of the *main feature* in a character's nature. The characters of Mr. Pickwick, Sam Weller, Pecksniff, Uriah Heep, Dombey, Scrooge, Bounderby and Mr. Podsnap were none other than *variations* of a particular psychological trait, elaborated in remarkable detail, with a mass of shades and implications, packed with realistic minutiae of morals and manners. The characteristic so emphasised might be hypocrisy as in the case of Pecksniff, or smugness as with Podsnap. Dickens's method differed from that of the classicists in that he was not studying an abstract passion as such, but was interested in the expressive side of human nature which to a large extent determines behaviour. Nor do Dickens's characters resemble the romantic heroes, for he *did not isolate* the features of human nature from *the objective world.* All his heroes are very much a part of the social environment which produced them, and have the outlook of the class to which they belong. The highly authentic presentation of a character, complete with all the concrete details, from description of his dress, habits, eccentricities, tastes, likes and dislikes, inclinations, intentions, aims, comportment, convictions, views, the circumstances and conditions in which he lives, trade or occupation, to his actual behaviour—coloured with powerful lyricism or criticism, exaggerated to the point of being grotesque or emanating an aura of the fantastic—creates the illusion of a complete and many-sided study of the character's psychology. Dickens's characters are so typified, and their social nature so fully defined that the author had no need to embroider on their psychology in the course of the narration in analysing their relationships with other characters or their reactions in various situations. Their moral qualities might alter—Mr. Dombey changes from a cold, soulless capitalist to a repentant and kindly old man, and the miserly old Scrooge becomes the epitome of kindness and generosity—but the inner course of these changes is not traced.

This principle of character portrayal is not at odds with

the realist method for it is based on social analysis and is thus a perfectly valid form of realistic generalisation of the real, genuine aspects of life reflected in the human consciousness. Gogol, for example, in *Mirgorod*, and especially in *Dead Souls*, created his characters solely on the basis of broad generalisation of their basic traits. Plyushkin, Nozdryov, Korobochka, Sobakevich, Ivan Ivanych and Ivan Nikiforovich, Shponka and Podkolesin are all highly typified and presented in their full social essence. In the course of the action they only reveal various shades and aspects of their already set natures. Psychological stability is also a feature of Thackeray's characters, presented against an extensive background of everyday life. Combining satire with description of manners and morals, Thackeray exaggerated certain aspects of his characters' nature and paid little attention to their psychological and emotional sub-stratum, being satisfied with stressing the social motives of their behaviour. Becky Sharp, the epitome of the selfish bourgeois go-getter, acts in conformity with her social nature throughout *Vanity Fair*, revealing *generic* psychological qualities in *various* circumstances, always remaining herself. She is more interesting for the energy with which she pursues her own advancement, than as a psychological study. The straightforward and honest Henry Esmond goes through his numerous adventures in wars and Jacobite conspiracies without changing psychologically. Nor is Pendennis at all changed by all the tricks spiteful Fortune plays on him. The embittered plebeian Heathcliff, the extremely striking hero of Emily Brontë's *Wuthering Heights*, who takes wrathful revenge for the wrongs inflicted on him by life and other people, and suffers prostrating personal tragedy, is the same gloomy, embittered outcast at the end of the novel as when he first appeared, and we only learn about what goes on in his heart from his actions and a few brief confessions and personal admissions.

Dickens's highly typified characters are the fruit of his thorough analysis of the fundamental motive processes in life. The years left their mark, and his early optimism gradually becomes clouded by gathering gloom, humour is replaced by tragic irony, and pure fun by angry satire, as he gradually becomes more and more aware of the negative aspects of capitalist progress and bourgeois democracy, which had attained maturity in England. The good-natured, superficial pattern of human relations reducing social contradictions to the struggle between the forces of good and evil, between good, kind people and cruel, hardened rogues, which characterised his early works and was somehow reconciled with a mercilessly truthful portrayal of the hard lot of the working masses, gradually collapsed under the impact of the writer's growing understanding of the nature of bourgeois social relations. Aware, like all critical realists, that society is a battle-ground of conflicting human interests, Dickens was not content to let the matter rest at that. In his later works, he no longer treats interest merely as a moral and ethical factor, but infused the concept of social struggle with real class content, discerning the clash of interests between the haves and the have-nots in life, between the ruling classes and the people, between the capitalists and the proletariat. From portrayal of individual shortcomings and criticism of certain aspects of bourgeois life, whether it was the position in workhouses and orphanages (as in *Oliver Twist*) or the state of education (as in *Nicholas Nickleby*), he passed to a critical presentation of capitalist social relations in their entirety, bourgeois marriage and family life (*Dombey and Son*), justice and the law (*Bleak House*), the machinery of government and the apparatus of coercion (*Little Dorrit* with its famous description of "the Circumlocution Office" and Marshalsea jail), and the factory system and the position of the working class (*Hard Times*). Dickens criticised bourgeois society from a democratic standpoint, endowing his favourite characters, characters from the people, with fine moral qualities, spiritual beauty and kindness, and making his representatives of the ruling classes ruthless, callous and aggressively self-seeking. Dickens presented the poverty and wretchedness in which the people at the bottom of the social ladder lived, deprived of even the most elementary human rights as the result of exploitation by the wealthy classes. He saw the most important and dangerous consequence of capitalist progress to be the dehumanisation of man due to bourgeois egoism and self-interest. "Oh! Ye Pharisees of the nineteen hundredth year of Christian knowledge, who soundingly appeal to human nature, see first that it be human," he exclaimed in *Martin Chuzzlewit*, referring to the various apologists of the existing order, from utilitarians and Malthusians to religious moralists and parliamentarians, in whose view the bourgeois system of social relations was perfectly in accord with the demands of human nature. "Take heed it has not been transformed, during your slumber and the sleep of generations into the nature of the Beasts."[1] The bourgeois outlook and morality with their bigotry and hypocrisy act like a corrosive acid on the human soul, making it cruel, callous and indifferent to the fate of others. This was the case with Mr. Dombey prior to his "conversion"—one of the most monumental figures of a capitalist to be found anywhere in world literature. It is true too of any number of Dickens's negative characters—Uriah Heep and Carter, Ralph Nickleby and Murdstone, Merdle and Jonas Chuzzlewit. But capitalism does not only distort and disfigure human nature: by enslaving the masses and condemning millions of working people to poverty and misery, and building the wealth and well-being of the possessor classes on their blood and sweat, it thereby produces in the social order of its own creation an insoluble contradiction between oppressors and oppressed, a conflict fraught with the direct consequences for itself. His analysis of life under capitalism and its very real contradictions led Dickens, as it did other realist writers, to the discovery in the very womb of history and life of a new contradiction of decisive importance for the fate of the capitalist system—the contradiction between labour and capital.

The blatant contradictions in capitalist progress came to light in the middle of the nineteenth century: everywhere the bourgeoisie had shackled the proletariat to the factory system, to a life of backbreaking toil and appalling hardships—whether the Welsh miners or the weavers of Silesia and France, the German artisans or the workers in

---

[1] Charles Dickens, *The Life and Adventures of Martin Chuzzlewit,* London, 1951, p. 224.

the iron and steel foundries of Sheffield. The cold, calculating brutality of exploitation exacerbated the class struggle and led to the development of a revolutionary situation, which came to a head in 1848, the Year of Revolutions, bringing new social forces into historical activity—the popular masses led by the proletariat. The conditions were created for the formation not only of *the revolutionary consciousness of the working class, but also working-class philosophical and political self-awareness.*

Bourgeois ideologists continued to consider capitalist production, with all its consequences—the class struggle, social inequality, the division of society into rich and poor, and exploiters and exploited—the perfectly normal, just, and indeed the only possible, system of production. But *scientific socialism* was already proving the possibility of *another method of organisation of production in place of the capitalist,* one which would create a new form of social relations based on the principle of *collectivism.* Grafted to the workers' movement, scientific socialism brought to it understanding of an aim and transformed socialism from a beautiful dream into a science that unravelled the secrets of historical development and the laws that guide it, thereby placing in the hands of the workers of the world a theoretical weapon that would enable them to effect a transformation of social relations. The ideas of scientific communism did not immediately achieve recognition in the working class movement, however. On the eve of the 1848 revolutions and in the years that followed, the movement was still influenced by manifold social theories and had still to cast off a host of bourgeois-democratic and revolutionary-democratic illusions. But it was in these years that the spectre of communism began to haunt the world historical arena, gradually assuming flesh and blood in heroic class battles, and becoming a reality in the feat of the Russian proletariat, the first to embark on the building of communist society.

Various views were current in the working class movement in the years before the Revolution, from the ideas of levelling communism stemming from the Babouvists, and taken up by the French egalitarians and the German supporters of what was known as "spoon communism" (Löffelkommunismus), to the ideas of Christian socialism and the theories of utopian socialism developed by Bazard and Enfantin, Theodore Dézamy and Cabet, and the petty-bourgeois theorists Louis Blanc and Proudhon, the father of anarchism. The working class had still not discarded faith in the possibility of bourgeois democracy and its capacity for development. It still believed that once the ruling classes fully realised the appalling plight of the people, they would come to their aid and help ease their burden. This kind of illusions were shared by the English Chartist movement, which Lenin described as the first broad, truly mass proletarian revolutionary movement of a political nature. In the verse of the movement's poet spokesmen—Ebenezer Elliott, whose poetry is largely connected with the struggle for the repeal of the Corn Laws, Thomas Cooper, Gerald Massey and Ernest Jones—revolutionary motives are interwoven with philanthropic ones, and opposition to tyranny is found side by side with non-resistance and universal forgiveness. Such illusions were also characteristic of the Weitlingers, the German levellers, and Herwegh and Freiligrath, poets connected with the workers' movement. They were reflected, too, in the poetry of Heine, who represents the summit of that second romantic movement called to life by the revolutionary situation. Heine, who was quite happy to be called "the defrocked romanticist" for his fierce attacks on reactionary romanticism and for his "unromantic" criticism of the bourgeoisie, said of himself: "Despite my murderous campaigns against romanticism, I have always remained a romanticist, and was much more of one than I ever suspected."[1] Yet he demonstrated remarkable historical perspicacity when he said of the Communists "that they are the strongest party in the world, that their day has not yet come, it is true, but patient waiting is no waste of time for the people to whom the future belongs".[2]

The contradiction between capital and labour was becoming the central issue of history, and could no longer

---

[1] Henry Heine, *De l'Allemagne*, T. 2, Paris, 1855, p. 243.
[2] Henry Heine, *Œuvres Complètes, Lutèce*, Paris, 1859, pp. XI-XII.

be avoided or ignored either by social thought or literature. It was natural that the issue should have first been
examined by the English realist novel, since England was
at the timo the most industrially advanced of the European
powers, and the contradictions of capitalism were consequently more sharply in evidence there.

Not only the critical realists—like Charlotte Brontë,
whose *Shirley* presents a fine picture of the spiritual
world of the working man, retaining a sense of human
dignity intact in spite of appalling hardship, or Elizabeth
Gaskell, whose *Mary Barton* gave a shockingly truthful
picture of the life of the Lancashire textile workers that
represented a strong indictment of the capitalist system—
but the bourgeois realists, too, were forced to investigate
the position of the working class in order to understand
the consequences its struggle for its rights might have for
the future of the bourgeois system. In his novel *Sybil*,
Disraeli displayed a sobriety and breadth of vision no
longer to be found among bourgeois ideologists today in
his portrayal of the terrible position of the English proletariat. He introduced characters who were members of
the Chartist movement, and was able to admit the division of society into two nations, the rich and the poor,
which he said were as far apart as if they lived on two
different planets. However, Disraeli suggested that the
class conflict should be solved by partial reforms, improvement of the lot of the poor and by making certain concessions to the proletariat. In this he was counting on the
philanthropic feelings of the ruling classes and the obedience of the workers. Harriet Martineau developed a
similar view in her cycle of works entitled *Illustrations
of Political Economy*. In the story *Weal and Woe in
Garveloch*, she made an open attempt to convince the
workers of the ideas of Malthus, arguing that large families were the cause of poverty. She called on the workers
to abandon organised political struggle (in *A Manchester
Strike*) and advised the bourgeoisie to reduce the burden
of taxation *(For Each and for All)* and increase private
charity *(Cousin Marshall)*. Written in a lively, interesting
manner, with a good knowledge of the working class
milieu and everyday life of the working people, and a

121

certain amount of sentimentality—but avoiding the exaggeration characteristic of the works of Eugène Sue or the novels of the "true communists"—Harriet Martineau's works enjoyed long popularity with the reading public.

The critical realists, who had discovered the meaning of the contradiction between capital and labour, were not clear as to how the conflict should be tackled and overcome. Elizabeth Gaskell and Kingsley, author of *Yeast* and *Alton Lock*, thought that the answer lay in Christian socialism. Charlotte Brontë and Dickens sought a counterbalance to the bourgeois system in man's moral qualities, humaneness and goodness. In *Hard Times* Dickens opposed the levelling power of the capitalist system—using the generalised image of the factory town of Cocktown to symbolise soulless capitalist civilisation and branding the sterile inhumanity of utilitarian theories in Gradgrind and Bounderby—with the humanity of Blackpool and the boundless kindness of Sissy, and also with the purity of his own moral standpoint, with a humanitarian indictment of capitalism.

The writers of the classical age of critical realism did not look deeply enough into the contradiction between capital and labour to discover the right way to solve it, the way, that is, which would lead to the ultimate victory of the proletariat, with which they sincerely sympathised. This was due partly to the hazy democratic nature of their own views which prevented them from recognising this prospect, and partly to the fact that the working-class movement was still ridden with numerous utopian, revolutionary-democratic and petty-bourgeois illusions. It took Marx and Engels with their genius to generalise its experience and, fusing it with *scientific socialism*, to create the revolutionary theory that paved the way to the victory of the proletariat.

However, critical realism in the classical period of its development *assimilated* the essence of the new capitalist order that had sprung up on the ruins of the feudal world. It penetrated and presented the conflicts of bourgeois society with merciless clarity and incomparable artistry. The realists turned their attention to every sphere of private and social life and, perfecting the realist method, left a truly encyclopaedic record of a whole historical epoch, its life and morals, and its ideas and types of people, generalising the lasting features of the capitalist system and of the bourgeois mentality. Their works are permeated with the idea of development—the concept of life and society as changing, moving, *developing* objects of literary portrayal. Thus their views and their works show an inherent *spontaneous historicism*, a quality that is lacking in present-day bourgeois thought. They presented the clash of opposing interests which divided and alienated people, to reveal the class struggle, the struggle of material interests. In the age of "free" competition, they mainly examined the consequences of capitalist progress which led to *division* and *alienation* and could devote far less attention to the *unifying* processes *within* the system.

The desire to interpret reality *synthetically* characteristic of progressive social thought in the first half of the nineteenth century was likewise a feature of critical realism of the classical period. But critical realism, failing to fully reveal the main contradiction of capitalist society, the contradiction between labour and capital, with all its historical consequences, did not succeed in achieving this synthesis. It was Marx's *Capital* and the theories of scientific communism which effected a *synthetic interpretation* of history, its general laws and tendencies and the real prospects of its development, and proved that the sources of class division and hence of the class struggle are to be found in the economic structure of society. It was the method of socialist realism, which inherited and carried further the achievements and aesthetic discoveries of critical realism, that was able to make a *synthetic portrayal* of reality.

Critical realism also foreshadowed socialist realism in the method of artistic investigation of reality and in the social views it expressed. An appraisal made by Marx and Engels of the legacy of French materialism is equally applicable to the classical critical realist tradition, and its importance for the formation of the socialist realist method. They wrote: "There is no need of any great penetration to see from the teaching of materialism on the original goodness and equal intellectual indowment of men, the omnipotence of experience, habit and education, and the influence of environment on man, the great significance of industry, the justification of enjoyment, etc., how necessarily materialism is connected with communism and socialism. If man draws all his knowledge, sensation, etc., from the world of the senses and the experience gained in it, the empirical world must be arranged so that in it man experiences and gets used to what is really human and that he becomes aware of himself as man. If correctly understood interest is the principle of all moral, man's private interest must be made to coincide with the interest of humanity.... If man is shaped by his surroundings, his surroundings must be made human."[1]

Similar views may be found in the works of almost all the classics of critical realism. Children of their age, unable to avoid the mistakes and prejudices engendered by the historical conditions which formed their consciousness, and with no clear political concept of how society might be transformed, they expressed the *protest of the masses* against the inhumanity of capitalism. The moral essence of their works was opposed to the apologist trends in bourgeois ideology, so that despite the limitations and occasional erroneousness of their political ideals, their art was essentially democratic, since it *objectively coincided* with the interests of the masses opposing capitalism's encroachments on human rights. A necessary stage in the development of literature, their works paved the way for a new aesthetic method—socialist realism.

Although the bourgeoisie managed to quell the 1848 revolutions, it had become clear to the bourgeois ideologists that the question of the workers was now the central historical issue on which the future of capitalism depended. The bourgeoisie sensed that despite scientific and technological progress, despite the stabilisation of capitalism, the flourishing of trade and the strengthening of the political positions of the possessor classes, a force was maturing within capitalist society which represented

---

[1] K. Marx, F. Engels. *The Holy Family*, Moscow, 1956, pp. 175-76.

a very real danger to the whole system of social relations based on exploitation. They could not help noticing that the decline of bourgeois culture had already set in.

Nietzsche, with his usual frankness, pointed to the workers' question as the main cause of the earthquake which had shaken the apparently firm edifice of bourgeois civilisation. In *Götzen-Dämmerung* he wrote: "The worker has been made fit to struggle, he has been given the right to form associations and the political right to vote, so that it is hardly surprising that the worker has begun to regard his existence as wretched. But what do they expect?... If you are striving to achieve a certain aim you must choose the appropriate means. It is only a fool who wishes to have slaves yet educates them as masters."[1]

Nietzsche was one of the first ideologists and apologists of capitalism to note the first symptoms of the decline of bourgeois democracy. He threw all the weight of his arguments into strengthening the positions of the ruling classes, attempting to arouse in the bourgeoisie a will to power, and to find the "appropriate means" to the end of turning the masses into obedient slaves. He was not, however, the only one to sense the approaching crisis. For while the shares remained high on the Stock Exchange and bourgeois politicians and economists were forecasting the permanent florescence of capitalism, while feverish economic activity was bringing its fruits in the form of the growth of industry and finance capital was creating powerful financial empires, stretching out their tentacles to overseas countries and subduing new lands and peoples in Africa and Asia, while this economic expansion created the impression of the inexhaustible power of the capitalist world, at the same time complicated processes and changes were taking place deep down in its social consciousness, which testified to the malaise of the whole capitalist system. Full-blown capitalism not only brought about general disintegration and the con-

---

[1] F. Nietzsche, *Werke in Drei Bänden*, Zweiter Band, München, 1962, S. 1017.

centration of the individual on himself but also gave a strong boost to the process of estrangement of the social force from man, a process that became a permanent feature of capitalism, especially in its monopolistic, imperialist stage.

In *The German Ideology*, Marx and Engels defined the essence of the process of estrangement as follows: "The social power, i.e., the multiplied productive force, which arises through the co-operation of different individuals as it is determined by the division of labour, appears to these individuals, since their co-operation is not voluntary but has come about naturally, not as their own united power, but as an alien force existing outside them, of the origin and goal of which they are ignorant, which they thus cannot control, which on the contrary passes through a peculiar series of phases and stages independent of the will and the action of man, nay even being the prime governor of these."[1]

This process of estrangement strongly influenced all aspects of consciousness, introducing numerous fetishist, illusory concepts of reality and man's relationships with it. It was aggravated by the growing complexity of social life, by the increasing division of labour isolating whole layers of people from one another, by the development of technology and industry, and the deepening of class national and cultural divisions. It became more and more difficult for the estranged human consciousness to take an *integrated* view of the phenomena of life, and instead they were perceived as *separate parts.* Lenin wrote: "Every individual producer in the world economic system realises that he is introducing this or that change into the technique of production; every owner realises that he exchanges certain products for others; but these producers and these owners do not realise that in doing so they are thereby changing *social being....* Social being is *independent* of *the social consciousness* of people. The fact that you live and conduct your business, beget children, produce products and exchange them, gives rise to an objectively necessary chain of events, a chain of

---

[1] K. Marx and F. Engels, *The German Ideology*, Moscow, 1964, p. 46.

development, which is independent of your *social* consciousness, and is never grasped by the latter completely."[1]

However, estrangement of man's productive and social, force was an historical phenomenon connected with the specific conditions of capitalist production. Examining the ways and means of overcoming estrangement in his article "On the Jewish Question", Marx wrote: "Only when the real individual man has retracted into himself the abstract citizen; when as an individual man, in his everyday life, in his particular work, and in his particular situation, he has become a *species being;* only when he has recognised and organised his own powers as *social* powers so that he no longer separates social power from himself as *political* power, only then will human emancipation be brought about."[2] In other words, man's estrangement from his social force will be finally overcome only in the conditions of communist society, when all the barriers between the consciousness of the individual and that of society will be removed, and the harmful consequences of estrangement will be *overcome in the course of the political struggle against capitalism.* Thus revolutionary consciousness, armed with the advanced theory of scientific communism, is *free* from those illusions which the process of estrangement introduces into consciousness as such. The progressive, revolutionary consciousness perceives reality as it actually is.

As for the consciousness of the masses, it perceives and apprehends the mechanism of social relations, the trends of social development and the nature of the views and convictions of the different classes not only in a period when class battles and conflicts are intensified, but also when this knowledge is introduced to it from without, by a revolutionary party wielding the theory of scientific communism.

Thus the process of alienation only develops fully in the bourgeois consciousness, which distorts reality pro-

---

[1] V. I. Lenin, *Collected Works*, Vol. 14, p. 325.
[2] K. Marx, F. Engels, *Werke*, Bd. 1, S. 370.

ducing false concepts of society, nature and man, and the relationships between them in various ideological spheres[1]. The concept of history and the forces that determine its course also change. The *idea of development* and the idea of progress that are a feature of bourgeois ideology in its early stage, give way in the period of mature capitalism to the *idea of the permanency* of social relations based on social inequality.

Bourgeois ideologists have come to accept as a self-evident and undisputable fact the idea that the final victory of capitalism has removed the need for the transformation and reorganisation of society. As the great Hungarian revolutionary poet Petöfi wrote, inveighing against the apologists of capitalism:

> False prophets claim that we have reached
> The longed-for shore of our endeavours.
> The promised land, they say, is here,
> The long, long road behind us.

Indeed, the French historians who first noted the class struggle, argued that it is *discontinued* with the victory of the bourgeoisie, while the positivist philosophers and sociologists treated society and consciousness as something *permanent* and immutable subordinate, according to Comte, to "changeless natural laws". The supporters of social Darwinism reduced the class struggle to a struggle for survival, thereby denying the possibility of any change in the social order, for the struggle they were referring to could, by its very nature, only continue within the existing system in the form of a battle for the highest possible level of material welfare. Those bourgeois ideologists who, like Renan, did recognise social change

---

Contemporary bourgeois philosophers, such as the French Jesuits Fathers Bigo and Calves, who deal with the revolutionary substance of the concept of alienation in their books *Marxisme et humanisme* and *La pensée de Karl Marx*, respectively, firstly try to eviscerate this concept of its revolutionary content, and secondly, in an attempt to show Marxism to be an ethical philosophy, reduce its content to the theory of alienation. These and similar views have been submitted to well-substantiated, shattering criticism in contemporary Marxist literature. Here we are *only* concerned with the problem of alienation in as far as it concerns the evolution of realism.

supposed that it could only take place organically, that is, without destroying the existing social structure. The *protective* character of bourgeois consciousness and the decline of bourgeois democracy in the mature period of capitalist development was brilliantly revealed by Dostoyevsky in his essay "On the Bourgeois", a chapter of his *Winter Notes on Summer Impressions.* He wrote: "Why has he (the bourgeois—*B.S.)* forgotten the high style in the chamber of deputies he was formerly so fond of? Why does he not wish to remember anything and waves his arms at you when he is reminded of something that was in the old days? Why this immediate anxiety in his mind, in his eyes, and on his tongue, when others dare to wish for something in his presence? Why, when he makes the foolish slip of suddenly wishing for something himself, does he immediately wince and begin to deprecate: 'Good lord, what *am* I doing?' and for a long time afterwards conscientiously tried to make up for his misbehaviour with diligence and obedience?"[1] This happens, Dostoyevsky continues, because he is afraid that "people may think that the ideal has not been reached . . . that perhaps one might wish for something more, and that thus the bourgeois is himself not completely satisfied with the order he stands for and forces on everybody else; that there are loopholes in society that need repairing".[2] Who is the bourgeois afraid of? Dostoyevsky answers this question too. The bourgeois is afraid of the communists and socialists. "Yes, these people he is still afraid of."[3] He is afraid because social welfare has not resulted from the ideals he declared in carrying out his revolution. "The immortal principles of 1789"—liberty, equality and fraternity—to which Flaubert's Homet had sworn like countless liberals with similar views in parliamentary speeches and from university Chairs, in philosophical treatises and in the daily press, had revealed their bankruptcy. "Freedom, what freedom?" Dostoyevsky wrote. "The same freedom for all to do anything at all within the bounds of the law. When can you do just as you please? When you have a

---

[1] F. Dostoyevsky, *Collected Works,* Moscow, 1956, Vol. 4, p. 100.
[2] Ibid., p. 101.
[3] Ibid., p. 105.

million. Does freedom give everyone a million? No. What is a man without a million? A man without a million is not one who does anything at all, but one with whom anything at all is done."[1] As for equality before the law, in the form in which it exists, the bourgeois "can and should take it as a personal insult". What about fraternity? In the Western, that is, bourgeois nature it "... has not appeared. What has appeared instead is the individual principle, the principle of the private man, increased self-preservation, self-advancement, self-entrenchment in the Ego, and the opposition of this Ego to the whole of nature and all other people as a law unto itself, perfectly equal and equivalent to all that there is besides himself".[2] In other words, capitalist civilisation resulted in the *alienation* of man, whose nature the bourgeois ideologists try to present as *immutable.* They assert that both society and man are static and constant, denying that society, and thus the consciousness of its members, could be reorganised on different lines. Herbert Spencer, who had a pathological hatred for socialism, basing his ideas on evolutionist theories, tried to make an absolute of class inequality considering it an immutable law of life. Although he sought the causes of the defects in the capitalist social order in capitalism itself, he attributed them to "human imperfection", as if this were something inherent and not conditioned. He rejected the idea of communist transformation of society on the grounds that: "The machinery of Communism, like existing social machinery, has to be framed out of existing human nature; and the defects of existing human nature will generate in the one and the same evils as in the other. ... The defective natures of citizens will show themselves in the bad acting of whatever social structure they are arranged into. There is no political alchemy by which you can get golden conduct out of leaden instincts."[3] Socialist humanism and the theory of scientific communism reject and refute such

---

[1] F. Dostoyevsky, *Collected Works,* Vol. 4, p. 105.
[2] Ibid., p. 106.
[3] Herbert Spencer, *The Man Versus the State,* London, 1914, pp. 38, 39.

misanthropical views of human nature. Lenin wrote: "We can only build communism out of the material created by capitalism, out of that refined apparatus which has been moulded under bourgeois conditions and which—as far as concerns the human material in the apparatus—is therefore inevitably imbued with the bourgeois mentality. That is what makes the building of communist society difficult, but it is also a guarantee that it can and will be built."[1] The guarantee of success in building socialism and communism lies in the fact that socialism enables the individual and the masses "display their abilities, develop the capacities, and reveal those talents, so abundant among the people whom capitalism crushed, suppressed and strangled in thousands and millions".[2]

The practical experience of socialist and communist construction in the Soviet Union and People's Democracies, and the spread of the ideas of communism all round the globe, confirm the sterility and mendacity of the opinions of Spencer, and of the contemporary bourgeois philosophers and sociologists, writers and propagandists who vainly try to prove the "immutability" of human nature, and hence deny the possibility of creating rational social relations.

The protective nature of bourgeois ideology was most fully and clearly in evidence in Nietzsche, whose views not only anticipated the views of contemporary bourgeois ideologists but paved the way for them. Nietzsche's philosophy reflected the essential features of the new phase in the development of bourgeois consciousness produced by the transition of capitalist society to the imperialist stage, with the increased alienation it entailed. The main features of the bourgeois outlook of the new phase, which cause us to define it as a decadent outlook, were formulated and defined in Nietzsche's philosophy. Decadence became the essential distinctive feature of the bourgeois consciousness during this period.

Like all bourgeois ideologists, Nietzsche took as his point of departure the immutability of capitalist society,

---

[1] V. I. Lenin, *Collected Works*, Vol. 28, p. 388.
[2] Ibid., Vol. 26, p. 404.

but he defended the immutability of existing relations so fiercely as to banish from history the very concept of development. He began his *Kampf* against the progress of socialism and humanism, freedom and revolution with scathing criticism of the concept of "historical man".

First and foremost, he detached man from all social ties and considered him as a sort of abstraction in his philosophising, as extraneous to all social and historical conditions. He also detached man from historical tradition, since, like historical thought, it was a legacy of the age of revolutions and thus hostile to the ideas and concepts that Nietzsche was infusing in the bourgeois mind, calling for a revaluation of values, and above all of those values which were in some way connected with the revolutionary and democratic movements past and present. With his view of man as a self-contained entity, independent of his environment and historical conditions, whose behaviour was determined by his will to power, Nietzsche nevertheless produced a fairly authentic picture of bourgeois civilisation and culture. While simplifying and vulgarising the social struggle past and present, he considered *slavery* to be the foundation of civilisation, the soil in which the culture of the chosen few grows and flourishes. According to his theory this élite of "supermen" is called upon to rule over the masses, or, to use his own term, "the herd".

Abstracted from history, Nietzsche's man is also extracted from the flow of time. His consciousness, essence and thought, his whole psychology are *extratemporal*. This attribution of an extratemporal nature to human thoughts and deeds, and to the whole human Ego, is a typical feature of *decadence* as a form of *consciousness*. No less characteristic of him is denial of rational cognition. Detached from the external objective world, estranged from reality, man is unable to fill the gap, the great yawning chasm between his subjective Ego and the outside world with the aid of reason, which only dissects and organises the chaotic stream of life, flowing its eternal course *alongside* man and washing against his soul. Only intuition can fill this gap. By suggesting a Dionysian approach to perception and apprehension of the world,

Nietzsche was opening the door wide to *irrationalism*, placing reason at the mercy of dark, cruel, "nighttime" instincts, and the ferment of wild passions. Bergson, who allotted the intellect the subordinate role of analyst and guide in the lower sphere of the material world, also considered intuition the supreme form of perception and cognition, since it embraces lasting motion in its entirety, and hence enables man to grasp not merely separate parts but the whole sum of phenomena of which the world is compounded. *Intuitivism*, an inherent feature of decadence, is an essential element of bourgeois consciousness and art and literature in the latter part of the nineteenth century, and likewise of all forms of decadent art in the twentieth century, beginning with symbolism and continuing in surrealism and abstract art. Just as decadence as a form of consciousness places the emphasis on the instincts and the sphere of the feelings, so the aesthetics of decadent and kindred trends in art—symbolism, for example—constantly strive to transmit vague, indistinct sentiments and sensations that are subjective and *particular* rather than to portray and analyse objective human thoughts and feelings with a universal significance. This hyperrefined transmission of the feelings of an alienated man is a feature of the poetry of Mallarmé, Wilde, Hofmannsthal, Sologub and George, an element uniting them all under one roof, so to speak, despite their very different personalities and artistic gifts, for it derives from the same *Weltanschauung,* produced by decadence as a special form of consciousness.

Viewing human nature as extratemporal, Nietzsche rejected the very concept of historical progress, replacing it with the theory of eternal recurrence. He countered the idea of development with the idea of "life, as it is, senseless, purposeless, but inevitably recurring, without a conclusive 'naught'—'eternal recurrence'. This is the most scientific of all possible hypotheses. We deny final aims: if existence had such an aim, it ought to have been achieved by now".[1] Thus, with the theory of "eternal recurrence" or "changeable constancy", where things and

---

[1] F. Nietzsche, *Ein Buch für Alle und Kuner,* Leipzig, 1900, S. 321.

phenomena change but their essence remains the same, Nietzsche proclaimed the permanence and immutability of the capitalist social relations, for the defence and protection of which the theory was indeed devised.

In *Also Sprach Zarathustra*, Nietzsche wrote: "All things eternally recur, and we with them.... We have already existed countless times and all things with us." But by denying development, Nietzsche was also denying the existence of historical time. Earlier, in his *Richard Wagner in Bayreuth* (1875-1876), he had written: "We experience phenomena so strange for us that they would be inexplicable, as if hanging in the air, as if going back into the depths of time, we were not able to connect them by analogy with Greek phenomena. Thus between Kant and the Eleatic philosophers, between Schopenhauer and Empedocles, between Aeschylus and Richard Wagner, there is such a close tie of kinship that the relative nature of all concepts of time is practically invisible: it begins to appear that many things are connected with one another, and time is but a veil screening this mutual connection from our view.... The pendulum of history has returned to the point from which it began its oscillation—it has returned to the mysterious distance and the depth of time. The picture of our modern world is by no means new. It must seem more and more to the historian that he is recognising old familiar features."[1] Along with the theory of eternal recurrence and the relativity of historical time, another of the main features of decadence was *anti-historicism*. Basically, all forms of modern bourgeois consciousness are affected by anti-historicism. Despite the fact that bourgeois consciousness has taken shape in conditions of crumbling social relations, in the period of the final collapse of bourgeois democratism, of the decline of the old colonial empires and the meteoric rise of the masses to activity, not to mention the scientific and technological revolution, it has practically lost all idea of the reality of history as a process. "Our critical cast," wrote Karl Joël on the eve of the First World War, "leads us to scepticism. This scepticism threatens to deprive us of the

---

[1] F. Nietzsche, *Unzeitgemässe Betrachtungen*, Leipzig, 1873, S. 22.

last and finest thing we inherited from the nineteenth century: our understanding of history. Nietzsche struck the first blow, with a book in which he intended to speak of the use and harm of history, but in which he in fact only spoke of its harm. Soon now the epitaph will be written: 'The death of a Science'." The neo-Kantians Rickert and Simmel subjectivised the concept of the historical process; Benedetto Croce simply denied that history was in any way a law-governed process, even to the extent of doubting the very existence of historical time; the determinist Spengler examined history as a sequence of separate, isolated cultures, each like a kind of organism whose life span was preordained, the features of their development being definable by analogy. Spengler, like Nietzsche, pointed to similarities between phenomena of different historical nature, thus rejecting in fact historical time: "Pergamum is the double of Bayreuth," he wrote. "Similarly, the illusionist painting of the Asian and Sicyon schools is purely a colourful episode corresponding fully to the Barbizon episode and Manet's school," and so on and so forth. If one adopted this approach one could continue such comparisons *ad infinitum*. Arnold Toynbee's philosophy of history is also related to this kind of thinking. If Spengler distinguished eight cultures as compounding the whole of history, Toynbee, the most influential of modern historians of philosophy, distinguishes no less than twenty-one. In his multi-volume work *A Study of History* he examines history not as an integrated developing process, but as a combination of various independent civilisations. Like Nietzsche and Spengler, he puts quite different historical events into the same category. Thus, he draws an analogy between Sparta and the Prussian state. Toynbee rejects the idea of the development of history in time, producing his own variant of the theory of eternal recurrence. Anti-historicism is not only to be found in the views of bourgeois historians and philosophers, but also in art and literature where the decadent outlook is present.

In *Ulysses* James Joyce compounded various historical periods, concentrating them in his hero Stephen Dedalus. The authors of "autobiographic novels", like André Maurois and Emil Ludwig, as well as many authors of historical novels, have *modernised history*, projecting modern social features into the past. The nature of this anti-historical trend in the bourgeois consciousness was noted long ago by Lenin when he wrote: "Nothing is more characteristic of the bourgeois than the application of the features of the modern system to all times and peoples."[1] The sense of history, which social thought acquired at the cost of such tremendous effort in the years after the French Revolution, is gradually lost in the age of imperialism, indeed even suppressed by the bourgeois consciousness, which no longer wishes or is able to see history *as a process*, and is unable to grasp the meaning and content of the changes taking place in the world.

Nietzsche's philosophy with its frankly voluntaristic and aggressive character, which made "free will" the prerogative of the Superman, in fact *denied freedom* to all, including those who belong to the chosen élite. Since there is no development, but only eternal marking time, "eternal recurrence" or "changing constancy", there is no real need for freedom, freedom of action or manifestation of will, since everything that goes on within man or outside him turns in a vicious circle and is predetermined by the wheel of life. Thus a frank, overt fatalism and slavish submission to fate creep onto Nietzsche's philosophy as a logical outcome of its very essence. With his characteristic rhetorical grandeloquence he calls this fatalism *amor fati*, that is, "love of fate". Nietzsche not only affirmed the enslavement of man in the conditions of capitalist society, but asked us to love social slavery.

The sense of unfreedom is the *fundamental* characteristic of the decadent world view. Estranged social force is perceived by the bourgeois consciousness as an extraneous power, mysterious, blind and inscrutable, as something which, far from being dependent on human will, actually directs and governs it. The proposition that man is not free is common to numerous sociological and philosophical theories and systems of the late nineteenth century, and of the present day too for that matter. The

---

[1] V. I. Lenin, *Collected Works*, Vol. 1, p. 154.

neo-Kantian Simmel wrote in *Jahrbuch der Gehe—Stiftung zu Dresden:* "In practice and in vague perception the individual may be to a greater degree than he is aware reduced to a *quantité négligeuble,* to become a speck of dust in the face of the tremendous organisation of objects and forces which gradually take from his hands all progress and all spiritual and material values." Such feelings also lie at the root of the deathly fatalism of Spengler, for whom the succession of civilisations, their birth and passing is subject to iron necessity. It is also the core of the existentialist philosophy, which views the external social forces as wielding dictatorial powers over the individual. It is an equally essential part of neo-Thomism, for which history is independent of the people who make it, depending entirely on the will of God, who pursues some grand design of His, so that people's behaviour is predestined.

Decadent art and literature faithfully reflected this proposition and man's lack of freedom was indeed to be its main content. Dorian Gray, an immoral character who was unable to distinguish between good and evil because he regarded beauty as superior to any moral values, belonged to the caste of the chosen, concerned only with the satisfaction of their own lusts and desires. His wealth and his disregard for the moral norms of the community appear to make a free man of him. In actual fact he is *not free,* either in his thoughts or actions. With the directness that is characteristic of decadent art, Oscar Wilde *materialised* his hero's state and sense of unfreedom, harnessing his fate to that of his portrait which absorbed all his base and sinful actions, and became his curse, reproach and secret master, one that Gray could not destroy without destroying himself.

Maurice Maeterlinck's characters, anaemic and fleshless, and reduced to vague, indefinite symbols, live and die as slaves of destiny. Foredoomed, and unable to escape their fate, not understanding what is happening to them, they either perish, like Tintagiles and Princess Maline, await their doom like the characters of the play *The Blind,* who symbolise mankind as a whole, or float away unresisting on the river of life into the unknown, without aim or purpose, and without hope of freeing themselves from the inscrutable power which controls their lives. Chance and fate rule the lives of Hofmannsthal's heroes. They dispose equally of people's destinies, appearing as two aspects of necessity, whose icy breath falls on that gay slave of fortune the adventurist Baron Weidenstam (in the play *Der Abenteurer und die Sängerin*) and the Madonna Dianora *(Die Frau im Fenster)*, who also becomes the victim of chance. Hofmannsthal reduces the wisdom and meaning of life to the following proposition: "All is inevitable, and great happiness lies in knowing that all is inevitable. This is the good, the only good."[1] It was quite natural that Hofmannsthal, in his *Electra* and *Oedipus*, should imitate ancient tragedy for which the theme of fate was an organic part of the action.

The life of Hamsun's heroes is spun of the unknown, illusions and solitude, the threads of their destiny woven and unwoven by some mighty invisible hand. Estranged from one another, seeing their own lives as an unsoluble enigma, they are slaves to their passions and love, which has the force of fate and embodies the power of fate. As if under the influence of some magic potion, they strain towards one another, but the destructive power of destiny prevents them from uniting. Hamsun replaces social antagonism which disunites people in real life with the antagonism of the sexes, biological difference, the love duel, generally ending in tragedy, for the heroes of his works are powerless to break the chains of passion which fetter them and deprive them of freedom of action and will. They pass one another by, like separate atoms, either in the glare of the night lights of the city, where dramas of poverty and hunger are enacted, or in some god-forsaken villages, to which, like an echo of the urban civilisation which Hamsun so detests, destructive passions reach out their tentacles, bringing anxiety and mystery to the simple life of people who are close to nature and whose hearts harbour nature's savage, hidden nocturnal passions. Hamsun hated the city and its civilisation, in-

---

[1] Hugo von Hofmannsthal, *Teater in Versen*, Berlin, 1905, S. 23.

cluding its offspring the proletariat, and observed with anxiety the decline of the *kulak* village, whose "pristine" power he extolled in *Growth of the Soil*, and the collapse under the impact of bourgeois enterprise of the old way of life of the peasants and fisherfolk, which he loved for its immobility and described in his trilogy *The Vagabonds.* This outlook drove him into the camp of political reaction and eventually to collaboration with fascism.

Man's sense of "unfreedom", as a fundamental feature of the decadent outlook, was organically linked with disbelief in the creative historical activity of the masses, and accompanied by a feeling of powerlessness in the face of social injustice.

> We're beasts in captivity,
> Each howling our rage,
> Yet lacking the courage
> To open the cage.[1]

Thus Sologub expressed his deep anguish and his renunciation of social struggle against the capitalist world. He even went as far as to reject the very possibility of helping the oppressed and humiliated who craved for true emancipation:

> Somebody cries out "Help!"
> What can I do?
> I myself am a poor, small man,
> I myself am a tired man.
> What can I do
> To help?[2]

We find the attitude that man is not free, but eternally at the mercy of irrational inscrutable forces, permeating the whole world view of Leonid Andreyev in the period after the defeat of the 1905 Revolution when he abandoned realism to become one of the originators of expressionism with his plays *Anathema, Man's Life* and *King Hunger.* Comparing history to a pendulum, indifferently marking the succession of very similar events, and re-

---

[1] F. Sologub, *Collected Works,* Vol. 5, p. 4 (in Russ.).
[2] F. Sologub, *Scorpio,* A Collection of Poems, 1904, Vols. III-IV, p. 5.

peating with depressing monotony "as it was, so it will be", Andreyev considered vain any attempt by the masses to change its course. The permanence and recurrence of everything in life rendered pointless any urge for freedom and revolutionary struggle, with the aim of changing the world for the better. The feeling that man is not free, paralysing the will and the mind and reconciling them to things as they are, is found equally in the governor (in the short story of the same name), who knows that a terrorist's bullet is waiting for him, and in the revolutionaries in *Tale of Seven Hanged*, who accept their end as a blessing, as the solution to their doubts, hopes and anxiety. The hero of *My Notes* subordinates human nature, freedom of thought, and the very idea of freedom to "the sacred formula of iron bars", comparing life and the world to a vast prison in which man is serving a life sentence.

Franz Kafka frankly portrays man as a "quaking creature". Caught in the clinging web of fear, the will-less plaything of unknown forces, man is regarded by Kafka as incapable of throwing off the chains of his fate, and is doomed forever to carry in his soul the curse of fear of the unknown. Finally, in the plays and stories of Samuel Beckett, a disciple and heir of James Joyce, life—and hence the affairs of men—are shown as senseless and absurd. His works are peopled not by real people, but by faceless abstractions. Isolated from the world of reality, having lost all idea of what life is about, crushed and paralysed by their fear of death, and unable to understand one another, they mutter disconnected, illogical thoughts, whose only sense is horror of the world, life and the cruel forces of history. Beckett's works represent one of the clearest examples of the crisis and malaise of the modern bourgeois consciousness affected by the process of alienation.

Declaring slavery to be the foundation of civilisation, Nietzsche saw his main task to be to educate masters who would be able to seize the various seething social impulses that cause social unrest with an iron hand and hold them firmly in check. Nietzsche's "Superman" was not to be bound by conventional ethics. Nietzsche gave free rein to his instincts and passions, cultivated cruelty in him, praising violence, war and bloodshed. This glorification of war and brutality was an essential feature of the decadent *Weltanschauung*, reflecting the growing brutalisation of man in capitalist society, where no quarter is given in the general free-for-all.

Literature was bound to reflect the brutality of life in a society where war and violence, crime and iniquity and individual and mass suffering were the permanent concomitants of progress. Previously, however, literature had regarded all this as the dark side of progress, and had not glorified evil for the sake of evil. It was only decadence, with its confusion of moral values, that began to look upon violence as an inalienable part of the new ethics that developed in the pre-imperialist stage of capitalism, and flourished in the hey-day of imperialism. For all his *serious* concern for the state of affairs in the world and his tragic dissatisfaction with it, in his *Les Fleurs du Mal*, Beaudelaire aesthetisised evil in its manifold expressions. Decadent art threw the veil of beauty over evil, violence and suffering, thereby *justifying* the brutality of capitalist society. The morbidness of Oscar Wilde's *Salomé* comes from the mixture of sentimentality and brutality, and self-torture and the desire to inflict pain on others characterise Hamsun's characters. Barres and Paul Adam created a veritable apotheosis to force and brutality, while the countless "colonial" novels full of racialist contempt for "coloured" peoples, cultivated brutality, thereby fulfilling the function of preparing soldiers for colonial wars and punitive expeditions against the peoples of Asia and Africa struggling for their freedom and independence. The glorification of violence and brutality is typical of such bourgeois realists as Kipling, whose works contain all the features of imperialist ideology with its aggressive optimism.

Nietzsche, himself decadent to the marrow, was a sharp critic of decadence as a way of thinking that served to weaken the class rule of the bourgeoisie, as an expression of the essence of bourgeois democracy which he thoroughly detested, seeing its negative aspects with the perspicacity born of hatred. Nietzsche's criticism of the bourgeois world was motivated by his desire to see the existing social structure strengthened, and the relative truth of his analysis of contemporary society was a demagogical cover for his apologia for capitalism. But there were many writers influenced by decadence who did not make any conscious apologia for capitalism. Rimbaud and Verlaine, Rilke and Apollinaire, expressed *the real tragedy* of life and man's inability to resist its power. This is why their works contain, alongside their natural, organic moods of despair and pessimism, anti-bourgeois motifs and moods of subjective, often anarchical revolt.

> Too long I have wept!
> How merciless the moon, how black the sun.
> May my keel be smashed on some jagged reef
> That I may sink and lie on the sandy bed.
> Enough of the wave's slow ripple around,
> Enough of the convoys, the sky for my roof,
> Enough of the proudly fluttering trade flags
> The twinkling lights on the convict pontoons.

Thus Arthur Rimbaud writes in his "Le bateau ivre", a poem whose tremendous bitterness and intense imagery expressed an individual's sensation of the collapse of the very supports of life, and a certain nostalgic anguish for the world he so hated and cursed. The crisis of the decadent *Weltanschauung* was a symptom of the general crisis developing in the bourgeois consciousness.

This crisis was bound to be reflected in the realist literature of the period, too, introducing features that had no place in the literature of classical critical realism. These changes were the result of fundamental changes in the historical development of bourgeois society. The period of revolution in Western Europe was coming to an end, and now Russia became the new centre of the world revolutionary movement. The new historical conditions brought about the decline of realism in Western Europe and its florescence in Russia. This process was to affect first and foremost the epic form, the very core of realism.

Gogol defined the novel as the epos of bourgeois society. He was obviously referring to the realist social novel, and his observation is basically correct, for the epic form was very much a feature of critical realism. At the same time the novel of critical realism was not epic in the true sense of the word. The true epic in folk literature—is based on the unity of the individual and society, which reflects the real nature of social relations in the early stages of historical development. The epic quality of the works of classical realism lay above all in the fact that the hero was the *product* of his social environment, and ultimately depended upon it. But the subjective element which invaded the epic narrative in modern times inevitably severed the individual's links with society. It was the conflict between the individual and his environment that underlay the action in works of critical realism, and this reflected the process of atomisation of bourgeois society, since the gradual advance of alienation also entailed a widening of the gap between the individual and his environment. The conditions for genuinely epic literature were only created in our own time by socialist realism, the main feature of which is analysis and portrayal of the process of reconciliation of the individual and society as a result of socialist transformation of private ownership social relations.

The growing conflict between the individual and society left its mark on all spheres of spiritual life in the latter part of the nineteenth century, injecting subjectivism into social consciousness and producing the tendency to look upon the thoughts and feelings of the individual, the isolated, alienated individual at that, as more "real" than external reality. Edmund Husserl, one of the forerunners of existentialism which has been one of the most influential philosophical movements in the twentieth century, remarked in his time that "all recent and most recent philosophy so inclines to anthropologism that it has become quite exceptional to come across a thinker who is perfectly free from the errors of this theory".[1] Indeed, metaphysical anthropologism was becoming a most characteris-

---

[1] E. Husserl, *Logische Untersuchungen,* Erste Thiel. *Prolegomena zur Reinen Logik,* Halle, 1900, S. 116.

tic feature of social consciousness in bourgeois society, although anthropologisation, anthropocentricity of consciousness reflects only one side of the process of historical development—the alienation characteristic of bourgeois society. However, in the age of imperialism, alongside this alienation, interdependence of men and class ties also make themselves felt more strongly.

The objective contradictions in social consciousness were naturally reflected in literature and art. Thus, impressionism was undoubtedly an offshoot of realism. The rejection of the smooth manner of academic painting in favour of generalisation and concentration of details, the presentation of the form of objects and the human figure by means of colour rather than line, the freedom and depth of perspective and sharp colour contrasts—all the innovations that the impressionist technique introduced—had as their aim maximum authenticity in the depiction of nature and the surrounding world. The impressionists dispensed with the superficially authentic traditional and artificial compositions of late romantic and classical art which had made a comfortable nest for itself under the protection of official academicism, and which was in fact hostile to realism and real nature with its conventional subjects, colours and compositions. The impressionists brought to art all the colour of life, simple unadorned reality, choosing as their subjects the everyday life and manners of the ordinary inhabitants of the big towns, their work and leisure. But their exclusive interest in *personal* experience made their art somewhat narrow, depriving it of social scope and impact, and confined it to the sphere of the subjective individual experience thereby undermining its realist foundations. In the paintings of the neo-impressionists and the divisionists we find the impressionist techniques, which originally enriched art and served to present real life, becoming an end in themselves, so that art's links with reality are dissolved.

One has only to compare the revolt of the impressionists against the established canons with that of the *peredvizhniki* in Russia, to see quite clearly the difference between the development of realism in Western Europe, and in Russia heading for revolution. The *peredvizhniki,* on the one hand, tried to present the texture of life and real objects and were thus the champions of truth in art, and, on the other, they were realists in the true and most precise sense of the word since social analysis and typification were major features of their art and were never sacrificed for the sake of experimenting with colour and light. It is because their art was rooted in the popular soil that in their best works the *peredvizhniki* and other artists who adopted their traditions, such as Surikov, rose above mere genre painting and achieved an epic quality. The realist art of Western Europe in the latter half of the nineteenth century did not so directly reflect the interests and views of the common people, and this was one of the reasons for the weakening of the epic element. Margaret Harkness, to whom Engels addressed a famous letter on realism, grasped very well the new features of realism and was to comment rather ironically on it, in her characterisation of the hero of her novel *City Girl.* He intended writing a novel in which he proposed to describe some strange episodes, interspersed with rather interesting psychological observations and which was to have no plot, for the plot had died out with Thackeray and George Eliot. Indeed it was true that "psychological observations" and "character study", having become an essential feature of realism in the latter half of the nineteenth century, often replaced the portrayal of the characters' relationship to their environment. In Hebbel's plays, which were based on classical and Germanic mythology, the action centres round two distinct points, reality and the psychological. Although all the plot and the conflict leading up to the final denouement was intended to reflect real-life relationships, a new quality had arisen in the character of his heroes: they had soared above the earth, so to speak, become too refined for reality, and against their tortured spiritual life and their complex psychological drama, the conflicts of real life seemed to lose their importance. In his petty-bourgeois drama *Mary Magdalene,* his characters' behaviour depends on social causes, but these causes gradually become less and less concrete, and the characters come to regard them as a series of chance misfortunes combining to form a hostile force. By introducing an element of fatality into the course of events, and thereby limiting the extent to which his heroes can exercise their will, Hebbel gradually destroyed the realistic foundation of his work. He reduced the social causes for the behaviour and actions of his characters to an initial impulse, which ceased to play any role whatsoever with the subsequent development of the plot, since from then on the dramatic conflict was produced not by a social conflict but by psychological conflicts in the characters themselves. His heroes were exceptional people, larger-than-life, with their strong, violent passions and desires. In Hebbel's view it is these inflated feelings and aspirations that make the world go round and determine the course of history. The fall of Candaules, the last of the Heraclids and King of Lydia, and the succession to the throne of Gyges (in the tragedy *Gyges und sein Ring*), marking a radical social change, hinged in Hebbel's play on the all-consuming passion of the two men for the Queen of the Rhodops. The fall of the Burgundian dynasty in *Die Nibelungen* hinged on the love conflict between Siegfried and Brunhild and Kriemhild's hatred for Brunhild. Hebbel's monumental trilogy concentrates on the royal love story, relegating the historical setting, the transition from pagan culture to Christianity, to the background.

Hebbel's strong characters—Herodes, Candaules and Etzel, are all children of the nineteenth century. They are all in the grip of destructive resignation, despite their tremendous capacity for action, and their spiritual worlds are highly unstable. They live in an atmosphere of suspicion and mistrust, having lost the ability to open their hearts to one another, to understand one another, condemned to perpetual isolation and loneliness. They are completely *ignorant* of one another's needs and feelings. In *Herodes and Mariamne*, Herodes, who doubts his wife's love for him, sets off to Rome condemning her to death if he should lose his life, not wanting her to give her love to another man after him. He does not tell Mariamne of his sentence, and she is very hurt when she finds out, for she loved him and was quite prepared to sacrifice herself for their love. Floundering in the dark, Hebbel's heroes perish tragically, this fatal ignorance and lack of trust between people being an expression of the chaos and disharmony in life. This is expressed with particular force in *Die Nibelungen*, where Hagen, Gunther, Etzel, Spielmann and the other characters are crushed by the titanic fury of Kriemhild's vengeance, through which all Siegfried's murderers come to a cruel, bloody end. But the fateful love of Brunhild and Siegfried is also doomed by her larger-than-life passion, and these proud natures are the *victims of ignorance*, for when Brunhild is baptised she loses the Valkirian gift of prophecy and is unable to foresee the tragic end of her love. Hebbel's later tragedies are tragedies of fate, and concentrating on passions and sufferings of individuals detached from their social environment, he largely abandons realism.

This gap between the inner world of man and external reality is an even more important feature of the works of Richard Wagner. The lyrical element which keeps breaking in with such insistence makes them lyric dramas instead of the powerful epics the composer intended. By expressing the intense pulse of life and its endless flow through human emotions and feelings, Wagner reduced the contradictions and social struggle of the objective world to contradictions and struggle within the human soul. "I see not the masses but individual people,"[1] he wrote to Malwida Meysenburg, and the tragic fate of individuals, their inner dramas, the hypnotic power of love are what he presents. The very rhythms of his music, their intensity, mobility and endless build-ups convey the battle of passions in the human heart, love torments and bewitching power driving Tristan and Isolde, the Flying Dutchman and Senta, and Siegfried and Brunhild not to happiness but to destruction. Wagner regarded the world as "a disharmonious chord". In Ring Cycle, which tells of the destruction of Siegfried, "the man of the future which we all cultivate and long for, whom we cannot

---

[1] *Richard Wagner an Freunde und Zeitgenossen*, Berlin und Leipzig, 1909, S. 306.

create but who will arise from our destruction",[1] Wagner believed, and not without reason, that the tragic finale of his opus magnum reflected one of the major conflicts of the age. Both the Ring Cycle and Hebbel's tragedies have two nuclei, two centres around which the action revolves: one in the sphere of the human feelings, the other in the external world. In the Ring Cycle we have the theme of love opposed to the theme of gold and the whole conflict of the drama, vested in abstract, mythological form, reflects the real conflict between man's spiritual needs, his great potential, his aspirations towards harmony and happiness, and the ugly prose of life, the lack of harmony in the world, which holds man captive and prevents him from exercising his powers. These heroico-pessimistic features of the Ring Cycle are most clearly evident in Wotan, who, in Wagner's own words, "...is like us down to the last tiny detail". If, as Wagner says, "all the ideas of our time are combined in Wotan",[2] then the outlook is bleak indeed, for the fruit of Wotan's reflections on life is that reality and human values are pure illusion, and man's only desire is "longing for the inevitable". "It teaches death": thus Wagner summed up the meaning of his colossal creation. Begun in the years of revolution, as an apotheosis of the radiant hero Siegfried, the Ring Cycle ends with the death of the gods, in a gloomy, pessimistic finale. "The main misfortune is not that the daughters of the Rhine reject Alberich," Wagner wrote. "...This was quite natural for them. Alberich and his ring could cause the gods no harm, if the gods were not themselves already on the path to destruction."[3] What relates the idea of Wagner's great work to the decadent world view is the all-pervading sense of the downfall of the ideals of the bourgeois democratic age and its approaching end, and the inner admission that the circumstances of life are stronger than revolutionary courage. The superb realism Wagner achieved in his characters in *Die Meistersinger* is diluted in his later works

---

[1] *Briefe an August Röckel von Richard Wagner*, Leipzig, 1903, S. 37.
[2] Ibid., S. 35.
[3] Ibid., S. 35.

by naturalist exaggeration, eroticism and ponderous symbolism. The political views and sentiments they express—just as in Hebbel's later dramas—were conservative in the true sense of the word, that is, both men were concerned with conserving existing social relations however unharmonious they might be, for the simple reason that they found it impossible to believe in change.

In narrative prose, too, the trend was towards the study of man's inner world, the latter becoming more and more an object of interest *per se* and no longer in relationship with environment. An early example of this is Flaubert's *Madame Bovary*, which is essentially an enlarged psychological study, and not a picture of morals and manners or an analysis of the anatomy of society such as we find in the novels of the classical period of critical realism. Viewing bourgeois life as a slough that sucks man down, swamping his energy and aspirations for happiness, Flaubert combines his description of the spiritual torments of an insignificant petty-bourgeois woman sinking lower and lower with a description of an equally banal and petty world, which serves as the trivial background to her trivial drama. He still adhered to the analysis of life that is such an important principle of critical realism, and also to the method of typification that realism had introduced. The main characters of the novel are full-blown portraits, not thumb-nail sketches, and the social picture he presents is consistent and uncompromising. The provincial doctor Charles Bovary and Homet, the chemist, and the other inhabitants of the provincial town are portrayed in a manner akin to classical critical realism. But the spiritual drama of the heroine, the loss of her romantic illusions, her love torments, her sufferings, fears and remorse for what she has done, her rapid swings from sentimental ecstasy to petty-bourgeois calculation tend to outweigh, both emotionally and by virtue of the importance Flaubert assigns to them, the depiction of the social environment—static and stagnating in hypocrisy, prejudice and selfishness. However, in the thorough analysis of Emma's feelings and moods, the hidden desires that ravage her heart and her essential duality, we find new realist features that were not present in the realism of an earlier

period. By his flexible, many-sided analysis of his characters' psychology Flaubert made up for the deficiencies
in the portrayal of social environment.

The mouthpiece for the social ideals of the milieu
Flaubert depicts is the liberal chatterbox Homet, with his
solemn appeals to the "sacred" principles of the French
Revolution, of whose ubiquitous degeneration the author
was only too well aware. The participants in, and wit-
nesses of, Emma Bovary's drama are isolated from one
another and are quite incapable of understanding the feelings of even those who are closest to them. Emma is a
closed book for her husband and her prosaic lovers alike,
while she herself sees others not as they are, but as her
imagination paints them. In fact, one of the main themes
of the novel is *loneliness* in a crowd, solitude in a densely
populated world where people are so indifferent to others
and so estranged from one another that real communication, spiritual contact, is practically eliminated. This theme
was new for realism, and must be ascribed to the development of the process of alienation.

Flaubert's family drama, although typified as a logical
phenomenon in the tragic conditions of humdrum existence of bourgeois society, ran its course within the closed
circuit of *personal, private* human relationships without
overspilling into social life, or in any way affecting it, and
had as its arena a stable, *fixed* system of social relations.
Flaubert did not regard bourgeois society as a stage in
human social development. For him it was an imperfect
but essential condition of human existence, a world order
corresponding to man's imperfect nature.

While the earlier realists had accepted the idea of development without question, Flaubert and many other
writers of the latter half of the nineteenth century had
serious doubts about the changeability of society and
human nature. The "progressive" Homet is a living refuta-
tion of the idea of progress. This acceptance of the stability of social relations and human feelings introduced
fundamental changes into the nature of realism in the
latter half of the century. *Madame Bovary*, like Maupassant's *Une Vie*, was heavily charged with social criticism.
But doubt in the possibility of perfecting human nature or

society prevented these and other great realist writersof their time from seeing the *trend of the historical process in its full dimensions and in true historical perspective*. Impassive portrayal of life began to replace analysis of the contradictions that were the motive force of social development. Instead of a full picture of reality in its totality Flaubert gives us a sequence of independent scenes. This characteristic feature of his narrative manner was to find its fullest expression in his *Tentation de Saint Antoine*, where the action is compartmentalised into a number of more or less self-contained episodes loosely strung together. The structure of this later work of Flaubert's testifies to the collapse of the epic form, where the world is treated as a *mobile entity*. Thus, Tolstoi's prose can be compared to a motion picture conveying the flux of life in all its tiniest details and thus presenting the processes of change in the human soul, in man's relationship with the outer world, and in that world itself. Flaubert's prose, on the other hand, is more like a magic lantern showing separate views of life, which only recreate the whole when taken together. The image of the world in Flaubert's works is like a mosaic, made up of numerous separate coloured pieces. Behind this manner of depicting reality lies a concept of reality as fixed and unchanging. It is therefore only natural that Flaubert should unconsciously compartmentalise motion suspending it even in the most dynamic portions of a narrative, as he does indeed in *Salammbô*, an historical novel in which he took great pains to reconstruct in minute detail the features of a lost civilisation and analyse the fierce love of the barbarian Mâtho for the daughter of Hamilcar Barca, the Carthaginian general. The following passage should suffice to illustrate this.

"...Suddenly the Carthaginian army appeared on the bend from behind the hills. The baggage slaves armed with slings were on the flanks and the first row of the main army was composed of legionaries in gold chain-mail mounted on fat maneless horses without ears or hair and with silver horns on their foreheads to make them look like rhinos. Between each squadron marched youths in small helmets with a javelin of ash-wood in either hand,

and wedge formations of heavy infantry brought up the rear. All these merchants had armed themselves as heavily as they could: some carried two swords and a spear, axe and club besides; others bristled like porcupines with arrows and carried unwieldy ivory or metal shields. Last to appear were the massive machines; slings, onagers, catapults and scorpions trundling along on wheeled platforms drawn by mules or teams of four oxen. As the army advanced the commanders rushed backwards and forwards breathlessly, shouting out hoarse orders, keeping the ranks from spreading or closing up too much. The senior commanders wore purple cloaks with magnificent long trains that got caught up in the straps of their sandals. Their rouged faces shone smoothly beneath their enormous helmets decorated with godheads. ...." [1]

We find this same immobility in the works of the Parnassians, and especially J.-M. de Heredia, and in Thomas Hardy's novels about rural England, where the tragedies of shattered dreams of people sunk in poverty, at the mercy of the cruel whims of fate, are played out in a completely static, stagnant world. We find this same static quality—a basic feature of naturalism—in Zola's *De la description* which *indicates but does not transmit* the flux of life. Tolstoi, on the other hand, who was writing in conditions of a mounting tide of revolution which threatened to sweep away the very foundations of society, when the struggle between opposed social forces was coming into the open, showed life on the move, as in the following passage describing an army on the move in a draft copy for *War and Peace.* "From all sides, from ahead and behind, as far as one could hear came the sound of wheels, creaking carts, and gun-carriages, the pounding of hooves, the crack of whips, goading cries, the swearing of soldiers, officers and batmen. All along the roadside at intervals were dead horses, some skinned, some not, broken carts with odd soldiers sitting by them waiting for something or other, or groups of soldiers who had got separated from their commanders, and were setting off for nearby

[1] G. Flaubert, *Salammbô*, Paris, p. 127.

villages or returning from villages carrying chickens, lambs, hay or bulging sacks. Wherever there was a slope up or down the crowds grew denser, and the din of shouting crescendoed. The soldiers, up to their knees in mud, pushed the guns and waggons. Whips cracked, hooves slithered, traces snapped and men shouted at the tops of their voices. The officers rode back and forth between the transport waggons giving orders to keep things moving."[1] What a collection of sounds and sights! The whole passage is seething with life and movement, full of noise and bustle. Mind, ear and eye are all vitally alive to the raging torrent of life that pours through the pages of this great epic.

The feeling that life was static, which is the determining factor in Flaubert's prose and is generally characteristic of West European realism in the last decades of the nineteenth century, testifies to a decreased sensitivity to the rhythm of history, the music of history, if you like, and the meaning of its deep-down processes. Take Flaubert's novel *L'Education Sentimentale*, in which he makes a subtle analysis of the exaggeratedly romantic love of his hero Frederic Moreau for the beautiful wife of the art dealer Arnou. This love is everything in the life of Frederic Moreau, which is essentially as colourless and anaemic as his passions. Flaubert makes fun of the romantic illusions of his spineless hero who floats like a splinter on the tide of events, and at the same time of the illusions of bourgeois liberalism, its social demagogy which Flaubert always so detested. He was equally scathing in his criticism of those true sons of the bourgeoisie, Monsieur Arnou with his love for copy-book truths and his knack for making money, and the banker Dambreuse, far more of a vulture, possessed of remarkable vitality and a great talent for dressing his sails to the wind. Thus, as long as the power of the propertied classes seems absolute and in no way threatened he is as hard as nails, but as soon as the mighty edifice of capitalism is rocked by popular

---

[1] L. Tolstoi, *Collected Works*, Moscow, 1951, Vol. 4, pp. 203-04 (in Russ.).

insurrection, as soon as the barricades go up in Paris and the people storm the "sacred" principle of private property, he does a volte face and immediately poses as a "friend of the people", nearly a proletarian himself.

Flaubert is quite well aware that the banker Dambreuse and the people are natural enemies and the struggle between them is inevitable, the aim for the bourgeoisie being the complete subjugation of the masses. The cultural and intellectual sterility of the ruling classes and the hypocrisy of bourgeois morality which hides immorality behind the cloak of respectability involve his scorn and derision. But social criticism is secondary in the novel to the portrayal of Frederic's limp passions, his arid, brain-spun love for the beautiful madame Arnou. The characters' personal life is somehow detached from real life, and runs an independent parallel course to it. It is more interesting for Flaubert than the events of the 1848 Revolution which he viewed as an isolated episode that was over and done with when the revolutionary explosion fizzled out, and not as a warning of what lay in store for the bourgeois order. This complete absence of faith in revolution and the creative power of the people was fundamental to his whole outlook. He was equally sceptical about the Paris Commune and the activities of the International. He did not accept socialism as a theory and did not believe in the possibility of a socialist society ever being established. Side by side with the hatred he harboured for the bourgeoisie went a deep hostility towards the working masses. This was what made Flaubert's attitude to society so complicated, and in this he was like many other critical realists of his day. He wanted to occupy an *intermediate* position between conflicting social forces and counterposed to the social ideals of both the bourgeoisie and the revolutionary people artistic values, beauty and the cult of form. Flaubert initiated the illusion that art was *independent of social life*, that the artist or writer could stand *aloof from class struggle*, which has survived right down to the present day. This illusion is based on the contradiction of a democratic, hence anti-bourgeois awareness, which was not, however, revolutionary, which could be critical of reality but had lost the sense of history involving change.

The anti bourgeois note is strong in Flaubert's works, but his range of subject matter was far narrower than that of his predecessors. A sceptical attitude towards the progressive ideas of his age and lack of faith in socialism one day achieving happiness for mankind, led him and several other contemporary critical realists, such as Ibsen, into an ideological impasse, leaving them wide open to the influence of decadence. The cult of form, doubt in the power of reason and science and rejection of the idea of social progress and development which came to the fore in Flaubert's later works, and especially in *Bouvard et Pécuchet*, weakened the realist texture of his art and introduced features of aestheticism. This crisis makes itself felt far more strongly in Flaubert's works than in the works of Maupassant, who greatly enriched the realist tradition with important aesthetic innovations.

For Maupassant—the greatest realist in West European literature of the latter part of the nineteenth century— life itself was the object of analysis and depiction. He still saw man and environment, character and the social conditions that moulded it, as inseparable and interdependent. Maupassant's prose engulfed all the processes of life and he typified them on the basis of analytical study of the *social nature* of behaviour, mentality, feelings, in short—people's whole individual cast. Peasants and soldiers, bureaucrats vegetating at their desks and enmeshed in red tape, young bourgeois bohemians, landladies, provincial gentlefolk and truculent prosperous farmers, grasping petty bourgeois counting every sou and making money the measure of all virtue, the proprietors of small restaurants, brothel keepers and whores, big businessmen and financial magnates, journalists and country priests, sailors and nuns, small traders and doctors; love, sordid and pure, the fierce clash of interests with no quarter given, the decay of family ties, the degeneration of feelings and of bourgeois society as a whole, patriotism of common people and venality of the bourgeoisie, the idiocy of country life, the endless struggle for wealth, monstrous cruelty in human relations, poisoning people's love and respect for their neighbours—Maupassant's works conveyed the whole colourful, motley scene of life in bourgeois society with all its contradictions and conflicts. Like his realist predecessors, Maupassant saw that the struggle between material interests was the mainspring of human actions and was aware of the class nature of these interests. He sought and found the root causes of Jeanne's tragedy in *Une Vie* and George Duroy's success in the objective conditions of bourgeois society.

Maupassant could see that the bourgeois order was hostile to man, destroying his finest qualities and turning him into a "two-legged animal", driven by the basest of instincts. He was horrified by the *brutalisation of man under capitalism,* which was to be the main theme of his whole œuvre. In the broad treatment he gave this theme, he drew on the objective features of life and generalised them as the destructive consequences of bourgeois progress. This latter, while being marked by a fast rate of development of science and technology and generally the material side of life entailed, as all advanced thinkers noted, and as Maupassant was clearly aware, a sharp contradiction between the material achievements of the capitalist system and its baneful influence on man's spiritual world.

The great unbridgeable chasm that yawned between the haves and the have-nots, which applied to cultural as much as to material values, was deliberately maintained by the former. The appalling conditions in which the masses, including children, worked to produce material values, the long hours leaving them no time for recreation and self-improvement, and all the attendant ills such as neglect of children and juvenile crime, prostitution and chronic alcoholism, the perpetual exhausting rat race, the stupefying propaganda of the ruling classes designed to consolidate the existing order and enlisting the services of the Church, schools, the theatre, the press and cheap literature which encouraged the basest instincts and fanned out national and racial hostility, the glorification of war and jingoism, the bribing of the skilled workers with the extra wealth derived from colonial plunder, the duping of the proletariat with the opportunist theories of "class harmony" and "class co-operation" (and later, in our own day—state capitalism), the punishment meted out to free thinkers and the institution of terror to quell the masses, in short the objective conditions of life in the capitalist world in their entirety led to the brutalisation of man, which found its expression in the atrocious colonial wars, the First World War, the bestialities of fascism and the merciless suppression of the resistance of the masses by the bourgeois "democrats".

Maupassant felt that this cruelty pervading every sphere of social life, and every aspect, big or small, of human relationships, constituted a serious threat to the human personality. He gave numerous examples of how it tainted even the most personal feelings: rich parents send away their child, the offspring of adultery, to be brought up in the country, condemning it if not to death at any rate to wretchedness; a peasant family frighten to death an old woman who had become a burden to them; a father meets his abandoned daughter in a brothel; and so on and so forth. His short stories are full of observations on the cruelty of life, full of examples of the debasement of human feelings, honour and dignity, which are just everyday dramas and tragedies. Maupassant was above all concerned with studying the *moral* and *psychological* consequences of the distortion of social relationships, analysing their effect on man's spirit, and in this he was typical of the critical realists of the latter part of the nineteenth century and of the new social consciousness that was the product of the intensification of the process of alienation.

Maupassant considered self-interest to lie at the root of the brutalisation of man, and the proprietary instinct seemed to him to be all-powerful. He himself gradually gave in more and more to the pressures of his age, and was later to become convinced that social evil springs from the imperfection of human nature. Character gradually ceases to be socially based in his works, and begins to disintegrate as the elements of which it is composed become increasingly disharmonious. They become not so much social influences as inherent biological factors, generic, inborn characteristics. In cases where the social is shown to be less important than the biological and even sexual factors, as in *Yvette* or *Fort comme la mort*, the latter lose much of their universality. With his tremendous sensitivity to all that was new in life it was only natural that Maupassant should have been deeply disturbed by the process of alienation which was gathering momentum. His famous story *Solitude* was a *cri du cœur* of a man who longed for contact with the world and other people and yet was prevented from achieving it by a great wall of incomprehension and estrangement. The theme of the story was a very actual one, and was to be developed in his later works, and notably in his novel *Pierre et Jean*.

While being aware of the process of alienation of man from his fellow men, his environment and the material culture he helped to produce, Maupassant was unable to grasp its socio-historical origin, and transposed it to the plane of inscrutable mystery, though fully appreciating that the phenomena connected with it constituted an essential feature of the new phase of history. It was at this time that the contradictions of imperialism began to reveal themselves, and they were reflected in Maupassant's philosophical story *Qui sait?* which describes how the things man has produced, his mute slaves, revolt and run away from people to lead their own independent existence. Maupassant's fear of the future which can be glimpsed through the weird irony of this philosophical parable is even patent in his fantastic story *Le Horla*, conveying the sense of unfreedom of the alienated man and forebodings of a new kind of bondage prepared by the mysterious, inscrutable forces of history erupting into everyday life.

Maupassant's contradictory view as expressed in his writings prevented his powerful criticism from breaking through the confines of the bourgeois system. He failed to see that there were powerful undercurrents in the bourgeois system itself that were capable of liberating man. In the long run the limitations of his bourgeois-democratic ideology, which had lost the sense of historical change, was to produce a crisis, decadent influences making themselves more and more felt in the ideas and style of his later works to the detriment of his realist method.

In English realist prose of the latter part of the nine-teenth century there was a shift of emphasis to the per-sonal and psychological, and the typical novel of the period was the psychological novel or the chronicle of family life. George Eliot, heir to the Dickensian and Thackeray tradition, treated the theme of the moral de-generation and regeneration of the individual, the theme of the power of egoism in combination with analytic por-trayal of social environment and its contradictions. But she tended to somewhat oversimplify these contradictions and her analysis lacked the broad scope of her predeces-sors. She generally reduced such antagonisms to a con-trast between the beauty and wealth of human nature and the consuming power of money. Silas Marner the weaver is estranged from other people by his egoistic passion for hoarding: "The gold had asked that he should sit weaving longer and longer deafened and blinded more and more to all things except the monotony of his loom and the repetition of his web. ...."[1] The thirst for enrichment proves the undoing of Hetty Sorrel, the heroine of *Adam Bede*, and of the Tulliver family in *The Mill on the Floss*, and is responsible for the sad downfall of the millowner's daughter Maggie. In *Middlemarch* George Eliot shows the erosion of family ties, the collapse of that bastion of bour-geois life, the family, and condemns egoism as the chief evil undermining the foundations of human relationships. But egoism becomes less and less of a class characteristic in her novels and more and more a negative feature of human nature which can, consequently, be overcome by education or moral example. Thus, social problems grad-ually give way to ethical problems and we find in her works *the illusion that society can be transformed through moral enlightenment of its members*, a fallacy that has persisted in critical realism down to the present day. George Eliot came to this false conclusion in a compara-tively stable period with few outbreaks of class conflict, and was no doubt influenced by the ideas of "class har-mony" preached by the positivists whose views she shared.

---

[1] George Eliot, *Silas Marner. The Weaver of Raveloe*, New York, p. 190.

The idea that moral education could be an instrument of understanding and changing life for the better or could serve the opposite end of deforming a human personality was also treated by George Meredith in *The Ordeal of Richard Feverel* and Samuel Butler in *The Way of All Flesh*. They combined it with scathing criticism of the official morality of the ruling classes, the stifling oppressiveness of bourgeois family life which was hostile to the natural aspirations of ordinary healthy human beings. Both these writers were critical of bourgeois democracy, the negative aspects of which they could observe for themselves in the life of their age. But they were equally critical of socialist ideas, and remained democratic radicals, being concerned with studying not the laws and trends of history and social contradictions but the contradictions inherent in their characters' natures. In criticising human defects they sometimes overlooked the fact that these were conditioned by society, and in condemning egoism (Meredith's *The Egoist*, for example) concerned themselves with its influence on human nature rather than with the external factors that engender it. They perfected methods of psychological analysis at the expense of social analysis, and lost sight of the dialectical relationship between character and environment, treating man's spiritual world as a separate entity, coexisting and running parallel with life as a whole.

Indeed there was nothing surprising in this approach for it merely reflected the fact that the process of alienation was affecting all spheres of consciousness. What is far more remarkable is that so many great writers of that age managed to remain faithful to the traditions of realism, when the objective conditions obtaining were a hindrance to its development, and it was persecuted by bourgeois ideology, for, as Oscar Wilde put it, the bourgeoisie's hatred for realism was like the fury of Caliban seeing himself in a mirror.

Thus, at the close of the nineteenth century there was an increasing tendency in realism to separate the hero from his environment, and the character from those very factors which made him what he was, a tendency which destroyed epic unity and prevented a synthetic portrayal of life with its main historical contradictions. Closely allied to this tendency was the one to ascribe an undue importance to environment, which was an essential feature of naturalism, a method that is fundamentally hostile to realism and was extremely widespread in the latter half of the nineteenth century.

The main tenet of naturalism was *verisimilitude*, the aim being to give a life-like picture of reality. In their attempt to remain true to reality, be objective and show life as it really is, the naturalists overlooked the importance of analysis. They described reality and classified it roughly in the same way as did the positivists—for positivism was the philosophical basis of naturalism—but did not attempt to reveal its contradictions or its movement, for both naturalists and positivists were prone to the metaphysical and non-dialectical approach inherent in bourgeois thinking. Naturalism imitates realism, but differs both in the absence of social analysis and typification, and in the way it *equalises* essentially different phenomena. While the realist method enables the writer to single out and stress the most important features of character or environment, and thereby understand and present correctly their trends of development, naturalism precludes the presentation of life as a changing category. The naturalist method, which stems from Emile Zola, has long since run its course as an independent literary method, but several features of it are still to be found marring realist works today.

Emile Zola considered naturalism to be the only way of properly cognizing life and portraying it synthetically. It accorded with his positivist views. Like many of the writers and thinkers of his age, he was acutely aware of a vast gulf between the observer and the object of perception, between subject and object, a gulf that widened as alienation increased. The decadents tried to bridge the gap by intuition. Zola tried to bridge it with the aid of objective facts, facts taken from books, newspapers, court proceedings and statistics, or directly observed. Anatole France made the following highly unflattering appraisal of Zola's method: "The artist's faceted, fly-like eye produces the most extraordinary impression: thanks to this all objects are multiplied for him as if he were looking through cut topaz".[1] Certainly, descriptions occupy an inordinately large place in Zola's prose. Quite often, as in his description of the shop window in *Au Bonheur des Dames* or his description of the cheeses in *Le Ventre de Paris*, they merely hold up the action and encumber the narrative with superfluous details. But Zola considered such descriptions as a means of cognizance, and used them to try to present life as it really is, with its features, facts and events that explain the development of society, whose historian and sociologist he set to be, and indeed was. In his anatomy of bourgeois society he frequently confused biology and sociology, which was in accordance with the spirit of his times. Positivism, with its cult of facts, its descriptive, cataloguing method, drew on the practical achievements of the natural sciences, in which mechanistic ideas were very strong, particularly in physiology. Many scholars and scientists in the period in question who were spontaneous materialists and were influenced by the ideas of the positivists, considered that the microscope and the scalpel would eventually yield the secrets not only of living matter but also of human social behaviour. Zola shared the tendency to ascribe men's actions to heredity and temperament, and this oversimplified scheme lay at the root of his naturalist theories, and was the idea behind *Les Rougon-Macquart*, a series of novels in which he intended to write the biological case history of two families who "physiologically ... represent the slow succession of accidents pertaining to the nerves or the blood, which befall a race...."[2] Yet, instead, he wrote a social history of the Second Empire. He could not force his art into the straightjacket of naturalist dogma, and for all its *organic unity* his work was really a battlefield on which naturalist and realist methods and trends clashed and fought with varying success. This battle reflected the deep contradictions of his outlook, which in turn reflected the contradictions inherent in the social awareness of his age.

Zola's desire to encompass the whole social reality of

---

[1] Anatole France, *La vie littéraire*, Première série, Paris, p. 229.
[2] Emile Zola, *La Fortune des Rougon*, Paris, 1955, p. 1.

an historical period, to reveal and assess the content of its determining processes, widened his thematic horizon and brought into his works aspects of reality which had never before been treated in literature. With his keen artist's eye he saw how the bourgeoisie had come into its own, crushing the 1848 Revolution, how it had entrenched itself and harnessed the state and democratic institutions to its own needs *(La Fortune des Rougon, La Curée, La conquête de Plassans, Son Excellence Eugène Rougon).* In the well-established bourgeois world money and profit became synonymous with the concepts of public order, prosperity and social calm, the measure of personal success, the real basis of virtue and the hidden mainspring of the official morality. He saw how the bourgeoisie formed an armed alliance against the people, how a *single class awareness* was common both to the financial oligarchy who stood at the helm of the ship of state and the bourgeois shopkeepers. The characters in *La Curée*, organisers and practitioners of shady financial deals, bureaucrats and big financiers had the same conservative ideology as the characters of *Le Ventre de Paris*, thrifty vociferous tradesfolk, with a fierce hatred for anybody that sought to shake the foundations of the established order that assured them a comfortable livelihood. Zola observed the emergence of the new kind of financier and finance capital beginning to coalesce with the apparatus of state, becoming linked to it by a multitude of invisible, but nonetheless perfectly material, interests. This was a new feature of the age, as was the character of Aristide Saccard who embodied it. Saccard and his more successful younger "brother" Cowperwood, the hero of Dreiser's trilogy, as well as the hero of Jack London's *Burning Daylight* embodied the tremendous initiative and organising drive of finance capital. Saccard's business affairs, always involving risk and relying on masses of petty-bourgeois investors, were all the fruit of his own initiative. Zola shows capitalism as it was before it assumed the faceless, abstract form of the trust period, as described by Norris or Vershofen. Nevertheless, side by side with Saccard, his bank exists as an independent force standing above the mass of people and influencing their lives like a *deus ex machina,* for the successes or failures of his Universal Bank is what determines the financial position of the investors and finally leads them to ruin. Zola also noted how the industrial power of capitalist society grew hand in hand with the growth of finance capital: how mines and factories invaded the peaceful countryside and the railways spread their web everywhere. So impressed was Zola by the scale and rate of capitalist progress that his critical ardour was weakened and he harboured the vain hope that in the long run the healthy forces of progress, which he himself was unable to define, would lead mankind onto the true path of prosperity and well-being. Nevertheless, he was not blind to the growing moral corruption of the bourgeoisie *(Pot-Bouille* and *Nana)* and the irreversible slide of the Second Empire towards collapse and ruin, which he described in *La Débâcle.*

Zola also realised that the development of bourgeois society would be accompanied by a strengthening of ties between people, and that social forces would tend not only to divide but also *unite* according to common class or property interests, common work or common sufferings. Zola tends to dissolve the individual in his environment, whose slightest tremor or disturbance sets up a wave which engulfs him. Hence his *collective portraits,* depicting the feelings and reactions of crowds, such as the procession of enthusiastic insurgents in *La Fortune des Rougon,* the crowd of enraged workers in *Germinal,* the terrified, demoralised soldiers in *La Débâcle,* and the avid crowd at the stock exchange in *L'Argent.*

Although he observed a great deal in the social life of his age, he often limited himself to pure *description* of what he observed rather than analysing it and revealing its contradictions and the contradictory relationship between man and his environment. While recognising the mutability of history and the fact of historical development, he at the same time asserted the stability of human nature, seeing man as biologically static, prevented by *heredity* from escaping the power of *social environment* and exerting an *influence on it,* to change it. Zola's insistence on the power of environment and heredity often approaches fatalism: thus the hereditary alcoholics Gervaise

Coupeau and her daughter Nana advance towards inevitable ruin; Gervaise, brought up among down-and-out illiterate workers in *L'Assommoir*, is also doomed from the outset, and there is the same fatal inevitability about Jacques Lantier's mad urge to kill in *La Bête Humaine*, and in the various abnormalities found in all the members of the Rougon-Macquart family. A typical feature of Zola's naturalism was his tendency to illustrate a particular social process by the actions and fortunes of his characters, rather than treat them as an organic part of the process, presenting man and environment as the indivisible whole they are. He thus often sacrificed historical perspective, substituting biological causality for social causality, thereby obscuring the real causal links in psychological and social phenomena. Zola's man is by no means always *historical man*: he was frequently the *mechanical product of environment*, branded with its evils and imperfections. Thus the peasants in *La Terre* are grossly simplified to the point of caricature, as are the workers ruined by drink and poisoned by the futility of their lives in *L'Assommoir*. The epic form of classical realism has disintegrated in Zola, and symbolism has begun to penetrate his works, as we also find in the naturalist works of Ibsen *(Ghosts, Rosmersholm* and *The Master Builder)*, and Hauptmann, and countless lesser writers, such as Huysmans, Holz and Verga. Naturalism gradually leads Zola to *animalise man*, placing him at the mercy of irrational instincts and animal passions.

Yet his keen powers of perception and his democratic outlook enabled Zola to see the social conflicts of his age, and particularly the main contradiction, that between capital and labour. He was not fully aware of all its implications, but like the majority of his contemporaries, he did sense that, despite its apparent stability, capitalist society contained the seeds of its own destruction, that a powerful force was developing which threatened the existence of the whole system based on the exploitation of man by man.

In *Germinal*, as he had previously done in *L'Assommoir*, Zola presented a mercilessly accurate picture of the appalling conditions in which the workers lived reduced almost to the status of animals and he recognised the *right* of the exploited to revolt, and showed in his novel how the "red spectre of revolution" loomed large, and was leading the working masses in its wake. But Zola, through the limitations of his outlook, was unable to perceive the *conscious* element in their movement. Though unable to understand the historical significance of the Paris Commune, he sincerely sympathised with the oppressed masses. The inhumanity and the injustice of the bourgeois order was all too clear to him, and he realised that the masses would not agree to be led by the halter forever. He had grave doubts about the continued existence of capitalist civilisation. In his later works, written in the opening years of the present century, *Les Quatre Evangiles*, he turns to a kind of *latter day utopianism* and in *L'Œuvre* (1901), draws a picture of the class harmony which should replace the class conflicts of bourgeois society.

It is hardly surprising that Zola's idea of socialism to which he came towards the end of his life should have been diluted with reformism, for the general trend in European socialism in the latter part of the nineteenth century had been a development *in breadth* with a corresponding loss in revolutionary intensity: the labour movement was spending most of its energy in the economic and trade union struggle. As a result of the spread of reformism in the socialist parties, they came to represent very little danger for the capitalist system, the Fabians in England, the French socialists and the German social-democrats having all retreated in their practical programmes from the militant principles of Marxism. The struggle was waged within the parliamentary system, using the legal opportunities offered by bourgeois democracy, and this led by the beginning of the present century to a revival of the illusion of bourgeois democracy both in the labour movement and among progressive thinkers, Zola among them.

However, Zola was too familiar with the true face of capitalism, had penetrated too deeply into the bourgeois soul to ever reconcile himself, even for a moment, with bourgeois reality. He began to look upon the masses as a force capable of leading mankind to happiness, but, as with many of his great contemporaries in Western Europe, this idea remained in the realm of pure speculation and did not find artistic expression in his works. For Zola the masses, including the proletariat, were an object of deep sympathy and pity, but not a conscious historical force: thus in *Germinal,* the proletariat revolts without understanding the meaning or purpose of its revolt. We find a similar picture in Björnson's play *Beyond Our Powers* and in Hauptmann's *The Weavers.* In those rare works of West European literature in which the position and historical role of the proletariat was examined at all, the presentation suffered from the same defects as were apparent in Margaret Harkness's *City Girl,* where, according to Engels: "...The working class figures as a passive mass, unable to help itself and not even showing (making) any attempt at striving to help itself. All attempts to drag it out of its torpid misery come from without, from above."[1] Thus, on the threshold of the twentieth century West European critical realism *had yet to undertake* the task of finding ways to the people and ideas renewing social life.

The feelings and hopes of the masses really came to occupy an important position in the literature of Russian critical realism, which developed against a background of preparation of a major revolution that was to forever transform the modern world.

The ethical power of Russian literature, its humanity and deep sympathy for the masses, its boldness in treating vital issues made it a carrier of the *awareness of the masses* and, once socialist transformation was underway in Russia, also of the *self-awareness of the masses.*

A typical feature of critical realism in the latter half of the nineteenth century was the great attention it devoted to man's inner world. Dostoyevsky submitted human psychology to mercilessly penetrating analysis in his novels, lit by the dim glow of the night lights of a big city, permeated with the smoky, dank atmosphere of St. Petersburg "lodgings" where powerful passions seethed, where pure hearts were singed by life's falsity and cruelty, where

---

[1] K. Marx, F. Engels, *Selected Correspondence,* Moscow, 1955, p. 479.

human baseness and wretchedness bred disbelief in the possibility of universal happiness and it was even blasphemously rejected, and where passionate faith was to be found side by side with militant unbelief. He presented the violent irruption into Russian life of the new bourgeois outlook, and showed the tragic contradictions of social progress. Dostoyevsky only examined the sick, twilight aspects of the human consciousness at various stages of affection because the normal state of the human mind interested him little and seemed to him to be *undramatic.* But he also presented the struggle between various *social psychologies,* thereby characterising both the environment and the central conflicts of social life. Dostoyevsky does not usually separate his characters from their environment: they are interdependent, and his characters have marked social features, although these are only presented through a character's spiritual world, in the conflicts between his own intellectual demands and interests and those of other characters, and the author is sparing of details of the environment. Thus the high degree of *intellectualism* of Dostoyevsky's novels determines their essentially play-like structure: the action develops from conflicting points of view, largely expressed in dialogues, and the psychological state of the characters determines the plot and denouement. Dostoyevsky investigated various forms of mental alienation and the ideas it produced, including Raskolnikov's idea of the "superman", Kirillov's idea of the "God-Man", and young Arkady Dolgorukov's "Rothschild dream". Dostoyevsky quite rightly links such ideas with bourgeois individualism. But in presenting the extreme forms of individualism, anatomising the human mind and spirit and penetrating the most hidden recesses of the human consciousness, Dostoyevsky, like other critical realists of the latter half of the nineteenth century, often imparted features of extratemporal *independence* to the spiritual life of his heroes. Svidrigailov, and especially the "last scion of the nobility", Nikolai Stavrogin, who although ostensibly diabolical, showed signs of an eerily grotesque parody of the extreme fatalism characteristic of Lermontov's gloomy hero Pechorin, have elements of strong inherent perversity and submission to instinct which Dostoyevsky ascribed to human nature. This view of human nature as the playground of dark, mysterious, irrational forces and the focus of inherent ungovernable instincts, for the most part base and destructive, that we find in Dostoyevsky's works was connected with his reactionary *Weltanschauung* and served him as an extra argument in his struggle against revolutionary ideas.

But in constructing his conservative positive programme for the organisation of society, out of religious dogmas, as the foundation of social morality and the back-to-the-soil idea, as the foundation of social relations, and advancing this programme as an alternative to capitalist progress and the views of the revolutionary democrats, Dostoyevsky based himself on an idealised image of the peasant and peasant life. His *muzhik* Marei, with his tremendous tenderness and humanity, lavished on the mass of the Russian people wallowing in the abomination of a life of violence and brutality, and calling them to peace, appealing to them to love one another, was ever invisibly in the background of all the complex philosophical edifices in Dostoyevsky's novels and the wild abstractions of his thought. The idea of *kinship with the masses*, though deformed by reactionary political views, underlay all his writings, imparting tremendous critical power and sympathy with the insulted and the injured. Even in his misinterpretation of it, this idea was able to give his works vitality: the very fact that he looked to the masses as a force capable of *resolving* all the contradictions of the human mind and history was in keeping with the spirit of the age. The idea that the masses are the motive force of history was making relentlessly headway in art and literature at that time.

This idea was the pivot of Victor Hugo's romantic epic *Les Misérables*, where the masses were presented not simply as an enslaved giant bearing on his shoulders the whole social edifice but as a giant in the process of freeing itself. The people was counterposing its own will to the will of the ruling classes and the whole apparatus of coercion created by the latter to defend their selfish interests—the State, the Army, the Police, the Law and the Church. Hugo presented the masses as suffering from want and earning their bread by the sweat of their brow, and he also showed them on the barricades, taking up arms to pave their way to the future. Hugo's epic was an historically accurate reflection of the *objective* side of the social process—the growing role of the masses in the life of society.

In accordance with the spirit of the romanticist method, Hugo universalised the characters of his heroes. Each one of them was an embodiment of a particular principle which absorbed the individual and the particular and gave the characters an abstract universality. Thus, Jean Valjean became the personification of goodness and virtue, Javert personified fantastic devotion to duty, and Thénardier—all that is base and vile. The conflicts are based on the romanticist principle of antinomy—the struggle between irreconcilable principles such as good and evil, brutality and mercy, and so on. Thus, objective truth was expressed in a somewhat abstract form, giving *Les Misérables* the declarative quality while indicating that the author's views were genuinely democratic.

In Charles de Coster's *Thyl Ulenspiegel* the masses are regarded and presented as the essential creative force in society, the motor of history. Here too the characters have a *symbolic* meaning, and embody various aspects of the soul of the masses. The epic quality of these two masterpieces of West European literature stems from the recognition of the true role and significance of the masses. Yet both belong essentially to the kind of epic where the *general idea* underlying the work does not find a unique, particular and individual expression in the characters. Dostoyevsky's characters, on the other hand, are highly particularised, each being endowed with highly distinctive characteristics. These are most carefully explored and the unique features revealed, not infrequently overshadowing the impersonal course of events and the objective development of life, those real conflicts which form the basis of the psychological conflicts that rack the heroes' souls. The essence of the epic quality of Dostoyevsky's works lies in the *objective logical necessity of what takes place* that is hidden behind the explosions of individual passions and feelings, and the complex emotional experiences of the heroes. But the general and the particular are not balanced: the individual, the apparently exceptional (for, despite its appearance of being exceptional and original, Raskolnikov's crime, or the murder of old Karamazov, or the tragedy of Nastasya Filippovna are in fact phenomena typical of class society) seems to drown out the historical content of his works. Dostoyevsky's "psychological realism" had its limitations: it was better suited to investigating and expressing in aesthetic form the special features of social psychology than to analysing and depicting the real everyday life of the people and the real social conflicts.

The life of the people was fully presented by Lev Tolstoi, in whose works the epic quality of realism rested on a balance between the individual psychological content of the hero and the historical sphere of his actions, presented in full concrete detail. The epic quality of Tolstoi's realism derived from his kinship with the masses, for, as Lenin put it, he "succeeded in conveying with remarkable force the moods of the large masses that are oppressed by the present system, in depicting their condition and expressing their spontaneous feelings of protest and anger".[1] Tolstoi's works, reflecting the mentality of the patriarchal peasantry in the age of bourgeois-democratic revolution, which developed in a relatively short time into *socialist revolution, directly express* the views and sentiments of the people, which was something totally new in nineteenth century literature. This identification with the people helped strengthen the epic quality of realism, this major quality, which was gradually being lost in West European realist literature of the latter half of the century.

Thomas Mann, remarking on the fact that it was the epic element that predominated in Tolstoi's prose, wrote: "It is the Homeric element, that I mean, continuously flowing narrative, half art half nature, enveloped in a naive grandeur, corporeality, objectivity, deathless health, deathless realism."[2]

---

[1] V. I. Lenin, *Collected Works*, Vol. 16, pp. 323-24.
[2] Leo Tolstoy, *Anna Karenina*, transl. by Constance Garnett with Introductory Essay by Thomas Mann, Vol. 1, New York, 1939, p. X.

For Tolstoi, the objective course of life, its continuous, uninterrupted flux, is also a major sphere of depiction. Historical conflicts, shaking and changing the destinies of peoples, gigantic collisions between vast numbers of people, personal dramas, the falseness of the official morality of the ruling classes, Church, Army and State, all came under his keen, searching gaze, and his ears were wide open to the sounds of life. Great and small things—the enchantment of a moonlit night and the sense of pleasure of doing a job well, minor details of peasant life, the colours and smells of the countryside in summer, the inhuman din of battle and the bubbling conversation in a society salon, the cracking of the ice in spring, the voices of convicts trudging eastwards—all were woven by Tolstoi into a vast and remarkably complete picture of the world. The powerful creative force of life moulded his language, his phrases, as ponderous and massive outwardly as they were essentially harmonious, and imparted extraordinary visual power to his three dimensional and impeccably authentic images. But as well as giving a remarkably vivid depiction of the physical aspects of reality, Tolstoi penetrated the innermost recesses of man's spiritual life and presented it no less vividly. Indeed it is this extraordinarily comprehensive analysis of the human soul revealing all its wealth and subtle shades, its real contradictions and almost imperceptible and inexplicable movements combined with complete portrayal of the objective processes of life that constitutes the distinctive *epic quality* of his works, deriving from his essential *kinship with the people.* Describing in true epic style the general bustle of human life, Tolstoi never lost sight of the individual in the crowd: all his characters have an intrinsic value and each is an individual world through which, however, there flows the endless stream of life, uniting the atoms of history, individuals, in a whole, called society. The masses of people who by their labour create the material and spiritual values of life, who fight and lay down their lives in battle to do the will of rulers, who bend over furnace or plough, sow and reap, mine coal and ores, build factories and palaces, the working millions, weary and oppressed, deceived and robbed, exhausted by inhuman labours, are all individuals for Tolstoi. The interests of Ivan, Pyotr and Marya, their separate wills, desires, feelings, hopes and plans, make up the desires, will, hopes and plans of the historical force called the people In order to understand the masses it is necessary to understand the spiritual and moral essence of *each individual representative* of the people. Thus, for Tolstoi study, analysis and portrayal of the life of society of necessity involves study of the spiritual life of the individual, for the upper classes, the rich, culture and art, power and coercion, the concepts of good and evil, religion and the State—everything that constitutes the content of the life of a given age, depends in the final analysis on the will of the people, and hence on the will of each particular member of the people.

Tolstoi took a great step forward in portrayal of the people, a step without which it is quite impossible to conceive the development of a new type of realism, namely, socialist realism. For Tolstoi the man of the people—above all the peasant—was not an object of detached observation and sympathy as he was for Turgenev or Leskov; nor was he the soulless property owner ruled by an all-consuming passion for making money and base, almost animal instincts, as he was depicted by the West European realists and naturalists, although Tolstoi did depict the "reign of darkness" in the consciousness of the masses with implacable truth. Nor did he present the man of the people as a paragon of virtue as did the Russian and French populists—although he certainly was wont to idealise the *muzhik* at times. Tolstoi's portrayal of representatives of the people—and in this respect only one writer was close to him, and that was Gleb Uspensky, one of the wisest of Russian writers—was based on a correct understanding of the real contradictions of life that made them what they were. Tolstoi's characters from the people, both such important ones as Tikhon Shcherbaty, Yeroshka or the soldier Avdeyev and minor, incidental characters—vagrants and beggars, impoverished peasants who have been reduced to extreme despair and embitterment, and the odd one who has been more fortunate—are accorded a place of equal importance with his characters from the educated and privileged classes, and are in many cases superior to the latter as regards moral integrity.

The ground ploughed so deeply by Tolstoi's realism has yielded an extraordinarily rich harvest. Without the fundamentally new approach to the portrayal of the people introduced to world literature by Tolstoi, who was capable of surveying history and bourgeois civilisation at once through the eyes of a consummate artist standing at the summit of European culture and through the eyes of the mass of the people, there could never have been *Gorky, who represented the character from the masses in the process of acquiring revolutionary self-awareness.* The Tolstoian tradition flowed organically into the literature of socialist realism and many characters in Soviet literature would have been impossible had not the ground been prepared by Tolstoi.

Tolstoi himself regarded his works as belonging to a new period in the development of realism, when "... the interest of details of feelings replaces the interest of events themselves".[1] This definition did not mean that Tolstoi denied the importance of events in literature, as is testified by his own works, which are packed with events. Thus, in *War and Peace* the drama derives from historical events of vast magnitude affecting the private lives of the heroes. *Hadji Murat* is rich in events; action in *The Power of Darkness* is dynamic, not to mention *Anna Karenina* and *Resurrection.* However, nowhere in Tolstoi's works—and this applies equally to his major works and his short stories—do events themselves form the basis of the plot and carry the action forward, as they do in the works of Balzac and Dickens, for example: they are always presented in terms of their influence on the inner world of the individual. The fortunes of Vautrin and Lucien de Rubempré or the secrets surrounding Arthur Clennam in *Little Dorrit,* or the adventures of Thackeray's Barry Lyndon and Philip are interesting and important in themselves. With Tolstoi events serve purely to impart authenticity to the narrative and reveal the spiritual content of the charac-

---

[1] L. Tolstoi, *Collected Works*, Goslitizdat, Moscow, Vol. 46, p. 188.

ters. In Tolstoi's writings psychological analysis does not merely serve to supplement and deepen social analysis, but becomes an independent means of investigation. The portrait of Tsar Nicholas in *Hadji Murat* which is so striking for its historical accuracy and the scathing criticism implied is achieved using the method of psychological analysis. Tolstoi's superb study of the tsar's character, revealing the motives of his behaviour and actions, showing his changing moods, his constant posing and habitual self-deception, at the same time represents a study of the social essence of despotism. The detailed account of the thoughts and feelings of the dying Ivan Ilyich, his frank self-analysis and self-confession, is at the same time a scathing criticism of the society and milieu in which the hero lived his dishonest, fruitless and unjust life, so typical of a dishonest, unjust society. By making psychological analysis serve as a major means of showing social contradictions, Tolstoi greatly enriched world literature, revealing new aesthetic and analytic possibilities of the realist method. Tolstoi's psychological analysis was more complex and flexible than that of Dostoyevsky, for example, especially because it always preserved an instinctive historicist approach. Besides, if Dostoyevsky portrayed intense psychological experiences of his heroes in a state bordering on the demented, Tolstoi presented various *natural* psychological states. While Dostoyevsky was wont to treat his characters' thoughts and feelings as eternal intrinsic categories, Tolstoi always presented the nature and emotions of his characters as socially conditioned, that is, as clearly reflecting their genetic link both with their environment and their time. Thus, spiritual movements of Tolstoi's heroes were not merely the interplay and conflict of personal feelings and desires, a kaleidoscope of emotions in the closed personal world of the individual, but could and did reflect the movements and contradictions of social life. Tolstoi, who sensed the impending collapse of bourgeois civilisation and felt the existing relations between people to be unjust and unnatural, did not view society as something static and immutable. Unlike the naturalists, he perceived the ceaseless *flux of history* in all spheres of social life, the "inexorable course of the whole", which Goethe had considered to be the realist's main task to portray. True, the reactionary and conservative elements in Tolstoi's outlook sometimes moved him to regard *causality of phenomena* as conditioned by an inscrutable force of fatal necessity extraneous to man. Tolstoi acquired this view of history also under the influence of the process of alienation, of which this illusion is a typical result, but it was never to prove strong enough to prevent him from portraying the phenomena of life in constant collision and development. For this reason, in the emotions of his characters too Tolstoi always strove to present the *incessant, uninterrupted working of thoughts and feelings characteristic of human consciousness.*

Attempts had been made in realist literature before Tolstoi to find means of penetrating the innermost recesses of the human soul. Lawrence Sterne and Jean-Jacques Rousseau made psychology an important element of narrative, but their method of presenting the inner world of their characters was purely *descriptive*. Thus, although Rousseau wrote his "Confessions" in the first person, he did so in a highly detached manner, so that one is more struck by the frankness of the account than by any feeling of immersion in the depths of the human Self. Literature at that time was not equipped to handle the process of the appearance, development and struggle of different emotions and thoughts actually within the human soul. A big step forward was taken by Stendhal, whose heroes act, think and try to explain their thoughts and actions. We hear the inner voice of Julien Sorel speaking, but this is still no more than the hero *commenting* on events. It was Tolstoi who first made the inner monologue serve as a means of presenting *thought processes actually going on*, and the complex workings of the human feelings, thereby giving literature an important new expressive device, opening up vast new possibilities of expression. This was a major break-through: without such scenes as the death of Captain Praskukhin in *Tales of Sebastopol*, Petya Rostov's "musical" dream in *War and Peace*, and Anna Karenina's inner monologue before she commits suicide— scenes of tremendous authentic power—the picture of life would have been very much poorer and its events would not have been perceived with the necessary fulness.

It was no accident that Tolstoi should have paid such attention to psychological analysis: it was dictated by the objective phenomena of life, for as social life of man becomes more complicated so does his spiritual life. Numerous new facts enter the sphere of his attention and he is only able to assimilate them all by developing his ability to associate different phenomena, with the result that associative throught becomes a most typical feature of the modern mind. Tolstoi perceived this tendency and reflected it in his works, without however raising it to the quality of an absolute or making it the universal principle of his presentation of psychological processes, as was later to be done by "the stream of consciousness" school. Joyce and Proust took the method of presenting the inner life of characters first introduced to literature by Tolstoi and made it universal presenting inner monologues (outwardly disorganised as in *Ulysses* or ordered and coherent as in *A la Recherche du temps perdu*) of alienated individuals as the only reality of life. As for Tolstoi he used inner monologues in order to increase the scope of his presentation of reality. Developing and improving psychological analysis as a literary method, he employed the device of *decomposing* the impression made by a particular character into separate impressions they produced in different characters. He stressed the need to "describe how this or that affects the characters".[1] In Tolstoi's works the main hero is presented through a plurality of views the other characters obtain of him. Then, to typify the character, he used the device of *adding together* all the different impressions of him that the other characters have already revealed in their judgements and inner assessments. Thus, in an apparently subjective appraisal of a character through the reactions to him of the other characters, we are in fact presented with an *objective* appraisal, since it is many-sided and thus remarkably complete. Tolstoi always typified his characters, stressing those psychologi-

---

[1] L. Tolstoi, *On Literature and Art*, Moscow, 1958, Vol. I, p. 319 (in Russ.).

cal and social features and qualities in them that were typical of the existing social relations. He created a vast portrait gallery of typical characters—poor peasants and rich peasants, day-labourers and *kulaks*, beggars, vagrants beau-monde pleasure seekers, country and town gentry, common soldiers and officers, servants, pettyfoggying court officials, and official dignitaries, liberals and conservatives, convicts and lawyers, society belles and prostitutes, workers and merchants, aristocrats and statesmen. The whole *seething stream* of Russian life, where the established customs, views and relations were breaking down, in the course of its *inexorable advance towards revolution*, was generalised and typified by Tolstoi. His tremendous psychological insight, combined with a correct understanding of the motives of human behaviour and an ability to see the organic link between men's inner world and their social environment enabled Tolstoi to perceive and present the processes going on in the human soul as the true, accurate reflection of the actual processes of life. Tolstoi did not draw up an inventory in his works of various facts and instances of social injustice and the terrible position of the working people, as the naturalists were wont to do. The distressing plight of the lower classes served as the natural background, the *historical undercurrent* of his works. Portraying the *continuous* struggle between justice and injustice, that is the content of life, Tolstoi studied the conflict between these two principles both in society and in the human soul. His criterion of what was good and just was what was necessary and useful for the masses, all that fitted into the outlook of the masses; and he viewed as unjust all that ran counter to the needs and outlook on life of the people. This is why he expressed his criticism of bourgeois society in ethical terms. He supported the ethics and morality of the havenots against the ethics and morality of the privileged classes, viewing the whole system of social relations, the personal and societal life of people in private ownership society through the sober and naive gaze of the working man. Tolstoi discovered that all the principles underlying bourgeois civilisation were false, unnatural and inhuman. Revealing their real essence, tearing off all manner of masks, Tolstoi ruthlessly exposed and criticised egoism and the pursuit of personal interests, and condemned the estrangement of people.

Unlike his West European contemporaries, Tolstoi did not make the basic conflict of his works property contradictions, the tussle between bourgeois outcasts for their share of the loot, or the destructive influence of instincts and heredity on people. The typical Tolstoian conflict is a moral conflict, and the whole mass of facts, events and testimonies that generally crowd his works and give them a convincing authenticity serves to highlight and stress the moral roots of the conflict. This does not mean that real-life material is of secondary importance in the narrative: realistic analysis enables Tolstoi to reveal the injustice and inhumanity of the existing social order, with its false, hypocritical official morality, its legalised injustice, vast apparatus of coercion—prisons, courts, Army, police, etc.—sanctified by the Church, with its division into rich and poor, oppressors and oppressed, to show it as alien to man and to normal, natural human relations. The existing social order corrupts human nature, makes man a slave of egoism and instills in him hatred rather than love for his fellows. We find a moral conflict in *The Power of Darkness, Anna Karenina, Resurrection, The Kreutzer Sonata* and *Father Sergius*, not to mention Tolstoi's didactic works. From his analysis of the contradictions of the personal and social morality that reigned in society based on private ownership and exploitation, Tolstoi came to the conclusion that this morality was *obsolete*, both because it was incompatible with the *natural* healthy movements of the human heart and because its social foundations and the forms in which human relations had been moulded by historical progress were outmoded. Indeed, presentation of the obsolescence and unnaturalness of existing social relations became the dominant theme in Tolstoi's later works, testifying to his *historicism*.

The bells still rang out from the countless churches throughout Russia, where prayers were recited for the health of the imperial family; and the foundations of the Empire, safeguarded with the whip and the bayonet seemed firm and unshakeable; the gendarmes were still all-powerful, and the man in the street supposed his whole life to pass under their watchful eye; joint-stock companies were still springing up overnight like mushrooms, and liberal professors and lawyers held forth on the benefits of parliamentary, constitutional government. Katkov's publications were still pouring forth unction and poison, Suvorin was laying the foundations of a Russian gutter press; famine was still stalking across whole regions, and the *muzhiks* were being taught to use guns so that they could be driven to the slaughter in Manchuria and later Galicia. The concessionaires still felt secure, confidently delving into the rich Donets coalfield and lining their pockets on Baku oil, and foreign creditors were still quite willing to support the dwindling finances of the Empire. The factory owners' dividends continued to grow at a time when millions of people of different nationalities were still deprived of the most elementary human rights, and the workers and peasants lived in indescribable poverty. But already the Empire was rocked by the terrorist acts of the "People's Will" revolutionaries and the world held its breath as the flame of Revolution sprang up in the East. Massive workers' strikes throughout the country already heralded the upheavals to come; the anger of the masses was already bursting to the surface—the countryside was seething with unrest and the time was not far off when the peasants would start setting fire to the landowners' country seats. In the depths of the workers' movement, Lenin was already at work forging a new type of Party, the instrument with which the Bolsheviks were to make a revolution in Russia and show mankind the path to the future. Indeed, the existing social order in Russia had outlived its day and its change by revolution was inevitable.

Tolstoi was a merciless critic of capitalism with its unjust, unnatural relations. Investigating such various social institutions as the family, the established Church, the courts, the police state, he showed the need for *changes at grass-roots level*, since all these institutions served to enslave and oppress people. He demanded the abolition of *private ownership of the land* and his ideal was to have the class state replaced by communes of free and equal small peasants. Tolstoi's conclusion that social relations resting on private ownership should be abolished—the objective conclusion his criticism implied—coincided with the socialist ideas, and Tolstoi basically posed in his writings those very questions of social development that were tackled by socialism. The vast mass of material from life that Tolstoi incorporated in his works, all the observations contained in them, argued cogently in favour of replacing the inhuman social relations that then existed with new ones based on humanitarian principles. Tolstoi's works reflected the spontaneously mounting tide of revolution, and, presaging the historic changes that were about to come, he submitted bourgeois civilisation to comprehensive criticism. Hence Tolstoi's urge to capture and fix in words the dominant features of life, which was reflected not only in the numerous actual events in which his works abounded but in the very fabric of the narrative. His long periods, and highly complex sentences with numerous dependent clauses, abounding in epithets and definitions, testified to a tendency to try and embrace life synthetically, define his characters from numerous angles and present a full picture of historical links. Yet his presentation of history did not embrace *all* the major *tendencies of social development*. This could only be achieved by a revolutionary consciousness, perceiving and investigating the whole of reality, all its forms, shades and the methods of struggle of *all* social classes and thereby *revealing the general tendency of social development*. With Tolstoi, on the other hand, as Lenin put it: "The exposure of capitalism and of the calamities it inflicts on the masses was combined with a wholly apathetic attitude to the world-wide struggle for emancipation waged by the international socialist proletariat."[1]

The sentiments of primitive peasant democracy imparted to Tolstoi's views and works not only tremendous critical power in exposing an unjust social order but also a certain passiveness. His heroes from the people display the submissiveness that had been instilled in the masses over centuries of exploitation and bondage. Tolstoi's

---

[1] V. I. Lenin, *Collected Works,* Vol. 16, p. 325.

humanitarian ideal, his great impassioned *plea for love* as the natural basis for human relations appeared in his works in contemplative forms, as preaching of non-resistance to evil. The prejudices of peasant democracy infused his outlook with a conservative element, pushing him towards Tertullian's condemnation of reason, progress, and the "superstition of science", and an ascetic condemnation of the needs of the flesh. Despite his closeness to the masses, a typical illusion bred by the process of alienation had crept into Tolstoi's outlook: he regarded moral self-perfection by the individual independent of the group as an effective means of resolving social contradictions and changing the unnatural relations that existed between people. This utopian view was to become one of the most typical illusions of democratic thought in the twentieth century. We meet it in Romain Rolland's *Jean-Christophe,* in the plays of G. B. Shaw, and in the works of almost all the outstanding critical realists of our century.

Nevertheless, the new features in Tolstoi's realism outweighed the conservative side of his outlook. His works ushered in a new stage in the development of critical realism. While before Tolstoi critical realism had been concerned with the relationship between the individual and society, the structure of society, the destiny of the individual in conflict with society, for Tolstoian realism, as for all twentieth century realism, *the destiny of society became the object of investigation.* The burning issue Tolstoi raised—how is a man to live in a society where falsehood, injustice, cruelty and violence reign, and where the masses are enslaved and deprived of the most elementary human rights—was to become the major ethical problem in the twentieth century literature. The idea that the existing social order must be changed, that is fundamental to Tolstoi's works, began to make its appearance in West European literature too. By the beginning of the twentieth century realism, having engaged in a fierce struggle with naturalism and various decadent trends at the end of the last century, had begun to gather strength, extending its field of vision to embrace new facts and contradictions of life that had been unknown in the last century.

The new century brought with it not sense of the prosperity, calm and stability of an established order, but a feeling of uncertainty and lack of faith in the firmness of the very foundations of capitalist society. The historical content of the twentieth century was and is determined by the greatest revolution in history—the complex, painful, vast process of transition from capitalism to socialism.

The First World War revealed to their full extent the glaring contradictions of capitalism at the imperialist stage of its development. The October Revolution in Russia ushered in a new era in the history of mankind and greatly accelerated the general crisis of capitalism, for which the period of decline now set in. The relatively calm, untroubled and steady development of bourgeois society was not only speeded up but rushed headlong towards disaster. All forms of ideology and consciousness became sharply aware of the impending disaster the historical process spelled for bourgeois society. In the face of the mounting class conflicts bourgeois ideology mobilised all its reserves, digging out of the philosophical archives Gobineau's racist theory of the natural superiority of the white race and its unlimited right to use violence to assert itself over other races. Nietzsche's inhuman philosophy came into its own and its ideas were made to serve as a justification for aggressive war and holding the masses in bondage, those essential features of the capitalist system. If Oswald Spengler had predicted the decline of Europe—bourgeois-democratic Europe, that is, or, as he put it, the "Europe of Manchester"—and called upon the ruling classes to display "firmness", paving the way for the dictatorship of imperialist reaction, his precursor Georges Sorel in his book *Reflection sur la violence* regarded contemporary history of the twentieth century and its future as an arena of wars and cataclysms, maintaining that the idea of war was an inalienable feature of the human consciousness. He ridiculed bourgeois democracy for its failure to hold the masses in check and proposed violence in the place of all legal methods of coercion as the only means whereby the bourgeoisie could hope to maintain their class domination. He proposed that the masses should be kept at a low level of spiritual development, that base instincts should be cultivated in them, and that they should be held in submission by unconcealed crude demagogy. Bourgeois literature created the image of a powerful and highly primitive hero, the lord and master relentlessly striding towards his goal knee-deep in blood and trampling the "coloured" peoples underfoot. The colonial, military and social novels of Claude Farrère and Kipling, d'Annunzio and Vershofen extolled the "strong" individual.

The sense of impending doom was equally strong among the critical realists. All the writings of H. G. Wells, for example, were pervaded with a sense of universal cataclysms about to destroy contemporary civilisation. The clashes between Man and the spider-like denizens of other worlds who nearly succeeded in enslaving mankind and destroying the Earth's culture; the fierce enmity between the degenerate classes of the future—the Eloi and the Morlocks; scientific discovery becoming a source of evil and misery; merciless battles between the haves and the have-nots, the masses and their masters, on the moving streets of the city of the future; the destructive battle in the air between Great Powers imperilling the very existence of civilisation—all Wells' pessimistic fantasies were to be traced to the atmosphere of intensification of the contradictions of bourgeois society. Even Jack London's works, where the mood is basically cheerful and optimistic contain highly tragic pictures of the relentless struggle between the workers and the financial oligarchy in *The Iron Heel* or of the collapse of the bourgeois order under the blows of a general strike in *The Dream of Debs*. This sense of impending catastrophe was present in prose works that portrayed concrete everyday life quite as much as in science fiction works where the conflicts were deliberately exaggerated and presented as larger than life. The ordinary everyday life of people, the serene, regular succession of births, marriages and deaths of old age in one's own bed, the daily round of work and play, was affected by historical forces producing deep and irrevocable changes in the very foundations of this regular life. Dramatic family chronicles became broad pictures of the decline and fall of bourgeois civilisation. Such was the subject of Thomas Mann's *Buddenbrooks* and Galsworthy's *The Forsyte Saga*. But as in Wells' science fiction, here too bourgeois culture and bourgeois life are still viewed as universal culture and life, so that the decline and fall of the bourgeoisie is regarded as the decline and fall of civilisation in general.

New phenomena of social life, its increasingly patent contradictory nature, its illogicality, the widening gap between the principles of official morality and fact, between the theory and practice of bourgeois democracy, forced realist writers to seek new means of presenting the changing world of reality. The critical realists of the twentieth century have wide recourse to the grotesque, to hyperbole, striving to convey the paradoxical nature of life by means of a paradoxical system of images. G. B. Shaw's plays were based on this method, whereby he strove to tear off the outward mask of respectability and expose the hypocrisy of the bourgeois system and its social contradictions. Heinrich Mann also made the grotesque a powerful instrument of his social criticism. He created a vast gallery of portraits of vicious German philistines, his crowning achievement being the "loyal subject" Diederich Hessling, in whom he embodied in exaggerated form the all too real features characteristic of the mentality of the German burgher of the age of imperialism. In his novel *The Head*, which contained scathing criticism of German militarism, and the ultra-nationalism and aggressiveness of the German bourgeoisie, he abandoned superficial likeness and made his characters parodies of their type. Irony, grotesque and paradox also characterise the method of Anatole France, whose works crowned the development of West European nineteenth century critical realism and absorbed its ideas and social ideals.

Adopting the view of progress as "the natural course of things" borrowed from Renan, Anatole France examined the changes this "natural course" had wrought in the society of his age. While the idea of development characteristic of the preceding stage of critical realism was by no means alien to him, it appeared in his works in a much more complicated form from the addition of new ideas typical of the philosophy of the turn of the century, by which he was strongly influenced. Various fallacious concepts of the nature of social development to which he adhered were also the result of the influence on him of the process of alienation.

Unlike his predecessors, who *depicted* the society and individuals of their age in minute detail, Anatole France preferred *reflection* to depiction as such, analytic study of manners to straightforward narration: he combined artistic presentation of reality with its philosophical interpretation, artistic imagery with the straightforward unadorned language of analytical philosophy, wise scepticism with the unassuming simplicity and native cunning of the born storyteller. These various elements were combined to produce his sparkling prose, full of irony, yet essentially sympathetic to man and people in general, and equally suited to a philosophical treatise, a satirical novel or a moralising novella. Anatole France's highly intellectual prose was infused with tremendous cultural content, and it was no accident that he attached such importance to questions of culture in the broadest and most universal meaning of the word. Witnessing the general decline of culture in the society of his age, the indifference of the bourgeoisie to culture as essentially hostile to its own narrow, selfish interests, Anatole France defended cultural values as the universal heritage of mankind from the primitivism of the bourgeois who was rapidly becoming a "two-legged animal" (Maupassant), the consumer and purchaser of cultural values. France defended humanism as well as cultural values. However, the idea of humanism that Pushkin associated with the ideas of liberty and struggle for emancipation, was originally regarded as an independent idea, unconnected with the struggle for emancipation by Anatole France and other major twentieth century realists and even those connected with the democratic movements of their time. To give Anatole France his due, it must be said that in the course of his spiritual development he did gradually overcome the illusion that humanism belonged entirely to the realm of speculative thought. However, in his works connected with the circle of ideas that were most fully expressed in *Le Jardin d'Epicure,* he treated humanism as a refuge of thought and culture rather than a banner of struggle and action. Early twentieth century philosophy in general tended to draw a line between action and speculation, between thought and deed. "Pure thought" was scornful of prosaic reality, and the man of action who was cultivated in bourgeois literature was disdainful of thought. The refined aesthete André Gide contrasted "pure thought" to "pure action", insisting that thought should not interfere with the solution of the practical problems of life and confining it to the sphere of speculation and abstraction, and using the theory of "pure action" to justify individual arbitrariness, and later on even fascist aggressiveness.

Anatole France destroyed the artificial antimony between thought and deed. The venerable old humanist Sylvestre Bonnard commits a "crime" by official moral standards in order to save a man, while Monsieur Bergeret, a respectable Latin scholar of the armchair variety, a humanist through and through, first revolts against the routine of day-to-day life, and subsequently joins the social struggle against the clerical-nationalist-militarist conspiracy to seize the key positions in the Third Republic. Anatole France sought to combine humanism with social action, the struggle to liberate man from religious, nationalist and other prejudices. He presented the real contradictions inherent in the society of his time, and showed how the Church, Army and State served to defend not the interests of the nation and the masses, but the selfish interests of the ruling classes who speculated on the Stock Exchanges, waged bloody colonial wars and used bourgeois democracy to safeguard their own privileges. The injustice, unreason and cruelty he saw in society sometimes caused him to be assailed by pessimism and to doubt the possibility of changing human nature and society for the better. However, these conflicts in his mind could not blind him to the movement of history and make him abandon the quest for social forces and guiding ideas capable of liberating man from all prejudices and all forms of slavery. His tremendous historical perspicacity enabled him to see in socialism and the working class movement the necessary basis for action to promote the welfare and emancipation of mankind. Connected as he was with the socialist movement in the early years of this century, it was only natural that he should have succumbed to the influence of some of the weaknesses that characterised it at that time. He was no revolutionary theoretician, and embraced socialism in the forms in which it was developing in most of the major capitalist countries. The opportunist, social-democratic nature of the socialist movement in the West led him to doubt the possibility of a complete transformation of society.

These doubts were expressed in his attempt to substitute the idea of historical rotation for the idea of development. In his major works, *L'Ile des pingouins*, *La révolte des anges* and *Dieux ont soif*, France drew the conclusion that history repeats itself, and human development passes through the same vicious circle repeated over and over again. He based this conclusion on his study of the results of revolutions that occurred at various periods, and especially the French Revolution. No revolutionary upheaval in the past had changed decisively and fundamentally the conditions of human existence. Every time exploiter classes retained power and the masses were defeated despite unparalleled examples, of courage and self-sacrifice displayed in the struggle for freedom. If Victor Hugo in his *Quatre vingt-treize* stressed the heroic character of the French Revolution, and practically ignored the more prosaic Thermidore aspect, Anatole France took the opposite line in his *Dieux ont soif*, avoiding rhetoric and concentrating on the objective causes that provoked the events of the 9th of Thermidore and brought about the downfall of the Jacobins. He shows no great enthusiasm for the bourgeois revolution, for he saw that it merely involved the replacement of the power of the feudal lords with despotic rule of money. This is also the dominant idea in Satan's dream in *La révolte des anges*, where the author shows how the overthrow of one form of tyranny leads almost automatically to the triumph of another.

Yet France combined misconceptions of the prospects of historical development with scathing criticism of that offspring of bourgeois revolution—bourgeois democracy. Only *direct* connection with the awareness of the masses could serve to free Anatole France and other critical realists of the time from their fallacious views of the prospects of social development. What he needed was not only a knowledge of the terrible conditions in which the masses lived, which he had, but also a knowledge of the potential *creative* powers of which the masses were the carriers, the ability to perceive the constructive element in the movement and struggle of the masses, that was capable of transforming the world. In short, what he lacked was that real understanding of the historical role of the masses that enabled Maxim Gorky to effect a qualitative change in the realist method. With a few exceptions, Anatole France never made the life of the masses the direct object of his attention: their interests and needs rather tended to be reflected indirectly in his works. Yet a sense of kinship with the masses, his inherent propensity as a humanist to assess life in terms of the interests of the masses, was the basis of his critical attitude to the bourgeois civilisation leading him to conclude that capitalist society was doomed. "One must not doubt the future: it belongs to us," he wrote towards the end of his life, having assimilated the experience of the First World War and the October Revolution in Russia. "The plutocracy will perish. The signs of destruction are already visible in its strong organism. It will perish because every caste regime is doomed to perish; the system of hire-labour will perish because it is unjust. It will perish, while still boasting of its power, just as slavery and serfdom have perished."[1] This conclusion was objectively deduced from critical analysis of capitalist society. Anatole France's political views underwent considerable evolution in the years following the October Revolution, and he came to believe that mankind's future lay in Communism. Yet, as a writer he proved unable to portray in literature the movement of mankind toward Communism. His creative method just as Tolstoi's lacked the qualities which might have enabled

---

[1] Anatole France's Preface to Jack London's *Le talon de fer*, Paris, 1933, p. 18.

him to reflect the new trends of historical development that were making themselves so powerfully felt in the twentieth century.

The objective development of the productive forces of society created real conditions for man to start becoming a "species being", as Marx put it, and to no longer "separate social power from himself as political power", for socialism to be translated into reality, for what Marx termed true "human emancipation" to put an end to man's alienation from his socio-productive force.

The transformation of capitalist society into a new type of society had begun. This process naturally found its reflection in art and literature. The time had come for critical realism to recognise the necessity for a change in existing social relations. It had amassed a vast quantity of facts showing that the social order based on private ownership was becoming outmoded and was at odds with the true interests and needs of man. But it was unable either to portray the forces capable of effecting, and indeed already preparing, the social changes that were in the making or to fully reveal the causes of the decline of capitalism and its inevitable collapse, and failed to perceive the actual prospects for the solution of the class conflicts of capitalism. It was inevitable in the very evolution of realism that it should give rise to *a new creative method* enabling it to take cognizance of and present the new factors at work in society that were preparing the reorganisation of the whole system of social relations on a socialist basis. The development of critical realism paved the way for a *qualitative* change in the realist method and led to the emergence of *socialist realism.* It should be stressed that this process did not represent a simple straightforward *transition* whereby critical realist tradition was simply developed and enriched, but involved important changes. Socialist realism inherited some, but not all, of the traditions of critical realism. As Lenin wrote in "Critical Remarks on the National Question": "The *elements* of democratic and socialist culture are present, if only in rudimentary form, in *every* national culture, since in *every* nation there are toiling and exploited masses, whose conditions of life inevitably give rise to the ideology of socialism."[1] These elements of democratic and socialist culture undoubtedly played a role in the development of the socialist awareness of the masses. They were present in the *Weltanschauung* of many great writers of the 19th and 20th centuries—Shelley, Heine, Morris, Tolstoi and Anatole France, to name the most outstanding in this respect. However, since they existed merely as *tendencies*, as aspects of the social views—philosophical, political, ethical, or economic—held by critical realists, and not as the sum total or dominant feature of *their whole outlook*, they did not, and indeed could not, result in the creation of a new method.

The emergence of socialist realism is connected with a tremendous growth of the *social self-awareness* of the working class, and in turn presupposes *full awareness* by the writer of the historical mission of the proletariat. In other words, *class* plays the *decisive role* in the development of the new method, which involves the writer's adopting the standpoint of the revolutionary proletariat which carries out a social and cultural revolution. The writer has to identify his outlook *wholly and completely* with the outlook of the working class in their struggle and victory, to be able to respond to life's phenomena in their entirety in the socialist spirit of the revolutionary proletariat and to accept Communism as the real prospect of historical development. Naturally, a creative method is more than an outlook, but it is based on an outlook and embodies its features. Thus, socialist realism cannot be unless the writer shares the outlook of the revolutionary working class, in the case of capitalist countries, or the outlook of the working class that is the ruling class in socialist countries.

Socialist realism was born in Russia. Centuries of autocratic government had led to the accumulation among the masses of tremendous revolutionary energy. Russian literature, with its legacy of heroic service to the masses paved the way for the emergence of the new realist method. Finally, the Russian masses produced a genius of the stature of Maxim Gorky. It was Gorky's works that

---

[1] V. I. Lenin, *Collected Works*, Vol. 20, p. 24.

marked the advent of a qualitatively new stage in the development of world literature, a stage corresponding to the socialist era in social relations.

After the triumph of the October Revolution in Russia and the building of socialism, at the juncture when a new social reality made its appearance in the world, with concomitant new relations between man and society, a new social ethic, a new understanding of the social aims and tasks of art and literature, a new literary method corresponding to the historical conditions and the historically-conditioned needs of the new society, socialist realism, began to develop. A similar process is to be observed in the people's democracies, where a new system of social relations fundamentally different from the capitalist, has emerged. Socialist realism is gaining ground in the capitalist countries, too, as the growth of the working class and democratic movement increases the influence of socialist ideology and culture. Aragon, Eluard, Nexö, Pratolini and Pablo Neruda—all writers with socialist views—have been logically led to adopt the socialist realist method, since the new processes going on in society cannot be expressed and cognized within the framework of the old creative methods, including critical realism.

The basic features of socialist realism were already clearly manifest in the writings of Maxim Gorky, which organically combined *universal, all-embracing* criticism of moribund capitalism with passionate affirmation of the new socialist social order that came to replace it.

Gorky's universal criticism of capitalist society was based on comprehensive analysis and portrayal of the life and relations of its major classes. The whole vast, turbulent current of life in tsarist Russia, rent by irreconcilable contrasts and howling contradictions, reverberating with the warning sounds of the greatest revolution in history, flowed freely across the pages of Gorky's books. The human driftwood of the mighty Volga, the human wrecks, battered and broken by life in the capitalist towns, "have-beens", the traders and dealers forcing upon the wild, refractory country the harness of forced labour, practically slave labour, and having the presumption to claim that by their depredations they were performing a noble mission and bringing progress to the country; the intellectuals alarmed by the thought of imminent revolution and boldly offering themselves to its cause in an orgy of "love for the people"; ruined peasants, torn up by want from their tiny holdings and finding themselves become disinherited proletarians with disconcerting speed; wealthy peasants, guarding their barns and pantries with the fierceness of watchdogs; the provincial petty bourgeois, wallowing in a slough of mental torpor and vegetating in their stagnant backwaters; secret police agents, soldiers, and all kinds of defenders of the tottering establishment of the Russia of the landowners and bourgeoisie; revolutionary workers, engaged in mortal combat with the autocracy and the power of capital; vagrants, monks and intellectuals who were hiding from the vital issues of life behind a wall of fine phrases; seekers after truth and justice in a world of falsehood and injustice; people who had lost their resemblance to human beings in the fierce struggle for existence with no holds barred; meek philistines and heroes paving mankind's way to the future; the extraordinary beauty of life and its most sordid wretchedness—Gorky overlooked no one, turning his fearless, penetrating gaze on life's awesome and enchanting countenance. Gorky saw and portrayed the whole of Russia seething as the mighty cauldron of revolution came to the boil, *at every level of society*, in its historic hour, the hour of the formation of *the self-awareness of the masses.*

Gorky showed with tremendous courage and merciless truth the depths of human degradation and brutalisation brought on by capitalism. Where even Tolstoi hesitated and stopped short at the nakedness of human sufferings and the shamelessness of man's abasement, Gorky went boldly on "to the end" ("The Watchman", "A Little Girl", "The Creepy-Crawlies" and "Caramora"). Gorky presented the horrors of the human condition under capitalism through simple, everyday facts treated as an *intrinsic* part of the system. His descriptions of various forms of brutality and violence were not an end in themselves, but merely served to demonstrate the inhuman nature of society based on exploitation. Gorky showed that the brutalisation of the working man was the result of the unnatural conditions in which he lived, while the boundless selfishness, greed and cruelty of the scions of the bourgeoisie, who would stop at nothing, not even crime nor the most immoral acts, to achieve their selfish aims, was but the natural expression of their class essence. For Mayakin, Vassa Zheleznova, Pyotr Artamonov, Dostigayev and other vultures, big and small, depicted by Gorky, there was not, nor could there be, any other law but personal gain, and awareness of the need to defend their personal interests made all the property owning classes automatically hostile to the masses, who were already ripe for making a bid for emancipation from the exploiter classes.

Gorky's heroes are always *types*, clearly expressing social class instincts and views. While portraying a character's individual features to the full, and refusing to reduce him to a social cipher, Gorky never overlooked his class essence. The outlooks of Boss, Bugrov or Mayakin are at once perfectly distinct and similar in that they are equally hostile to the masses. The division of society into rich and poor, oppressors and oppressed, was the natural order of things for Gorky's capitalists, which they would never allow to be changed without a fierce struggle. Their outlook being based on the instinct to conserve the existing order, they form a single social unit in the struggle of interests going on all the time in society.

Unlike the critical realists, Gorky did not limit himself to a statement of the existence of class struggle and its influence on individual members of society. He saw and depicted the *natural consequences* of the class struggle for the fate of capitalist society as a whole. For the first time in world literature, in Gorky's works the prospects of social development as perceived *subjectively* by the writer coincided with the *objective* movement of history and social development, and indeed this is the essential feature of socialist realism.

Gorky did not need to find his way to the masses, he was himself of the masses. His critical realist contemporaries were clearly aware of this feature of his art, something totally *new* in world literature. Stefan Zweig was quite right when he noted that in Gorky's works the people itself acquired the gift of speech. "From out of its own flesh it created itself a mouth, and of its own speech its own spokesman, out of its own midst a man, and this man, this writer, its own writer and champion, it brought forth from its gigantic womb that he might make known to all mankind the life of the Russian people, the Russian proletariat, the humiliated, the oppressed and the persecuted."[1] Gorky's social views, his whole *Weltanschauung*, enabled him to see capitalist society not only *from within*, but *from without* too, from the standpoint of the future that was relentlessly approaching, heavy with revolution and the collapse of capitalism. As a revolutionary writer, standing *outside the system of the bourgeois consciousness*, free from the illusions born of bourgeois ideology and the process of alienation, Gorky revealed the real contradictions of the capitalist world and was able to submit all the principles underlying bourgeois society to truly *universal* criticism. Gorky's historical perspective was based on his understanding of the inevitability of the replacement of capitalist social relations by other. Unlike the historicism of the classics of critical realism—and this was a basic feature of the new creative method— Gorky's historicism was not limited to the portrayal of characters and types in accordance with objective historical truth, which was the great achievement of realist art as a whole. Gorky, for whom both as a revolutionary thinker and a writer the idea of development was organic, portrayed life, and thus history, in *ceaseless movement*. He portrayed not only the concrete forms and aspects of its movement visible to his contemporaries, but also the direct natural results of this movement, which was paving the way for the final triumph of the working people. That is why *historical optimism* is a basic feature of Gorky's works and of the new creative method, an optimism based not on the writer's own subjective views and sentiments, but deriving from perception of the objective process of social development, an optimism of a new type, that did not involve glossing over the contradictions and tragic aspects of life, as bourgeois liberal thought is inclined to do.

[1] Stefan Zweig, *Begegnungen mit Menscher Buchern Städten,* Berlin, 1956, S. 98.

Gorky's optimism was marked by a straightforward, sober view of life and people, a refusal to ignore the tragedy and drama that constantly arose in and from social reality. Behind the chaotic course of events, all the various manifestations of life's cruelty, injustice, misery and suffering, Gorky perceived the relentless movement of cause and effect paving the way for the elimination of misery and suffering from man's life. It was Gorky's kind of optimism, the new principles of portraying reality the founder of socialist realism introduced to literature, that engendered the essential optimism of Fadeyev's *The Rout*, Vishnevsky's *Optimistic Tragedy* and the best works of Soviet literature about the war. It is from Gorky's kind of optimism that socialist realist writers in the capitalist countries have derived the courage with which they portray the horrors of capitalist exploitation and the enslavement of man by the bourgeois system.

The new historical perspective that is to be found in the works of Gorky predetermined the new kind of *causality* that is a feature of socialist realism. Take Thomas Mann's portrayal of the decline and fall of the bourgeois family in *The Buddenbrooks.* He deliberately equated the fate of his burghers and the fate of bourgeois society as a whole in analysing the objective causes that led to the ruin of the Buddenbrooks, and ascribed a secondary importance to the social aspects of the process. He described the ruin of the Buddenbrook business and dynasty with tremendous artistic skill but confined the narrative almost entirely to the sphere of family ties and the personal lives of his heroes.

Gorky, on the other hand, in *The Artamonovs,* also describes the decline and fall of a powerful family of entrepreneurs. But in presenting the downfall of the Artamonov business, the business, that is, of the whole Russian bourgeoisie and the social system they support, he adduces a vast mass of facts drawn from the social history of the age. For Gorky the degeneration of the Artamonovs, the weakening of their "blood", is a secondary factor. More important for him by far in determining their fate is the *mass movement.* Revolution is the basic cause of the downfall of the Russian bourgeoisie, and it sealed the fate of the Artamonovs, the Bulychovs, the Dostigayevs and other scions of the bourgeoisie.

Thus, in the new creative method, the investigation and interpretation of the causal links operating in society involves determination and clarification of their social nature.

In analysing and depicting the life of bourgeois society, its inherent contradictions, Gorky felt bound to define the motive forces of social development. Unlike bourgeois ideologists, who take a metaphysical view of the historical process, Gorky saw the sources of class antagonisms to lie in the material conditions of life, regarding the masses as the motive force of social development. In Gorky's works—and this is an important feature of socialist realism—the masses are presented as the force that makes history and produces all spiritual and material wealth. This makes his works a real encyclopaedia of the life of the masses, providing an exhaustive account of both their everyday life of need and deprivations, and their heroism and creative potential. For Gorky regarded the consciousness of the masses to be a major factor in the creation of culture. He pointed out how the powerful, inexhaustible spiritual and creative resources of the masses found reflection in the gigantic images, created by popular fantasy, such as Gilgamesh, Prometheus, Mikula Selyaninovich, Vassilisa the All-Knowing, Faust and Thyl Ulenspiegel. In the years preceding the October Revolution Gorky insisted that the culture of the future would rest on popular culture, and in the years following the Revolution, he worked with equal persistence to help create that culture of the future by participating in the practical organisation and effectuation of the cultural revolution.

It was this new understanding of the historical role and mission of the masses that determined Gorky's new portrayal of the character of men from the masses, fundamentally different from that to be found in the works of the critical realists. Men and women of the people in Gorky's works are highly "intellectual", not in the sense that they are "well-read" and "educated", which is so often confused with intellectual ability, but in that they have a keen mind when it comes to finding their way in the complex situations in which life abounds, and in their attitudes to life. Gorky's heroes, in their relationships with one another and society, in their attempts to determine and find their place in society, always exercise their active probing minds. They not only ponder over questions of love, death and conscience, and the work at hand; they also think about life and society, trying to work out for themselves where they are heading. Gorky's heroes, all kinds of different people he has met in the course of his long wanderings through the towns and villages of Russia, are all the time pondering seriously on how life can be changed and in what direction. They are constantly straining under the burden of exploitation, oppression and coercion, and they understand that it is impossible for life in Russia to continue as it is. They slowly but surely become *aware* of the fact that it is necessary and inevitable that the existing order should be changed, and the best of them pass from spontaneous protest, spontaneous rejection of social injustice, to the higher level of *conscious* protest against capitalism, joining the ranks of active opponents of the bourgeois system.

Gorky presents the formation of *the self-awareness of the masses* above all as a *process*, a complex, tortuous process, starting from a correct understanding of the objective position of man in capitalist society and passing through the overcoming of illusions engendered by the existing order, and instilled by traditions and human alienation, to finally arrive at inner liberation from the private ownership mentality and egocentrism and fusion of the individual interest with the common interests of the working masses struggling for their emancipation from capitalist enslavement. Basically, the most important thing for Gorky is the *theme of man's emancipation* from all forms of spiritual and material slavery. Gorky's tremendous interest in man, which was expressed in his very first works and the anthropomorphism characteristic of his whole literary output, derives directly and is inseparable from the revolutionary, emancipatory nature of his world-view. While in the bourgeois consciousness anthropocentrism was the outcome of greatly increased alienation both among individuals and between individuals and society, Gorky's anthropomorphism reflected the process of overcoming those objective conditions that gave rise to alienation and associated illusions. Gorky contrasted the freedom and beauty of man, the lord of the universe, with the miserable existence of man under capitalism. In order to become the *real master* of his destiny, man must *struggle for freedom.* Gorky portrays a whole host of characters representing in vastly different ways the awakening of the self-awareness of the masses, from those heroes like Smury, Konovalov and Gvozdyev, who are constantly pondering over the meaning of life, to those who have already raised the banner of revolution. Gorky's revolutionaries differ greatly as to their level of social self-awareness. Alongside Nilovna, moved by her maternal instinct and sense of justice intrinsic to a worker to embrace the revolutionary cause, we have her son Pavel, dedicated working-class revolutionary, one of those who stood in the vanguard of the Bolshevik struggle. Along with Nil, opposing the will of the working class and faith in its ultimate triumph to the will of the ruling exploiter class, we have the Bolshevik Kutuzov, a man armed with a mature mind and vast knowledge and experience, who crushes his spiritual and political opponents with the strength of his ideas and manages to smash the complex phraseology whereby the bourgeois intellectuals attempted to protect themselves from the inevitability of revolution. Gorky did not reveal all the aspects of the revolutionary at one go, but did so gradually, widening and deepening his portrayal as he himself gradually, with the expansion of the revolutionary struggle, came to know the typical features and qualities of revolutionaries. Gorky—and this is another major feature of socialist realism—attributed tremendous importance to the matter of creating convincing images of those in the forefront of the freedom struggle, rightly considering them to be the supreme expression of the finest qualities of the masses. The ideals of the critical realists were expressed in their *moral standpoint,* and only rarely in positive characters, and even then these usually lacked power. This was the case with Balzac's Bénassis, Tolstoi's Karatayev, Dostoyevsky's Alyosha Karamazov and Father Zosima and so on. In Gorky's aesthetics, however, the aesthetics of a new type of realism, the problem of creating the image of a hero possessed of that exemplary moral strength which would help mould the character of the participants in the struggle of the masses was a problem of primary importance.

Gorky's greatest achievement was his portrayal of Lenin, the leader of the Revolution, something that could only have been accomplished with the help of the new creative method, which made it possible to make an objective appreciation of historical phenomena in their real relationship with social life. Gorky perceived and depicted Lenin in revolutionary perspective, as a creative person, *transforming the world*, as a thinker, possessed of remarkable historical perception and acumen, as a man of action, inseparably linked with the people, and able to sense the slightest motion of the popular masses, and finally as a statesman, realising exactly where and how to lead the masses.

Gorky's portrayal of men and women of the people was remarkable for its completeness and vitality, and wealth of feelings and ideas. Gorky was a consummate master of psychological analysis, and in many ways carried forward the Tolstoian tradition. However, for Gorky, psychological analysis was more than a means of criticism, more than a surgeon's scalpel dissecting the human soul and exposing all that was hidden under all manner of masks and poses, for him it was also a means of presenting the richness of human nature, the great variety of human sentiments and thoughts about life and the world. Gorky used psychological analysis to reveal the latent wealth and power of the mind and spirit of the ordinary people prevented from manifesting themselves properly by the unnatural social conditions. In portraying characters of the masses Gorky constantly stressed not only the vast reserve of practically untapped moral energy, but also the vast creative potential. The people of the masses are united by strong ties of brotherhood and fellowship, by gradually perceived *common goals*, an essential prerequisite for revolution. He shows how capitalism *disunites people*, in the sense that it "desocialises the personality", as he put it, but at the same time serves to produce solidarity among the masses. This new *collective spirit* that had arisen among the masses could only be perceived and expressed by an exponent of the new creative method. Gorky shows the manifold ways in which the creative energy of the masses is revealed—now in spontaneous outbursts of fury and revolt, often reckless and foolhardy, against the bourgeois order, the moribund establishment protecting the rights and interests of the possessor classes, now in purposeful constructive activity, in moments when the people begin to *work freely*, selflessly engaging in creative work. The *poetisation of labour*—a new, major feature of socialist realism—made its first appearance in Gorky's works. Gorky showed how natural it is to work and create, and what great joy creative labour can bring to free men who have thrown off the capitalist yoke.

Man cannot acquire true freedom without freeing himself from those views, habits and illusions that capitalist society instils in him. For Gorky it was perfectly obvious that the main feature of the bourgeois outlook was individualism, resulting from a rift and antithesis between man and society. He made a penetrating study of the process by which illusory views of life arise in the consciousness of people who perceive themselves as individuals alienated from the objective world, which appears to the self-centered individual as a mesh of insoluble mysteries and hostile forces. Gorky devoted two extremely important works to the problem of alienation, the stories *Blue Life* and *On Cockroaches.* The illusory perceptual anomalies that afflict the heroes of these stories—Konstantin Mironov, returning to his normal routine of philistine existence and money-grubbing after a violent spiritual crisis, and Platon Yeryomin, dying "on his feet"—are the direct result of the abnormal, unjust social order.

The heroes' illusions and misconceptions as regards the world, life and other people are the consequence of self-immurement from the processes going on in life around them and complete absorption in their own personal world. Gorky made a comprehensive analysis of the social essence of this phenomenon in *Klim Samgin* where he portrayed and submitted to universal criticism the most typical aspects of the bourgeois mentality.

Gorky embodied in this, his last novel, a whole complex, eventful period of history, beginning in the years leading up to the First Russian Revolution culminating in the events of February 1917, a period including the years of reaction and the years of the upswing of the revolutionary movement, marked by the ideological collapse of the autocracy and the destruction of the illusions of Russian bourgeois democracy, a period that abounded in grandiose class battles, violent strikes, the burning of landowners' estates, the brutal mowing down of defenceless demonstrators in Palace Square of the imperial capital that came to be known as Bloody Sunday, the adventurism of the social-revolutionaries, the provocations of tsarist secret police, selfless, consistent agitation by the Bolsheviks at factories and plants, a period of ideological ferment and vacillation among the intelligentsia, its division along the lines of political sympathies and antipathies.

Gorky omitted no detail of the social setting. It was all there: merchants and bureaucrats, Narodniks and Marxists, the students and their search for the true values, the aberrations of decadent art, the revolutionary struggle and the sectarian distractions of the intellectuals, rejecting revolution, the activities of secret police agents, and so on and so forth. The completeness with which Gorky portrayed the social environment enabled him to give an exhaustive presentation of the intellectual and spiritual life of Russian society on the eve of the revolution. The tone was set by the mounting tide of revolution, which made itself felt in every sphere of social relations. radiance lit up the furthest recesses of life and of the bourgeois consciousness, showing up for what they were really worth—all the pathetic efforts to postpone of truth in the sphere of spiritual values made by the bourgeoisie and its offspring—half-baked democrats, cowardly liberals, newly-baked Nietzscheans, apostles of pure beauty and art for art's sake, energetic entrepreneurs and provincial thinkers, all out to probe the immutability of the existing order of things.

Simple truths were taken wholesale and, eviscerated of their true content, woven into a sticky web of words, concepts and phrases: the masses should be loved as the carriers of divinity, but they were not yet ready for freedom and needed guidance and protection; revolution was necessary, but the masses were too ignorant to be entrusted with the task of carrying it out; people were estranged from one another, and this was an eternal, immutable law of existence, and so on and so forth. Such false ideas, corrupting heart and mind, became part of Klim Samgin and those like him, and he was no longer capable of distinguishing between truth and falsehood, or good and evil. Spiritual and moral values had become confused and *devaluated* in his mind, and while guessing that underlying the "system of phrases" in which people envelop themselves, underlying all the falsehood on which human relationships, love, the family and friendship, were based was fear of the truth of that which was approaching, fear of an uprising of the masses, fear of revolution, Klim Samgin nevertheless tried to put off that fateful moment for he was *hostile* to it. Klim and those like him are unable to make a correct assessment of the historical prospects or the real position that obtained as a result of the developing revolutionary situation. Isolated from the real needs of the masses, centered entirely on themselves, they embrace with open arms all sorts of illusions, which have one thing in common— they are all of a *protective, anti-revolutionary character.*

Historical truth, the totality of real relationships, can only be grasped by the revolutionary consciousness, the consciousness of the masses. Peasants and revolutionaries, workers and progressive revolutionary intellectuals look the truth of the age straight in the eye. In the course of the revolutionary struggle, in the struggle with the bourgeoisie and tsarism, man takes cognizance of the tendencies of history and social development, and by *recreating and transforming the world,* becomes master of his alienated socio-political force. Kutuzov understands perfectly well what is going on in life and what the outcome of the struggle between the working masses and the bourgeoisie will be. In this lies his strength and the guarantee of victory.

Gorky also submitted to extensive criticism the ethical principles of bourgeois society. His art, glorifying the emancipation of man, is fundamentally humanitarian. Gorky's humanism, as distinct from the reflective humanism of many of the critical realists, and above all Tolstoi, is active. It is the culminating point of the vast humanitarian tradition of Russian literature beginning from Pushkin, who first linked humanism with the struggle for freedom. The principle underlying Gorky's humanism is activity directed towards human welfare, activity designed to help man practically, activity to destroy unjust social institutions and *free man from suffering*. Gorky invariably took as his point of departure man's *real interests*, and it is from this that his humanism derives its power. This humanism determined the *particular kind of epic principle* in his works.

Gorky is a writer of epic caste not only by virtue of his tendency to write works of vast scope, or even because the underlying theme of his work was the revolutionary transformation of bourgeois society and the growth of the social self-awareness of the masses, but above all because of his great love for the physical world, for the beauty of the tangible fabric of life. His palette contains thick, rich colours. His prose is full of remarkably expressive and strikingly authentic details. Yet despite this love of the concrete, physical fabric of reality and his comprehensive portrayal of the social forces at work in society, the human personality is never lost sight of, never swamped in the narrative, and a marked lyric strain runs throughout his works. A major feature of Gorky's works is fusion of the lyrical and epic elements, to form *a synthetic whole*. In his autobiographical trilogy, this synthesis of the two vastly different principles enabled him to present a large variety of people, a complex, comprehensive picture of life, and reveal the conflict between different social classes while at the same time creating a *lyrical hero of giant spiritual stature*.

Gorky was able to perceive and distinguish all the various social forces acting and conflicting in the society

moving, man's place in the changing world, his destiny in modern society which is *in a state of revolutionary transformation*, naturally became the main object of attention, and was reflected, either intentionally or spontaneously, in the works of artists and writers of the most various trends. Literature and all other forms of social ideology recognised the need for a synthetic perception of history in the making. This is why bourgeois social thought tried to develop a universal conception of life that would explain the "secret" of human relationships in the modern world (although this "secret" had been revealed long since by Marxism) and the nature of the relationship between man and the world of natural phenomena.

The most common feature of modern philosophical theories, for all their essential differences, is undoubtedly a gravitation towards synthesis. Freudism elaborated a universal conception of culture where everything is derived from sexual urges. In their philosophy of culture, the Freudists tried to explain the motives of human behaviour and the nature of social conflicts in terms of basic biological factors and evolve a system for controlling man's individual and social behaviour. The tendency towards a synthetic interpretation of the world is even more manifest in the views of the British and American neo-realists of the cosmological trend and especially in Whitehead's activistic philosophy of process, which regards life and all that exists as a process, where the individual is part of the whole and at the same time, a condensation of the whole. On the basis of this view of things, Whitehead developed what he considered to be a comprehensive, all-inclusive philosophical model of the world, history, sociology, ethics and aesthetics, all based, in the final analysis, on God, and interpreted accordingly not only natural scientific, "pan-physical" processes, but also questions of practical politics. Whitehead regarded history as "adventures of ideas", that is as a process of changing human views of the world, society and God, changing and moving history itself. He held that ideas, rather than material factors underlay historical progress and tried to develop a system of views more appropriate to our age than the collection of old concepts evolved back in the nineteenth century. Whitehead realised that unless the old society was provided with new ideas, and unless it changed its old methods of controlling the masses, sooner or later the passions, desires and feelings of the masses would burst forth in revolt and the result might well be a socialist revolution. He himself was a supporter of liberal evolutionism in politics, and held that it was preferable to satisfy certain of the most pressing needs of the masses than to radically alter the existing order.

Neo-Thomism is another philosophical movement that makes a claim to universality and is as conservative in the original meaning of the word. The neo-Thomists posit that God is the all-embracing essence of the world and eternal existence, and every mortal creature is comprehended in the essence of God. Despite their declared belief in free will, they are in fact denying it, since, according to their theory, man, like everything else in life, depends on divine will.

The neo-Thomists reject the view of history as a senseless, chaotic, and aimless movement of heterogeneous forces, an uncontrolled stream of events, as it was presented by Theodor Lessing, author of *Geschichte als Sinngebung des Sinnlosen* which caused a furore in the twenties, and by other representatives of "the philosophy of life", who denied causality and interdependence of historical phenomena. On the contrary, they hold that God organises, synthesises and guides history towards some goal, and that this goal, which may be cognized through faith and revelation, has nothing at all to do with the social ideal affirmed in life by revolutionary socialist thought.

In art and literature the tendency towards a synthetic comprehension of reality exerted a strong influence— sometimes fruitful, sometimes destructive—on form, and served to somewhat erode the boundaries between the different arts. This was also promoted by several new factors, such as the development of the cinema, whose aesthetic idiom draws on the theatre and makes use of words, music, colour, and the visual image, as well as devices from painting and narrative prose.

The synthetic nature of the cinema, now universally recognised, was realised early on by some of its most outstanding exponents. After the appearance of the colour film, the major Soviet film director Alexander Dovzhenko wrote: "The tremendous advantages of the colour film over black and white are as obvious as the prospects for its development are unlimited. If we called the cinema before the appearance of colour a synthetic art, now that it has received new expressive means, including the vast possibilities of the art of painting, this definition will become applicable in full measure."[1]

The specific features of the cinema, such as dynamic movement of the subject in time and space, free transposition of events and the fact of there being no obligation to adhere to strict chronological sequence, the frequent change of angle of vision and distance, the possibilities of contrasting episodes and grouping facts in montage has had a noticeable influence on modern prose.

There has been considerable mutual influence between other genres, for instance, poetry and prose. Andrei Bely began to combine the techniques of prose and poetry back at the turn of the century, and there are strong poetic undercurrents in his prose giving it an added expressiveness and producing inner rhyme, alliteration and the organisation of the period on the poetic pattern, the latter thus acquiring the independence and emotional completeness of verse. The influence of poetry is strong in the works of several modern writers. Some of them, like Sean O'Casey, combine features of poetry and prose to evolve a highly original, striking and expressive style, rich in rhythmic transitions, brilliant alliteration, internal rhyming and assonance in lyrical or solemn passages, and lyric poems in prose included here and there as emotional highlights. Prose, in its turn, has been energetically invading poetry. Many poets have begun to feel the classical forms and metres inadequate for conveying the rhythms of modern life and have thus resorted to prose verse.

This is true of a number of major revolutionary poets, such as Gastev, Berthold Brecht, Eluard, Pablo Neruda, Nazim Hikmet and Mieželaitis.

---

[1] A. Dovzhenko, "The Colour", The Art of Cinema, Moscow, 1948, Nos. 2-3, p. 6 (in Russ.).

Partly under the influence of the Walt Whitman tradition, the new prose verse has gradually been adopted by British and American poets, from Lee Masters in the twenties, through W. H. Auden, Cecil Day-Lewis, Carl Sundburg, Archibald MacLeish, down to the younger generation of poets, including Allen Ginsberg. French poetry, developed independently but in the same direction, modern exponents including Jean Cayrol and Saint-John Perse.

In prose verse, the tendency is to abandon straightforward prosody and rhyme for a language that outwardly (but only outwardly) resembles prose, poetic metre being replaced, as the cementing principle, by melodic rhythm. However, the image in prose verse remains strictly poetic, without expansion into detail that is characteristic of narrative prose. This form is perfectly viable since it enables the writer to base his poem on a sequence of associations and develop the poetic idea in a strictly logical fashion. It also opens up wide possibilities for epic and lyrical development of the theme.

While the mutual influence of prose and poetry has not greatly affected the structure of the artistic image, the opposite is true of attempts to associate arts with such vastly different expressive techniques as sculpture and painting. In their attempt to achieve a synthetic representation of the world, many painters have resorted to a combination of techniques and devices of these highly dissimilar arts. Cézanne who devoted a great deal of thought to the question of the relationship between volume and space in a painting, conceived the idea of presenting nature by means of the cylinder, the ball and the cone, that is by means of three dimensional geometrical figures, believing that in this way it would be possible to fully capture the physical depth of nature. He himself only took the first steps in this direction, but his ideas fell on well-prepared ground, and were taken up and developed by many other artists, especially the Cubists—Gris, Braque, and above all Picasso, who, quite unconcerned about the consequences, set about dissecting the world into geometric elements attempting to capture their volume, to depict all sides of a model at once and present it to the viewer from every angle simultaneously. Basically, Picasso was trying to do the work of the sculpture. He produced paintings where the natural proportions of objects were distorted, all their sides and surfaces being superimposed upon one another or crossing one another at various angles.

Picasso's painting, like that of the other Cubists, deformed and distorted the real appearance of objects. Twentieth century bourgeois art has been going much further along this road of distorting reality, representing it not as it actually appears, in its materiality, but through various abstractions. This perception and representation of the world and the development of life is becoming a characteristic of the modern bourgeois consciousness, which attempts both to embrace the whole of reality and at the same time to break it down into certain abstract elements. This is expressed, for example, in Husserl's phenomenology, where the world is seen as a collection of ideal substances, each of which can be defined and determined by logical analysis. The adherents of "creative evolution", notably Bergson, held that rational (non-intuitive) perception, being analytic by nature, splits the stream of events into separate concepts, transforming the essence of things into symbols. Bergson's views served to pave the way for the penetration of abstraction into art. Bergson considered rational thought to be capable of distilling a phenomenon from its concrete nature and viewing it as an abstraction. An example of this is a film, which transmits the impression of movement by the sequence of immobile images. In order to reproduce the motion of the world latent in it, writes Bergson in *Creative Evolution*, it is necessary to extract "from all the movements peculiar to all the figures an impersonal movement, abstract and simple, *movement* in general, so to speak: we put this into the apparatus, and we reconstitute the individuality of each particular movement by combining this nameless movement with the personal attitudes. Such is the contrivance of the cinematograph."[1] By introducing the concepts "impersonal", "abstract", "movement in general", Bergson thereby

_____
[1] Henri Bergson, *Creative Evolution*, London, 1913, p. 322.

opened up to art the possibility of conveying not real phenomena but *ciphers* of these phenomena. As for the film, it does not "extract" some impersonal, abstract movement from a sum of static images, but combines these images, imparting to them a live causal relationship by means of movement, by means, that is, of a real process....

However, the tendency towards an all-embracing depiction of the world, so strong in twentieth century art, did not, and indeed could not, lead to the emergence of syncretism, since art in our age is not developing on a homogeneous social foundation. All one can say is that in certain arts there has been a growing desire to achieve a synthesis of reality. But while revolutionary democratic art makes, as Aragon put it, the "real world" the basis of artistic synthesis of life, bourgeois art bases its attempts to achieve a synthetic depiction of life upon the alienated individual consciousness. For this reason all attempts of bourgeois social thought and art to achieve a synthesis of the contemporary world only resulted in *pseudo-synthesis*.

For example, the Freudian philosophy of culture, with its claims to universality and to an exhaustive explanation of the facts of history and sociology, is based on an extremely meagre unhistorical concept of man as an unchanging and unchangeable biological creature, whose instincts, physical desires, lusts and neuroses are supposed to determine the whole course of history, the main features of modern civilisation and the nature of contemporary social conflicts. Not only does Freudism fail to explain our age, either the nature of its contradictions or the meaning and content of the changes in progress: it deliberately reduces the real variety of life to the narrow, limited outlook of the individual, a creature assailed by fears and moved by aggressive urges, giving a free rein to his animal lusts and instincts and dark passions, a slave to a possessive, egoistic ethic.

Neo-realism, a highly respectable philosophy leaning heavily on the natural sciences and mathematics, won great popularity in the West by virtue of its apparent objectivity. Yet the explanation it offered of the phenomena of the material world was based on the identification of the real object of reality, its abstract idea, with individual perception of it. Basically, the neo realists were returning to some of the concepts of idealist Naturphilosophie.

Although he insisted that he was regarding nature as a continuous, incessant process, in terms of duration, Whitehead was in fact unable to perceive things in their collective unity, since he extended the atomisation of his own perception to the whole universe, dividing it into separate events, thereby viewing collective unity and "duration" as the sum of separate events. Whitehead, like the other neo-realists, equated perception with the object of cognition, and regarded the real world as the product of the human perception: he was thus subscribing to the subjective idealist views and, like Bergson, making intuition the instrument of cognition. Whitehead's philosophy of the nature of things was thus built on very shaky foundations of the alienated individual perception, detached from live connections with the world, and was thus unable to produce a synthesis of the world. As for the systems of the neo-Thomists and other fideists (Hartmann, Alexander, Häberlin and others), they demonstrated great flexibility and a capacity to adapt to the social requirements of present-day capitalist society, and altered the nature of their arguments to correspond to changes in social conditions.

Neo-Thomist philosophy recognised the reality of the world, but investigated not that reality which exists objectively, but the strange pseudo-reality formed of "actual" and "potential" existence, invented by the isolated, self-centered consciousness of the alienated individual. This latter "reality" admits of the existence of a static immortal soul, as the basis of human nature. This concept of "reality" admits of revelation and various other concepts that belong more to the dark ages of theology, scholasticism and demonology than to our age of great social transformation and scientific discovery. The fact that the neo-Thomists accept the reality of the material world does not mean that they explain the essence of existence by material factors. For them, material factors are of secondary importance, since God is regarded as the origin of all things. Thus, they hold that man's perception of things can never be complete since man perceives not the real

213

essence of things or processes but merely their likeness formed in his mind, so that he approaches cognition of the truth by way of these simulacra. Perception is never complete for the added reason that it is independent of time and space, that it is "pure" and non-concrete, and, we might well add, thereby unable to take possession of its object. Thus, despite the fact that it is the avowed aim of neo-Thomism to examine and perceive reality, in actual fact it is powerless to do so.

Realist writers who are in some way or other under the influence of the Catholic outlook—writers like Mauriac, Bernanos or Böll—are thereby limited and hindered to a degree from perceiving the real conflicts of life. Their works, while giving a largely authentic panorama of personal and social life (Mauriac less than Böll, since he mainly confines himself to the bourgeois family), nevertheless tend to treat social conflicts as a struggle between "pure" good and evil, eviscerated of their real social content.

The basic theme of the works of Mauriac—an extremely profound writer in the realist tradition, whose "novels of character" reveal an outlook divergent from the official Catholic set of standards—is the struggle against all manifestations of evil. The aesthetic ideal underlying his works is born of the desire to free man from all the baseness and evil in which he wallows in everyday life. Mauriac has never acknowledged that man's moral code of behaviour can only be changed as a result of changes in the social conditions in which he lives, so that in this sense he was and remains within the framework of the traditional bourgeois philosophy. Nevertheless, his ethical ideal calls forth extremely pungent criticism of evil, which he presents most vividly, sometimes investigating and depicting quite hair-raising details as in *Thérèse Desqueyroux*, where a young woman who has made a marriage of convenience slowly poisons the husband she does not love or *Sagouin*, describing how a wretched, ugly child perishes as a result of the cruelty and callousness of a bourgeois family. Mauriac has a wealth of realistic detail to build up the mundane dramas of mundane bourgeois existence— the collapse of family ties, and the destruction of the personality through egoism and self-interest, the gradual erosion of the better aspects of a man's nature by the overwhelming urge for personal gain, the numbing of the heart, personal despotism, secret crime—and produces a picture of striking power and authenticity. However, in all cases these are purely human dramas, brought about because people had failed to apply the ethical principles of Christian morality, and this makes Mauriac's realism narrow both in the subject matter embraced and the conclusions drawn. The shrewd observations of life his works contain constantly seem to strain at the confines of his ethical ideal towards a wider system of views on the sources of human misfortunes and the ways of putting them right. But Mauriac has never taken this step.

In the case of Böll, his sharing of the sentiments of the democratic strata in West Germany, his irreconcilable hostility to all the consequences of nazism, his clear memories of the days of the national disaster and his opposition to neo-nazism and reaction, gained the upper hand over his Catholic illusions, making them hardly noticeable, so that his works reflect the real conflicts of life and genuine social contradictions.

Genuine realist literature could not derive sufficient sustenance from the views and sentiments expressed in neo-Thomism or other religious outlooks on life.

There is another reason why the tendencies towards synthesis in the bourgeois consciousness were destined to be unfruitful, and that is that the anthropocentric and anthropological approach to interpretation of the processes of life, asserted itself in new forms. Typical in this respect are the sociological conceptions of Max Scheler, whose philosophical views along with those of Husserl had a marked influence on existentialism. Scheler foresaw the growing role of élitism in capitalist society, and thus regarded the problem of "leadership" and "following" as the basic problem of sociology and the philosophy of history. He sought to justify the rule of a minority over the majority, the rule of an "élite" over the masses, by the so-called "law of small numbers" invented for precisely that purpose by the Austrian sociologist Wieser. In *Die Vorbilder und die Führer*, Scheler wrote: "The law of leadership (*Führerschaft*) and following, or rather, the law whereby any group, whatever it might call itself—family, tribe, clan, people, nation, commune, cultural circle, class, professional association, estate, robber band gang, of thieves—falls into two parts, the minority that rules, and the large part that follows, is a natural and universal law of sociology...." Further on he says: "The group as such reveals a strong analogy to a living organism.... Each multicellular organism has vital organs of different value: there is a hierarchy of leading, dominant and subordinate, performing organs and functions."[1] Since Scheler regards the division of society into a ruling élite and a subordinate mass to be an organic law of existence, depending neither on the class structure of society nor on consequent inequality, he holds that there must be basic carriers of *permanent qualities* of representatives of the ruling hierarchy. Hence Scheler's idea that anthropological qualities fall into definite categories which he views as the motive principle of social progress and an expression of "the eternal and immutable" in man himself. "Here is a possible scheme of models, or as I would put it, archetypes: the saint, the genius, the hero, the leading mind of civilisation, the practical man."[2] Scheler holds that these models exist in life as soul models, predetermining certain forms of human behaviour valid in all times and ages. However, while attributing great importance to the hero type, Scheler in fact associates heroic qualities with the type of man produced by bourgeois society. "These are the main types of hero—the statesman, the military leader and the coloniser,"[3] he writes.

Echoes of Scheler's classification are to be found in the writings of numerous modern bourgeois philosophers and sociologists, while the idea that qualities of human nature are unchanging and immutable is a hallmark of the contemporary non-socialist consciousness and is frequently to be met with in art and literature.

This idea gives rise to an abstract view of human nature, entailing loss of contact with reality and an exaggerated

---

[1] M. Scheler, *Schriften aus dem Nachlass,* Bd. I, Bern, 1957, S. 260.
[2] Ibid., S. 268.
[3] Ibid., S. 314.

emphasis on psychological analysis. In the works of many twentieth century writers man's inner life is treated as something perfectly independent of the outside world, developing according to its own laws, reality merely serving to provide an outside impulse for the auto-development of the human spirit. This was the approach of Marcel Proust, undoubtedly one of the greatest bourgeois writers of the century. Such writers as Virginia Woolf, Gertrude Stein and Eugene O'Neill divorced psychology from the environment and social circumstances that condition it neglecting social analysis, and thereby weakening the realist element in their works. But even writers who were, on the whole, realists but failed to give due attention to social analysis of reality frequently regarded the spiritual and biological aspects of human nature as something autonomous, and substituted *biological* or *instinctual* motives for *social motives* of human actions and behaviour: Sherwood Anderson did this all the time, and William Faulkner did it very frequently. The works of these two very different writers present a fairly full, authentic picture of American provincial life, of people entirely absorbed in their own narrow interests, their family and business worries, motivated entirely by the pursuit of gain and profit, which disfigures them morally and spiritually. For Anderson this thorough, accurate presentation of the real conditions of life of American provincial philistines, callous and embittered, ruled by racial and religious prejudices, crass hypocrisy and avarice, is simply a background for the terrible personal dramas of his alienated, lonely heroes. Anderson saw his heroes for what they really were— little people with trivial passions, unsatisfied cravings, and unrealised dreams—but regarded them as persons rather than social types, as individuals revealing each in their own different way an immutable, extratemporal human essence, which is ruled by instincts, sex, passions, a sense of fear or joy, but above all fear, fear of life and the people around them. He was interested in exploring the dark crevices of human nature, supposedly free from the influence of social factors. Sex, the instinct to reproduce, repressed or fulfilled, is what motivates the actions of many of Anderson's heroes, both in his novels, like *Dark*

Laughter, and his stories in "The Triumph of the Egg", or "Winesburg, Ohio".

In Anderson's works, natural social causality often gives way to irrational, impulsive causality of psycho-physiological phenomena. The characters' actions are often unexpected and largely inexplicable, as the reader has not been prepared for them. This approach to the characters naturally affects the narrative manner, which is adapted to convey capricious changes in the characters' sentiments and emotional state, and as a result the external logic of events is often sacrificed without any inner logic acquired. Anderson is often unwilling to see a phenomenon in its entirety, complete with its causes. As a result there is little action in his short stories and their conflicts, if any, are left unresolved. The heroes tend to make their appearance in the narrative with already formed characters outwardly independent of their social background and environment. That they are products of their environment is a matter for the reader to guess, for this is masked by the author's appeal to their "eternal human" qualities. Thus, Anderson fails to make full use of the realist method, and elements of naturalism and decadence penetrate his works, to the detriment of its critical power.

Faulkner's manner is extremely original. If Stendhal compared the novel to a mirror, being carried along a highway, Faulkner's novels can be compared to a cart travelling along the dusty street of a small provincial town. Aboard the cart are several grey-haired people, local old-timers, who know everything there is to know about all the local inhabitants, know all the latest gossip and scandal, which are discussed in the local drugstore, know every single person's past, and what they are about to do before they've done it. They know what the important townsfolk are doing, what speculation is going on in cattle, grain, property and land, what plans are in the offing at the local bank. They also know all the secrets, all the heart-rending dramas, played out in the silent nights beneath the roofs of the peaceful homes, in the nearby forest, from whence an occasional shot is heard and there is one citizen less. The old-timers look around and each in turn tells all he has seen, slowly, unhurriedly and in great detail, in time with the slowly moving cart. They talk about the same event, but each in his own way, with his own little details, sometimes repeating what another has already said, but always adding something new to the account. And as they talk on about their hometown, about their district, about the nearby farms, about blacks and whites, about wealth and poverty, about good deeds and crimes, about love and misfortunes, a picture of everyday life, a routine, hard, joyless, busy life, gradually emerges from their slow, leisurely talk. A light dust from the wheels of the cart covers the faces of the narrators, a scorching sun roasts their backs; the wheels creak, and the wind carries to their nostrils the odour of ripening corn, smoke from the chimneys of the homes, and the acrid smell of horses. This is a saga of oppressive life in a stagnant rural backwater in the American Deep South.

For a long time this element held Faulkner in its grip: he gave himself up wholly to the tide providing a precise photographic copy of life's harshness and coarseness, presenting man not so much as a social being, but rather as a biological creature hostile to all others, as an unintellectual being, ignorant, uneducated, acting out of self-interest, and influenced by purely physiological factors— a mixture of neuroses, pathological abnormality, repressed or unrevealed sexual desires and pursuits. Time past and time present—landowners and metayers, tenant farmers and day-labourers, the vestiges of aristocracy, Negroes who can still remember slavery, and whites nostalgic for the old plantation days, hired labourers and provincial lawyers salesmen and local councillors, policemen and convicts, murderers and their victims, prostitutes and pimps, confidence tricksters and enterprising traders, housewives up to their eyes in domestic chores and tramps, cranks and cattle drovers, war veterans and small-town intellectuals, Ku Klux Klansmen and Left-wingers, bankers and informers, and many, many more besides, crowd the pages of his books, presenting a dense, bustling, lively and curiously gloomy panorama of life, at times realistically full-blooded, at times naturalistic, decadently weird, painfully cruel, bestial and hopeless.

An exaggerated attention to the instinctive, hidden, irrational side of human nature, moving a person to behave illogically and the extension of this to the narrative, as well as a naturalistic "copying" of emotions, account for the incoherence of many of Faulkner's works, with events presented out of order, in a highly confused manner. Faulkner's own perception of life was transferred to his works, which abound in confused inner monologues and condensed emotions of characters crazed by fear of life or death, thirsting for violence, exalted by saccharine-sweet noble emotions or pursued by the most trivial, mundane worries. Faulkner's own disorganised, chaotic outlook made for works that were equally disorganised, chaotic and not easily intelligible (viz. *Go Down, Moses* and *A Fable*). Sometimes the symbolism overcame the realistic element, as weeds strangle a wheat stalk, sucking all the live juices out of it.

Faulkner's concept of human nature determines the structure of his works. If man's inner, spiritual world cannot always be subjected to rational analysis, and man sometimes remains a closed book even to himself, then the truth of life, the real nature of relationships, events, and facts, that is, the cognizable sphere of people's practical behaviour cannot be regarded as an entity, something which has only one meaning, but is regarded as the sum of the varying views of different people. This explains why Faulkner's novels became a string of personal monologues, with the voice of the narrator woven into them (viz. the Snopes trilogy—*The Hamlet, The Town, The Mansion)*, or an investigation undertaken by the author together with the characters (as in "Absalom, Absalom!").

The realist foundations of Faulkner's works were undoubtedly somewhat shaky: nevertheless, in his best novels the realist element got the upper hand, the result being works of serious content, with important conflicts presented objectively, that is, following the true movement of life, and allowing it to determine the characters' behaviour. For a long time Faulkner wrote exclusively of the American Deep South, his native country, an influence which extended to his views and prejudices. In his later novels, however, and particularly in *The Mansion*, the main theme became the social order itself, rather than Yoknapatawpha County and its inhabitants. Faulkner evolved towards critical realism, gradually freeing himself of his decadent-naturalist view of the world. Realistic trends developed and came to the fore in his later works under the impact and pressure of the processes which in America as everywhere are gradually weakening the positions of capitalism.

There is a constant conflict in his works between decadent-naturalist tendencies and critical tendencies on the one hand and idealising ones, on the other. He attempted to counterbalance the lack of ideals, the eminent practicality, utilitarianism, and amorality of American provincial life with some positive social ideas and their carriers, since he realised that man was becoming dehumanised in the society in which he lived.

He realised the importance and nobility of Communist ideas but was unable to accept them, finding them totally alien to his own nature. He regarded Communism as a beautiful dream completely unrelated to real life, and this was his main mistake, which prevented his works from acquiring an objective historical perspective. He was completely given over to the ideas of bourgeois democracy—not to be confused with that which rules in America today and reflects the interests of the monopolies, and which Faulkner regarded with irony and suspicion. His own social ideals were deeply rooted in the past, they were that system of ideas that were defended by the Southern democrats in the mid-nineteenth century—federalists and constitutionalists like Stephens, Calhoun, and Liber, based on patriarchal relations between people, between master and worker, white and black—democrats who defended the rights of the proprietor, and thus held in esteem the personal freedom of the individual—provided he was white, and a man of property. They staunchly defended the interests of the owner classes, and were fierce critics of the overt capitalist production of the Northern states, attempting to prove that slavery, preserving the patriarchal way of life, was more humane than the factory system.

Clearly these outdated ideas were assimilated by Faulkner in a somewhat modified form, as a tradition transformed by modern conditions. But his criticism of callous greed and cupidity, as poisoning all humane, moral qualities—personified in his works by Snopes and Snopesism—is very much in the spirit of his predecessors. The heroes, who stand for the patriarchal traditions of the South (Gavin, Ratcliff, Judge) are all but sugar-coated, while all the author's anger and scorn are visited upon the carriers of "Snopesism". But Faulkner sees the essence of Snopesism as irrational, and inherent in human nature rather than deriving from objective social conditions. Basically Faulkner considered the democratic spirit of the Old South—an illusory spectre—to be the only force capable of opposing the corruptive, corrosive influence of Snopesism and the ugly, one-sided morality it engendered. In portraying people's hardships and sufferings, their joyless daily tasks, he did not believe they had it in them to change the conditions of their own existence. He likened the ordinary working folk—tenant farmers, metayers, hired labourers etc.—to moles or termites, with the reservation that if moles could burrow through the foundations of a building, and termites eat their way into it, making the building unstable, people are incapable of shaking the established order, since they possess neither the individual determination of the mole nor the collective determination of termites. His lack of belief in the creative, revolutionary potential of the masses blinded Faulkner even to the features of American life that were perceived and presented by Steinbeck in *The Grapes of Wrath* and by Erskin Caldwell. Naturally, this concept of stability and the impossibility of fundamental change in society ruled by Snopeses—except, of course, for minor internal changes and modifications within the framework of that society—prevented Faulkner from producing a synthetic picture of the real contradictions of contemporary bourgeois society and contemporary history. His works are rather like a sombre fresco, in places mercilessly truthful, in places phantasmagorial. The main thing is it is incompleted and patchy, not because the author lacked the time or patience, but because he failed to perceive the full flow of historical progress behind the movement of everyday life, and did not present those features of live history that are essential for a full-blooded, realist epic.

Faulkner diluted and transformed the realist method, but not to the extent that the realist writers of undivided bourgeois affiliations did, as a look at the works of Proust will immediately show.

Proust's epic work *A la recherche du temps perdu* is generally regarded as a literary offspring of Bergsonian philosophy. There is no doubt that Bergson had a strong influence on Proust's outlook, as indeed he did on that of many other bourgeois intellectuals. However, Proust's works were not simply a direct application of Bergson's philosophical views in literature, since the influence of philosophy on art and literature is always mediated, being passed through the prism of the artist's personal experience. The views of Proust show a great deal in common with the ideas of Bergson, but this is rather the result of a common outlook produced by similar social causes than the result of direct influence.

There are certainly similar features in the approach of Bergson to the study of the material world and the approach of Proust to the study of society. Bergson might well have been referring to Proust's creative manner when he wrote in *Matière et Mémoire*: "...Restore the link between the separate objects of your everyday experience; then dissolve the static continuity of their qualities in vibrations on the spot; concentrate on these movements, ignoring the divisible space that supports them, and note only their mobility, fixing only this indivisible act by your mind; you will then have a vision of matter, that may be exhausting for your imagination, but pure and free from all that life's needs add to your perception."[1]

Bergson regarded perception as a combination of past and present, where the past never disappears but enters the present, continuing its existence there thanks to memory. This simple, and when all is said and done, rather banal idea, is to be found in Proust's novel, which is constructed on the basis of reminiscence or recollec-

---

[1] Henri Bergson, *Œuvres*, Paris, 1959, p. 343.

tion of the past, which comes to play a more vital role for the author than the actual present. Proust regarded memory, combining past and present, as an instrument reproducing the past in the present. He sees no division between them, and views the boundaries between past and present to be extremely imprecise and fluid.

Bergson termed the process by which memory unites past and present, imparting actuality to the past, and adjusting the past in the present, "duration", and was in fact substituting this speculative concept, which but imitated the actual movement of life for real development. Proust also resorted to the adjustment of the past in the present, seeing the main aim of his work in reproducing the stream of life as a stream of consciousness. In other words, Proust believed that by making a thorough study of the inner world of his hero Marcel and the other characters of his novel, by investigating and analysing their reactions to the world and describing their perception of things, he would thereby be presenting a full picture of the life of society, that is, of the life of the wealthy French bourgeoisie in the period extending from the end of the last century up to the First World War. Proust undoubtedly regarded himself as a chronicler of society life and manners. In fact, however, reality was dissolved in his novel in the individual's perception of life, and objective truth became as flexible and fluid as its reflection in the narrator's consciousness. This dissection of life into events in progress, experiences, memories, feelings and impressions, and so on, emerged from Proust's view of the individual perception of the external world as a mobile, incessant, indivisible process, in the way William James had done before him. "Consciousness ... does not appear to itself chopped up in bits," James had written in his *Psychology*, which can by rights be regarded as a pragmatist theory of knowledge. "Such words as 'chain' or 'train'," he continued, "do not describe it fitly as it presents itself in the first instance. It is nothing jointed; it flows. A 'river' or a 'stream' are the metaphors by which it is most naturally described."[1] James insisted that sensations transmit the

---

[1] William James, *Psychology*, New York, 1900, p. 159.

reality of things to the mind. "If there be such things as feelings at all, *then so* surely as relations between *objects exist* in rerum natura, *so surely, and more surely, do feelings exist to which these relations are known.* ...If we speak objectively, it is the real relations that appear revealed; if we speak subjectively, it is the stream of consciousness that matches each of them by an inward coloring of its own."[1] Proust's view was basically similar to that of James in this respect, and he concentrated on subjective illumination of life's phenomena through the stream of consciousness, thereby depriving them of their reality.

Proust did not destroy the material fabric of the world—his roman fleuve is full of authentic details of everyday life, morals, habits, interests, occupations and pastimes showing great perception and most expressively conveyed, and his characters were by no means ciphers, but had the depth and completeness of real people. Nevertheless, their mainspring, their inner essence, somehow escapes us. The characters reveal themselves as different personalities in different spheres of life, and it is extremely difficult to decide which is the real "they". Odette Swann, a vulgar harlot, appears now idealised by Swann's love for her, now as a refined society lady, now as a protagonist seeker of adventure, now as a wife and mother. Swann, too, changes according to the company he is in at a particular moment, altering from society dandy to a stodgy bourgeois. Albertine, the woman loved by the main character and narrator, Marcel, is also an enigmatic character, and many of the minor characters are extremely elusive. Even the scene of action, the landscapes and interior settings, vary constantly according to Marcel's changing perception of them.

Proust believed that by presenting his heroes in this fashion he was conveying their constant development and movement in time, and at the same time reproducing the flux of life. In point of fact in so doing he was violating the fundamental principle of realism, since such an approach to the object of portrayal presupposes the absence of a true objective essence in phenomena and events. This view was far from new or original. Nietzsche had written

---

[1] Ibid., p. 162.

long before him: "There are different kinds of eyes ... and therefore there are many truths too, and thus no truth at all." Proust, like Whitehead, for whom the world consisted of separate events in collective unity, divides the integral process of the movement of life into separate moments, whose boundaries are fixed by various discrete personal mental states. A line is viewed as a succession of dots. Duration, which is supposed to be transmitted by means of reminiscences of the past on the one hand and highly involved syntax on the other—in other words, by the very form of the narrative, adapted for the purpose of transmitting the flux of events—actually appears in the novel as a succession of separate events perceived by the narrator—and having for him equal significance, whatever their real significance and scale. The movement of life was adjusted and strengthened by the perception of the individual, whose spiritual experience was incomparably narrower than the world in which he lives. For Proust, however, it was *individual experience* that was the object of investigation and portrayal and not real life, which in fact gives birth to that experience and is inseparable from it.

Proust destroyed the epic fabric of art not only by refusing to depict the fulness of social conflicts, preferring to present the circumscribed, spiritually arid life and lax morals of the wealthy classes, but also by perceiving and treating human nature in a dualist manner. While regarding the human essence of his characters as an unknown quantity, which could not be submitted to social analysis and realistic portrayal, he at the same time considered this essence to be fixed and revealed in the one permanent and stable element there is—class-conditioned behaviour and self-perception. Proust viewed bourgeois social relations as the only possible form of human relations, and class differences as a norm. This view helped to counteract his epic's hermetic insulation from the outside world and open it to the events of real life. Proust presented a detailed, enthusiastic description of the select world of wealth and aristocracy, and the inhabitants of that world, with their relationships, their views and feelings. He poured cruel irony upon those, like Bloch and the Verdurin couple, who tried to climb the social ladder into the world of high society. But at the same time he could not help showing that this world was unstable, that the social barriers were breaking down, as illustrated by the career of Odette Swann, Madame Verdurin, or Robert de Saint-Loup's marriage. This world corroded from within by gross immorality was also shaken by social events—the Dreyfus affair, and signs of the approaching imperialist war. Criticism has a place in Proust's novel, albeit of a very different kind from the social criticism of G. B. Show, Thomas Mann, Romain Rolland and other critical realists. In his latter writings, especially in *Le temps retrouvé*, Proust gradually came to the conclusion that the way of life he so cherished was seriously threatened: the high waves of social battles and cataclysms had begun to beat insistently against him too. In poeticising a moribund way of life, Proust used the old well-tried tactic employed by all champions of the bourgeois system, that is, self-criticism in the interests of self-preservation and conservation. The alienated individual, who considered himself to be the measure of all things and the hub of the universe, felt the need for a social support. It could not be otherwise, since alienation of the individual from society can only take place within society, and is especially marked in a highly-developed society. While describing the shadier aspects of the life of the social hierarchy, Proust began to extol the military and pay tribute to nationalism, showing ostentatious reverence for Robert de Saint-Loup, who dies a hero's death in battle in the name of the imperialist interests of the French bourgeoisie.

Although the social aspect of Proust's novel was over-shadowed by his preoccupation with psychology, its importance was considerable nonetheless as an example of the way the bourgeois consciousness—however refined in form and aloof from practical life it might appear to be—was beginning to practise determined self-defence in the new historical conditions that arose in capitalist society after the First World War, when its political structure was undergoing a transformation under the impact of the October Revolution and its ideas and under the influence of its inherent contradictions. The complex processes that took place in the spiritual life of the twentieth century were a reflection of equally complex processes in social life.

The far-reaching historical events and changes in our age of transition from capitalism to socialism affect the existence of every single inhabitant of our planet, taking him along in their irresistible course. All the old, outmoded institutions, ideas, views and principles are being transformed before our very eyes, and the future can be seen in the making in the workshop of history, so that the consciousness that the ideas of the old society are *obsolete* and are on the way out has become a characteristic feature of the spiritual life of our age.

As a natural result of all this, modern man is faced as never before by the need to *choose* and *define* his place in the social struggle that is under way, the ultimate sense and content of which is the socialist transformation of social relations based on private ownership. Today, nobody can live like Robinson Crusoe on a "desert island". Neither a man's outlook nor his practical activities can remain without *social supports*, as independent perception or independent action. They are bound to form a part of the complex, highly involved system of social links, dependent relationships, conflicts, interests and aims of which life is made up.

The bourgeois consciousness can no longer be integrated, clearly-defined and unassailable by doubt. As for the non-bourgeois consciousness that has not yet become socialist, the problem of its alignment with the forces that exist and conflict in society at the present time is of decisive significance. Hence its heterogeneity and instability, its inherent contradictions and inconsistencies, its illusory concepts of the world. Hence also its outward complicatedness, with a system of myths erected in an attempt to consume and dissolve reality. But behind all these illusions and figments of an alienated consciousness stands—in various forms in each individual case—a sense of the instability and vulnerability of the existing order of social relations.

One of the most widespread forms of rejection of contemporary society is criticism of it from the standpoint of a pseudo-naive individual, endowed with a "childish", spontaneous perception of the world. This kind of criticism is generally associated with a spontaneous democratic outlook when life is seen through the eyes of simple folk, as in Hašek's *Adventures of the Good Soldier Schweik* or the comedies of Charlie Chaplin. But in the bourgeois consciousness in the proper sense of the word, the sense of obsolescence and instability of existing social relations often receives a curious slant, being expressed in rejection of the technological progress of the machine age and the hectic urban life of modern civilisation, saturated with all kinds of machines.

This attitude has found expression in modern art in a taste for the primitive, a keen interest in prehistoric art forms, or the art of peoples still at the tribal stage of development who have not been seriously affected by modern civilisation. However, bourgeois artists remove this wholesome art from the living context and historical background which gives it its real power and meaning and vulgarise it by concentrating exclusively on the *formal elements*—such as laconic, formalised style, exaggeration of certain physiological features and expressiveness of nature—deprived of their original religious or cult significance. Bourgeois artists thus *primitivise* folk art that is really far from primitive, regarding it formalistically, which is only natural since the very concept of "primitive" as an artistic form and the attitude to the art and culture of the non-European peoples as something *exotic and savage* arose out of a primitive and oversimplified understanding of the conflicts of contemporary life and the ways of their solution.

Primitivised art was incapable of generalising, let alone synthesising, life with its real contradictions and of conveying its real complexity. Primitivism as an artistic movement (whatever name it was given—Dadaism, Expressionism, Surrealism, Cubism, etc.) was a symptom of the decadence of modern bourgeois culture. It merely served to confirm that the contemporary bourgeois consciousness is lagging behind the development of life and is less and less capable of grasping its determinant features.

The attitude to urbanisation, mechanisation and technical progress was incomparably more complex in content and social mood in literature than in the fine arts or music, although the latter was also affected by the tendency for primitivisation. Study of the effects of the urbanisation on man's personal and social life and observation of the contradictions accompanying material and technological progress inevitably prompted in a writer an urgency to grapple with all the problems connected with the subsequent development of capitalism, with the objective course of modern *social progress.*

Even before the First World War, Joseph Conrade described the colourful, scintillating world of the South Seas—tranquil lagoons glowing red in the light of the setting sun, luxuriant coral islands, dozing to the eternal murmur of the surf—a fresh, outdoor unspoiled world—as the only refuge for man languishing in the civilisation of cities and machines, carrying in his soul, like a curse, the evils, the views and habits, the hopes and disappointments it engendered. Conrade and his heroes—for all that they were undoubtedly strong-willed people—no longer believed in the viability of the society they had left, setting out for the sea. But the world in which they sought refuge was very different from their own idea of it. Conrade realised that the life he presented, in the exotic form he so admired, would soon be a thing of the past. Light sailing boats were being replaced by motor vessels, and the bold, adventurous individuals forging their own happiness at their own risk were giving way to the cynical agents reeking of blood and whisky and representing faceless, merciless concerns and trading companies. Conrade's contrasting of the rugged beauty of pure, unadulterated passions, a virile, healthy spirit and integrity with the ever more complicated life of civilised society with its mounting pressures did not solve any social conflicts but merely revealed the writer's disillusionment with the results of social development that brought alienation, sowed distrust among people, and cast everyone into a solitary cell of suffering.

The tragic note we find so often occurring in Conrade's works was by no means a feature of all the bourgeois realists and was wholly alien, for example, to his younger contemporary G. H. Chesterton. Chesterton's heroes have none of the psychological complexity or spiritual fragility and inner drama of Conrade's characters. Nor do we find in Chesterton's works any of Conrade's psychological realism. For all his inclination towards the grotesque and the paradoxical, Chesterton was a traditionalist as regards form. His works have none of Conrade's free, loose composition, with sudden changes in pace and departures from chronological sequence. Chesterton was a blatant optimist. Nevertheless, the conflicts in his works were based on the same rejection of modern urban civilisation. His favourite heroes, artificially simple-hearted and naive, like Father Brown and Innocent Smith, strive desperately to understand the confused world around them hoping to catch a glimpse of a colourful, exciting world they hope is lurking somewhere behind the façade of everyday humdrum existence. Chesterton and his heroes longed to inspire energy into anaemic feelings, plans and desires of modern man and cursed society for levelling and impoverishing the human personality. However, Chesterton went no further in his defence of the personality than routine radicalism and really did no more than to revive the philanthropical traditions of Toryism, whose most noteworthy representative in the nineteenth century was Carlyle. Chesterton's alternative to mechanical progress was a romantic version of the Olde Englande of the guilds (*The Napoleon of Notting Hill*, *The Return of Don Quixote*, etc.). In practice his vociferous radicalism proved extremely mild and somewhat conservative, since, like his hero Innocent Smith *(Man Alive)* he merely "disregarded the conventions but kept the commandments". Conrade showed how technological progress ravaged the human spirit. Chesterton—and this was symptomatic of the bourgeois outlook in general—was opposed to it on the grounds that it involved the strengthening of the working class, and thus increased the danger of revolution. He still hoped that it might be possible to turn revolution into a joke *(The Man Who Was Thursday)*, hoped, in other words, to dilute the revolutionary sentiments of the masses with bourgeois liberalism. After the October Revolution, however, he was forced to abandon this consoling illusion, and during the thirties sought refuge in other illusions, flirting with the forces of political reaction. By appealing for a return to the "good old days", he was revealing the weakness of his own outlook, his inability to grasp the meaning and content of historical changes, and opened the door for the penetration of non-realist fantastic elements into his writings which distorted reality.

The social views reflected in Chesterton's works—the appeal for a return to the supposedly happy and simple life of the Middle Ages—however paradoxical, were by no means so unusual as one might imagine. Many bourgeois ideologists today have come to doubt the very concept of progress and are incapable of perceiving and understanding the major tendencies of modern historical development. They try to reduce the real picture of the contradictions of social development and the real complexity of social conflicts to a few primitive principles that suit them.

Such *gross simplification* of real conflicts was also characteristic of early twentieth century bourgeois realism, which had begun to depart from social analysis.

Realism—and in this lies its superiority to other artistic methods—is capable of perceiving and reproducing the real complexity and full content of life in its free and natural development. But bourgeois realists of early twentieth century were wont to *schematise* life.

A simplified understanding of social contradictions led and continues to lead bourgeois realists to a one-sided view of human nature. They tend to *animalise* man; most typical of them, the English writer D. H. Lawrence, underwent an evolution in this direction. Lawrence began as an artist with an extremely keen perception of real life, fully familiar with the monotonous existence and joyless labour of simple working folk, with their small joys and big sorrows. He described the collapse of the foundations of English country life under the relentless pressure of the expanding industrial towns and machine civilisation, the decline of the old traditions, which he sincerely regretted, and the gradual levelling and impoverishment of the human personality this process entailed. His characters are always presented in close, if not always perceived, relationship with their social environment. In his later works written in the late twenties, however, he made a clear attempt to detach his characters from their environment, and began to treat the social factors underlying human relations as being of minor importance, placing his characters at the mercy of passions and instincts, and above all the sexual instinct. The psychological approach so characteristic of his earlier works, like *Sons and Lovers* or *The Rainbow* gives way to analysis of instinctual motives, and subtle depiction of love as an emotion is replaced by depiction of sexual sensations. True, Lawrence denied all the criticism of his works as being excessively erotic. He contended that his novels were not sexy but phallic. Sexuality, he went on to explain, is something that comes from the mind, producing mental reactions, whereas phallic reality, on the contrary, is valid in itself and full of warmth.

"Phallic reality" screened for Lawrence, and indeed for many other writers, genuine live reality with its irreconcilable antagonisms and fierce conflicts, which Lawrence was intent on ignoring. Lawrence would see twentieth century man as wholly divorced from the world of people, abandoned entirely to body instincts, standing face to face with the universe, the flesh and nature, rejecting the burden of civilisation and all social ties and obligations.

Unlike the Freudians, who considered human nature to be essentially sick and neuropathical, Lawrence regarded and presented man as a healthy animal, principally engaged in satisfying his sexual appetites. But Lawrence's illusion of the individual apparently free and independent of society—an illusion born of alienation—could not remain a "pure" idea, and with time acquired a marked social colouring. In *The Plumed Serpent*, set in exotic Mexico, the sexual feelings of the heroes are complicated by the *thirst for power*, and animalisation of human nature inevitably leads, for it could not be otherwise, to the glorification of strong personalities capable of driving and leading the human herd.

Individualism Lawrence so frankly extolled revealed kinship with the political reaction that, in the twenties, was beginning to play a prominent role in the capitalist countries. Lawrence's praise of individualism, on the surface completely apolitical, in fact linked his work to the burning political issues of the day. As for the "phallic" principle which Lawrence regarded as the motive force of human actions, it simply led to impoverishment of the picture of the world to be found in his works and to gross vulgarisation of human nature.

In reducing all the numerous spiritual and intellectual aspects of the human personality to a handful of basic instincts, Lawrence shut the door to himself for conveying a full picture of reality. He substituted a primitive diagramme for the world in all its variety and complexity, and resorted to symbolism and heavy rhetoric in his attempt to present the secrets of the life of the flesh, which severely undermined the realistic structure of his works.

Lawrence's opposition of instinct to civilisation was but one of the forms in which bourgeois realists expressed their disillusionment with progress. Aldous Huxley went even further in contrasting the two, with his insistence on cultural decay, which for him, one of the most "highbrow" of writers, was tantamount to the decay of civilisation, the two being for him synonymous.

If Nietzsche, one of the master masons of the edifice of imperialist ideology, *revalued* all values, Huxley tended to devalue them. When Flaubert produced his *Dictionnaire des idées reçues,* he did not claim that it included the whole of human culture and was perfectly aware that the *Dictionnaire* was simply the wisdom of your average bourgeois. Huxley, on the other hand, regarded all culture other than that created by the "chosen few" to be simply a collection of truths and knowledge that have become compulsory maxims and are thus dead and uncreative. He divorces culture from the people, viewing it as the heritage and creation of the "chosen few", and regarding the masses with contempt and hostility.

He made a clean break with the humanitarian tradition which is based on love for one's fellow men and belief in their creative powers. He even broke with the liberal tradition, with its pity for the disinherited, relegating the working masses to the role of mute slaves in the service of a small spiritual élite. Huxley cynically rejected the need to educate the people, insisting that it is quite sufficient for them to be taught a few practical skills and habits, such as how to behave, how to work and obey. According to him, knowledge and culture are quite unnecessary to the ordinary person, since they would only serve to confuse him—in other words, to give him ideas about changing the existing order of things and achieving real freedom. Huxley was terrified by the prospect of fundamental historical changes, and in the interests of preserving the capitalist system in the century of the greatest revolution in history he rejected the expediency of the revolutionary transformation of society, insisting that political freedom (and indeed any other kind of freedom) was unattainable. Mankind as a whole cannot possibly be free: true freedom is the prerogative of a handful of persons—those who wield power and who are superior to the general mass of people by virtue of their wealth and property, and their abilities. The man in the street has no need of freedom; it is a burden to him, and he does not know what to do with it. He feels far happier under the familiar yoke of subservience. Therefore, if mankind is powerless to attain freedom and does not even require it, social progress is impossible, and the existing capitalist system of relations should and must be preserved and adjusted to the development of history—which Huxley does not dare go so far as to deny. However, the adjustment of bourgeois society to new conditions can, and indeed must, be achieved by giving more independence to chosen individuals and increasing the bondage of the masses.

Huxley warned his contemporaries of what he considered to be excessive flirting with the masses and the ideas of democracy, predicting a gloomy future for the individual personality if they persisted—its subjection to the power of the crude, ignorant crowd. Like Lawrence, he saw a danger in technological progress, but instead of rejecting machine civilisation outright, he attempted to examine and interpret the influence of social contradictions on the individual. At the height of the Great Depression, in the years when fascism was relentlessly advancing to suppress the last democratic freedoms of the Weimar Republic, at the time when the class struggle had intensified and the anti-bourgeois sentiments of the masses were mounting in the capitalist countries, Huxley, extremely perturbed at the turn events were taking, ascribed all the world's ills to technological progress and the growing activity of the masses. In *Brave New World* he drew an extremely gloomy picture of the world of the future, insisting that this was what lay in store for mankind unless it overcame what he regarded as the aberrations of historical development. Faithful to his conviction that the masses can only be happy in bondage, he presented the world of the future as a state with an extremely rigid hierarchy, that was based on American-style soulless conveyor-belt technology, and had implemented unificatory ideas, supposedly typical of Communism. Huxley was not concerned about the masses being reduced to the state of bovine happiness, as he described it in his novel, but he was concerned for the fate of the bourgeois individual, who might be deprived of his personal freedom and his privileged position.

Evaluating all the events of life, history and social struggle from the standpoint of a man with an alienated consciousness, and championing the principle of the absolute value of the individual, Huxley often directed his criticism against the progressive ideas of the age and those social forces that were undermining the foundations of the bourgeois order. His suspicion and hostility were aroused not only by the course of historical events, but also by the creative, constructive side of human nature that leads the masses forward, into the unchartered future, to the heights of scientific knowledge. With malicious satisfaction Huxley denigrated man, presenting him as lustful, stupid and spiteful creature, preferring anarchy to constructive work.

In the years leading up to the Second World War, and in the post-war years, the powerful social ferment and great historical changes he witnessed convinced Huxley that mankind would be unable to calm the forces of destruction that had been unleashed and went as far as to reject the very idea of social progress. While proposing a refuge from the storms of the age for the few in mystical self-absorption, he prophesied a disastrous future for man-kind as a whole. He held that man's inherent animal instincts cannot be curbed or changed, and that people would descend to the level of wild beasts *(Ape and Essence)*, and these instincts would eventually gain the upper hand and drag mankind backwards. Regarding the social activity of men, states and parties and all kinds of social institutions to be essentially hostile to man, their development only leading to levelling, unification, and the dehumanisation of the human personality, Huxley denied the usefulness of people's social activity and strongly attacked the idea of social progress. In *Brave New World Revisited* he presented the idea of the rational transformation of society as a pure illusion. The future, as he sees it, bodes ever greater tyranny and suppression of individual freedom. Like all bourgeois ideologists, Huxley when he uses the word "man" is referring not to the whole human race, but a tiny part of it—bourgeois man. According to him, this suppression of individual freedom would be effected with the aid of Pavlov's reflexology, through mass media, such as modern advertising. Huxley regarded population growth as another threat to individualism. Thus Huxley's ideological evolution has described a full circle, from scepticism to out and out nihilism and capitulation to reaction, since he refused to recognise the existence of any forces capable of opposing and breaking it.

Huxley's prose has always been full of irony—irony of a very different brand from that benevolent, generous irony that spiced the prose of Anatole France, or the irony of scathing social criticism characteristic of the great satirists Swift and Shchedrin or again from the irony used by the German romantics to soften the conflicts and contradictions of life. Huxley's irony was the product of a weary civilisation, and had as its target everything that is noble and fine in life, human nature and culture: in the words of the Russian poet Nekrasov, it is the irony of "those who are moribund without ever having lived". Imbued with senile coldness it mocked human feelings, deprived people of hope in the future, and concentrated on defending the lonely individual who rejects the principles of humanism, despises morality, and denies knowledge, progress and freedom. The only small comfort that this lonely individual was offered was a kind of mystical retreat from the world which was as pathetically ineffective as a means of combating the progress of world history with its inexorable advance towards new forms of social relations as an attempt to melt the Antarctic with a match. Huxley's consciousness reflected the most typical features of modern decadence, and although in his earlier works he employed a realist manner of writing, ridiculing the non-realist trends that were then fashionable, in his latter years he abandoned even that insipid realism he had adhered to in his youth. His heroes lost all semblance of real flesh and blood characters and became ciphers, embodying ideas. Their feelings became arid and were replaced with a collection of rational motives and impulses, and their spiritual and intellectual content was reduced to sterile, bookish erudition. Sententiousness, didactics and abstraction gain the upper hand in his works, and his talent is no longer able to control them. Overburdened with bookish knowledge, afraid of reality, and rejecting all ties with other people, he sinks deeper and deeper into the mire of cold nihilism.

The contemporary bourgeois consciousness was fully aware of the fact that the individual is not only juxtaposed to society, not only sets his own personal interests in opposition to it, but is also a part of a vast system of relationships thereby participating in the struggle between heterogeneous interests of a social, suprapersonal nature. It was impossible to ignore the existence of various trends towards unity, the concentration of economic, political and spiritual forces in contemporary society, reflecting the process of transition from monopoly to state-monopoly capitalism. Naturally this process was perceived indirectly and obliquely. It undoubtedly underlay those systems of thought that regarded man as a self-contained individual entity but nevertheless as existing in the element of all kinds of relations with people and the world. The primary and most primitive philosophical expression of these unifying tendencies to be observed in social development was unanimism, which included the One, the personality, the individual in "universals", "forces". The unanimists, and especially Jules Romains, were wont to dissolve the "Ego" in "We", the individual in the group. For them anything at all could be treated as "We" or the "group": a crowd of factory workers on their way home from work, a company of soldiers or a group of idlers. As Jean-Paul Sartre wrote, not without malice, *"We observe an event, we take part. That is unanimism, which Romains wished to present in Vie unanime or in Vin blanc de la Villette."*[1] By substituting various kinds of group relations for class relations, the unanimists were able to treat the members of casual groups of people as sharing common interests *overriding* social interests—and indeed to reject the existence of *different social interests* in each person—and to equate the objective content of the aims pursued by the individual members of the group with the aims of the group itself. In *Vin blanc de la Villette,* Jules Romains extends the unanimity of the strikers to each individual striker. But he draws no distinction at all between this feeling and the enthusiasm, and sense of comradeship the soldier feels marching through the streets of Paris with his battalion to quell the workers. The result of this approach was to stress the transient nature of class differences and the *permanence* and *omnipotence* of those spontaneous *unifying* principles that operate in bourgeois society, and which Romains and his heroes give preference to making man a *collaborator* with these forces, which draw him into their orbit. Thus, social factors are rejected by the unanimists in favour of the concept of the unanimity of human wills as the underlying motive of human behaviour. These wills, engulfing man, are directed towards the *preservation* of existing social conditions and hostile to the class interests opposed to "unanimity".

In other words, the idea of *unanimity* was used as an instrument in the struggle against anti-bourgeois forces, as confirmed by the evolution of Romains' major work, the twenty-seven volume *Les hommes de bonne volonté.* Begun as a broad portrait of life and manners, a multi-levelled panorama of society on the eve of the First World

---

[1] J.-P. Sartre, *L'être et le néant. Essai d'ontologie phénoménologique,* Paris, 1943, p. 485.

War, it gradually degenerated, along with the evolution of the political views of the author, to become a reactionary pamphlet against contemporary progressive social movements, and especially Communism. It was not only his reactionary views that prevented Romains from creating a synthetic picture of life, but also the artistic means of depicting people and society that he evolved under the influence of these views.

If groups are indifferent to the personal interests of the individuals that compose them, these heterogeneous interests being masked by "unanimity", it is logical that there should be no main hero as the ideological and spiritual centre of a work. "The need to relate everything to a central figure is linked with a perception of the world centred on the individual, and which it would be more correct to call not individualistic but 'individuocentric', just as there once existed the geocentric system of the universe", Romains wrote. "But this becomes a relic when the real subject is society itself or a large human agglomeration composed of various individual destinies, each moving independently, not knowing one another for a large part of the time and not asking whether it would be more convenient for the novelist if they all meet by chance at one particular juncture...."[1] Thus Romains proposed replacing the traditional novel built on the principle of the interaction of hero and social environment by the "roman fleuve", in which parallel subjects, characters and events develop side by side without being linked and related.

Such a view of life and history is patently false, for Romains, insisting on the casual and undetermined nature of events or historical phenomena, overlooked the real law-conditioned tendencies of the historical process and the fact that events and human actions are far more interrelated and interdependent than meets the eye. Unanimism failed and was discarded for the simple reason that it presented an oversimplified, primitive interpretation of the relationships between the individual and society. An in-

[1] Jules Romains, *Les hommes de bonne volonté*, V. I, Paris, 1932, p. XIII.

comparably more complex picture of these relationships is provided by existentialism.[1]

Despite their very different political sympathies, the existentialists have provided a pretty convincing *description* of the modern world and contemporary bourgeois society as it *appears* to the bourgeois perception. This is the secret of the success, popularity and wide acceptance of existentialism, which is to be regarded more as philosophic publicistic writings than as a coherent system of views. Hence its influence on those realist writers who portrayed life in basically existentialist terms.

Existentialist philosophising is concerned above all with the position of man in the world and society, and his relationships with life, society and other people. This does not mean that it successfully reproduces a genuine picture of social relations, since its analysis of contemporary life and human psychology and assessment of events is based exclusively on the experience of bourgeois man. Although they do not wish to remain within the bounds of anthropocentric thought, the existentialists are unable to free themselves entirely from its influence since their own views are a product of the process of alienation, and they make the individual personality their point of departure, the "One", as Jaspers puts it. But this "One" exists along with other people, for itself and for others: hence what the existentialists call "co-existence".

However, the existentialists regard existence together, in society, as the existence of socially equal units. They are thus regarding man in the abstract, thereby making an abstraction of social relations, depriving them of concrete historical content. For the existentialists self-perception is the content of co-existence.

According to the existentialists, co-existence arises only together with the concept of the "You-relationship" (Marcel), "communication" (Jaspers), or "being-with-Another" (Sartre), that is, when the One perceives the existence of Another and enters into a relationship with him. In his article "Über Bedingungen und Möglichkeiten eines

---

[1] Viewed here only in as far as it concerns literature and the subject of realism. (Author's note.)

neuen Humanismus", Jaspers tries to prove that individualism is the foundation of humanism. He writes: "Our analysis of struggle for inner freedom views man as One. Does this not make it sound as if the One is everything? On the contrary, the One ceases to exist as an individual in the course of things and remains the One only insofar as he enters into communication with other Selfs (Selbstsein) and the world."[1]

It might be thought that by communication Jaspers means those complex forms of social relations that underlie and determine all the other forms of human relationships. But no, Jaspers regards as communicative those relationships in which man reveals his potentialities. Jaspers regards as one of the most important kinds of communication—and here the influence of Scheler is clearly discernible—*leadership and service*, including such highly different forms of relationships as subjection and responsibility, fidelity and kindness. In other words, Jaspers presupposes social inequality in this kind of communication a priori, viewing an historically transient phenomenon as eternal. Other kinds of communication are *communicability*, being the basis and prerequisite for the possibility of human relationships, *discussion*, promoting greater mutual understanding, and *political relations*, to which, however, he ascribed a secondary importance, insisting on the fallacy that the One is independent from politics.

Sartre also extracts man from the element of social relations in his philosophical works. In *L'être et le néant*, whose basic propositions Sartre has never abandoned, he described the kinds of relationships that exist in the world as he sees it. They do not differ on matters of fundamental principle from those of Jaspers.

According to Sartre, the One is separated from Another or connected with him above all by virtue of his *views*, a concept with the significance of a category. *To view and be viewed* means to perceive oneself as an object for Another, or more precisely rather consider Another as an object for oneself. The knowledge that I am not Another

---

[1] Karl Jaspers, *Rechenschaft und Ausblick*, München, 1951, S. 292.

comes from the body which comprises what may be called "my world". Relationship between "my world" and Another is also effected through *language, love, masochism, sadism, indifference, desire and hatred*. It is these forms of relationship that Sartre regards as determinant. Existentialism replaces social aim or interest—the real motive force underlying human activity—with the concept of *project*, which includes a person's possibilities deprived however of concrete social content. As true children of the twentieth century, the existentialists do not reject technological progress. "...Technology is the destiny of our century,"[1] Heidegger said. However, to prevent the bourgeois consciousness from wallowing in narrow practicality and to ensure its *development*, they campaigned for the spiritualisation of technology with art—the most typical example being Heidegger's treatise "Wozu Dichter?" Nevertheless, their concept of man is pessimistic and calls for stoicism.

The existentialists argue the need for stoicism on the grounds that man exists in the face of death. This is not a new discovery, and throughout his history man has had the courage to ceaselessly create and make use of the available benefits of life, although perfectly aware that he must one day die. For the existentialists however, this knowledge that man stands face to face with death (nothingness), and that he bears nothingness within him, gives rise to the idea of the absurdity of life based on fear and anxiety. They are only concerned with the freedom of the One, and remain indifferent to the fundamental matter of how this freedom will be achieved. One gets a vague idea that they incline towards bourgeois democracy—even Heidegger and Jaspers in his later years, who were at one time reconciled to fascism.

The gloomy nature of existentialism, its tendency to separate "purely human" emotions and mental states from their underlying social motives, the view of man as a creature cast into an abyss of fear, anxiety and anguish, and the substitution of "purely human" ties for social rela-

---

[1] Martin Heidegger, *Vorträge und Aufsätze*. Günther Neske Pfullingen, 1954, S. 33.

tions—all reflect a tendency that is current not only in philosophy but also in contemporary art and literature.

Despite its claim to be a "new humanism", existentialism is in fact far removed from the real genuine humanitarian searchings and aspirations of our age. In his treatise *Über Bedingungen und Möglichkeiten eines neuen Humanismus,* Jaspers frankly admitted: "Humanism is not the final end. It merely creates the spiritual space where each and every man can and must struggle for his freedom."[1] Thus, only the activities of the individual directed towards the satisfaction of his own personal interests are recognised, since the struggle for *personal freedom* alone renders impossible the struggle for the creation of a harmonious system of social relations in which a person, retaining and enriching his own individuality, would not feel a need to defend his freedom from society.

The existentialist interpretation of freedom, combining a strange form of fatalism with patent voluntarism, inevitably destroys historicist thought. Heidegger says that "freedom is the sphere of fate", and this idea is natural for existentialism, since the alienated consciousness constantly feels unfree. At the same time freedom is regarded as personal self-will, since the individual is opposed to the world, to the whole sum of social and economic forces, and not dependent on it. The logical deduction from such a self-awareness is Sartre's proposition that man is *condemned to be free.*

The existentialists inevitably link the problem of choice with the concept of freedom, treating it, however, as "purely human". They hold that existence always occurs in a particular situation, and that therefore man is constantly faced with the necessity of making a choice. This is fairly obvious to anyone, and there is nothing original in the idea in itself. However, the existentialists regard the need for choice as an affirmation of an individual's willfulness. They divide situations into those that can be resolved and what they call "frontier situations" (*Grenzsituationen*). Historical existence, where a man is aware

---

[1] K. Jaspers, *Rechenschaft und Ausblick, Reden und Aufsätze,* 1951, S. 284.

of himself as a person and *thus, through himself*, perceives time or *historicism*, is viewed as belonging to the latter category. While a man is capable to some extent of cognizing his personal existence, he is unable to cognize suprapersonal, universal features of historical existence, that is, frontier situations, and is unable to overcome them and resolve them. Thus personal experience sets the limit in cognizing historical experience.

Generally speaking, not only has existentialism been unable to provide an ideological basis for realism, but when its theses begin to dominate a work of literature they corrode a realistic view of the world, leading to schematisation, rationalising and naturalism. Above all these theses obstruct perception of the real underlying *motives* of human behaviour, and the social factors that condition them.

The colouring of real-life processes, events, human actions and social conflicts with existentialist theories is an essential feature of the works of writers, who deal with important socio-political themes, such as Sartre and Camus, Salinger and McCullers, Simone de Beauvoir and Iris Murdoch, Catherine Anne Porter and Ilse Langner, and numerous other writers who share the existentialists' views or have come under their influence to some extent. Their works are generally characterised by a certain duality in perception and presentation of reality, causing their stories to have two planes, as it were—the real and the existentialist—with the result that the social content of the contradictions of contemporary life that are treated becomes quite vague. Some of these writers hold anti-bourgeois views. However, this critical attitude to bourgeois society, strongest of all in the works of Sartre and Salinger, never amounts to total rejection of the system that condemns man to suffering and sows evil in life, since the ultimate causes of man's fear, worry and anxiety are mystified by their philosophy.

Roquentin, the hero of Sartre's early novel *La Nausée* like many of his characters, is rather a peg on which to

---

[1] M. Heidegger, *Vorträge und Aufsätze*. Günther Neske Pfullingen, 1954, S. 33.

hang ideas than a real person of flesh and blood. Roquentin finds himself at variance with his normal routine life, for reasons of which he himself is only vaguely aware, after being suddenly gripped by a strange sense of nausea and repugnance for "existence with others". Although one may agree with him that the sated and sordid world of "others" he is referring to is indeed rather repugnant, he is surely wrong in feeling this way about life as a whole. Roquentin's feeling leads him to decide that the existence to which he is "abandoned" is absurd. The novel gradually degenerates into an existentialist treatise, examining the behaviour of a man in the situation of "the absurd", and the author concentrates on the description of his hero's feelings, which are as uninteresting as they are insignificant.

Sartre's three-volume *Les chemins de la liberté* represents another attempt to study human self-perception and the various possibilities of "choice", this time in the setting of French life on the eve of the Second World War. The hero is seeking *"inner"* freedom, in the existentialist sense of the word, that is, *"the necessity of choice"* to which man is condemned, to define himself in different situations. Mathieu is trying to defend his right to personal freedom, and therefore rejects participation in the political struggle of his time, considering it futile and pointless—this applying equally to the struggle against fascism and the war waged by the ruling classes. He does not wish to join the Communists, since he believes that by joining the Party he will be forced to renounce his personal freedom. And in the name of this same "personal freedom" he breaks with his mistress and remains alone.

Sartre treats the relationships between his hero and the other characters in the novel from the existentialist point of view, and devotes a great deal of space to the description of sexual relationships that are not without a pathological tinge. But it is not only love relationships that link the characters of the novel. Since the absolute freedom towards which Mathieu aspires according to the existentialist view is impossible, he is condemned to "existence with others". Practically speaking, this meant that war drew his "existence" too into its orbit. Sartre shows the various relationships with other people in which his hero finds himself on becoming a soldier in the army: friendship, hatred, fear, subordination, command and so on. The people, including the soldiers, are presented as a collection of "existences" crushed by fear of the future and therefore giving way to their instincts. Sartre's existentialist views prevented him from perceiving the *heterogeneity* of the sentiments of the masses and the different currents that flow in the popular sea, the existence among them of truly progressive elements. Thus, the Communist Brunet is presented as Mathieu's constant counterpart and opponent. Brunet is shown to be remarkably purposeful, hard and devoid of emotions, isolated from the masses by whose name he always swears. His convictions for him are like a fortress in which he takes refuge from the complexities of life.

Les chemins de la liberté is a collection of incidents and situations loosely strung together, and their motion in time and space gives only a pale imitation of the real motion of life, since their real causes are ignored. The epic principle of a novel is destroyed, since the objective theme—the people's struggle against fascism—is replaced by the searchings of isolated individuals involved in the system of existentialist relationships with the world for their own *personal* paths to absolute freedom. While Mathieu's path ends in true existentialist fashion—although not believing in the ultimate aims of the liberation struggle he dies in a hopeless battle against the nazis, thereby affirming his inner Self, or in existentialist terms, finding himself in a frontier situation he defines his existence in death—the socio-historical situation presented in the novel remains incomplete, for Sartre did not finish the planned cycle (writing only the first three parts— *L'age de raison, Le Sursis, La mort dans l'âme*). The novel is a novel of moods, full of the symbolism that is so characteristic of existentialist writings. Sometimes this symbolism is very straightforward, as in the novels of the American authoress Carson McCullers, who for the purpose of demonstrating the eternal loneliness of man and the complex, painful tangle of human relationships, makes her characters either spiritually sick or physically handicapped. Sometimes, however, existentialist allegory is laid on as a gigantic complex structure, as in K. Anne Porter's *Ship of Fools*, where the voyage from South America to Europe of a ship significantly called *Faith* symbolises the advance of human society towards the Second World War and the relations between the passengers the relations between people at that time, people consumed by national hatred, mutual hostility, competition, antipathy and so on.

Symbolism is not necessarily incompatible with realism: it can serve to intensify images and thus as a means of realistic characterisation. But in this case it must on no account be allowed to become an abstraction, to substitute absolute concepts for real individuality of a thing or phenomenon, its historically-defined meaning. Realist symbolism reveals this meaning in sense-object expression, and not in the form of idealised abstract universality. Thus the symbolism of Shchedrin's satire, despite the outward lack of resemblance to reality always preserved the inner truth of a phenomenon, its concrete substance and significance. The existentialists use symbolism to ascribe extra-social universality and permanence to a phenomenon, and thus dimming its historical basis. This kind of glossing over of the concrete social outlines of a phenomenon is typical of Albert Camus, whose dry, didactic prose, while ostensibly transmitting the outward texture of reality, attached to it some hidden mystic sense. This occurred not because his imagery is too far-fetched and figurative—on the contrary, it is extremely clear and almost commonplace—but because his existentialist views prevented him from gaining a proper understanding of the underlying conflicts and processes of life and seeing things in their historical perspective.

If Sartre uses the term "nausea" to convey the relationship between modern man and society, and this abstract concept prevents him from revealing the true state of society, a similar function is fulfilled in Camus' works by the concept of "the absurd". According to Camus, the human tragedy—the tragedy of man "in general", of the "One"—consists in the absurdity of life. The tragic absurdity of existence arises not from the fact that man exists in the face of death, but because he lives amid chaos, irrationality and injustice, *aware* of the absurdity of this situation and unable to achieve the *clarity* necessary to escape from this irrational state of affairs. Man has no hope of changing the absurdity of his existence and this gives him the right to freedom, the right to revolt against moral dogmas. If we remove the philosophical coating from Camus' reasoning, we can immediately see the social origins of his metaphysics of the absurd and his defence of individual anarchy. As a radical Camus opposed political reaction and fascism, but as a writer and thinker he was spiritually crushed by the historical events of our grandiose and harsh age—its revolutions, wars, fascist terror, the defeatism of the ruling classes—its countless conflicts and multifarious disasters. He was only conscious of the dramatic and dark side of the modern age that has brought people so much suffering, and refused to recognise that the positive creative forces of reason and historical progress are capable of changing, and indeed are already changing, the structure of the world we live in. Camus rejected any view of the prospects of social development but the one deriving from the situation of the absurd, and rejected above all the prospect of a Communist future for mankind. Hence the profound pessimism of his works. Any appeals for action they may contain were fruitless, since he regarded human actions as taking place entirely in the situation of the absurd, in other words, a social situation that was not subject to any change. Camus' man, remaining within the framework of what already exists, is condemned to futile action, like that of Sisyphus, who in the Underworld was condemned to roll uphill a huge stone that always toppled back again. Unable to perceive the real processes going on in life, and, like all the existentialists, substituting analysis of various "relationships" of fear, despair, enmity, duty, culpability, subordination, and so on, that arise between people in the situation of the absurd for proper analytical investigation of life, Camus announced: "My generation knows that it will not transform the world." His major novel, *La peste*, was devoted to demonstrating the futility of all man's attempts to resolve this inescapability of absurd situation.

The outbreak of plague in an Algerian town symbolises above all the rise of fascism and totalitarianism, crushing individual freedom. The characters—both those like Doctor Rieux, the clerk Grand, the social worker Tarrou and their helpers who try to combat the plague, and those who are the plague's accessories or indecisive people unwilling to struggle against it—reflect the various political forces and sentiments of the time of anti-fascist struggle. There are also parallels between the actual course of the struggle against the plague and the real events of these years. At the same time, the symbolism is meant to be much wider than this. The plague is an inscrutable, inhuman evil, which man is condemned to face throughout his existence, being forced *to act to defend himself* from it, which involves recognition of others. Camus completely ignores the concrete historical motives that lead people to struggle against evil, treating evil purely as an abstraction. Thus the concrete motives of the anti-fascist struggle become metaphysical in his novel. Evil comes and passes away again. Like the tides, it advances and recedes, but it is indestructible, for its bacilli live in people themselves. The plague passes, but neither Camus nor his heroes believe that it has gone for good, that its forces, the forces of social evil, will ever be defeated once and for all.

In the works of Camus, as of other existentialists, contemporary bourgeois realism demonstrates its impotence in the face of the real complexities of life, its inability to understand the real facts and prospects of social development. This departure from social analysis, the major, determining feature of the realist method, and its replacement with symbolical metaphysics, are characteristic features of contemporary bourgeois realism.

Many bourgeois writers are aware of a decline in the creative possibilities of this method, but seek to restore its former power not by deepening social analysis, but by experiments in form that merely serve to hasten the decline and disintegration of the bourgeois realist method.

One such attempt is represented by the so-called "new novel" school, essentially an offshoot of existentialism. Its members energetically reject this connection, for unlike the existentialists they retain faith in reason. However, their "reason" remains an abstraction, since they are far from accepting historical reason, far, that is, from understanding the objective tendencies of the historical process. It is thus more accurate to regard them as a current in the existentialist stream. They make extensive use of existentialist concepts, especially ones like "view", "you", and so on. The role of "view" is especially important in Robbe-Grillet's novels *Le voyeur* and *La Jalousie,* where the *event*—a crime in the former, a double-cross in the latter—are presented to the reader not through action but through a lateral "view", a subjective assessment of what happens. The concept of "presence" is equally important for them. As in Sartre's *Nausea,* things and people (likened to things), reveal in their novels their "presence", suppressing the characters' personalities and outlooks. As the result Robbe-Grillet's novels, for example, rather resemble price lists or registers, spiced with a semi-detective plot.

The "new novel" writers consider that modern society has entered an "age of suspicion" (the title of a novel by Nathalie Sarraute) due to a growing divorce between the form and substance of human relations, between the form and substance of social institutions and morality, between word and deed. Society is not what it pretends to be: it is utterly false and phoney. This deduction that gives a critical flavour to the works of "new novel" writers means that they recognise the obsolescence of the bourgeois social order, but this does not make them critical realists, since they reject the fundamental principle of the realist method—the portrayal of types. Their "characters" are deprived of individuality and personality, the essential basis for presenting the typical; they are but abstract ciphers.

The portrayal of social types is a sine qua non of realism. The members of this school, however, whose thinking is patently non-historicist, abandon analytic portrayal of the real relations between the individual and society and between people within society, rejecting the need for "characters" as an aesthetico-cognitive category in the novel. They ignore real human ties and examine not genuine social relations but their surrogate, just as the existentialists do. They thus substitute for *social analysis* the *description* of things (Robbe-Grillet), of insignificant emotions (Nathalie Sarraute), of changes in a character's mental state in the process of self-perception and self-discovery (Butor), and so on. Like the naturalists, they break up the process of life into static elements and try to overcome the stationary nature of their own vision of the world through an imitation of movement, that is, by constantly altering the angle of vision of the action, shuffling events around in time, using interminable inner monologues to reproduce the stream of consciousness of their characters, and frequently resorting to symbolism. They derive their technique from Joyce, Proust and Kafka, and also employ certain devices from Faulkner. Their works fail to reveal the real contradictions of contemporary life, for the simple reason that their limited understanding of the nature of human relationships does not permit them to perceive the movement of history.

In order to grasp the true underlying causes of historical events it is necessary to perceive and reveal the real forms of human and social relations, and not imaginary ones, the real forces at work in society, and not ephemeral ones. In other words, it is necessary to make a realistic study of society, a proper social analysis of events and relationships in it, and compare the facts and observations derived from such an analysis with the objective movement of history in order to infuse real-life content into a literary work.

The bourgeois realists are fast losing the ability to investigate the world objectively, with the result that the pictures of life we find in their works are but a vague approximation to reality. Bourgeois realism shows itself incapable of synthetic perception and presentation of the modern world, since it loses sight of the real content of present-day social relationships. These relations are analysed and portrayed in their movement and development by realist literature arising on another, non-bourgeois ideological basis.

The study of social relationships is a fundamental ideological and aesthetic task for literature whose aim is to understand and take cognizance of life. Realist literature, by studying these relationships in their movement and development, relating them (but not identifying them) with the social order that has conditioned this or that form of human relations, has been revealing the specific features of society, the actual characteristics of a particular social structure and of the changes that have taken place in it, are in progress or are likely to take place. Realism employs the study of human relationships as an instrument for cognizing and presenting society. At the same time, profound investigation of society, its conflicts and contradictions, provides the key to cognizance of man himself, in all the complexity of his personal and social manifestations.

Many-sided study of social ties and relationships has always been of primary importance in literature, and the greatest literary achievements of the past were all based on portrayal of the relationships between man and society. Today, in contemporary historical conditions, such study has assumed a special importance, for it alone enables literature to perceive, understand and depict the objective conditions which are already *putting an end to the state of human alienation*—that is, preparing and accomplishing, the establishment of social relations that remove the antagonism between the interests of the individual and those of society, bringing them into harmony and giving the individual every opportunity to develop his abilities and potentialities to the full.

The practical foundation for the evolution of such relations was laid by the October Revolution and the subsequent process of building socialist society in the USSR. But the bourgeois world, too, has already reached a level of development where, as Lenin pointed out, state monopoly capitalism means full *material preparation* for socialism. The general crisis of capitalism has produced fundamental changes *in the spiritual sphere, in mankind's intellectual life.* Today we are witnessing the establishment of a *new human self-awareness,* free from the illusions and attitudes engendered by the old society, and communist in nature and character, accompanied by resolute *criticism and reassessment* of all the social views produced by capitalism.

The transformation of the world is a reality of our age, and as such no longer remains a secret to the bourgeois consciousness. The defenders of the moribund system of capitalism are taking all kinds of measures to try and protect the pillars of private ownership relations from the great tide of historical change that is threatening to sweep them away. While the more aggressive and ignorant part of the bourgeoisie are placing their hopes in force and thermonuclear weapons as a means of halting the advance of history, bourgeois and social-reformist theorists recognise the inevitability of change and are seeking ways and means of containing the process of social change within the framework of the existing system of social relations, and thus perpetuating this system. Hence the numerous formulas of social reform, plans for reorganisation of administration such as the "New Frontiers" policy of the late John Kennedy, or the "Great Society" concept proposed by US ex-president Lyndon Johnson. Hence the attempts to introduce limited planning into capitalist economy characteristic of Gaullism, for example, and all the current ideas of technocracy, partial nationalisation and so on and so forth.

Some eager minds—H. G. Wells, for example, in his later works such as *Phoenix* and *You Can't Be Too Careful*—have insisted that the world revolution had already taken place and modern science, communications, mass media and transport have transformed mankind into a great universal family. True, there remained a few outstanding matters to be seen to—such as the abolition of class and national discord, the causes of war, social inequality and so on—but Wells considered that such minor details could easily be taken care of by technocratic administration. The more practically-minded ideologists of big business place their hopes in "people's capitalism", trying to corrupt the class consciousness of the proletariat by inculcating private ownership habits into the workers, making them "co-owners" of the means of production, shareholders and participants in the share-out of dividends. Naturally the share and role of small shareholders working in production is quite negligible and exerts no influence at all on the course of production. However, the theory of "people's capitalism" sows the illusion that class conflict is on the wane in contemporary capitalist society, and the fallacy that socialism can be grafted on the capitalist system.

Similar ideas are propagated and introduced in practice by the so-called "public relations" system, where the aim is to abolish social conflicts arising between workers and employers in capitalist concerns. Arising at the time when the automation of production is beginning to fundamentally alter the occupational structure of the working class, when the new system of production organisation requires a larger number of skilled workers, when the intense strike struggle of the working people is forcing the employers to make certain concessions, "public relations" are called upon to give the workers a personal interest in the success of production. The idea is that a worker who understands the aims of production, a worker who is treated politely, will have no grounds for conflict with his employers so that relations between employers and employees can be based not on hostility and enmity, but on reasonable mutual concessions, a kind of ideological coexistence.

But the supporters of this system carefully conceal the simple but irrefutable fact that however well he may understand the aims and tasks of production, a worker remains the object of exploitation, a source of profit for the employer. "Public relations" system glosses over the contradictions between labour and capital but is no more able to prevent the exacerbation of the class struggle than any other attempts to soften and take the sting out of the social conflicts of contemporary bourgeois society.

The same vain purpose was pursued by the American sociologist Galbraith with his theory allotting the capitalist state the role of arbiter and regulator of the antagonistic interests of the monopolies and the working class in his *American Capitalism. The Concept of Countervailing*

Power, which was very much to the taste of big business circles. The same aim was pursued with the idea of the "integrated society" expounded by the late Pitirim Sorokin, based on the totally unhistorical thesis of the possibility of the ideological and economic merging of capitalism and socialism to form a future social order "integrating" features of the two systems that are currently in a state of conflict and competition.

Such theories have various origins: some of them derive from illusions and unwarranted hopes of the possibility of "cheating" the logic of history, and halting its irreversible objective course, its development from capitalist to socialist relations. Others represent a patent demagogical attempt to distort reality and deceive the masses, instilling in them views and habits that are alien to them. But whatever the origins of such theories, they invariably reveal the fact that contemporary bourgeois thought is incapable of grasping the sum total of the contradictions of the modern world and correctly assessing the prospects of the historical conflict between the moribund capitalist system and the socialist system that is steadily affirming itself.

Only scientific communism, Leninism, has proved able to define and analyse the real scale and complexity of the historical process of the transition from one social system to another now in progress. Moreover, it in itself is a great force by means of which the modern world is being transformed. The whole spiritual life of mankind today is subject to its influence. It provides the key to perceiving the meaning, nature and characteristic features of the modern age, to understanding its conflicts and contradictions, to determining the trends, direction and major purpose of the historical process. It also provides the ideological basis for the new literature of our age, socialist realism, which represents a qualitatively new stage in the development of the realist method.

But scientific communism, being a universal philosophical doctrine, merely provides literature with the general ideological principles which the writer has to apply to reality, to the course of life with its changes and inherent conflicts, *in each individual case*, each time *perceiving* and investigating new features that appear in the constant flux and development of life, generalising what he has perceived through *thought in images.* Such generalisation is always an *indivisible creative act,* where cognition and expression are inseparable. It is on no account mechanical application of sociological concepts on a particular and unique, live novel phenomenon. The ability to perceive the deep connections between human desires, feelings, passions and interests and the social factors underlying man's inner world, the ability to see life from a *socialist, revolutionary standpoint,* is only possible where a writer's socialist outlook has been based on his own *personal* experience.

It is this socialist outlook that determines the creative method of the new literature, which examines and depicts the emergence of new relationships between people in the modern world as an historically determined, inevitable process of succession of essentially different social orders. Thus *conscious historicism* is the main, determining feature and sine qua non of socialist realism and its creative method.

The inevitability of the transition from capitalism to socialism is *sensed* by all the big writers of our time who have not lost touch with reality and shut themselves up in an ivory tower, blindly serving art indifferent to the world's needs. At the very beginning of the October Revolution, the poet Alexander Blok wrote: "The artist must realise that the Russia that was has gone never to return. The Europe that was has gone and will never be again... The world has entered a new era. *That* civilisation, *that* statehood, *that* religion—all are dead. They may return and exist again, but they have lost their being...."[1]

The sense that the old world is beginning to lose its *historical* being, has been penetrating the consciousness and works of writers of other countries too. As early as the mid-twenties, when many politicians and people in the world of culture had a far less clear idea of what the October Revolution involved than they do today, Thomas

---

[1] A. Blok, *Collected Works,* Moscow, 1962, Vol. 6, p. 59. (in Russ.).

Mann had the courage and perspicacity to declare: "We all feel and know that a mighty wave of change is sweeping over Europe, what is known as 'World Revolution', a radical change in our way of life, and all kinds of means are being employed to realise it—moral, scientific, economic, political, technical and artistic; this change is advancing with such speed that our children, born before the war or after it, basically live in a totally different world which remembers little of our old order. The world revolution has become an established fact. To deny it is tantamount to denying life and development; to persist in conservatism in the face of it is tantamount to voluntarily placing oneself outside life and development."[1]

Similar ideas were expressed by Theodor Dreiser, who wrote: "Russia's embarking on the path of socialism lit up in a blinding light the social inequality existing in America, so that alongside books whose only aim is to divert the reader carefully avoiding social problems, there inevitably appeared other books showing the need to change the social order."[2]

This kind of awareness, which was extremely widespread after the October Revolution, could not possibly have remained passive. It frequently became the point of departure for a movement of democratically minded writers away from *spontaneous* historicism, from intuitive understanding of the need for social change, towards *conscious historicism,* which naturally entailed a fundamental change in the realist method. Such changes in aesthetic method are natural and inevitable: they are inherent in the very essence of realism and testify to its capacity to develop, for *a method is a sum of principles of ideological and aesthetic cognizance of life and its expression in images, principles that are historically conditioned and enriched in creative practice.* If the historical basis of a method changes, then the method itself is bound to change too. It was perfectly natural that the major social

---

[1] Thomas Mann. *Zwei Festreden,* Leipzig, S. 35-36.
[2] L'Association Internationale des Ecrivains pour la Défense de la Culture. Conférence extraordinaire tenue à Paris le 25 juillet 1938, Paris, 1938, p. 18.

conflicts of our age should have found their fullest re-flection and interpretation in the work of writers wielding the method of socialist realism, since it gives the writer the maximum *opportunities* for historical, comprehensive, *synthetic* depiction of life and society, man and his rela-tions with society.

The new creative method helped the writer to free himself from illusions and misconceptions about life and society, since in presenting life as a process of develop-ment and formation, with its real conflicts affecting the destiny and interests of millions upon millions of people, he could fall back on the achievements of progressive social thought, which contributes to the transformation of the world, helping people renew social relations. Natur-ally so, since the spiritual progress of mankind is not re-ducible to the accumulation of new facts and knowledge of the world, but is essentially the elaboration by man of concepts of the Universe, society and himself that cor-respond to the truth and are not simply the product of his imagination, the creation by human reason of a true picture of reality, true in both the general and the par-ticular.

Such development towards a more perfect understand-ing of the objective content of life is characteristic of all forms of human creative activity—science, studying the various laws of natural phenomena; social thought, which has armed mankind, thanks to scientific communism, with knowledge of the laws and tendencies of historical de-velopment, and the arts to an equal degree. Naturally, progress in literature is never straightforward. But when all has been said and done, one is bound to admit that it has been advancing and becoming enriched in our age. This is understandable, for literature is a source of aes-thetic pleasure, a means of expression and satisfaction of man's aesthetic demands, and at the same time it is a great chronicler of life, a kind of vast collective memory of mankind, the repository of mankind's feelings, thoughts and hopes. Literature is improved and enriched because man's aesthetic-cognitive ability is improved and enriched.

The new historical situation, the revolutionary cata-clysms and changes that swept through the world, engendered socialist realism. The emergence of socialist realism was a response to the profound organic demands of history. The revolution brought about by socialist realism in literature and art was thus more than a revolution in aesthetics: it affected the basic, major and determining sides of the arts as an independent form of man's spiritual activity. The essence of the revolution effected by socialist art and literature consisted in the resolution of the conflicts treated in pre-socialist art and literature and then viewed as insoluble, and also in the affirmation and depiction of the new, socialist relations between people, and between the individual and society. Thus the novelty of the new creative method is not reducible to its aesthetic features or the content of the works created on its basis. Socialist realism contains a natural, non-mechanical unity of ideological and aesthetic principles, so that it is not a simple aesthetic innovation but an independent kind of artistic thinking. This unity of ideological and aesthetic principles in socialist realist literature and art derives from the unity of the system of views underlying the new method, from the conscious historicist thinking of writers subscribing to its ideological-aesthetic principles.

If the spiritual aspirations of the critical realists frequently led them to perceive and reflect—though often in an extremely indirect manner—the sentiments, views, hopes and spontaneous protest of the democratic masses who experienced the oppression of private ownership social relations, the socialist realist writer directly and openly expresses and defends the fundamental, historically progressive interests of the masses. The emergence and establishment of socialist realist literature is organically related to the determinant historical feature of the twentieth century—the growing role of the popular masses, the force underlying all the major social developments of our age.

Socialist realism is thus the art of the masses emancipating themselves or already emancipated from exploitation and risen to conscious historical activity. It is of the masses because it is revolutionary in spirit, because it considers that historical development is bound to lead to the harmonious classless society of communism. From this socio-political ideal socialist realism derives the conception of man it affirms, a conception in full accordance with the humanitarian nature of socialism. This conception is most completely and clearly revealed and realised in Soviet literature, which is the most mature and developed product of socialist realism.

Marx pointed out that man is a dual being in antagonistic class society: he is at once a social being and a private being, a private man, whose interests and demands do not correspond with, but are opposed to, the interests of society. "Where the political state has reached its truly developed form," he wrote, "man not only in his thoughts, in his consciousness, but *in reality, in life,* leads a dual life, heavenly and earthly, a life *in a political community* in which he recognises himself to be a *social being,* and a life *in a civic society* in which he acts as a private person, regarding others as a means, reducing himself to the role of a means and becoming the plaything of alien forces."[1] As a result, he finds himself in conflict with his fellows and with society as a whole, suffering from the disharmony of life and the cruelty and chaos of human relations.

This conflict between the individual and society was depicted with remarkable penetration and artistic expressiveness in the works of critical realism. Socialist realist literature has dealt with a different social process—the abolition in the course of the practical work of building classless socialist society of the gap between the personal and the societal aspects of man, between his personal individual interests and the interests of society as a whole, the people as a whole. The main theme of critical realism was the depiction of the discrepancy between the demands and aspirations of the individual and the social conditions in which he exists, which often led to his moral downfall or physical death. Socialist realism has been reflecting the process of creation of more favourable conditions for the development of the individual, since the main goal of communism is the *welfare of each person.*

The motive force of events in critical realist literature was man struggling for his existence, his dignity and his

---

[1] K. Marx, F. Engels, *Werke,* Bd. 1, S. 354-55.

ideals. In socialist realism, for the first time in history, the masses appeared as the force engendering events. Revolutionary action, the movement of the masses, became the central themes of Soviet literature in its early days when the new art and the new artistic method was in a process of emergence and development. The heroes of *The Iron Flood* by Serafimovich, Fadeyev's *The Rout* and Sholokhov's *And Quiet Flows the Don* were not simply individual representatives of the struggling masses: the hero of such works were the people themselves, the masses in revolt, defending new social ideals and new relations. For the first time in the history of world literature, the masses were presented not as a passive element on the margin of events, within which the lone individual acts, but as an independent force possessed of a single united will combining separate wills, a single collective interest, a force rising in the process of revolutionary activity to a higher level of social self-awareness.

The real hero of *The Iron Flood* is the column of the Taman Army led by Kozhukh—an initially disorganised, chaotic, undisciplined crowd of people, which is gradually transformed in the course of fierce struggle, into a close-knit entity inspired by a common will and ideal. They move along, tortured by hunger, thirst and scorching heat, under sultry skies, between mountains clad in an impenetrable tangle of thorny bush and the sea beating against the rocky shore, to a continual hubbub of cries of joy and sorrow, pain, suffering and despair, to the creaking of cart wheels and the neighing of exhausted horses, the crying of children and the wailing of women, storming pass after pass amid a hail of machine-gun bullets and heavy field-gun fire, sweeping aside Cossack covering detachments and overcoming White Guard regiments. Serafimovich—and this is a feature of the new method—studies and depicts with scrupulous fidelity to historical truth every slightest oscillation in the sentiments of his collective hero, the rise and fall of its energies, the complex psychological changes that take place in it, the emergence and strengthening in it of the new, *socialist* self-awareness, which helps it to overcome the habits and prejudices that have become ingrained in it over the centuries. This new self-awareness born in social struggle frees the rank and file participants in the Taman campaign—poor peasants, day labourers and newcomers from non-Cossack areas—of their views and illusions engendered by the old society they had lived in. The new self-awareness is the product of the great aim and purpose that arose before them, the task of liberation from all the fetters of the past, the fetters of society based on private ownership. They translate the *possibility* of a new, more just life, corresponding to the interests and needs of the masses into a *reality*. They are fashioning history with their own hands, and the gradual understanding of this indisputable fact enables them to develop a qualitatively new criterion for evaluating the past and perceiving the sources of the injustice they constantly came up against throughout their former lives, and accept without reservations, as the only one possible, the prospect of a new life worthy of man that the triumph of Soviet power brings them. They rise to conscious creative historical activity, and history loses the aura of mystery the bourgeois consciousness and bourgeois ideology impart to it, and appears to them in its concrete, practical form. They are naturally still unable to give free, clear expression to their own self-awareness, for the burden of the past—ignorance and illiteracy—still weighs heavy upon them. But they have glimpsed the possibility of understanding and transforming life, changing its course, altering its basis, and this is a guarantee of and a foundation for the further spiritual growth of the masses, of their inevitable rise to the heights of world culture.

Only a writer with a socialist outlook, depicting the life and struggle of the popular masses and guided by the socialist realist method could see the masses in this light. The people were the real hero of many other works besides *The Iron Flood*. The real hero of *The Rout* is neither Metelitsa, nor Morozka, nor even Levinson, but the *unit* to which they all belong, sharing a common destiny, sharing dangers, misfortunes and hopes. The portrayal of the people as the major force of history is a characteristic feature of socialist realist literature as a whole, and it became clearly defined at an early stage in the development of the new method. In exactly the same way, the hero of Barbusse's *Fire* is not any particular soldier of the First World War but a whole troop of soldiers. This innovatory feature of the works created according to the new method was astutely perceived by Stefan Zweig, a writer who developed in the channel of critical realism. Writing of Barbusse's novel, he said: "Instead of the two methods of portrayal that had hitherto existed in literature—the subjective and the objective—Barbusse chose a third: the collective.... Barbusse increased the observing, sentient Ego tenfold, so that it acquired a new oneness: he speaks and writes not through an individual but in the name of seventeen companions, which a hundred weeks of common sufferings in the furnace of war have fused into a single whole.... Dissolved in a fraternal community, he no longer perceives anything separately, personally, but whatever he feels, he feels it with seventeen souls."[1]

In both Barbusse's *Fire* and Serafimovich's *The Iron Flood* the portrayal of individuals is secondary to the main task—the portrayal of the group, the masses. Hence complete correspondence between the inner world of individual characters in these epic works and collective hero, that is the people, the masses, the people composing the group that is the object of portrayal. Hence the complete absence of barriers between the few individualised characters that emerge in the narrative and the other characters, both the incidental, episodic characters and those comprising the group whose portrait is presented. Hence also the directness of the links and relationships between the characters and the environment in which they move and act. Kozhukh, the leader and commander of the Taman column, hardly differs at all from the men he leads into battle and towards the new life. He knows exactly how they think and feel, just as they feel him to be a part of themselves—even the better part of their nature, for Kozhukh is by no means dissolved in the group he leads, but represents a higher stage of social, political and organisational awareness.

---

[1] Stefan Zweig, *Begegnungen mit Menschen, Büchern Städten*, Berlin und Frankfurt am Main, 1956, S. 209, 210.

All the members of the march have clearly defined relations with the group to which they belong. The fact that in the epic novels by Serafimovich, Barbusse and others these relations are presented in general terms and not dissected or greatly differentiated must not be taken as meaning that portrayal of the group replaces or submerges analysis of the individual. In actual fact, in socialist realist literature the presentation of the life of the group, the life of the masses, goes hand in hand with close investigation of the forms of social relations that link the individual and society, man and the people, in social conditions that are qualitatively different from those obtaining in bourgeois society. Thus, the ability of socialist realist writers to perceive and depict the masses as the motive force of social changes, the constructive factor of history, does not mean that the masses or the group are regarded as homogeneous, unified and undifferentiated. The group is treated as being composed of individuals, each with his own different level of social awareness, in accordance with reality to convey which is the supreme aim of socialist realism. This explains why the socialist realist writers have succeeded in portraying *the spiritual growth of the masses*, for they have given scrupulous attention to the spiritual growth of man in social struggle, in the practical building of socialism.

The individual may have a less complete and pure social awareness than the whole group to which he belongs, since he retains features of the past and of the environment in which his character and views were shaped. Socialist realism therefore presents the *elevation* of the individual to the ideological, ethical and moral demands of the group in all its authentic complexity, without simplification of the tortuous process of spiritual growth that attends a man's adoption of a higher social consciousness and higher moral concepts than those he had previously known.

Lenin often warned against a simplified, primitively straightforward view of the shaping of a socialist consciousness. At the same time, he was equally critical of those sceptics, who doubted the feasibility of creating a new socialist culture, and hence its creator and bearer, the new man. He wrote: "The old utopian socialists imagined that socialism could be built by men of a new type, that first they would train good, pure and splendidly educated people, and these would build socialism. We always laughed at this and said that this was playing with puppets, that it was socialism as an amusement for young ladies, but not serious politics."[1]

Lenin's faith in the triumph of socialism and socialist culture was firmly based on his profound knowledge of the real inherent potentialities of the masses, of the oppressed man, of the people. These potentialities revealed in the course of the struggle for socialism and its practical achievement, were perceived and depicted by socialist realist literature which has profound faith in the creative talent of the working masses. Socialist realism's most important innovatory contribution to world literature has consisted in the depiction of the strengthening and development in people of the best aspects of human nature—creative endeavour, humanity, and so on—and the expulsion from the human consciousness of all that is base, brutal, animal, and egoistic, all that human nature inherited from the age-long struggle for survival, the struggle of man with his fellows in private ownership society.

Apart from the power of habit and tradition, another basic factor that generally motivates people's attitudes and behaviour in private ownership society is personal interest, frequently degenerating into unbridled avarice. Other motives begin to determine the activities of people who have arisen to struggle against exploitation of the masses involved in the process of building socialism. The interests of society gradually become their own personal interests or begin to coincide with them. This complicated process, involving enrichment of man's spiritual world, his moral and ideological growth, and development of new criteria for evaluating himself and his environment was captured by socialist realist literature at a relatively early stage of its development. The theme of man's moral growth and assimilation of higher social interests, was

---

[1] V. I. Lenin, *Collected Works*, Vol. 29, p. 69.

already the central theme of Gorky's *Mother*. The first successful attempt at this theme in Soviet times was undoubtedly Fadeyev's *The Rout*, the significance of which lies in the way the social awareness of the masses is shown to grow to maturity through individual destinies, characters and relationships.

The collective hero of Fadeyev's novel, the partisan unit, is presented not as a monolithic body but as compounded of individual elements: it is a collection of different personalities, destinies, passions, views and hopes. Yet despite the comprehensive and many-sided portrayal of the members of the unit and their commander, despite the detailed psychological analysis of the thoughts and feelings underlying and determining the partisans' activities, the main thing about every one of these characters is their sense of belonging together, which materialised in the unit, in the group they form. The idea dominating all their practical activities, the supreme criterion of their actions, and the invisible but internally conditioned basis of their behaviour is the collective ethic of the unit, reflecting the ideals of the emancipatory struggle of the masses. The members of the unit embrace these ideals and regard them as their own personal ideals, as a result of their own personal practical experience of life. They all have a very different past, and yet it was similar in one important respect—they were all among the insulted and the injured, the exploited masses suffering from social injustice.

The new social ideals illuminate with the stark, merciless light of truth the old discredited motives and goals of human behaviour born of exploiter society, the egoism that was a regular feature of human relationships, and the individualist approach to social interests and to those tasks that history had placed before the working masses building the road to socialism and true human freedom. Scathing criticism of the morality of exploiter society is a major feature of the novel, for in socialist realism affirmation of the new goes hand in hand with criticism and rejection of all that is opposed to socialism and hinders its practical implementation in life.

The individualist morality of Mechik and the private

ownership mentality of the quiet old man Pika are defeated by the higher social ethic of which the collective hero of novel is the carrier. But the defeat of their ideological and moral principles is presented not as personal refusal to accept the ideas of the revolution—that would be a gross oversimplification of the complex process of the emergence of the new social awareness—but as a result of the incompatibility between the values to which Mechik and Pika adhere and which are connected by numerous spiritual threads to the moribund old world and the values asserted by the revolution. There was bound to be a conflict between the carriers of these different ideological principles, and it is presented in the novel with full social and psychological motivation, as is characteristic of works produced on the basis of the socialist realist method.

Powerful artistic generalisation achieved by the major exponents of critical realism was due to the spontaneous historicism of their thinking which enabled them to see and portray their heroes as an aggregate of social and psychological features and present the social factors underlying human psychology and man's spiritual world. Socialist realism has inherited this achievement of critical realism, and is enriching it, since conscious historicism makes possible a more complete understanding and reproduction of the unity of social and psychological features in man without separating the psychological element from the social basis and environment that engenders it, as the twentieth century critical realists have been doing. For the socialist realist writer man is the point of intersection of active social forces. In examining the psychological features of the individual, socialist realist writers at the same time investigate the social factors that shape his spiritual world, so that portrayal of the individual is intrinsically combined with depiction of society and social processes.

The conflicts in the best socialist realist works acquire an epic quality, not necessarily by virtue of their scope, although scope is an essential feature of portrayal in socialist realist works, but rather by virtue of the manifold links between the characters and real life. The study of society is active, and reality itself is active in socialist realist works and not simply a static background against which the vicissitudes of the characters' relationships take their course. The presentation of life as a neutral *background*, the presentation of social environment as a static, self-contained element is typical of naturalism. It is even characteristic of the works of such outstanding writers as Zola and Norris, not to mention the lesser adherents to the method. In socialist realism, environment is not treated as overwhelming fatality with man entirely at its mercy and purely the product of its conditions. Works of socialist realist writers present it, in accordance with historical truth, as fluid and changing, with its development consequent upon the struggle of different social tendencies, which influence the characters' lives and their relationships with one another and face them with new problems and tasks that they have to resolve always reckoning with the objective trends of historical development. Man is treated not as a function of his environment, but as the active principle of social development, a motive force of history, and hence is presented as exerting an active influence on his environment and history, changing them, and combating those conditions and circumstances that are hostile to him. Consequently, life's real conflicts and contradictions are objectively reflected in socialist realist works, not only in the depiction of the grouping of social forces but also of the relationships between the characters, their views and understanding of life, and man's duties and obligations.

The conflict between Mechik on the one hand, and Morozka, Levinson and the other members of the unit on the other in *The Rout*, highly personal and well-motivated psychologically, revealed a more profound conflict, the clash between genuine revolutionary spirit and petty-bourgeois rebelliousness, between the collective urge for real freedom and the wilfulness of the individual who places his personal interests before the interests of society. The study of the anatomy of Mechik's psychology in the novel is at the same time a study of a certain type of social behaviour in revolutionary conditions, the kind of behaviour that was typical of a rather wide section of the petty bourgeoisie, who only accepted the revolutionary changes up to a point, beyond which they abandoned the cause and began to oppose it. Fadeyev did not reveal the social roots of Mechik's mentality and behaviour intuitively or purely speculatively. He approached the character and the social problem it represented, equipped with a new literary method that enabled him to create a really authentic character whose mentality reflected the interweaving of social and psychological contradictions of his time.

The question of petty-bourgeois revolutionariness was also examined by other, non-socialist realist writers. But they treated the problem as a personal tragedy, the tragedy of the individual swept into the maelstrom of historic events. Lion Feuchtwanger attached far more importance to the distress caused Thomas Wendt, the hero of his expressionist novel *Neunzehnhundertachtzehn* by his limited petty-bourgeois revolutionariness than to the tragic events of the ill-fated Bavarian revolution, which provides the background for the spiritual vicissitudes of his hero. Many of the Soviet works written around the same time as *The Rout*—the novels and short stories of Ehrenburg, Klychkov, Sobol, Pilnyak, Alexeyev, Bulgakov and others—treated these problems in a similar manner. Where *The Rout* differs from them is in the fact that Mechik's limitations bring about a tragedy *for others*, for the other members of the unit, who pay with their lives for his desertion of the cause. Conscious historicism that sustained the new creative method enabled the author to see and portray the true, objective nature of petty-bourgeois revolutionariness and collate it with the genuine revolutionary spirit of the downtrodden masses, who face incredible hardships and are prepared to make the greatest sacrifices in order to transform the conditions of human life to make them worthy of man. Mechik as the carrier of a particular social tendency, was observed by the author in the thick of life and revolutionary struggle, and therefore his image is so full-blooded and not a mere cipher.

Conscious historicism enabled the writer to grasp and present the germination and development of new, essentially socialist features in the characters of ordinary rank-and-file participants in the revolutionary struggle.

Socialist realism, recognising and reflecting the masses as a creative force moulding events, thereby acquires highly democratic features. As befits a genuinely revolutionary art form it has grasped new, progressive features in the psychology of the masses and the individual working man. Genuine democratic spirit and conscious historicism, these two organic elements of socialist realism, are what gave rise to the specifically socialist realist concept of "hero".

In socialist realist literature the hero's character is not simply a plurality of features and qualities of equal merit and significance. Nor is it a tangle of unhealthy passions, complexes, various neuroses, lusts and fears, or a vessel of hereditary diseases. Nor again is it a "hermetically sealed" system of instincts and rational impulses completely independent of social environment. Finally, it is on no account made up of permanent characteristics of "human nature" that has remained unchanged since Adam.

Socialist realism regards character above all as an individual phenomenon, which the most diverse social influences have helped to shape. In this respect socialist realism inherits and develops the concept of character found in critical realism. There, however, the similarity ends, for socialist realism perceives and brings out the *social dominant* of the hero's character, whereby the individual is connected with the transformation of life, with life's historical movement and change, the factors which predetermine and condition the struggle of passions, interests and inclinations in the human spirit and a man's attitude to social struggle and the conflicts of his age. Conscious historicism enables the socialist realist writer to see the character's social dominant as the basic factor of his spiritual development. Socialist realist literature has created a great multitude and variety of characters for the simple reason that it has reflected the complex process of establishment of new social relations and the awakening of the new social awareness of the masses. It presents, analyses and investigates far more complicated relationships between the individual and society than does critical realism.

Basically, the chief form of relationship between the individual and society presented in critical realism long remained within the bounds of Balzac's famous formula "victim or hangman". The conflict this formula embraces was resolved either by the collapse of the individual's illusions, by his death, or, finally, by surrender to the society he had been struggling against and betrayal of his own ideals. The fates of Lucien de Rubempré, Julien Sorel, Raskolnikov, Eugene Witla or Martin Eden are vivid examples of the kind of conflict generalised in Balzac's formula. This kind of conflict possessed real depth and drama conveyed by many major works of critical realism. It provided the opportunity for the individual to pass his sentence on the society which stood opposed to him as a hostile, irrational force.

But naturally, this formula failed to embrace all the forms of conflict between the individual and private ownership society. And when history confronted realism with the special task of examining the objective destiny of that society itself, the conflict between the individual and society in critical realism underwent a change. The hero began to evolve an attitude not only to society but to its historical prospects and values, the ethical and moral principles of human behaviour, and the duty of the man who rejects the traditional demands made upon him by society. This increase in the scope and depth of the conflict between the individual and society is to be found in the most outstanding critical realist works of the twentieth century, beginning with Romain Rolland's *Jean Christophe* and Thomas Mann's *Der Lauberberg* and ending with the novels of Hemingway and Graham Greene. These writers greatly expanded the spiritual world of the individual, giving him an increased sense of dedication and concern for the fate of his fellow men, which moved some of their heroes to act in defence of freedom—like Jacques Thibault in *Les Thibaults* by Roger Martin Du Gard and Hemingway's Robert Jordan in *For Whom the Bell Tolls*—or forced them to make a reassessment of the spiritual values of bourgeois culture, like did the heroes of Romain Rolland or Thomas Mann

Socialist realism presents different relationships between the individual and society, relationships that are not antagonistic but, on the contrary, of increasing accord and closeness. The characters are therefore portrayed not only as growing richer spiritually and intellectually, but as advancing towards a higher level of social awareness, with all the other aspects and qualities of their nature following in the wake.

The individual's growing realisation that his interests correspond to those of society in the most important, decisive respects and his mounting awareness of the needs and interests of the whole of society and the state was apprehended by socialist realist literature in the very early stages of socialist transformation of society. It was portrayed as the awakening of great moral powers in the people of the first years of the revolution. In reflecting the individual's advance towards a higher level of social awareness, socialist realism shows his moral potential as revealed in his actions and his attitude to his social duty. The noble moral potential of Morozka, although his nature had been crippled by the world of property, enabled this very imperfect and simple man to free himself from the scab of the past and accomplish a truly heroic feat.

The crystallisation of a new, socialist outlook in people invariably entails development and enrichment of their moral qualities. Metelitsa, a platoon commander in the partisan unit, who has been led by his own experience to realise the need to struggle against the old order, and who hates all forms of oppression, humiliation and social injustice, is far from an ideal at the beginning of the story. It is in the course of the struggle, as a participant in the revolutionary movement, that he overcomes within himself the remaining features of self-contained individualism and becomes commander fully conscious of his responsibility towards people, a person capable of self-sacrifice for the common good. To accomplish this common good, which he regards as his own personal good, he took up arms and left his home and land, leaving behind

18—0801   273

him too the individualist outlook and views he inherited from his peasant ancestry.

The essentially democratic spirit of socialist realism does not mean that it sets its sights on some "average" level of culture and self-awareness of the masses. It consists rather in the ability to comprehend and reflect the fundamental interests of the masses, and promote the moral education of the people.

Socialist realist literature never regarded or presented the revolutionary movement of the masses as an explosion of elemental forces, spontaneously fermenting passions and uncontrolled impulses. It has shown the existence of a guiding social force, which was at work in the revolution and ensured the success and triumph of the revolt of the masses.

The masses, who had tasted to the full of the old order of capitalists and landowners, who had shed their blood on the battlefields of the imperialist war, had suffered from hunger and direst want, and had been exposed to daily insults and humiliations from the powers-that-be, had come to realise the need to change the conditions of their existence by revolution. The role of the Party of the proletariat, introducing class consciousness, organisation and understanding of the goal into the revolutionary movement of the masses was thus of decisive significance to their destiny and the revolutionary cause.

The masses had come to understand the need for revolutionary action, but it was the Communist Party that showed them *what was to be done, and how and for what purpose.* Many people were moved to enter the revolutionary struggle by a feeling of hatred for the oppressors and a thirst for justice. It was much as the Italian socialist realist Pratolini wrote of his hero who came to embrace the ideas of revolution: "You wouldn't be in the Party if you didn't trust your heart. Have you read a single line of the book called *Capital*? Why did you join the Resistance? Because you understood the theory of surplus value, or because you felt insulted in your heart?"[1] The

---

[1] Vasco Pratolini, *Cronache di Poveri Amanti*, Vallecchi Editore, 1955, p. 324.

Communists, however, brought the higher socialist awareness to the masses, and taught them to understand the real meaning of what was happening.

Pantelei Chmelyov, the hero of Leonov's *The Badgers,* meets a stranger one starry night on a road in devastated Russia. The stranger helped him, a future chairman of a village Soviet, one of the millions of people trying hard to understand the meaning of their life and the events taking place in their motherland, to finally make his political and human choice and embrace the true cause the Bolsheviks were bringing the masses.

Commissar Klychkov in Furmanov's *Chapayev* gave a great deal of patience to the political education of Vassili Ivanovich Chapayev, one of the most colourful figures of the Civil War and a true representative of the revolutionary peasantry. By personal example and through daily association Klychkov fostered his spiritual and political development and growth of social awareness helping him to attain the stature of a new type of military and political leader, once his talents and abilities were awakened by the revolution.

The commander of the partisan unit in *The Rout*, the Communist Levinson, is the bearer and champion of the highest social awareness of his time. He exerts a tremendous influence on the psychology, views and behaviour of the men under his command, who have entered the revolutionary struggle in answer to the call of their hearts without fully understanding its real aims. These aims are perfectly clear to Levinson, and he manages to make them clear to the rest of the men because he understands their way of thinking, their needs and abilities so well. Although he lives the same life as his men, he is at the same time ahead of them, just as the scout goes ahead of the unit, leading the way through unknown dangers. Levinson's socio-political outlook is far, far wider than Kozhukh's in *The Iron Flood* and he generously shares his experience, political and otherwise, with the men, and the seeds sown by his firm, sure hand sprout in their hearts and minds.

His experience of leadership, his demand for strict discipline, exactingness and shrewd understanding of men's psychology have a beneficial influence on Metelitsa, helping him to free himself from his anarchist inclinations. Levinson's personal influence and the truth he is the carrier of help new social sentiments take root in Morozka, and contributed to the feat Morozka accomplished for the common cause.

Levinson plays an exceptionally important role in the novel because he reflects the objective significance and role of the Party's leadership in the life of the masses.

The Party, leading and directing the masses, from the very outset of the revolution worked for the closing of the gap between the personal and social aspects of man, between his personal interests and the interests of society as a whole. Socialist realist literature reflected this new feature of life at a very early stage, and later, in full accordance with historical truth, continued to present Communists as bearers of the new, higher social awareness, bringing it to the mass of the people.

The theme of the development of social consciousness in man became the dominant theme of socialist realism. It presented the process of the shaping of the new man, the eviction of views inherited from the past, in both the individual mentality and that of the masses with all its complexity and drama, all the essential attendant conflicts.

Sholokhov's *And Quiet Flows the Don*—one of the most monumental works of socialist realism—reflected and generalised on an epic scale the process of man's settling with the past and overcoming the age-old views and habits inculcated by the old order; as well as the collapse of the old, outmoded system of social relations.

The epic quality of the novel arose not only from the particular talent of the author, who is a born realist and sees man and nature, the human soul and the life of society, in their true, natural form, undistorted and retaining all the sensual, plastic beauty of real life. The fact is that the author's thinking was based on conscious historicism, enabling him to perceive and transmit an accurate picture of the social contradictions in old Russia that engendered the revolutionary explosion, the revolt of the masses, and to present the influence of major, decisive historical events on the life of both the individual and the people.

In *And Quiet Flows the Don*, even more than in *The Rout*, one feels the powerful breath of the Tolstoian tradition, demonstrating the continuity between the two creative methods, their inner connection and the uninterrupted evolution of realism, this major trend in world literature. This tradition finds expression in Sholokhov's great attention to the "dialectics of the soul" of his characters, the exhaustiveness of his analysis of their psychological states and their inner world as a whole and the full-blooded, remarkably plastic, and tangible depiction of life. He portrays historical conflicts and irreconcilable contrasts and contradictions which determine the characters' destinies, their interrelationships, and their place in the current of history, carrying everyone and everything along.

The Tolstoian tradition in Sholokhov's novel is not an imitation but an *inheritance*, a point of departure, from which the writer's own independent thought starts the examination, from a new social and personal standpoint, of historical events and their influence on the mentality of the individual and the masses.

Sholokhov perceives life's contradictions and dramas, the psychology of his characters and the motives underlying their behaviour from the inside, as it were. This is not simply because he was in fact living amidst certain factual material that formed an essential part of his practical and spiritual experience, but also because he viewed life as a writer identified with the people, adhering to a revolutionary, socialist system of views and appraising history from the point of view of the masses and their revolution.

Sholokhov begins his analysis of society entering the period of the collapse of the old exploiter order and the birth of new social relationships between people, his presentation of the socialist revolution, with a description of the personal lives of his heroes, an analysis of the position of the individual in the old social system that was on the way out. Sholokhov chose this approach to the depiction of the decisive turning point in the life of the people because he understood that the scale and significance of the social changes that occurred as a result of the revolution could be presented with full force not only by depicting class battles into which the millions are drawn but also by examining the personal destiny of an individual, which is always linked by numerous threads to the destiny of society as a whole. This ability to reveal the general through the particular and fundamental social antagonisms through conflicts that appear to be of a personal nature is the most outstanding achievement of Sholokhov's method.

To begin with Sholokhov shows his heroes in the steady stream of everyday life, in the element of Cossack life, which is highly traditional and for all its original features similar in essentials to that of the ordinary peasantry. His characters' interests and concerns do not extend beyond their own household and adding to it, the cycle of work on the land, requiring intense physical effort but at the same time animated by simple, healthy poetry, family matters, and the various requirements connected with service to the tsar which gave Cossacks a sense of occupying a special position among the social strata of tsarist Russia, a sense that was strengthened by certain privileges. Their outlook was limited by concepts of their military duty and a code of military valour cultivated over the centuries and which made it compulsory that the Cossacks should participate in all the military actions of the tsarist government, a concept which in the minds of the ordinary Cossacks was confused with the idea of defending their country. This illusion was carefully cultivated by the Cossack hierarchy and the Orthodox Church. The characters' mental horizon was further limited by their hostility towards the non-Cossack peasants whom they regarded as a threat to their own welfare.

The world in which the heroes of Sholokhov's novel lived was not united and monolithic. Material inequality and its result—the different social interests of the poor and prosperous Cossacks—deprived it of unity, and Sholokhov showed with keen discernment how the knots of social contradictions were tightened in the set pattern of life that had held its own for centuries, contradictions, which were only to be resolved by the revolution and the following years of building a classless society.

Sholokhov adopted an historical approach to the factual material that forms the basis of his novel, refusing to tone down irreconcilable conflicts or make his heroes' entry into the world of new social relations easier than it actually was. *Conscious historicism*, that fundamental principle of the new method of socialist realism, underlies the triumph of realism Sholokhov achieved with his novel.

Basically, this principle consists in the author's understanding of the basic, major trend in the development of social relations, in his conviction that the capitalist system based on the principle of private ownership is disintegrating, that it has outlived itself and is giving way, and indeed must give way, to a more perfect form of human relations—socialism. From this understanding of the course of social development other important features of socialist realism arise, such as new criteria of assessing people's views, actions and behaviour, and an ability to combine analysis of the same with analysis of the social situation, which the socialist realist writer always views in the light of the general prospects of social development.

This is why Sholokhov does not limit himself to depicting the vivid, colourful way of life and family relationships conforming to patriarchal customs. He studies the relationships between the individual and history, which has sprung into tumultuous, revolutionary motion, and shows how stifling is the society based on private ownership for the individual who does not wish to dissolve in the slow, regular stream of mundane existence, who refuses to submit to the power of mouldy traditions and the established morality called upon to bolster up the decaying old order and to be guided exclusively by self-interest. The story of Grigory Melekhov's and Aksinya's passionate love for each other illuminates the stagnating and cruel old social order with a merciless clarity. Proud and noble in their love, they were prepared to flout the old customs and ossified traditions. Their relationship, their struggle for happiness together, laid bare the inability of the old order to satisfy the finer spiritual and moral requirements of the individual.

This kind of conflict, the conflict between two people

and society, has never been regarded in major works of world literature as purely personal. In depicting such a relationship, the two lovers' spiritual vicissitudes and their struggle to be the masters of their own destiny, great writers always presented major social contradictions, and criticised the imperfections of society. The fate of Romeo and Juliet, Manon Lescaut and de Grieux, Ferdinand von Walter and Louise Miller, Julien Sorel and Madame de Rénal, Carmen and Jose, Anna Karenina and Vronsky, the lovers in Chekhov's *Lady with the Dog* and so on, despite all the difference in character, the age they live in and the circumstances of their drama, all testify to the inability of society to solve the conflicts according to the natural inclinations of human hearts thirsting for happiness and endeavouring to defend their right to it in an unequal struggle against the opposing world. The fact that almost all the heroes of these dramas perish shows clearly that these conflicts, not socially crucial and apparently easy of solution, just could not be solved in the conditions of a social order based on private ownership.

Grigory's love for Aksinya descends on the Melekhov household like a major disaster. Their powerful, passionate feelings raised the lovers above their relations and fellow villagers for whom the prosaic demands of everyday existence were incomparably more important than wild, uncontrollable passions.

Pantelei Prokofyich's domestic calculations and plans become highly precarious, for they are built on the shaky foundations of his son's heart which is in the grip of an all-consuming passion. The system of values Grigory and Aksinya are being pressed to submit to internally and objectively contradicts their aspirations, hopes and desires, and they rebel although life arrays against them its most tenacious and stultifying forces—habit, family traditions and the interests and requirements of the household economy and privately owned land. Actually, at the beginning the power of land over Grigory's peasant mind is so great that he refuses to follow Aksinya's bold, independent call to abandon everything and begin a new life somewhere far from his home hearth.

Grigory and Aksinya's love brings nothing but suffering to those around them. For Stepan Astakhov, Aksinya's departure is a hard blow, for all that he never understood her passionate independent nature. For Natalya, at first far removed from Aksinya and Grigory's relationship, her marriage to Grigory, arranged by their parents for material, economic considerations, became a great human tragedy that ruined her life and her rich personality. She was capable of great unselfish love, and eventually made an effort to revolt in her own way against misfortunes and injustices that plagued her and her family. Natalya is a truly poetic and tragic figure. Her sad plight confirmed the inhumanity and ruthlessness of the world order in which she lived, an order in which human dignity and the individual's real needs were subordinated to self-interest. The hero and heroine, too, Grigory and Aksinya, by abandoning themselves to their powerful feeling such as is only given to a man to experience once in a lifetime also drink the cup of sorrows to the full.

Grigory and Aksinya's drama arises from the objective conditions of their life. Following the dictates of their hearts, they ran counter to established ways, customs and traditions of the society they lived in. Sholokhov makes no attempt to idealise them. They both contain within them many features from the psychology of their environment and the social morality against which they have revolted. They become the victims of this morality, and occasionally submit and subscribe to it, renouncing their inner freedom and only finding themselves again by *rejecting* this morality, rejecting all that binds them to the way of life based on material interests. But they are incapable of resolving their conflict on their own. They cannot defend their love and dignity *within* the existing system of social relations, and often bow to circumstances and forego both. But the fact that they sometimes compromise with life, themselves and their conscience, does not mean that their conflict with society can never be resolved. If society fails to give people the opportunity to live a full life worthy of man, then society must be changed and rebuilt. The conflict between Aksinya and Grigory and society can only be resolved outside the old system of social relations. It will be resolved when these people and others like the macquire freedom, when everything that mutilates the human spirit has been rejected, and man liberates himself from the cancer of the past and overcomes the views, habits, concepts and norms of behaviour he has inherited from the old order. Thus Sholokhov presents in the relations between two individuals—and this is a characteristic feature of socialist realism and the criteria by which it judges life's phenomena—a major social problem of the age, confirming the incompatibility between the old social order and a human being's real needs.

But transforming society is a complicated painful business involving fierce struggle. Sholokhov presents all the real drama of the process, by placing his heroes face to face not only with the moribund, obsolescent traditional way of life, but with the movement of History itself.

In the words of the nineteenth century Russian critic Belinsky, the inner qualities of human nature become particularly evident at *critical* moments in history. Such a major event as the October Revolution revealed down to grass-roots level all the irreconcilable conflicts and antagonisms of the class society of bourgeois-landowner Russia, set in motion the best aspects of the spirit of the masses and raised the awareness of the masses to a qualitatively new stage, by introducing to it in practice the ideas of socialism, social equality and freedom.

Not a single person was able to stand aside from and remain uninfluenced by the revolutionary processes that changed the old world in the face of its fierce resistance. The events of those years had a profound impact on human nature. The importance of Sholokhov's novel as a work of the new realist method consists in his investigation and presentation of the socio-psychological changes in the awareness of the masses not only in the socio-historical aspect but also in the sphere of the personal life of the individual, since for Sholokhov man is not the object of history, but the subject, the active principle at work in it, the maker of history.

Thus, in Sholokhov's novel characters are presented as existing and developing in the unity of the individual and the historical, the personal and the social. This is why the two major threads of the narrative—the historico-analytical and the personal vicissitudes of the heroes—are not opposed or parallel to one another, but merge into a single stream, powerful and deep. This ability to perceive the individual and the social as interrelated and interdependent enables Sholokhov to portray both the course of the revolution and at the same time the life of ordinary people who became participants in historical events, which determined their destiny.

Like millions of others, Grigory goes through the hard school of the First World War, a war that was imperialist and expansionist on both sides.

To begin with, like his parents, grandparents and great-grandparents before him, Grigory did not pause to reflect on what was happening and, accepting everything that came into his life and the lives of his near and dear ones as a result of the war as an inevitable evil, as part of the normal pattern of existence, faithfully served the interests of the Empire. Brought up to honour duty and obey authority, he performs his military obligations, without bothering to ask himself the fairly obvious question of why he was fighting, in whose interests he was called upon to continually risk his life, rot in trenches and make desperate assaults on a better-equipped enemy. Grigory's awareness is at the same level as that of millions of Russian *muzhiks* thrown by the tsarist government against the Kaiser's armies and Krupp guns. He is a typical representative of the masses, who were to come to understand the futility of the imperialist war through their own bitter and bloody experience, learn that the war was contrary to the interests of the people and cast off the illusions which still persisted after the 1905 revolution and the following years of fierce reaction. Thus, Grigory's vacillations and his painful reflections in the interludes between battles largely reflect the vacillations and changes in the consciousness of the masses, who advanced from disillusionment with the tsarist government and rejection of tsarism to revolutionary ideas.

In accordance with his creative method, Sholokhov presents the growth of the awareness of the masses through highly individualised characters, projecting, as it were, historical events onto human hearts and minds, focussing the profound historical significance of events in the personal destinies and emotions of his heroes.

In his very first battle, while overcoming his horror of death and doing what the other soldiers do, Grigory at once senses that the war which has the blessing of official morality and the Church is a terrible, inhuman business. Illusions about heroism and patriotisme instilled in soldiers by officers and the Church are dispelled for Grigory and others like him when they realise the falseness of the official ideology that glorified war and called upon the masses to patiently bear the misery and hardships that fell their lot.

The human suffering and the violence and injustice committed in the name of war bring Grigory to the realisation of the bitter truth that the imperialist war entailed the brutalisation of man and confusion of the concepts of good and evil, justice and injustice. He could smell the mould and decay that accompanied the death agony of the Russian Empire. He was aware of the rusing tide of wrath of the masses and was himself full of hatred he had developed during his years at the front for the order that cast people into senseless, futile sufferings and refused to take into account man's real needs.

Grigory was unable to determine with the necessary clarity who was to blame for the misfortunes of his people, himself and his near and dear ones. But he meets with people of greater social awareness than he himself possessed, and from them—from Garanzha, for example— learns to evaluate events correctly. Garanzha's forthright, empassioned words about the war and those who brought all these sufferings on the people bring home to Grigory the horrifying truth and teach him to grasp the social, class nature of the events he is taking part in. Grigory takes the first step towards spiritual freedom, towards shaking off the burden of views and concepts that society has instilled in him. But this step did not make him a fighter for the people's cause. He cast off many of his illusions but not all of them, for habit and tradition were still too strong. Thoughts of his own land had a tenacious hold on his mind, arresting his ideological development and confining him to private interests and preventing him from understanding the common interest being born in relentless struggle with the forces of the old society. Having broken with the past, Grigory had no clear idea about what the future offered him and did not really believe that it would bring him any good.

Socialist realist writers present real history as a battlefield of social forces in constant movement, whose nature the writer can perceive, just as he can perceive—not in its concrete forms but in social perspective—the final outcome of the struggle between these forces. Singling out the main, determinant trend of history, in accordance with the objective course of historical development, the writer does not isolate it from other aspects and trends of the social process but presents their mutual influence and the resistance of the reactionary social forces to the main trend, that of social progress. For this reason, the picture of life is not one-sided. It is shown in all its colours and facets, all the interplay of light and shade, and not through rose-coloured spectacles or dark glasses. Thus Sholokhov showed how the power of the past weighed heavily not only on Grigory's spirit, but on Aksinya's life too. Submitting to circumstances, unable to resist them, she shifted with the tide allowing humdrum existence to overshadow her love for Grigory, that great unruly passion that had filled her whole being and enabled her, an illiterate woman, deprived of all rights, to revolt against the power of her husband, the power of custom and the social order.

But the past does not only fetter and enslave people's inner world. It is never passive in the face of historical changes. At an historical moment, when the masses led by the vanguard of the working class, the Bolshevik Party, were rising to conscious historical activity, breaking the machinery of state by revolution, reviewing and rejecting fundamental ideological principles of the old society, the scions of the old society—deprived by the revolution of their former privileges and the possibility of living as parasites on the masses—took up arms to crush the forces of the future in a desperate effort to retain their power. Sholokhov gives a broad, comprehensive picture of the forces of counter-revolution—the White officers, brutalised in the trenches of the First World War, morally degenerate and spiritually bankrupt men, for whom their own people have become a more dangerous and hated enemy than the German imperialists, since they have arisen against the age-old privileges of the ruling classes with the demand for rights for the masses instead of rights for a few. The Cossack autonomists, their leaders and inspirers, are also presented with realistic completeness and differentiation, as the Cossack wealthiest who waged a fierce struggle against the new people's rule and the poor Cossack masses, who have begun to realise that only Soviet power can lead them out of the chaos of war, to real freedom. Sholokhov needed to present these antipopular forces in his novel in order to make it perfectly clear that the ideas guiding the Russian counter-revolution were doomed and futile, and also because without defining and describing the social environment and the antagonisms at work there, it is impossible to show the evolution of the human spirit, man's inner struggle, vacillation and development objectively and in the spirit of real historicism.

Grigory has already broken away from the old views and concepts inculcated in him by the old society: he hates the ruling classes who have led the people into a senseless war and are preventing them from choosing their own future. He longs for peace and tranquil, constructive civilian life, but the idea of people's rule, in the name of which the revolution was accomplished, the only valid idea of the age, expressing its wisdom and concentrating in itself all the positive, constructive aspirations of the time, remains unacceptable to him, for, as he and his fellow villagers, and other Cossacks who have taken up arms against Soviet power, understand perfectly well, this idea will totally demolish the old way of life which to Grigory and his fellows seemed the only possible, natural, time-hallowed form of human society. Grigory fights for its preservation, devoting his life to the defence of an historical illusion and gradually becoming aware of the futility of this struggle. As the result he suffers a shattering inner defeat and pays for his errors the terrible price of losing his family, losing Aksinya, losing his faith in the old world, its power and its promises. Ever since Grigory, a son of the working Cossacks took up arms against Soviet power, against the people, against the creative forces of history, a continuous reappraisal of the thoughts, sentiments, hopes, which had once seemed indisputably correct, was going on in his mind until he gradually came to appreciate their real worth.

The image of Grigory Melekhov in all justice can be called a triumph of socialist realism for its comprehensive content, significance and exceptional psychological authenticity. For Grigory's tragic destiny reveals naturally and vividly the crisis and obsolescence of the private ownership outlook, the fact that it is historically doomed and the difficulties a person has to overcome in order to free himself from the power of the views and concepts inculcated by the world of private ownership. Before Grigory's mind could be freed, his own inner aspirations, which had not yet fully crystallised, had to fall into line with the movement of history, which was largely obscure to him, but of which he could perceive the salient, determinant features. It was the joint action of these two factors—the inner, subjective, and the external, objective—that brought Grigory to the decision to break with the past which had such a tenacious grip on his heart and mind. From the crucible of the Civil War, where everything that had led him astray along the tortuous paths of history was consumed, Grigory emerges to reassess his past, and hoping he can still begin a new life and perhaps even make amends to the people. The path ahead through the virgin lands of history will be long and difficult for him, he will have to wage a hard struggle with himself, for the new life he is embarking upon is based on very different principles from those by which he has hitherto been guided. He renounces everything that had made him renegade, and this new Grigory undoubtedly deserves our sympathy.

Grigory, like other misguided representatives of the masses, begins to understand that the truth is on the side of those against whom he had fought so long and unsuccessfully. He becomes convinced—and this is presented in the novel very strikingly—that the erstwhile masters of Russia, the scions of the ruling classes, could only advance a *conservationist, defensive* idea in the new historical conditions, one in defence of a doomed, moribund, unjust and obsolescent social order. The new revolutionary forces brought into the world an idea *transforming* life. The light of this new truth, like a light from the future, illuminates the tragic events of the novel, the destiny of the characters, introducing new, higher criteria of assessing historical events and human actions. The torch of this new truth is carried by people of a higher social awareness, the Communists Stockman, Podtyolkov, Koshevoi and others, many of whom pay with their lives for their dedication to the revolutionary cause. Sholokhov does not idealise them: he shows both their qualities and their defects. But their thoughts and deeds are devoted to active and selfless defence of the new.

These characters give the necessary perspective to the generalised picture of life the novel presents, reflecting the main tendency of the historical process by the very fact of their presence in the narrative. They define the true scale of Grigory's personal drama, the degree and depth of his errors, and indicate the spiritual heights he must reach. They also show that the solution of these seemingly eternal and insoluble social conflicts is possible and can only be achieved through transforming the whole social system that engenders war, property inequality, the enslavement of some men by others, and all the manifold aspects and forms of oppression and social injustice. These characters bring into the novel the new socialist ethics, new principles of behaviour towards people, dictated by love for the working masses and concern for their interests.

For a long time Pantelei Prokofyich, Grigory's father, tried to oppose the advance of time, protecting his family and farm from its destructive influence. His son Pyotr died defending the existing order, and his other son Grigory was torn between the two conflicting camps, going from one side to the other. The old family, based above all on property interests, was unable to withstand the pressure of the changes and a new morality that overcame the power of prejudices asserted itself—the free love of free people, of Dunya and Mikhail Koshevoi.

The new social ethics revealed the inhumanity of the opposition to the popular masses put up by their numerous enemies like generals Kaledin and Krasnov, Fomin and others, and reflected the creative, constructive aspirations of the masses who long for peaceful labour, for work for the benefit of man and society. The new social ethics, its ideas, hopes and ideals the socialist revolution has brought into life become the foundation of the criticism inherent in the new literary method.

In socialist realism, which investigates and presents the real contradictions of society and man's inner world, criticism is inseparable from the affirmation of the positive social ideal introduced by the socialist revolution, the tasks of building socialist and communist social relations. Socialist realism subjects to uncompromising, comprehensive and substantiated criticism the social relations based on private ownership and the consciousness they give rise to, and also everything that impedes the advance of the free socialist world towards communism. Socialist realism is partisan for the simple reason that it forthrightly rejects capitalism and the phenomena of mankind's societal and spiritual life engendered by capitalism. Socialist realism forthrightly defends and expresses the ideas of communism, and therefore combats all expressions of bourgeois ideology in socialist society. Socialist realist literature assesses and examines real life in the light of the tasks of building communism, and therefore criticises those forces and phenomena that hinder the process of socialist construction and interfere with the strengthening and improvement of the socialist system.

The image of Grigory was presented *critically* in the novel, the author being perfectly aware of the objective causes that brought him into conflict with the positive, constructive forces of history, and deeply sympathising with his tragic destiny. The tragic nature of *And Quiet Flows the Don*—one of the masterpieces of socialist realism—derived from the author's understanding of the incompatibility of the individual's aspirations and objective capabilities and demands with the obsolescent social order, which not only impedes the spiritual and moral growth and enrichment of the individual, but can keep him in the bondage of its old illusions, habits, traditions, customs and views.

Socialist realism does not reduce tragedy to a single formula, revealed in Vsevolod Vishnevsky's *Optimistic Tragedy*, where we are shown the conscious self-sacrifice of heroes in the name of the common good, in the name of noble, supra-personal social interests. The tragedy in *And Quiet Flows the Don*, or to be more precise in the destiny of Grigory Melekhov, derives from the same sources as does the tragedy in the destiny of Andrei Startsov in Fedin's *Towns and Years* or Dmitry Vekshin in Leonov's *The Thief*. It arises from the conflict between the surviving power of the past in the consciousness of a man who has already broken with it, who realises that it is unjust and doomed, and a qualitatively different social and personal ideal which is irresistibly asserting itself. This tragic conflict is rooted in the objective contradictions of social life, of live history in the making, and will gradually be resolved as the structure of society is altered and society solves and overcomes the social contradictions that gave rise to such conflicts. Thus, historicism in understanding the drama and tragedy in the relationship between the individual and society is an important intrinsic feature of socialist realism.

However, socialist realism never absolutises the tragic, never makes it metaphysical, for it always takes account of the fact that human tragedies are the product of the concrete social conditions in which people live, and that as society is transformed and reorganised on a rational, just principles, the sphere of tragedy will be reduced, since socialism and communism are capable of removing its root causes from life. But this can only be achieved on condition that man actually becomes the conscious creative, constructive maker of history.

Bourgeois ideology regards tragedy as a natural element of life, just as it regards fear to be an essential, inalienable feature of human existence. This is a fundamental idea of the pessimistic trend in the bourgeois conscience, which has been expressed in differently shaded formulas by numerous bourgeois ideologists from Schopenhauer, Kierkegaard and Hartmann and to contemporary pessimists who, reflecting the crisis of bourgeois society, regard the tragic as a universal, all-embracing form of man's relationship with life and human existence in society. Thus, for the existentialists, existence in general is existence for death.

Nobody, of course, would suggest that there is nothing dramatic or tragic about death. However, this does not mean that man realises his supreme potential in death or lives for death, rather than in order to express himself in life, in deeds, making his life, which has its natural beginning and end, meaningful and joyous, and a source of personal satisfaction and happiness. By treating tragedy metaphysically, existentialism deprives it of concrete substance, of social causality, and rejects the possibility of its removal from life. In these circumstances man is left with no other choice but to stoically bear all the hardships of existence, for, as Albert Camus wrote in *Le mythe de Sisyphe*, man's awareness of the absurdity of existence, his inability to reconcile the irrationality of the world with his desperate longing to acquire clarity, leads him to admit the invincibility of the existing circumstances and to act like Sisyphus, that is, in conditions that render your actions perfectly futile and pointless.

This idea is diametrically opposed to the humanitarian fundamental idea of socialism, the conception of the individual as well as the masses ascending to constructive activity, and by this activity, making their life meaningful, changing life and themselves. This historically new process, pervading every sphere of life in socialist society, was perceived and presented by socialist realism truthfully and comprehensively.

Among the most important results of the triumph of the socialist system in this country were a general acceleration of social development, the creation of the objective prerequisites for the removal of class distinctions socialist society inherited from capitalism, and progressive unification of heterogeneous social layers and groups in a classless society, devoid of class struggle or class antagonisms. The building of socialism and the erasure of class distinctions went hand in hand with industrialisation, with the fundamental transformation and restructuring of the economy. This involved not only the creation and predominance of modern industry in a formely prevalently agrarian country, and the strengthening of ties between the working class—the most progressive and highly organised class—and the peasantry, but also the collectivisation of agriculture, and the creation of a uniformly socialist economy.

Along with industrialisation, a cultural revolution was carried out, in the course of which literacy and culture were brought to the *popular masses.* The formation of a classless society—by no means a painless process, since it involved the reshaping of long-established views, habits and relationships, which the revolution had begun to break down—led to the closing of the gap between personal and societal interests, a process that had a tremendous impact on the social psychology of the masses and the individual.

In his article *How to Organise Competition?,* Lenin wrote: "The workers and peasants are still 'timid', they have not yet become accustomed to the idea that *they* are now the *ruling* class; they are not yet resolute enough. The revolution could not *at one stroke* instil these qualities into millions and millions of people who all their lives had been compelled by want and hunger to work under the threat of the stick. But the Revolution of October 1917 is strong, viable and invincible because it *awakens* these qualities, breaks down the old impediments, removes the worn-out shackles, and leads the working people on to the road of the *independent* creation of a new life."[1]

From their participation in work for a common cause of building socialism, the popular masses began to become aware that they themselves were the *ruling* force, capable of *independent* creativity. This development of awareness in the whole people and in individuals from the masses of their role and importance in the state building socialism was captured by socialist realism. Illumina-

---

[1] V. I. Lenin, *Collected Works,* Vol. 26, pp. 409-10.

tion and explanation of various aspects of this process was for a long time a major task of the new literature, which investigated and presented the development of the ordinary man-in-the-street towards a higher level of social and civic consciousness.

Pyotr Soustin and the former coffin-maker Ivan Zhurkin in A. Malyshkin's *People from the Backwoods* flee from the depths of provincial Russia, from the changes that are breaking down the familiar way of life with its accustomed poverty and spiritual slough, flee through cold and night into the unknown, throbbing faraway where a gigantic new construction project is under way. Fear is their companion, fear of the irreversible changes, and memories of their life in their native Mshansk, which although far from easy was as familiar as the ABC they had learned in childhood. They were used to that life and the relations with the world and other people that were part of it, to the simple, hard relations of a world ruled by the simple mechanics of buying and selling, where the ideal was accumulation, and the supreme consummation of all dreams to have one's own little business, lucrative if only in a small way, and one's own little house isolated like an island in a river at flood time from everything that was going on around.

Pyotr and Ivan flee from life in provincial Russia, nor is this comfortable, sated provincial life, as colourful as a Russian woman's shawl, depicted by the artist Kustodiev, but that depicted by Gorky in his *Okurov Town*, with people wallowing in ignorance and superstition, prejudice and cruelty, concerned entirely with and ridden by the task of earning their daily bread, doped by vodka and church bells, informed about the great wide world only from the wild gossip of the womenfolk. It was a life where a major event was a fair and where shopkeepers and *kulaks* felt like fish in water, past masters at currying favour with the local authorities and endeavouring to outwit Soviet power itself.

But the two men carry with them very different memories of the past. While Pyotr remembers above all the markets with the sharp aroma of bast baskets, the winy scent of ripe apples and the thrill of bargaining, Ivan remembers the hungry eyes of his children and his wife's patient submission. And it is quite logical that in the new life the cunning Pyotr who has not forgotten his trading habits should suffer defeat while Ivan, freeing himself from the time-hallowed sense of his own inferiority should square his shoulders and become a rightful builder of life.

In *People from the Backwoods*, A. Malyshkin gave an extremely accurate portrayal of the process of man's moral enrichment by socialism, of the struggle of new ideas and new experiences people acquired during the building of socialism with their previous experience of life that isolated them from the mainstream of history. Their erstwhile conceptions gradually gave way to an understanding of the new forms of relationship with the world in which they live and act. Socialism enabled them not only to accede to a higher level of material welfare but widened their spiritual horizon, aroused their intellect from slumber, and made them aware both of their rights and of their responsibilities towards society.

For Ivan Zhurkin the giant construction project becomes far more than a place where he earns his living. It gives him something else besides money and material benefits: he comes to realise the importance of the project for the people as a whole, its historical importance, if you like. The dam rising higher and higher above the clayey ground represents for him the power of the new life that is erecting barriers against the past, and since he hates that past, he rejoices in the fact that his labour has contributed to this dam built at the watershed between the streams of the past and the future.

Awareness of the fact that his work is part of a collective effort, that it is for the *common good,* changes Zhurkin's psychology, giving him a formerly unknown sense of responsibility for the common cause of socialist construction. This growing awareness of the importance of their own work as an essential part of the work of all leads other characters to throw off the burden of old concepts. Among them is Tishka who chucks away a second-hand priest's furcoat he had bought for show and takes the wheel of a lorry, Polya, who escaped from female bondage to lead a life of her own, and the seasonal labourers who shaved off their luxuriant beards and became permanent workers. Their new attitude to their own work opens up to them a rough but wide road forward.

The historicist approach characteristic of socialist realism is also based on an understanding of the prospects of social development. Historical perspective is thus one of the major socialist realist criteria of assessing the events, conflicts and phenomena that characterise a particular stage of development of society and relationships between people, and hence relationships between the characters of a literary work. This perspective makes possible a correct analysis of the essence, features and potentialities of the characters and their conformity with reality.

Ivan Zhurkin and the other characters in Malyshkin's novel were perceived and presented by the author in historical perspective. What Zhurkin achieved was not the final result but simply the point of departure of man's development in socialist society. Zhurkin is a man who makes very modest demands on life, despite the fact that he has accomplished so much, casting off the fetters of his provincial past. Although his demands are limited, he has already traversed one stage on the road the masses had to traverse in their irresistible advance to knowledge, culture and a life worthy of man.

The many-sided investigation of the profound changes taking place in human psychology, the new understanding of man's potential, and the presentation and explanation of the objective changes that socialist construction had brought about in life revealed the strength of the new creative method, which made it possible to analyse the relationship developing between the individual and the socialist life that was taking shape and reveal the new conflicts engendered by history in the making.

Socialism not only presented man and society with new great aims, but changed the underlying stimuli of human behaviour and activity. Personal motives were gradually relegated to the background and man's mentality changed under the impact of social interests, the impulses inculcated by the new socialist order that was being affirmed through the work and activities of the masses.

Ivan Zhurkin begins to realise the need for the individual to take account of social needs, the moral demands of society. Between his former total absorption in his own petty affairs and his present work on the construction site lies a whole historical epoch, which the Soviet people has passed through with extraordinary rapidity, accelerating the course of time, as it were, creating a powerful industrial base, collectivised agriculture, a new intelligentsia, and a new socialist culture.

Socialist realism perceived and depicted how the actual process of labour and construction instils in man social motives for his activities. The description of a single day on a giant construction site in Valentin Katayev's novel *Time, Forward!* shows how creative, constructive activity becomes the main content of life for the builders. The cement-layers, the engineers and the management are all engaged in ceaseless search for solutions to the problems that arise every day, every minute, to complex organisational and ethical questions. They are all involved in the conflict between moribund habits and methods of work, views of life and human relations on the one hand, and the new life on the other, or in other words, between the old traditions that no longer correspond to the pace or scale of the epoch, and the traditions born in the course of building socialism. The most advanced people working on the project are engaged in creative exploration. The depiction of *their work process as a creative process*—the powerful, innovatory feature of the novel—reflects the changes that have taken place in the awareness of the masses, in their social psychology. Socialist realism never treats man as an abstraction or extracts him from social relations, but always makes man reveal himself, his essence and his personality, through his actions, through his active relationships with society, environment, time and history. Labour in socialist society is one of the major spheres in which a man reveals his essential features, his personality, his moral and ideological content, for labour crystallises many of a man's qualities, enabling him to renew himself, enrich and improve his own personality, in the process of transforming life.

Lenin wrote: "...the proletariat represents and creates a higher type of social organisation of labour compared with capitalism."[1] Further on, he stressed: "The communist organisation of social labour, the first step towards which is socialism, rests, and will do so more and more as time goes on, on the free and conscious discipline of the working people themselves who have thrown off the yoke both of the landowners and capitalists."[2]

Socialist realism, in accordance with the truth of life and history, showed that major, decisive changes in the life of socialist society, in its economic and social structure, take place on the initiative of the Party with the conscious support of the masses, for these changes are intended to ensure a fuller satisfaction of the people's material and spiritual requirements. That major turning point in the history of socialist society, the collectivisation of agriculture, was accomplished successfully because it was in accordance with the needs of socialist economy and the fundamental interests of the working peasantry, who had begun to realise that collective economy was the only way to eliminate want, close the gap between town and countryside and produce the material values necessary for the building of socialist and communist society. Collectivisation dealt a blow at the main carrier of non-socialist and anti-socialist views, illusions and aspirations, the property owner, and brought the peasantry out of the circumscribed world of the private economic interests to take part in collective labour for the community, enabling them to combine personal and community interests. It brought the peasantry to a higher stage of economic activity, to technical progress, changing the face of the countryside by introducing urban culture, and fostering the development of a new rural intelligentsia.

Transformation of the countryside and the closing of the gap between town and country is one of the most complex processes in socialist construction, involving the solution of a multitude of economic, organisational, psychological, moral and ethical problems. It has been a constant theme of socialist realist literature right down to the present day when elaboration of today's problems of country life is combined with historical study of the vari-

[1] V. I. Lenin, *Collected Works*, Vol. 29, p. 419.
[2] Ibid., p. 420.

ous stages of collective-farm construction and assessment of past successes and mistakes. This theme will naturally be developed in depth and breadth as the literature of socialist realism as a whole develops, but the main question—why was it that the system triumphed?—has already been answered in the works dealing with the emergence of the collective-farm system.

It triumphed because collectivisation was supported by the whole Soviet people, because of the firm union, welded by the revolution, between the working class and the working peasantry. It triumphed because the basic classes of Soviet society agreed about the ways of establishing socialist relations in the countryside.

Davydov, the hero of Sholokhov's *Virgin Soil Upturned,* symbolises this union. A worker, he learns through his own experience and daily search how to lead the peasant masses to acceptance of the ideas of collectivisation and an understanding of the advantages of the collective-farm system. The author shows Davydov grappling with the real difficulties and conflicts that arose in the countryside in the process of collectivisation, and shows how he surmounted these difficulties. As the result he achieved a remarkably complete and authentic character which generalised the actual experience of foremost promoters of collective-farm construction.

Davydov had personal experience of the opposition of the *kulaks;* he had to crush the sabotage by some of the wealthier peasants and help the middle peasants to overcome their doubts. He had to struggle against ignorance and prejudice, and in practice evolve methods of organising the collective farm management. He and his helpers and comrades-in-arms—Maidannikov, Nagulnov and Razmyotnov—had to resolve problems that had never confronted anybody before, correcting their mistakes as they went along. The collective-farm system triumphed because the idea of collectivisation brought forth a host of gifted, dedicated organisers and leaders, who, like Kirill Zhdarkin in Panferov's *Bruski,* Ivan Sipayev in Makarov's *Blue Fields* or Ivan Fedoseyevich in Yefim Dorosh's *Village Diary,* swayed the waverers and doubters and led them along. The collective-farm system triumphed because, despite mistakes and extremes, the mass of poor and middle peasants realised the advantages of the new economic system, which enabled people who had hitherto been oppressed by want and harassed by petty worries over their unproductive private economies, to enter the mainstream of life and to see the connection between the country's economic development and their own prospects, and to recognise opportunities for society as also opportunities for themselves. The social changes that took place produced corresponding changes in the outlook and sentiments of millions of people, and the images in *Virgin Soil Upturned* (Ustin, Dubtsov, Arzhanov, Shaly and Varya Kharlamova) reflected typical processes taking place in the consciousness of the masses as they arose to constructive social activity.

Socialist realist literature has observed and presented one of the most important of conflicts, and one of the most difficult to eradicate—the contradiction between the property instinct and the needs and demands of a collective society for which private ownership and the whole system of views, concepts and habits it engendered are a negative factor which society combats with all the spiritual and material means at its disposal. The power and tenacity of the property instinct, its capacity to transform and adjust itself was presented by socialist realist literature in its various aspects. It has captured both the craven cruelty and hostility to the new system of people like Ostrovoy, and the callous selfishness and mean calculating attitude to others of people like the Ryashkin couple in Tendryakov's *A Misfit*. If Ostrovoy's conflict with the new society should only have ended, as it did, with his downfall, the Ryashkins, while not being actively hostile to Soviet society are exposed as carriers of ideas that are opposed to its ethics and moral norms.

Fyodor, the son-in-law who enters Ryashkin's household, rebels against the psychology of the Ryashkins and their way of life not because he fully understands the sources of their views or the fact that their way of life represents a survival of property relationship in socialist society. He condemns this alien way of thinking from the standpoint of ideological and moral criteria that have become a part of himself, which he has acquired from his own experience of life in Soviet socialist society. Different criteria of assessing moral and ethical qualities of man and his goals, different stimuli to activity hold sway in Fyodor's everyday environment than those which govern the little world of the Ryashkins and others who have not broken their spiritual links with money-grubbing.

Socialist realist literature has not only investigated and depicted such new motives of human behaviour but has shown how they are established in life as an organic part of man's practical experience and his personal life, gradually ousting moribund views and concepts from his consciousness. This process has not proceeded without a struggle. It is complicated and fraught with conflicts, sometimes extremely acute ones: but it is irrepressible, ensuring as it does that the consciousness of the individual and the masses does not lag behind the development of society and its economy. Socialist realism has reflected the new conflicts whose nature is determined by the energetic strengthening and affirmation of the ideological and ethical principles of socialism in all spheres of life. Sometimes these conflicts develop in a dramatic manner, but, in accordance with historical truth, the principles organically connected with socialism and most fully expressing its active, creative, constructive essence invariably triumph in the end, despite all the difficulties.

Such new conflicts, deriving as they do from the very nature of socialist relations and hence only possible once the new social order has emerged, have been scrupulously examined by socialist realist literature. Typical features of the new ideological and ethical principles determining relationships between people and between the individual and society were vividly expressed in, for instance, Yuri Krymov's novel *The Tanker Derbent*, which analyses the psychological effects of the change in a man's attitude to his own work and his personal duty to the collective and hence to society.

The hero of the novel, the mechanic Basov, is presented in sharply conflicting relationships with many people, with his work-mates and the factory management, and the general consensus is that he is rather a misfit. Assigned by the factory management to the shabby oil tanker *Derbent*, he still refuses to resign himself to routine and indifference and his behaviour and views of man's duty and purpose remain unchanged. But his discord with his fellows has far-reaching effects: his personal life is disrupted, his wife whom he loves dearly left him and he finds himself alone among strangers, who comprise the crew of the *Derbent*, alone with the inhospitable Caspian Sea and monotonous work, with nothing to break the endless tedium of routine repetition. On the surface the conflict of the novel is somewhat similar to the typical conflicts of non-socialist literature, describing man's loneliness in the world, in society.

Bourgeois ideology, art and literature tend to treat human loneliness as total and unamenable to the meagre means of communication—fear, sex, the thirst for violence, the urge to command or obey—the kinds of ties that allegedly dominate the whole system of human relationships. Democratic literature has often treated the theme of human loneliness for the purpose of showing the incompatibility of man's moral and spiritual aspirations with the opportunities provided by society. In presenting the tragedy of human loneliness, democratic literature was criticising society itself.

Basov's loneliness is fundamentally different in character. He is not at odds with society, with the *social system* in which he lives and acts. His philosophy of life, his social views, his very feelings, are rooted in socialism and his character has been moulded, shaped and tempered by the socialist system. What we have here is the *apparent* loneliness of the man who rebels against routine and apathy, against the inability and refusal to keep up with the rhythm of the time with its changing, growing demands. Basov enters into conflict with his work-mates and the management because he represents a new, higher level of socialist awareness, and his actions are stimulated by the desire to make fuller and more active use of the opportunities the socialist system offers people, above all in the sphere of work, which is transformed from fulfilment of a task to a creative act. A special feature of this conflict is that Basov's opponents are not at loggerheads with the social system either and are convinced that they are acting for its good. However, Basov undoubtedly renders greater real service to society with his work than his opponents, so that the objective conditions are there for Basov to emerge the victor in the struggle of views and attitudes to duty he has embarked upon, responding to the demands of the time.

For a creative attitude to work to be implemented in practice, it is essential to fight routine, and keep up creative ardour at all times. This is a difficult task, demanding constant spiritual uplift and necessitating the struggle of a man with himself to resist the temptation to take it easy, as well as with many people around him. Basov has a hard time, because not only his work-mates but his wife too regard this attitude to duty and work as exaggerated and excessive. But the logic of events shows that his understanding of personal responsibility should become the general principle of behaviour in socialist society. Basov could never have emerged victorious in the conflict had he really been alone. But many other people share his attitude to life and Basov merely reflects and expresses in his behaviour a widespread spiritual process. He could not have won had he been isolated from the collective which took shape aboard the *Derbent,* where people gradually came to understand the meaning of their work and its social importance and adopt a creative approach to it.

Basov is the carrier of a new social ethic, a new socialist attitude to duty and work, and the ethical principles by which he is guided contrast sharply in their humanitarian essence with the individualist ethics to which those two relics of the past adhere—the Captain Kutasov and the navigator Kasatsky, who abandon drowning men to save their own skins.

The new ethics fosters a creative attitude to labour and lies at the root of the collective feat performed by the crew of the *Derbent,* when they rescue their fellow sailors from the flames of the blazing tanker.

Basov was the moving spirit of this feat, Basov, who embodies many features of the Soviet character. It was men like him—people who did not lose heart in the gravest circumstances, who were entirely dedicated to the cause of socialism, who never evaded personal responsibility—that became commanders of companies, battalions and regiments during the Great Patriotic War, bearing on their broad firm shoulders the colossal weight of the initial defeats and the daily hardships of war, which paved the way to Victory.

Socialist ideology, like socialist art and literature, are profoundly and organically international by nature. Soviet literature, a multi-national literature, reflects the integrated process of establishment of socialist relationships and concepts within the nations that once stood at very different levels of social and cultural development. The affirmation of socialism, an integrated process for all the nationalities inhabiting the Soviet Union, is effected through the development of the democratic cultural traditions of each people, so that Soviet socialist culture is really a harmonious confraternity of interrelated cultures mutually enriching one another. This new form of relationship between peoples is reflected in socialist realist literature, which wages an uncompromising struggle against all kinds of ultra-nationalism and chauvinism, those inherent features of bourgeois ideology and the bourgeois concept of international relations.

Socialist realism regards contemporary socialist life as a sphere where personal requirements for action and creativity are achieved, as a sphere offering ample opportunities for the satisfaction of human material and spiritual demands. At the same time, the new socialist reality is regarded as the historically-conditioned consequence, and direct logical outcome of the previous development of society, as the triumph of constructive, democratic forces of history within every national culture. Therefore, along with works reflecting the contemporary historical process, history in the making, socialist realism has organically engendered works presenting the significant events and contradictions of the past that illuminate and explain the path trodden by the masses during their historical existence. The spirit of historicism, inherent in socialist realism, has determined the approach of socialist realist writers to past.

A central theme of Soviet historical novels has naturally

and logically been popular movements, events connected with peasant uprisings in Russia, with the struggle of the masses for social and national emancipation. A great deal of attention has been devoted to analysis of the relationship between the individual and history, the complex problem of the individual's perception of the historical process, the relationship between the individual and the State, the development in the consciousness of advanced people of the past of emancipatory ideas and aspirations. Chapygin's *Razin Stepan* and Vyacheslav Shishkov's *Yemelyan Pugachov*, the novels of Olga Forsh, Alexei Tolstoi's *Peter the First*, Mukhtar Auezov's *Abai*, S. Borodin's *Dmitry Donskoi* and V. Yan's cycle of novels about the Tatar invasion all contained a new view of history as the collective creative activity of the popular masses and the arena of their struggle for freedom against oppressors.

In the bourgeois historical novel history as a rule has been regarded either as a vast theatre wardrobe from which historical costumes were borrowed for characters who bore no relation to real history except for the external attributes of the past, or as an irrational, inscrutable sphere in which the powerful isolated individual pursued his personal interests, regarding all others as instruments to be used for their attainment. The socialist realist historical novel is opposed to this kind of view and refutes the idea of individual wilfulness and the various theories justifying cruelty committed in the pursuit of personal goals. V. Yan's novels are typical in this respect, providing as they do a comprehensive picture of the Mongol invaders savaging civilised lands, wiping whole cultures from the face of the earth and destroying and enslaving peoples, in many cases arresting their general cultural development. The brutality and inhumanity of Jenghiz Khan and his successors—a feature common to other conquerors—was presented by the author as the result of a supreme indifference to the value of human life and the benefits of civilisation, which makes for more human relationships among people and provides opportunities for the development of the human personality. The humanitarian idea that is the keynote of the novels throws in starker relief the destructive, disruptive role of Jenghiz

Khan in history, the illusory grandeur of his dark deeds, the barbarous cruelty that accompanied his conquests.

While the critical realist historical novel regarded the lone individual and his humanitarian aspirations as the prime mover of the historical process, socialist realist literature shows that he who wants to leave his trace in history must defend the progressive ideas of his age and express the aspirations of the masses. The critical realists sought in history the confirmation of their views of life, society and man. They frequently presented history as a collection of facts and events through which they were able to express their attitude to their own time, to contemporary life. For them past and present were essentially similar, not because the present was regarded as inheriting certain traditions from the past, but because they looked upon both as the scene of an eternal struggle between reason and unreason, humanity and inhumanity. This was the approach of Lion Feuchtwanger, as a logical result of which his historical hero—the bearer of reason and humaneness—was isolated from the masses, since the latter, lacking the culture and education of the individual humanist, were prey to prejudices that closed their minds to historical reason.

The revival of "the hero and the crowd" theory, which is totally alien to Marxism, as a result of the personality cult, had an extremely adverse effect on the historical novel, as indeed on the development of other genres in Soviet literature. In many cases the masses faded into the background, historical conflicts were simplified and the spotlight was on the idealised figure of this or that historical personage, even such as Ivan the Terrible, who, as his name implies, did not earn the affection of posterity.

The "no conflict" theory, whose influence was to be felt especially oppressively in novels on contemporary themes, banished class conflicts from the historical novel and adjusted the past to the burning topics of the day: the role of the State was excessively idealised and the masses, the makers of history, were relegated to the role of executors of the designs of individual personalities towering above them. But these views that are alien to Marxism and socialist realism were opposed by the entire experience of Soviet literature and the live traditions of the October Revolution, which continued to be a powerful source of inspiration. Nikolai Ostrovsky's novel *How the Steel Was Tempered* had a powerful ideological and aesthetic impact for it not only contained a character whose passionate, wholesome nature and view of life were moulded in the crucible of the revolution and the struggle for the establishment of Soviet power, but presented through episodic characters, a collective portrait of the heroes of the revolution years, whose life and deeds served as a vivid moral example to the succeeding generations.

The hero of the novel—on the surface a simple straightforward story, but really a most profound and complex work—won people's hearts above all with the purity of his ideals and convictions, in the name of which he was prepared to perform, and did perform, great deeds of self-sacrifice, as well as with his fairness to other people. For Pavel Korchagin the world consisted of clear, straight lines, and not because he simplified the real complexity of life, but because he was able to grasp the essence of things, to tell the important from the secondary, and to perceive the true nature of the conflicts he was involved in. Thanks to his integrity, his clear-cut, partisan views, he would never compromise with views and behaviour that were alien to him, and never allowed himself to be misled by Left-wing pseudo-revolutionary phrases or the ideological and other enticements of the old order.

Korchagin was a man of a heroic bent, and his heroism was not the product of irrational, reckless courage, but arose from his selfless voluntary service to the great revolutionary cause. Awareness of the great aims of socialist society was an organic part of the outlook of people of the age of socialism and produced that remarkable phenomenon that came to be known as mass heroism which was a major factor which contributed to the Soviet people's victory in the Great Patriotic War.

Nikolai Ostrovsky's novel was an early and successful attempt to present in full dimension this new social phenomenon brought about by the great movement of the masses, their awakening to conscious historical activity.

Ostrovsky constructed his novel as a generalised description of the life of the ordinary rank-and-file participant in the revolution, with a main current connected with Pavel Korchagin and interspersed with numerous episodes providing a glimpse of fighters for the revolution some of whom were of the same cast as Korchagin and some showed features testifying to a more mature experience of life and political struggle. The revolution's fighters of whom the novel provides a collective portrait, were, like Korchagin, distinguished by lucidity of views and an ability to orientate themselves in the changing political and social circumstances. They were all engaged in conscious creative historical ability and not simply executing the will of some superior, supposedly infallible mind.

All the episodic characters in the novel, despite the differences in their personal fortunes and individual natures, were ruled by the same social dominant, rooted in organic heroism. Yet in presenting heroism as an inalienable feature of people who have taken up the standard of revolution Ostrovsky never separated the heroic from the real-life conditions and circumstances, the historical situation in which his characters lived and acted—thereby revealing the historicism of his aesthetic thought, which is an essential attribute of socialist realism.

The extraordinarily acute sense of reality that is present in the author's portrayal of even the most unusual, exceptional situations in which the revolutionary period abounded, enabled Ostrovsky to convey the objective movement of life, to depict the genuine contradictions that Korchagin was called upon to resolve and the real obstacles he had to surmount. The real-life background of the novel—and this is one of its chief merits—has the maximum authenticity while at the same time radiating a powerful energy that inspires men to great deeds. The fine thoughts and feelings of the hero and secondary characters derive from the struggle for socialism in which they were engaged. The novel taught readers courage and fortitude and the ability to defend one's views. The hero belonged to the galaxy of fighters for the revolutionary cause who arose in full awareness to defend and affirm its ideas, having been prepared for this by their whole experience of life. They measure people's actions, their own included, against the yardstick of the revolution and its ideals, valuing above all independent thought, and the ability to constantly feel one's own responsibility for the success of the cause. Adhering unswervingly to the new socialist ethics, they regarded it as one with the interests of the State, realising that in the conditions of socialist construction the State principle must serve to strengthen and develop the socialist ethics, making it the ethics of the whole people, part and parcel of the spiritual experience and moral world of people at different levels of social awareness, including some starting right at the bottom of the ladder.

Ostrovsky's novel revealed with tremendous power the intrinsic heroism of people making history and remaking life. This was in accordance with the spirit and purpose of socialist realism, which affirms the noble features of human nature, the qualities that enable man to free himself from base instincts and habits implanted in him by the society based on private ownership.

Like other socialist realist works, Ostrovsky's novel was pervaded with deep patriotism, as is only natural, since the socialist revolution, investing state power in the people, destroyed, among other myths of the old society, the myth that patriotism automatically unites the interests of the ruling and oppressed classes—a false thesis used to justify chauvinism and imperialist annexation and oppression. The socialist revolution brought forth the profoundly internationalist idea of defence of socialist society and the gains of the revolution. This was also an essential idea of socialist realist literature, which took part in the patriotic education of the masses and prepared them to bear the unparalleled hardships and trials that fell to their share during the Great Patriotic War.

The events of the war, which decided the question of the very existence of socialist society, greatly strengthened Soviet man's sense of unity with his socialist homeland. This found reflection in the literature of the time which presented the intense and dramatic experiences of the people fighting for their freedom.

The socialist realist method made it possible to capture

and reflect new features in the consciousness of the masses called forth by the tragic events of the war years. Literature was thereby able to examine the growth of the people's awareness of their historical responsibility for the destiny of the nation. In the process Soviet people acquired a deeper understanding of the basic organic links between the aspirations of the masses for freedom and the quest for social justice that had inspired progressive people in the past, and the revolutionary experience of the Soviet people who made the first attempt in history to put the ideals of socialism into practice. Thus, the idea of defence of the socialist homeland was organically fused with the ideas of defence of national cultural achievements, which greatly enriched the people's understanding of themselves and their historic mission and intensified their feelings for their homeland. Soviet patriotism, an organic compound of the progressive traditions of the past and the traditions that had become established in the life and consciousness of the masses during the years of socialist construction, was the seedbed of the heroism with which the Soviet people defended their achievements.

The aim of the war was perfectly clear to Soviet people, as were its causes. They were perfectly aware that it represented a clash between two fundamentally different social systems.

To fascist ideology, based on theories of racial superiority and intended to perpetuate class inequality, and the fascist morality, really a form of amorality, justifying all kinds of cruelty, unleashing base passions and instincts, encouraging violence and coercion and devaluing man, reducing him to the level of a beast, the socialist morality opposed high ethic and moral values and the idea of social and personal freedom materialised in the course of socialist construction.

Socialist realism, which absorbed the complex system of thoughts and feelings of Soviet people and spoke with tremendous sincerity and warmth of the people who took part in the greatest struggle in history, while conveying the burning hatred of society as a whole for the enemy, not only did not forego the principle of the international brotherhood of the working people but expressed the most humane ideas of the age—the ideas of human freedom.

Socialist realism expanded the sphere of investigation of life and penetrated the spiritual world of its heroes who defeated the enemy in fierce combat, focussing attention on those features and qualities of Soviet man's spiritual world in which the social experience of the builders of socialism, the sons of the new civilisation, was crystallised.

During the war years one of the major themes of Soviet literature was, as it were, brought to completion, the theme of the struggle of the masses and the individual for the ideals of the revolution, characterised by a study of the process of man's entry to the new life, which he created with his own hands, by his own labour. The literature of the war years, which, like all aspects of Soviet ideology at the time, was mobilised to accompany the soldiers on the battlefields, and to extol their feats of valour, *took stock* of Soviet man's moral progress made during the period of socialist construction, for in those harsh years history put to the test both the material and moral achievements of socialism. Soviet literature passed this test with flying colours, for it presented in all genres, as did socialist realist art as a whole, the hero *equal to* historical events of unprecedented complexity and gravity, the hero whose spiritual world and experience were adequate to the experience of history and enabled him to understand the essence of what was happening, its historical meaning and character.

The hero of Soviet literature—and this was one of the most telling qualities of the new literary method—felt his own actions to be a part of the historical action of the whole people, but he retained his individuality and vital authenticity never becoming a mere personification of an abstract idea. The sharp, blown-up characterisation, often dispensing with the detail found in the war years literature did not contradict either the psychological or the social truth of the time. This applied to many characters—the complicated Panfilov and Momysh Uly in Bek's *Volokolamsk Highway*, the scouts in Kazakevich's *Star*, the soldiers in Platonov's and Dovzhenko's stories, the partisans and popular leaders in P. Vershigora's *Men with a Clear Conscience,* the tankmen reflecting on the destiny of their country and the world and nature of good and evil in Leonid Leonov's *The Capture of Velikoshumsk,* Konstantin Simonov's and G. Beryozko's portraits of military commanders, and the doctors and nurses in Vera Panova's *Fellow Travellers.*

The close attention paid to man's inner world in the literature of the war years, the study of man's moral nature and the roots of his character, link the Soviet literature of that period with contemporary literature in a single, uninterrupted tradition not only in subject matter —the war theme still occupies an exclusively important place in socialist realism today—but in the way it presents the growth and strengthening of communist features in Soviet man. There are of course obvious differences in the scope and degree of reproducing these features and the moral questions facing man found in the literature of the war years and today, but the difference is to be ascribed to historical experience and not to the approach to the subject, which is the most important for socialist realism.

Naturally, with an accent on man's moral experience the lyric element was strengthened in the literature of the war years. The poetry of those years spoke with remarkable spiritual purity of the innermost thoughts and feelings of people finding themselves face to face with history, of their attitude to life and death, love and hatred, of their feelings for their country and their sense of duty towards it. The verse of Olga Bergholtz, Alexei Surkov, Nikolai Tikhonov, Mikhail Isakovsky and others conveyed the tragedy of the times without any sense of doom and were imbued with faith in victory and unshakeable belief in the justness of the cause for which men and women were fighting at the front and in the rear. *Universal feelings* uniting man with his fellows, the age and the people took the place of *personal* feelings in the lyric poetry of those years. There was a strong lyric element in such major epic works of the time, as Pavel Antokolsky's *Son,* Margarita Aligher's *Zoya* and especially Alexander Tvardovsky's *Vassily Tyorkin.*

The combination of lyrical feeling with epic scope in the presentation of the essential aspects of the psychology of the masses enabled Tvardovsky to create the image of a *typical Soviet soldier* of the Great Patriotic War.

Lyrical feeling rich in subtle shades and imbued with intense grief and pain for the suffering homeland and the optimism deriving from the people's unshakeable belief in victory was tested against the experience of the masses reflected in that of the hero, making *Vassily Tyorkin* a truly epic work. The determinant feature of Vassily's character, discovered by the author in the very thick of the mass of soldiers, and expressing the sentiments, thoughts and hopes of that milieu, was that he was a typical Soviet working man, educated and formed by the socialist system, drawn by the course of historical events into the war and fully aware of its decisive importance to his country and the whole of mankind.

There is no barrier between Vassily and the people, he is himself of the people and this inseparable fusion between the hero and the fighting masses represents a new historical phenomenon, the unification by socialism of all layers of the nation in the defence of the gains of the revolution.

A son of the socialist system, Vassily possesses a high sense of personal, human and civic dignity, a high level of social awareness. Casually, as it were, without undue emphasis, with a sly smile, but never departing from the truth, the author showed the historical scale of his hero, who throughout the hard times of war managed to retain a sober appraisal of the disposition of forces, not only on the battlefield but in the arena of history. He is fully aware that it is the people who must tip the balance in their own favour, for only the people are responsible for the present and future of the way of life and social order they have chosen.

The presentation of the hero's mind as capable of fully grasping the essence of the historical time is one of the major achievements of socialist realism, for in works based on other creative methods the hero frequently fails to achieve this. Critical realist works rose to this height when the author's spontaneous historicism widened his

outlook and enabled him to perceive and present the leading, determining contradictions of the time.

Vassily Tyorkin's clear and lively mind of a man of the
people, together with his authentically national character,
account for the charm and impressive strength he emanates. Vassily is thinking all the time as well as acting,
like the author, who embodied in the poem his philosophical reflections on life and death, man's behaviour in
the unnatural conditions of war, on the aim and purpose
of the war, on the past and present. This intellectual element that pervades the poem is clearly seen through the
apparently simple texture of the narrative, concealed behind the simple talk, banter and lyrical digressions. It is
constantly felt in the vivid generalisation, and in the very
atmosphere of the poem, which is infused with the high
moral purity. The breadth and depth of the hero enabled
the author to convey through him the people's understanding of the vital values he is defending in mortal combat with the enemy.

For Vassily socialism with its established system of relations, everyday life, institutions and social structure is the
concrete reality which he himself has created with his own
hands, his own everyday environment, the air he breathes.
He cannot imagine himself outside socialism since for him
and millions of other working people the new system of
social relations is the natural form of social existence.
What Vassily appreciates above all in socialism—as befits
a man brought up in socialist society—is the personal human freedom it provides, the opportunity to be creative
and engage in constructive activity. This key idea of the
poem is revealed in the highly significant dramatic scene
of Vassily's battle with Death, who tempts him, a man
bound by numerous threads to society and his fellow men,
to break these threads and abandon the most important
thing in his life, constructive work, which for him would
have been tantamount to death—both physical and moral.

Tyorkin opposes Death's temptations—its insidious
demagogy, its attempt to instil doubt and lack of confidence in his own powers into the hero's soul, its call for
submission and resignation and its promises to remove
from his shoulders the excessive burden history had

placed upon them—with longing for action, for creative, constructive activity. His faith in his own ability to put right and restore what the war had destroyed, his firm belief that a man's purpose in life is to act rather than to vegetate, enables him to reject Death's false temptations, behind which Nothingness lies.

This praise of constructive activity, found in many of the works written during the war, this ability to perceive and accentuate the determinant quality in the character of people in socialist society—the creative principle—is a link between the literature of those years and present-day Soviet literature, whose major task is to present the creative, constructive element in man, which is being moulded by the new social relations. This theme is organically connected with processes going on in society, with the appearance of new problems determining the relationship between man and society in conditions of mature socialism, in the period marked by the beginning of communist construction.

The changed conditions of social life have introduced qualitative changes in the relationship between man and society, accelerating the formation of a collective awareness in Soviet man and erasing the difference between personal and social interests. Major socio-economic changes have produced the prerequisites for the emergence of the phenomenon Marx and Engels called "real community". As they wrote in *The German Ideology*: "The illusory community, in which individuals have up till now combined, always took on an independent existence in relation to them, and was at the same time, since it was the combination of one class over against another, not only a completely illusory community, but a new fetter as well. In the real community the individuals obtain their freedom in and through their association."[1] Consequently, man can only acquire real freedom in society on condition that he does not separate himself from it but transforms it from a conglomeration of class antagonisms and conflicts into an association of individuals united by a collectivist self-awareness and overcoming the distinctions engen-

---

[1] K. Marx, F. Engels, *The German Ideology*, Moscow, 1964, pp. 91-92.

dered by class, property and national inequality, the opposition between town and countryside and differences in
culture and educational standards. The strengthening of
"their own association", that is, of socialist society provides objective conditions also for a harmonious development of personality for preservation of its integrity and
its spiritual enrichment. As Marx and Engels pointed out,
"only in community [with others has each] individual the
means of cultivating his gifts in all directions; only in the
community, therefore, is personal freedom possible."[1]

The socialist collective and the relations existing and
developing in it are the highest type of human relations.
Not one of the forms of class society is capable of elimi-
nating estrangement, competitive struggle, and lack of
trust between people. These features of human relations
between people characteristic of class society also determine the dominant form of relations between its members
struggling with one another and existing in various forms
of antagonism with one another.

In the socialist collective a different form of relations
between the members of society is created, based not upon
mutual enmity and the struggle of individuals for their
own personal, not infrequently antagonistic interests, but
upon concord, which gradually replaces other forms of relations bearing the stamp of the transitional period of socialism.

The transformation of society from a sphere where antagonistic contradictions are at work into a collective association based on concord and capable of solving the
inner contradictions of its development to the advantage
of the whole of society, and hence of the individual too,
is only possible when in the course of social evolution the
objective material factors of social progress are gradually
brought to approximate to the subjective factors, that is
the individual consciousness, which becomes aware both
of the historical necessity of the socio-economic changes
taking place and their expedience, their benefit to man.
This two-sided, but essentially integral process, determines
the development and growth of socialist society and

---

[1] Ibid., p. 91.

creates the objective prerequisites for its transition to a different, communist level. This extremely complex objective process, abounding in inner contradictions and marked by numerous difficulties, has now become the chief theme of socialist realist literature, which is investigating its concrete historical forms and the phenomena accompanying it and engendered by it in the social psychology and the inner world of men, who is changing himself in the course of changing society. Socialist realist works do not *illustrate* this process, following the outward chronology of events, but *reflect* it capturing and presenting above all its consequences for the spiritual experience of the individual.

The advantages of the socialist realist method, namely, that it permits a synthetic analysis of both social phenomena and man's inner world with all their interconnections and isolation of their dominant features were made broad use of by the exponents of the method in generalising and reflecting the determinant features of the spiritual make-up of Soviet people who lived through one of the most terrible, destructive wars in human history.

For the bourgeois consciousness the ideological consequences of the war, which ended not only with victory over Hitlerism but with the ominous mushroom cloud, involved disillusionment in man's abilities and objective value, and in his capacity to overcome the power of his baser instincts over the humane aspects of his nature. Prevalently pessimistic views of human nature have predetermined the success of existentialism, the spread of the "philosophy of the absurd", the strengthening of irrational concepts in the philosophy of history and the endeavours of bourgeois ideologists to blame man rather than the system of social relations for the dehumanisation of life in capitalist society.

Socialist realism, reflecting as it does the objective features of life, the humanitarian character of the socialist system and its moral principles, has presented a totally different picture of man—man who far from having lost his humanity in the unprecedented trials of the war actually increased his spiritual wealth. The boundless sufferings he went through failed to deprive him of the ability to sympathise with other people and understand the true measure of their pain. Andrei Sokolov, the hero of Sholokhov's story *The Fate of a Man*, who, like thousands of others, fought the war in the ranks, drained the people's cup of sorrow to the dregs and knew from his own bitter experience what the nazi New Order meant, knew the stifling oppressiveness of nights in a concentration camp, the atrocities of the fascist butchers and slave labour for the Reich, did not regard saving his own life as an end in itself—he had looked death in the face too many times for that. Amid inestimable suffering and torment people like him preserved something far more important, their human dignity, their courage and will fed by the knowledge that they were fighting a war of liberation, their firm belief in the necessity and justice of the social system they were defending, which for them was inseparable from the concept of homeland. People of their cast—and that means the vast majority of those who bore the brunt of war on their shoulders—came to victory acquiring tremendous confidence in man's indomitability and capabilities, and devoted their energies to restoring their country after the ravages of war.

The decisions of the Twentieth Congress of the CPSU, which removed the vestiges of the personality cult and restored the true Leninist norms of social life, resulted in an increase in the objective value of the individual, his initiative and creative powers, for concrete social reality came to reveal the humanitarian essence of socialism ever more fully. This basic fact of the contemporary history of Soviet society has been submitted to all-round scrupulous investigation and found expression in socialist realist works, where the moral conflict has come to the fore in recent years, the accent being on portrayal of the development, struggle and triumph in the individual consciousness, social psychology and human self-awareness of new moral and ethical principles continuing and enriching all that is best in universal human morality and ethics. This humanitarian theme runs like a golden thread through works with very different subject matter, making for the ethical significance of socialist realism as the literature of the new civilisation.

However, the moral conflict does not replace the task of investigating and analysing social life and presenting the relationships between individual and society in their fullness, and showing the struggle of socialist ideology with the private ownership ideology. The moral conflict is interwoven with this type of investigation as an essential element, permitting the writer to achieve a more profound and clear understanding and presentation of the inner world of contemporary people, members of mature socialist society.

Despite the unity of basic views underlying socialist realist literature, it does not lead to uniformity of aesthetic and stylistic features. The new literary method is based on the individual freedom of the writer in understanding and hence depicting those aspects of life he examines and submits to aesthetic interpretation. Without prescribing any rules or any particular expressive devices to the writer, or restricting him in any way in his quest for new expressive means, socialist realism enables him to perceive and understand the truth of history and penetrate its innermost recesses where social relations are interwoven and social changes mature. The socialist realist method enables a writer to avoid utopianism and prevents him from confusing what ought to be with what is.

The importance of socialist realism in world literature lies in the fact that by presenting the determinant social problems of historical development and showing the inevitable emergence and development of new, socialist relations, it has proved man to be capable of overcoming the obstacles to social progress and creating a just society on a rational basis.

Critical realists have also examined the basic social conflicts of our day and age, and have investigated—though less directly and consciously than socialist realism—the objective process of the transformation of contemporary society from capitalism to socialism. This is only natural, since critical realism reflects the sentiments of the broad democratic masses, thus absorbing both the strong and the weak aspects of the democratic outlook, which give rise to illusory concepts of history. But through studying social relations, presenting the changes under way in society and investigating the position of man in the contemporary bourgeois world, the foremost critical realists came to the objective conclusion that the capitalist system is obsolescent and incapable of solving the contradictions by which it is torn, that it produces monstrous forms of coercion and enslavement and is capable of destroying civilisation.

This conclusion, which is reached by the foremost critical realists, is not always backed up by analysis of social factors that have a direct influence on the development of society and the course of contemporary history. It generally derives from reflections upon the causes of the collapse of the ideological and ethical values of bourgeois society, that is, analysis of the *effects*, testifying to the degeneration of society and its social structure. This conclusion is based on a study of individual human destinies, the make up and the motives underlying the behaviour of the scions of contemporary bourgeois society, its ideological life and family relationships, on the debunking and exposure of the illusions society engenders.

It became obvious to the critical realists that bourgeois society was beginning to hamper man more and more, depriving him not only of general but also of personal prospects. The illusion that bourgeois society can progress endlessly and that man can enjoy unhampered personal success and advancement within its framework had been lost forever. In his trilogy, Theodore Dreiser presented, against a broad background, the rise to wealth of an enterprising, strong-willed man Frank Cowperwood, who never gave way to setbacks and was undismayed by failures. Encouraged by his own philosophy of life—the strong will make the better of the weak—he strode forward confidently to success, climbing to the very top of the social ladder and becoming a leading financial magnate. Cowperwood embarked on his career in the years when the capitalist system appeared to offer unlimited opportunities, and the road to wealth seemed open to all. After some severe setbacks and blows to the capitalist system struck first by the outbreak of the First World War and later by the October Revolution, the future of both the capitalist system and the individual who lived under it appeared in a somewhat different light. Personal success and advancement became rather problematic. Clyde Griffiths, the hero of *The American Tragedy*, one of the masterpieces of critical realism, also longs for wealth and self-advancement. But if Cowperwood, at the end of the road, having overcome all obstacles, came to reflect on the vanity of life and the fortune he had amassed, Clyde Griffiths was awaited at the end of the road by the electric chair. This was not because he was a weaker biological creature than Cowperwood or less unscrupulous in his choice of methods to secure his advancement, but because the social conditions in which he acted had changed.

Though naturalist elements were clearly discernible in Dreiser's works, he did not regard the life of society and the struggle in progress there in the Spencerian spirit and did not substitute biological for social motives of human behaviour. He realised that the struggle going on in bourgeois society was clearly a social struggle, a struggle of interests and that it determined a man's behaviour, his character and views. Clyde Griffiths, who is prepared to commit a crime in the interests of his own self-advancement (although he does not actually murder his mistress, he wanted to be rid of her and made no attempt to save her when she was drowning in the lake), and later himself became a victim of the machinery of the law, the object of a clash of interests, intrigues and careerist and selfish aspirations, is by no means an inveterate immoralist. He is an ordinary denizen of the bourgeois world. There is nothing special or unusual about him: he fully ascribes to the views, prejudices and illusions of the society in which he was bred. Rough and uncultivated, he has been used since childhood to the rat race going on around him, used to seeing those people prosper and lord it over him, who were able to grab a good slice of pie for themselves. For him, as for others around him, personal success and assertiveness mean everything, and moral principles, of whose futility and fruitlessness he became convinced from personal experience, are driven into the background. Thus his amorality which led him to try and destroy his mistress who barred his way to success was the product of the amorality of society itself, and

Dreiser made it amply clear in his novel. He showed unambiguously how amoral and inhuman the relationships were within the Griffiths family, the rich branch of which, ignoring all feelings of kinship and purely human duty, left Clyde's unfortunate parents, street preachers, hawkers of religious morality, in the lurch, and put Clyde himself in conditions that objectively set him on the path to crime. Equally amoral is the mockery of justice that was played around Clyde, for in investigating the circumstances of Roberta's death, nobody was interested in the basic motives of Clyde's action. Not one of the participants in the tragic events is prepared to give a moment's thought to society's responsibility for corrupting man. Dreiser's novel refutes one of the most widespread and cherished illusions of bourgeois society, the demagogical thesis of bourgeois propaganda that everybody has unlimited opportunities for personal success and advancement. The bourgeois world turns a blind eye to those who lose out in the rat race and persists in enticing its denizens with the false glitter of success, firmly and mercilessly defending the class interests of the wealthy. Dreiser was bluntly outspoken about it in his novel.

The strong critical charge in the novel ensured that it came to occupy an exclusively important place in contemporary critical realist literature, signifying a turn towards investigation of the nodal contradictions of present-day bourgeois society. Dreiser opposed to the amorality of the bourgeois world the simple morality of the working people free from the blind pursuit of self-interest which held Clyde in its grip. They are capable of resisting the temptations which the world of social inequality offers them in such abundance, and preserving their human dignity. Roberta Alden, Clyde's lady friend, was one such person, and the author contrasts her morality with the other characters for there was much in her attitude to life that derived from the moral principles of the working people. The vivid contrast between different types of social ethic greatly strengthened the critical element in the novel.

The American Tragedy presents a merciless analysis of life in bourgeois society. Moreover, the author made a comprehensive analysis of the mechanism of the collapse of moral values in the consciousness of people in bourgeois society, treating this moral degradation as a social norm. This process also found reflection in Sinclair Lewis's novel *Babbitt*, written somewhat earlier.

Mr. Babbitt, a successful businessman from the flourishing American town of Zenith, symbolises a different aspect of moral degradation from Clyde Griffiths. Whereas Griffiths encroaches upon the Law, Babbitt regards anybody who doubts the Law as scum and a rebel against social prosperity. Whereas Griffiths comes from the lower echelons of bourgeois society, Babbitt is firmly in the saddle. But the difference is purely superficial, for both are products of the same culture and civilisation, of the same way of life. Griffiths' inner world is reduced to the thirst for success. Babbitt is also a spiritual pauper, but he fills his moral vacuum and his futile existence with worship of things. The root cause of this phenomenon had been indicated by Marx as follows: "Private property has made us so stupid and one-sided that an object is only *ours* when we have it. ... In place of *all* these physical and mental senses there has therefore come the sheer estrangement of *all* these senses—the sense of *having*."[1]

The joy of possession—the possession of his own house, full of characterless, standard, sturdy furniture and other domestic items, the possession of his own family, with a defeminised, dehumanised wife and not too obedient children who remain an enigma for Babbitt's standardised mentality, the possession of his own car and office, where his employees toil away, working cogs in a machine, for whose human qualities he has no time at all; the possession of a collection of stereotype, commonplace concepts of democracy, the advantages of private enterprise and the American way of life, fill Babbitt's spiritual void, and give him the illusion of leading a full life. In rare, brief moments of illumination, he senses, without fully realising it, how meaningless his life is. He does not dwell on these anxious sensations, however, but is immediately caught up

---

[1] K. Marx, *Economic and Philosophic Manuscripts of 1844*, Moscow, 1959, p. 106.

again in the routine of everyday humdrum existence. Babbitt, a typical bourgeois that he is, has no personal, human attitude to life: he thinks and acts within the framework of standardised forms of private and public thought and behaviour. His atrophied individual qualities and loss of independent characteristics are not peculiar to him alone: they are the result of permanent and active factors of bourgeois society that lead to a levelling of individual distinctions.

Babbitt has no firm moral principles of his own, but subscribes to generally accepted maxims which are convenient in that they form a shell under which he can hide his self-interest and egoistic calculations, dirty deals with his own conscience, dishonest business practices, which Babbitt refers to as good business sense and so on, and a host of other sins which do not bear close scrutiny.

Literature, philosophy and pedagogics have long tackled the question of the morality of the individual, his ability to develop true moral criteria for assessing his own and other people's behaviour, his ability to create inner barriers to destructive external influences. In its early days the bourgeoisie strove by means of religion, education and the arts to instil in the consciousness of their sons the virtues necessary for personal and civic life, in contrast to the corruption, frivolity and amorality of the aristocracy. However, the bourgeoisie did not adhere to strict puritan morals and Roman virtues for long: once they had seized power from the old society they acquired the latter's failings, to which were added their own. The need to hold on to power, mercilessly oppressing and exploiting the proletarian masses, enslaving the peoples of the colonies and displaying boundless hypocrisy and pharisaism, led to the cheapening of moral values in the bourgeois life and consciousness. Nietzsche scorned and mocked the accepted morality as a morality of slaves, of the herd, and offered in its stead a morality for masters, which was in fact total amorality. Decadent art and literature, flaunting its immoralism, made virtue of vice.

However the corruption of man by capitalism had very dire consequences. Amorality, like a cancer in the body of capitalist society, poisoned even the healthy cells.

Babbitt's moral indifference, so shrewdly observed and portrayed by Sinclair Lewis, was by no means a harmless phenomenon. A quarter of a century later another American writer, Arthur Miller, examined in his play *All My Sons* a typical case of bourgeois amorality culminating in treason, for the industrialist Joe Keller who had made a fortune during the last war supplying the US Air Force with faulty and substandard aircraft parts, was responsible for the death not only of his pilot son but of many other airmen in combat with the nazis. In the final analysis, Joe Keller collaborated with the nazis. The corruption of moral values and the collapse of moral fortitude in property-owning society is also responsible for the downfall of Ethan Hawley, the hero of Steinbeck's *The Winter of Our Discontent,* who from being a respectable pater familias and conscientious worker becomes a blackmailer responsible for the death of his friend, a cruel, merciless scoundrel. Hawley's transformation, that seems unexpected and inexplicable at first sight, in fact reflects the most serious process of alienation from man of his finest qualities.

But despite the fact that Babbitt's moral essence is completely amorphous and his inner world is a vacuum, that vacuum can be filled with highly dangerous stuff. The lively philistine bursting with vitality, the unscrupulous businessman, Babbitt regards himself and his confreres as the ideal model of what a man should be—the perfect citizen, the eminently sensible, law-abiding citizen, the standard citizen, which everybody should endeavour to imitate, for the "Babbitts" can offer them a decent Christian life. Babbitt is a fanatical champion of private property interests, with a fierce hatred for all whom he suspects of being opposed to them. Armed with an automatic pistol, in the ranks of some national guard or a unit of the Honest Citizens League—the prototypes of the present-day Minutemen or John Birchers, Babbitt, like all the other Babbitts, the host of businessmen, industrialists, bankers, store owners, restaurant proprietors and other „sensible", "law-abiding" citizens of Zenith, all standardised and depersonalised by bourgeois society, is prepared to destroy those whom he regards as opponents of his way of life—unarmed intellectuals, socialists and proletarians.

The first fascio, the organisation that gave its name to the most dangerous and reactionary political movement of the twentieth century, was formed in Milan in the spring of 1919. In the same year a hysterical demagogue who called himself Hitler was peddling the national-socialist "ideas" in Munich beer halls and at workers' meetings. Among those who were swept off the rails by the First World War, the ex-soldiers, ruined shopkeepers and declassed proletarians, reduced to desperation in a fierce struggle for survival, the future führers of fascism enlisted supporters and party cadres, preparing for an offensive against socialism. To begin with fascism posed as an anti-capitalist movement, skilfully juggling with Left-wing phraseology, but the critical realists—and this was the great service and testimony of the strength of realism as a creative method—perceived and divined its profoundly reactionary character, and the terrible threat it represented to mankind.

In Sinclair Lewis's *Babbitt* there is a premonition of this danger. In several of his subsequent works, *It Can't Happen Here* (1935), *Gideon Planish* (1943) and *Kingsblood Royal* (1947), Lewis made a more thorough analysis of the growth of the fascist menace in America. Other critical realists also examined the dangerous process, which testified to the profound crisis of bourgeois society that made the ruling classes adopt terrorist methods in order to retain their power and privileges. The essence of fascist ideology, the content of its demagogy, was revealed with tremendous acumen in Thomas Mann's *Der Zauberberg* and Lion Feuchtwanger's *Erfolg*. In presenting the emergence and development of the fascist movement, the critical realists naturally probed to discover what it was that enabled fascism to corrupt vast numbers of people. They pointed, as the most important of the causes, to the amorality of bourgeois society, the distortion of the moral values current in it, the loss of moral standards by many people, dehumanised by capitalism, the moral vacuum in their consciousness which fascist or pre-fascist ideology was quick to fill, as in the case of Mr. Babbitt.

The growth of amorality in the capitalist world was associated with the degeneration of the ideals of bour-

325

geois society, the absence of a noble idea capable of inspiring the individual and the masses to constructive historical activity, for the practical business ideology is powerless to do so. The bourgeoisie is capable of fighting to retain power, and has a vested interest in material-technological progress but it is incapable of advancing a constructive idea to solve the inherent contradictions of capitalist society.

Bourgeois literature had long since felt the lack of re-vitalising ideas in the society which had produced it. On the eve of the First World War André Gide formulated the ambiguous and dangerous concept of "pure" or "un-selfish" action in *Les Caves du Vatican*, action, that is, devoid of a concrete and visible goal and clear meaning. The idea of "pure" action was blowing in the wind, testifying to the crisis of the bourgeois consciousness. Gide took as his point of departure a perfectly natural situation: man is an active creature, therefore he cannot remain inactive. It is all a question of how and to what purpose he is to act. If people alarmed and enraged by the situation in bourgeois society sought ways to socially meaningful activity, Gide and others offered a sophist trap, by encouraging them to act and at the same time freeing them from the fetters of morality. The hero of the novel, the young Lafcadio, pushes an old man off a fast train in the name of "pure" action and afterwards feels at peace with life.

The fascist movement and fascist ideology, vociferously proclaiming their "dynamism" and "activeness" offered people thirsting for action a surrogate of historical activity and an ersatz idea of national superiority, giving "selfless" action a perfectly clear conservative aim, filling the vacuum contained in the concept of "pure" action with the brutal, aggressive system of fascist views.

But democratic thought, like the masses resisted reactionary ideology, its corruptive influence, and embarked on a more active search for socially meaningful action capable of resolving the terrible conflicts of our age and freeing man from the burden of suffering and misery engendered by the moribund social system. The powerful workers' movement, the rise of the anti-fascist struggle, and in the post-war yeare the peace movement and the struggle for socialism and national independence, in which the masses and the intellectuals have become involved, helped purge the democratic consciousness of many illusions and misconceptions about the course of historical development and its real prospects and produce a high level of social ethic, which has become a feature of the democratic outlook.

However, perception of the nature and sources of the chief contradictions of our day is fraught with grave difficulties, for the historical process itself has become incomparably more complex. The true difficulties of shaping the new social awareness were reflected by the art of critical realism.

Critical realist writers considered it inevitable that this kind of self-awareness should be developed, and this deduction testified to a grasp of reality which was entirely historical and which was given to literature only by realism. The detailed and many-sided exploration of the real world, of the true history of society, of the life of the human spirit and of the struggle of the various intellectual trends of the time, all lent weight to the deduction of critical realism that it was essential for man to move away from the way of life which ossified and killed personality, and which engendered the inhumanity, violence, and bitter social antagonisms of our age. The criticisms of society contained in the works of the outstanding representatives of contemporary critical realism by no means in every case or consistently rejected the private property system of social relations, and not infrequently were confined to aesthetic problems. But their spontaneous historicism of creative thought enabled the critical realists to catch and reflect, behind the personal human destinies or conflicts raging within the bourgeois family, behind the contradictions of private and social psychology, the substantial and universal social processes at work. The study of human relations and connections inevitably turned into an exploration of contemporary life and made it possible to establish the interdependence between conflicts maturing in the depths of the private sphere of human activity and the general historical conflicts of the age.

Man's growing dependence on processes at work in society was clearly perceived by critical realism, and this compelled the writers to reformulate and solve anew the problem of the relation between the individual and society, concentrating on problems of man's social responsibility for what was happening in the world. A similar preoccupation was characteristic of all the major works of critical realism in the twentieth century, and it was organically linked with the revolutionary processes taking place in contemporary society and stripping bare its glaring contradictions.

Exploring the relations between man and society in our age, Galsworthy, Thomas Mann, Sean O'Casey and Roger Martin du Gard based themselves on actual social experience, and subjected the existing way of life to extremely sharp and well-founded criticism, often progressing from the analysis of aesthetic conflicts, from the exploration of the sources of the moral and spiritual decay of bourgeois society, to an analysis of the social causes behind these phenomena, of the social contradictions which, in the final analysis, are what drive man to act this way and not otherwise. Consequently, twentieth century critical realism did not lose its ability for sweeping social generalisations characteristic of critical realism in the earlier stages of its development. This found expression in the big epic novels which have become typical of contemporary critical realism, inasmuch as the growing complexity of the historical process with its many motive factors, demanded a broad scope of presentation. The epic, naturally, did not displace the other narrative genres, but gained new stimuli for development in our age, fraught with social convulsions. The broader presentation of reality in the epic novel, the upturning of new layers of that reality, so to speak, involved the exploration by the realist writers of the historic destinies of the bourgeoisie, the central problem for contemporary critical realism, irrespective of whether their works depicted social processes, personal human destinies, or internal family conflicts reflecting conflicts of a more general and historical nature.

A monumental personification of bourgeois morality and consciousness emerges from the pages of du Gard's epic novel in the character of M. Oscar Thibault, who considers himself a guardian of public order and the sacred principle of private property, a pillar of the state and the church, and a defender of the bourgeois way of life against onslaughts by such natural foes of the privileged classes as socialists, atheists, proletarians and other champions of disorder. Roger Martin du Gard, in creating the capacious and significant character of Oscar Thibault, endowed him with the features inherent in and typical of bourgeois consciousness, which may also be observed in Soames Forsyte, or in Ferdinand and Amélie Boussardel in Philippe Hériat's *Famille Boussardel.*

The determining trait of Oscar Thibault's character is his conviction that the property owning order of things is the only one possible in life. According to M. Thibault, social inequality is an inevitability and, in its way, a kind of blessing. His feeling for property has driven out all other feelings, has distorted them and dehumanised them, giving his outlook an external semblance of orderliness, harmoniousness, and logically, all of which mask, his inhumanity. Similar phenomena are portrayed by Martin du Gard in *Vieille France,* where he shows how the "sense of having", to use Marx's term, dehumanises man, turning him into a selfish, avid and frenzied beast. Oscar Thibault, the founder of a corrective institution for juvenile delinquents to which he has had his own son sent on the strength of a vile suspicion, a family despot, a mainstay of political reaction, a law-abiding toady, has become a shell of a man who has lost any human personality he could call his own. But the order which he so stubbornly and unswervingly upholds is a pseudo-order seething with irreconcilable contradictions. Trouble is brewing in M. Thibault's family and his sons turn against him. The bourgeois family regarded by M. Thibault as an unshakeable institution, a citadel of order, is undergoing appalling disintegration, which has to be hidden under a mask of hypocrisy and bigotry. The society which M. Thibault has considered the acme of creation was inevitably heading for explosion, for a world war which has to shake the foundations of capitalism and summon into existence the socialist revolution.

The demon of private property, served by M. Thibault with such fanatic devotion, radiates a deadly emanation which poisons the hearts of men. With superb mastery of psychological analysis, du Gard shows how a way of life founded on the principles so dear to the heart of Oscar Thibault corrupts people in various ways, either depersonalising them, as in the case of Gise, or endowing them with the egoistical amorality which becomes second nature even to so outstanding and brilliant a personality as Rachel, or turning them into practical men whose vision is limited by a narrow social horizon, as happens to Antoine Thibault, who wants to adjust to the world in which he exists without reflecting on its imperfections, and who pays for his social blindness with his life.

A consistent and comprehensive portrayal of the dehumanising nature of the bourgeois world order naturally entails the question of man's relation to capitalism as a social system. Thus, du Gard's novel brings up the problem of choice, central to human existence in our time. Du Gard presents it by exploring the nature and causes of the conflict between Jacques and Antoine Thibault and their social environment, their protest against their father's authority and against the authority of the society in which they have grown up. The problem of choice naturally leads to the search for socially meaningful action.

Externally, the problem of what man is to do in an imperfect and cruel world has solved itself easily for Antoine. He is a children's doctor, a man in a humane profession, and he brings comfort to human beings by everyday activity. His hard and self-sacrificing labours, which are a source of great satisfaction to him, are described in the novel with real inspiration. The logic of a realist writer, however, exploring personal human destinies in their close interrelationship with the historical process, in other words, the spontaneous historicism of du Gard's creative method, enables him to demonstrate that Antoine's decision to limit himself to this kind of activity is essentially a false one, for it does not give him the opportunity to loosen or slash the tight knots of social contradictions, of the real conflicts of life, and encourages man to adapt to an environment whose meaninglessness he fully realises. History, moving inevitably and implacably onwards, does not allow man to escape or hide from its influence. This is confirmed by the tragic fate of Antoine and his brother Jacques.

Martin du Gard's epic is devoted not so much to the exploration of the bourgeois family, although this aspect is certainly there in the novel, as to elucidating the historical destiny of bourgeois society. The central part of the novel explores the details of capitalism's preparation for its greatest crime against the masses of the people— the First World War, which signalled a crisis in the whole social system of capitalism. For Roger Martin du Gard, the injustice of the property owning social structure is self-evident, and he realises the need for socialist revolution. Revolution as a means of establishing justice on earth is discussed by the Thibault brothers, and the writer does not conceal his agreement with the theories of the revolutionarily inclined Jacques. But, in a mature and highly developed capitalist society, the possibility of putting revolutionary ideas into practice seems to him impossibly difficult.

The embodiment of rebellion and protest in the novel, Jacques, who rises up against his father's authority, against the hypocrisy of the official morality and, ultimately, against society itself, is thirsting for socially meaningful action, and, after long spiritual wanderings, he seeks union with the European socialists who, by all the logic of things, should be implacable enemies of capitalism. But, at the crucial moment, they betray the revolution and become social patriots, supporters of war to a victorious conclusion. The path taken by the theoreticians and practitioners of the Second International proves false. The opportunists and social traitors opposed the solution of the radical problem of the age that was proposed and brought to fulfilment by Lenin, struggled with unbelievable ferocity, deceiving and corrupting the masses, entering into shameful deals with capitalism, perverting and slandering the ideas of the Bolsheviks. Millions of people whose tendencies, if not revolutionary, were at least anti-capitalist and anti-war, were deafened, deceived, disorientated by chauvinist and anti-communist propaganda, by the incredible howls of fury raised by the troubadours of national-ism. It was therefore extremely difficult for the masses to arrive at an understanding of what was happening. The fate of Jacques clearly demonstrates this complexity of the movement of an individual towards an historically grasped and socially meaningful action.

Totally disillusioned with the social opportunists and longing to put an end to the madness of the war, he turns in despair to individual struggle against social evil and, in the vain hope of addressing the hostile armies over the heads of their governments, dies a senseless death, shot by a gendarme. The path of individual strug-gle also proves to be a false one.

It is Antoine who takes stock of all that has been ex-perienced and thought. While he is dying, poisoned by gas on the front, he reassesses all the values by which he and his society lived and comes to the conclusion that his life and the lives of many people of his generation were lived wrongly in many respects, for they shirked social responsibility, did not intervene in what was happening, and allowed the grasping, self-interested bourgeoisie to decide the fate of the world.

Antoine and the author of the novel place their hopes on man's individual search for solution, but this search is aimed at understanding the historical truth, and there-fore the call to action in Roger Martin du Gard's epic, far from being an abstract one, is a real humanist call, offering the individual the opportunity of accepting the ideas of a radical reconstruction of property owning so-ciety.

The final section of du Gard's epic was written on the eve of the Second World War, and many ideas which found expression in the *Epilogue* were engendered by the new historical situation, which differed considerably from the one depicted in the novel. The writer does not at-tempt to modernise history, however. He observes a strict historicism, throughout the narrative which externally conforms to the traditional form of the novel. In *Les Thibaults* the author of *Jean Barois*—a novel with an experimental form which anticipated the modern cine-matic novels—does not experiment with form, but nevertheless his epic is the offspring of a new stage in the development of critical realism. Adopting some methods of naturalist aesthetics, du Gard actively introduces documentality into the narrative, yet he does not reflect the true facts and events of live history passively or descriptively, but includes them in the sphere of intellect of his characters, making the question of the paths along which history moves the subject of tense, sharp debate. The intellectual element pervades the novel and the discussions which take place in it touch upon the most important aspects of life.

Thanks to the flexibility of its creative method, critical realism was able to show the different aspects of the general crisis of capitalism, and it did so with a number of different literary means and devices.

Just as the brutal age of the Thirty Years War gave birth to the tragi-comic character of Simplicissimus, whose adventures and reflections exposed the meaninglessness of what was taking place, and the cruelty and brutality of the nobility, contrasting the lawlessness and anarchy which prevailed in a country ravaged by the Landsknechts, with the commonsense and humanity of the ordinary people, so the cruel, tragic years of the First World War produced the character of the good soldier Schweik, whose adventures and extremely sober reflections on the happenings in a world gripped by fear and hate, exposed the myths created to justify the capitalist system which had plunged mankind into the catastrophe of war.

Hašek's *The Good Soldier Schweik* gave a broad panorama of the decay of the old society—its law and order, morals and religion, public and private morality, state system and all the myths created by the ruling classes in defence of that state system. Nationalism and chauvinism, the idolisation of power and the justification of the right of the few to rule over the many, the cult of the army and violence, the principles on which bourgeois democracy rested, were subjected in this book to merciless ridicule and uncompromising rejection. Such a work could only be created by a revolutionarily inclined artist, who was fully aware that the old world was doomed, who possessed an enormous store of historical optimism, and whose talent was truly of the people. Under the effulgent and simple-hearted gaze of the good soldier Schweik the pet slogans of the quasi-patriots, the champions of war, the defenders of social relations which had outlived themselves, faded, lost their attractive colours and revealed their obsolescence, their hostility to man, to his natural, rightful needs and requirements, to his reason and the feeling of brotherhood which united the oppressed masses, but which had been corrupted and distorted by property owning society.

Twentieth century critical realism has produced few works to match *The Good Soldier Schweik*'s power to strip the social consciousness of its myths, cleanse it of illusions, give a true assessment of social phenomena, and tip off all the various masks from a society approaching collapse. Powerful, life-affirming laughter dominates Hašek's satire, and shakes the edifice of the old society to its very foundations. The actual literary manner in which *The Good Soldier Schweik* was written demonstrates the inexhaustible artistic potential of realism as a creative method, the widely varying means of expression.

Exposing the unreasonableness of what exists and is taking place, Hašek reduces to absurdity, to total nonsence, the outwardly logical arguments, concepts and situations typical of the everyday consciousness, morals and customs which the property owning way of life inculcates in people. The satirical hyperbole and grotesque condensing of the characters, the tenseness of the situations in which the heroes of his satirical epic find themselves, the concentration of the plot to the laconic terseness of an anecdote, the abundant introduction into the narrative of inset novellas, the polyphonic structure of the plot, the generalisation and enlargening of the characters, the rich and refined multiplicity of shades in the texture of Hašek's writing, all these features served the main aim of his narrative—to expose the essence of the social contradictions, to reveal the abnormality and sterility of a social structure which had unleashed the war and was incapable of satisfying human needs. All aspects of reality and social life were subjected by Hašek to subtle and flexible social analysis, making it possible to typify the criticised phenomena and suggesting the conclusion that it was logical and necessary to change a social system which had outlived its use.

The revelation in *The Good Soldier Schweik* of the incompatibility of the ruling social order with the personal and social aspirations, needs and requirements of man, which gives Hašek's epic a humanist tenor, was the form of criticising capitalism characteristic of twentieth century critical realism. In Hašek's work the social background is extremely broad, the writer's gaze penetrates into various spheres of life, illuminating with the light of merciless criticism the decrepitude of the old social order, and consequently the juxtaposition of the individual and society, man and the social system, is not turned into an abstraction. The central conflict of the work is revealed in historically concrete forms. This distinguishes realist art from the many non-realist trends of the twentieth century (expressionism, surrealism, and the school of the absurd, for example), and enables critical realism even in the portrayal of personal dramas or human relationships which would appear to bear on the private sphere of life, to show the deep-lying social causes and to reveal the inner inhumanity of the bourgeois world.

The drama depicted by Hemingway in his novel *A Farewell to Arms* opens in a beautiful natural setting defiled by the roar of guns, by senseless, savage slaughter. The retreating army, abandoning its waggons, strewing the path with the dead bodies of mules and soldiers, discarded weapons and silent machine-guns, loses its illusion about the justness of war, its faith in the reasonableness of everything which nationalist propaganda has drummed into the heads of the soldiers. The senselessness of what is taking place is also revealed by the fact that the victors—the Kaiser's troops—have gained an isolated victory in a lost war, after which will follow revolution, the Treaty of Versailles, the hungry years of inflation and the fascist takeover. Among those who lose all their illusions is the hero of the novel, "Signor Tenente" Henry, an ordinary person, one of the many whom the war has dragged into its maelstrom. All he is able to set against the tribulations inflicted upon him is his craving for peace and quiet, for simple human joys. He does not know how to think politically and analyse the link between cause and effect, but he says "that's enough" to war, thus liberating himself from the burden of arguments justifying his participation in the fratricidal combat. Hemingway sets the great power of love, human closeness, the joy and fullness of life, against the cruelty of the historical events from which his hero wants to find refuge in the sphere of private life. But this attempt at being a modern Robinson Crusoe, at escaping from the inexorable contradictions of life, ends tragically. Consequently, the death of Catherine is not an accident of fate. The tragic end of the novel, which is full of a high lyricism and compassion for man, reveals the incompatibility of man's aspirations and desires with the objective conditions of his existence. Therefore, in spite of the outward concentration on portraying human feelings and emotions, Hemingway's novel carried a great charge of social criticism, forcing his readers to reflect on the causes of human adversities and compelling his hero to seek for an answer to the inescapable question with which life confronts him and to define his attitude towards the forces at work in society. This need to study concrete social reality became clear to the critical realists, because the historical situation which developed after the First World War and the October Revolution in Russia, sharpening as it did the contradictions between the individual and society to the utmost, made the fate of the individual dependent on the outcome of the clash of conflicting social forces in bourgeois society.

Critical realist writers, sensing the instability of society, observing the changes taking place in it, noting the all-round moral and social degradation of the capitalist system, carefully studied the turning of the bourgeois to terrorist forms of preserving their own class rule. It was the ideological justification of the need for the ruling classes to turn to new forms of domination that Hans Castorp came up against, the hero of Thomas Mann's novel *Der Zauberberg*, the first realist work of the twentieth century to give an analysis of the phenomenon of fascism, its ideological sources and its methods of influencing people's minds.

Thomas Mann diagnosed the terrible disease from which the property owning society of his time was suffering. This disease, in his opinion, was an organic one of a social system which had entered the period of its decline, and Mann investigated the spiritual symptoms of the disease with highly refined methods of literary analysis. His realist mastery, which represented the peak of modern critical realism, injected new blood into the realist tradition, elaborating a literary language capable of conveying the variable, changing spiritual life of our times, the chaos and confusion reigning in the consciousness of people confronted with the irreconcilable contradictions of modern history, with the irrational element which the decline of the old order introduced into life and social development.

While retaining an extremely acute feeling for real life, a full-blooded awareness of the actual substance of existence, Thomas Mann, in his artistic generalisations, expands his portrayal to the scale of a symbol, simultaneously endowing an abstract idea or a sociological concept with real concrete substance and giving a concrete, definite phenomenon a broader meaning. Life in the Berghof sanatorium, high up in the mountains, where the novel's hero Hans Castorp finds himself by force of circumstances, symbolises the life of property owning society. Just as the lines of force cross an electric field, the processes taking place in real life cross the existence of the inmates of Berghof and are reflected in the sphere of the spirit, in the intellectual atmosphere surrounding Hans. The long battle for his soul between the representatives of different social and political trends in modern bourgeois thought, between Ludovico Settembrini, the humanist and adept in bourgeois democracy, and Leo Naphta, the advocate of totalitarianism, the philosophising Jesuit, who develops the tenets of fascist ideology, between committed protagonists who are determined to become Hans Castorp's tutors, this battle, which symbolises the battle of ideas waged for the "European soul", enables the writer to depict the real, objective condition of the social forces supported by Hans' self-appointed mentors.

Ludovico Settembrini, the refined orator, advocate of the ideas of the European humanists of the Renaissance, who sincerely believes in human progress and the power of education, who is the enemy of anarchy and disorder, the champion of reason, who is convinced that in the last resort reason will bring people to the promised land, to the universal victory of democracy, clearly perceives the threat to his own existence, to the "European soul" posed by the cruel, blood-thirsty arguments of Leo Naphta. But Settembrini himself reveals a lamentable discrepancy between word and deed, an excessive faith in the power of the word, and the conviction that the influence of the word can check the dark stream of reaction flooding the countries of Europe and threatening to destroy the social and political institutions so dear to Settembrini's heart.

A great deal in Settembrini's views was very close to Mann's own views. But his tremendous historical sense, his allegiance to the truth, his striving, typical of realism as a creative method, towards a profound understanding of the social processes determining the course of life, enabled him to reveal the historical limitations of Settembrini's social and political ideals, their sterility and incapacity to cope with the real difficulties facing man's social development.

His opponent and antagonist, the Jesuit Naphta, is a product of property owning society in the same way as Settembrini, a champion of the principles of degenerating bourgeois democracy. Naphta's ideology is engendered by imperialist reaction which was preparing to attack not only bourgeois democracy, but also the rights of the masses and the individual. He rejects universal human morality totally, categorically, regarding it as a manifestation and justification of human weakness and contrasts it with immoralism, the true core of the morality of the tyrants. His ideological creed is a mixture of Nietzscheism and irrationalism, an apologia for violence and the cult of suffering, contempt for reason and an appeal to instinct. For him there is only one aim—to preserve from destruction the social relations based on exploitation of man by man—and to further this aim he is prepared to stop at nothing. In praising the inquisitors Torquemada and Conrad von Marburg, the dark champions of spiritual and social despotism, Leo Naphta also praises the acts of the Holy Inquisition, regarding the burnings at the stake and executions as a most weighty argument in the struggle against all dissidents, against those who dare to defend and uphold the rights of man, human freedom and dignity. And whereas Leo Naphta confines himself to theorising, formulating and working out the fascist ideology, his followers, who could not care less about theories and were ready to accept the simplified truths proclaimed by "theoreticians" of the Naphta type—and there were more than enough of them—turned from world to deed, burning books in the squares of German towns and shooting workers and intellectuals. Bawling their militant songs they prepared their campaign for world dominion.

With remarkable sagacity Thomas Mann perceived the great danger posed by imperialist ideology and anti-humanist art which echoed it. The sinister character of Naphta was a warning against this danger, and the novel's hero Hans Castorp, equally wary of both the loquacious Settembrini and the demagogic incantations of Naphta, reserves his right to historical choice.

But there is one more force which acts on the mind and heart of Hans—the spontaneous force of the revolution which presents itself to him in the character of Klawdia Chauchat, a Russian patient at Berghof in whom restless anti-bourgeois and anarchist love of freedom and primordial power of love are fused into a strange blend which fascinates Hans.

Mann followed the Russian Revolution with great attention, sympathy and interest, but there was much in its character and motive forces that he did not fully understand, as show the novel *Der Zauberberg* and the literary-philosophical treatise *Goethe and Tolstoi*. Having passed through the test of love and urge for freedom, the hero of his novel remains on his own, alone with the future, independently seeking a path to the future. This solution of the hero's fate denotes not only the writer's inability to transcend the ideological limits of the democratic consciousness, which was true of many critical realist writers, but also reflects the objective difficulties of historical development in the highly developed capitalist countries, and the difficulty in understanding it.

The decline and disintegration of bourgeois democracy were obvious. And this indisputable historical fact became particularly striking in the years of economic crisis which shook the edifice of the capitalist economy. However, neither the crisis nor the disintegration of bourgeois democracy led to the creation of a revolutionary situation. After suppressing the revolutionary movements in Western Europe, the bourgeoisie declared a crusade against communism and resorted to new forms of maintaining class rule. It unleashed the fascist reaction on the populations of the weakest links in the capitalist system —Italy and Germany—physically destroying the most conscious and revolutionary sections of the nation, stupefying and deafening the people with nationalist and racialist slogans, and encouraging dark, base instincts in the masses.

The profound process of the transition from capitalism to socialism was very difficult to grasp for the democratic consciousness, which found it extraordinarily hard to understand the general, overall meaning of these historical events and the dialectic of historical development behind them. However, confronted with the obvious symptoms of the organic crisis in the capitalist system, the critical realists made a correct diagnosis of what was taking place.

Whereas Thomas Mann's *Der Zauberberg* analyses the ideological aspect of fascism, examining and criticising primarily its theoretical arsenal, the novels of Feuchtwanger, particularly *Erfolg* written just before Hitler came to power, depicts the practical side of fascism, so to say, its methods of putting into practice the abstract arguments of the theoreticians of force.

Erfolg presents an extremely broad picture of life in post-Versailles Germany which is turning to fascism. As the main symptom of this fatal process, Feuchtwanger points to the decline of bourgeois-democratic institutions, the gradual transfer of political power to the industrial and financial circles behind the professional politicians and administrators. He notes how afraid the bourgeoisie, the strong of this world, are of the people, who emerged from the flames of war with hopes of changing the existing order and are embittered by the hard years of inflation which the propertied classes used to put their financial affairs in order. He shows that this fear forces the industrial and financial bosses to support the National Socialist movement, called the movement of the "true Germans" in the novel, and its Führer Hitler, who appears in the novel under the name of Rupert Kutzner. Next to this vain demagogue, whose character is conveyed by satire and grotesque, the writer, true to history, places the figure of General Vesemann, in which it is easy to recognise his prototype—General Ludendorff, thus revealing the organic link between the ideologies of the military clique and fascism, and showing that one of the sources of the fascist reaction was the revanchism, the nationalism of the German bourgeoisie, whose aggressive cruelty and historical limitedness are also portrayed in the works of Heinrich Mann, Leonhard Frank and other critical realists.

Rupert Kutzner recruits to his cause all the dregs of society—hired assassins, thugs, petty bourgeois caught up in the grip of inflation—brutalised, hating everyone and everything, and ready to commit any foul act. Poisoned by war, by the ideology of war, trained for one trade only —to be a soldier, and fit for one thing only—to kill, a section of the younger generation who had not learnt to live in peace and was impatient with unemployment and inflation, offer their services to the fascist bosses.

The atmosphere of falsehood, hysteria, cruelty and bitterness spread by fascism stupefied people. The fascist agitators offered extremely simple ways of solving social contradictions, and the simplicity of their social recipes won over many who were undecided. Another reason why the lies spread by fascism, its social demagogy supported by terror, were effective was that bourgeois democracy had revealed its bankruptcy and obsoleteness.

In Germany it was incapable of transforming and adapting itself to the new historical conditions, as it did in other highly developed countries, and its disintegration during the years of the Weimar Republic was depicted with great accuracy and merciless authenticity in *Erfolg.*

Feuchtwanger showed that the democratic republic was just a façade behind which dark forces were rampant. And while the supporters of classical bourgeois democracy, so to say, who were brought up on the legal concepts of the time of its youth and could not adjust themselves when lawlessness became the law, died out like antediluvian reptiles caught in the Ice Age; while there were people like Dr. Geyer, who realised that the old forms of the state system were collapsing and tried somehow to deaden the onslaught of the capitalist reaction, the majority of bourgeois politicians were only too ready to compromise and come to terms with fascism, clearing its way to power. The characteristic features of a bourgeois democrat, who has embarked on the path of collaboration with fascism, are to be found in the novel in the retired Bavarian minister of justice, Otto Klenk.

The writer criticises society sharply, but his criticism has a very complex ideological basis, and the internal contradictions, characteristic of Feuchtwanger's world outlook, which have left their mark on his criticism, were also common to other critical realists, for their world outlook corresponded to the level which democratic consciousness had reached at that time.

Erfolg reflects a profound doubt in the creative abilities of the mass of the people, a distrust in their historical reason, common to many critical realists. The revolutionary struggle of the working class found itself almost completely outside the writer's field of vision, and peasantry was depicted as an amorphous, bigoted mass—the natural soil of rising fascism. Feuchtwanger, like many other critical realists, sensed the strength of the ideas radiated by the October Revolution. The fact that the revolution and the ideas accompanying it had exerted a most profound influence on the property owning world was becoming clear to him. He introduced the engineer Kaspar Pröckl into the novel, the bearer and representative of the most revolutionary ideas of our age. Nowhere does he express a hostile or negative attitude towards Pröckl, but the whole structure of Pröckl's world outlook is alien to the writer.

Feuchtwanger recognises the strength and viability of the Communist Kaspar Pröckl's views, but does not believe that they have a proper place in the intellectual and social life of capitalist Europe. To his mind these views are only one of the items in the parallelogram of historical forces, only one of the elements composing the mosaic of the spiritual life of modern society. He does not accept Pröckl's views, because he believes that the liberating idea which Pröckl serves is incompatible with humanism. Feuchtwanger did not see the humanist content in revolutionary ideas and subscribed to the liberal-democratic reflective brand of humanism. While recognising the need to change reality because it is devoid of reason, Feuchtwanger thought that the word could be the instrument of change, i.e., the gradual education of man in a humanist spirit, which, as he thought, would make it possible to rebuild the world without destroying the existing system of social relations, that is, without resorting to revolution. The method of overcoming social contradictions proposed by Feuchtwanger—and in this case he was expressing a viewpoint typical of critical realism—reflects the crisis of historicism characteristic of modern bourgeois and democratic consciousness. This crisis forced Feuchtwanger, in spite of his highly accurate observations on concrete life, to give a less than adequate picture of reality, and this inadequate portrayal of modern history, mobile, changing reality, this inability of critical realism to grasp and synthesise in art the image of the world, was felt very strongly by many critical realist writers.

Some of them, like Dos Passos, for example, solved the complex task of portraying the dialectic of the relations between history and man, the interconnection between the hero and the living stream of history, by resorting to montage. He inserted into the narrative various newspaper reports containing all sorts of information about events in society. This method which he called the Camera Eye was supposed to convey the sensation of the passage of time, to reproduce the distinctive aura of the age, its uniqueness. But the mechanical separation of real historical events from the human destinies of the heroes did not make the picture of reality more profound, and degenerated into a mere literary device. The very principle of portraying the parallel, non-intersecting destinies of the various characters, all taking place at the same time, which dominates in his trilogy *U.S.A.*, comprising *The 42nd Parallel* (1930), *Nineteen Nineteen* (1932) and *The Big Money* (1936), demonstrated the writer's inability to grasp *in toto* all the links of historical causes and effects determining the development of society and conditioning human destinies. The separation of man from the stream of time, from history, was not only a symptom of the crisis of historicism, for that in itself was engendered by more general causes, including the absence of a revolutionary situation in the developed capitalist countries and the critical realists' vague ideas about the future path of social progress. For Feuchtwanger, for example, history was the tragic balance of the forces of reason and unreason. Ernest Hemingway arrived at a stoic view of life.

The monstrous experience of the world war cheapened for him many of the social and ethic values of bourgeois society, revealing the falseness of its ideals, but this experience made his awareness of life remarkably acute, increasing his ability to delight in the simple joy of being alive. The tense leap of a trout caught on a hook, the light rippling of a forest stream, the scent of dry pine needles and a bonfire of juniper, the sudden rapture of passion, the affirmation of human bravery and dignity in difficult, sometimes highly dangerous, situations—boxing or bull-fighting—this is what Hemingway set against the meanness, cruelty and senselessness of life in a world which gave birth to terrible wars, which devastated man and deprived him of happiness, which took away from him all joy in being alive and hardened his soul. Hemingway sensed and conveyed most acutely the breach which exists between man and the world in which he lives and acts, between the requirements of the individual and the social order, which condemns man to senseless suffering.

Valuing courage, fortitude, the ability to defend one's own dignity and to preserve a feeling of human brotherhood and solidarity in difficult, soul-destroying conditions, Hemingway placed his hopes on personal human fortitude, regarding human striving to withstand the pressure of circumstances, the onslaught of life and injustice, as a necessity and a moral duty. However harsh and unjust, cruel and inhumane life may be, you must not give in, but bear all its adversities with stoic dignity, firmly, bravely keeping on to the end, without being afraid or making compromises, fighting and resisting that which is striving to conquer and crush you.

Stoicism became the keynote in Hemingway's writing, not just in the stories (for example, *The Undefeated, Fifty Thousand, The Short Happy Life of Francis Macomber, The Snows of Kilimanjaro,* etc.), but the long novels *To Have and To Have Not* and *For Whom the Bell Tolls* right up to the tale of *The Old Man and the Sea,* supplemented by new ideas, naturally, but nevertheless colouring the whole narrative. Hemingway's stoical personal and social position led him to concentrate on studying human behaviour and intensified his interest in psychological situations which force a person to decide to act in accordance with the requirements of his stoic moral duty. This explains the writer's tendency to study reactions to danger and risk of death, and look for subjects in a somewhat exotic sphere, very different from the everyday, ordinary, prosaic lives which most people live, which undoubtedly restricted the social range of his works, for the life of a boxer, bull-fighter, tramp, professional hunter, wealthy tourist on safari or seeker for thrills and excitement is only a tiny fraction of the social activities in the property owning world, and the conflicts developing in this narrow sphere are of a specific, restricted nature.

The stoicism of Hemingway's world outlook also determined the stylistic peculiarities of his narrative manner. Inner reticence, reserve, concentration on oneself, reluctance to show one's feelings—characteristic features of Hemingway's heroes, who clench their teeth and take their solitary stand against life and circumstances—also produced a special manner of communicating with one another. The characters do not express their thoughts and feelings openly. Only echoes reach the surface, signs or ciphers concealing the hidden life of their feelings and emotions. Thus the use of implication became a predominant feature of Hemingway's narrative art, endowing the outwardly simple subjects of his works with a wealth of meaning.

However, stoicism very obviously restricted the social action of the author's heroes. By defending their dignity, bravely withstanding the blows of life, or dying morally victorious, his heroes solved private problems and rarely, sometimes never, thought about more general questions of social being on which in the final analysis their own destinies also depended. They acted within a given social system, resisting its pressure, but not attempting to change it and not thinking of removing the forces hostile to man. For a long time Hemingway's creative development was hampered by the poverty of his feeling for history, by the fact that he could not see an historical goal capable of inspiring man and mobilising in him all the forces of his spirit and reason, giving his life a meaning that was not only important, but of universal importance. The crisis of historicism in the consciousness of critical realist writers, could be overcome only by turning directly to the vital, active forces of history, only by overcoming the illusions of stoicism which in the final analysis was proof of a limited social understanding and of the inability to detect in life the positive forces capable of changing society and opening up the path to historical creativity.

Hemingway's faith in man and love for him, the democratic nature of his views on society, enabled him eventually to advance to a more historical view of the world, which expanded the social range of his realism. This made it possible for him to include the main social contradictions in his portrayal of the time and to overcome the belief, engendered by stoicism, that man is able to fight social evils on his own.

This illusion was nourished not only by the atomisation of human society, the alienation of human interests, man's concentration on his private interests which separates him from the other members of society. Illusions of this kind were also nourished by the weakness of the working-class movement in the developed capitalist countries, its lack of unity which prevented the working class from taking concerted action against the capitalist system and was a most serious obstacle to the formation within the working class of a revolutionary, collective consciousness. This lack of unity led to the strengthening of social-reformist tendencies in the working-class movement and the activisation of the conciliatory activity of the right-wing opportunist Social Democratic parties, which deflected the working class from the political struggle and encouraged it to concentrate on defending its economic interests alone. Therefore, although they depicted the position of the masses of the people and gave a most authentic picture of the consequences of capitalist exploitation, its inhumanity and cruelty, the critical realists also reflected the immature social consciousness of the masses, their incapacity to make a correct historical choice.

The same inevitable question—whither now—confronted the heroes of Hans Fallada, the author of a tragedy about a "white-collar worker", set in the period of the most acute economic and political convulsions in the capitalist system, the metayers and tenants driven from their land, whose dramatic fates were depicted by Erskine Caldwell in his grim stories and novels, full of sorrow and compassion for the poor, and the hunger-driven unemployed in one of the greatest social novels in American literature, Steinbeck's *The Grapes of Wrath*. And it also confronted the critical realist writers themselves who by no means always and in all respects transcended the level of consciousness of their heroes.

Pinneberg, a lowly office worker who tries to live the ordinary life of an ordinary person, that is, work honestly for his boss in order to support his family, clashes with the soulless, discordant mechanism of a social system which is indifferent to his desires, hopes and plans. Slowly but surely he descends to the lower depths and is forced to live on the outskirts of the town in the wretched barracks built for those who have lost their homes and their jobs. For the employers he was a means of acquiring profit, for the trade unions a troublesome client, who irritated their officials and the labour exchange by his appeals for help.

Fallada showed that the very way of life in property owning society, the daily grind to earn a living, devastate man ruthlessly, not only depriving him of the simple joys of life and the chance of spiritual development, but also preventing him from understanding his position more clearly, from getting to the root of causes which have cast him into this disastrous situation. Pinneberg, the hero of Fallada's novel *Kleiner Mann was nun?* is reduced to despair, to total moral apathy, but this is the final stage in his evolution—the next would be hatred and resentment for everything and everybody, for life and the world. In real life the Pinnebergs tried to find a solution to the complicated social situation in which they found themselves by turning to fascism, i. e., by making a wrong historical choice. The writer did not realise that his hero was capable of embarking on this dangerous, self-destructive path. He hoped that the kind, humane qualities in Pinneberg's nature would protect him from making a fatal mistake, from surrendering blindly to the social demagogy of fascism, its promises and pledges, for which a bloody, expiatory price had to be paid, as history was to show. The writer's error was caused by the crisis of historicism which restricted his artistic thinking; the fatal decision made by the Pinnebergs was to a large extent the result of their limited social consciousness and showed how painfully difficult it is for historical truth to penetrate people's minds, what tremendous resistance it encounters and with what enormous suffering people pay for their meek submission to the reactionary forces of history.

Whereas Fallada's novels show people crushed by the weight of social contradictions and losing their power to resist the capitalist system, Steinbeck in his novel depicts people who are continuing to resist and defend their simple human rights against a social system indifferent to their private fates. At the very best they are necessary to society as a reserve labour force, a source of cheap labour.

With a host of unemployed like themselves, who have been driven from hearth and home, the Joad family journeys on in a rickety car, burying their old along the roadside, under the scorching sun and torrential rain, in search of the promised land where they will find shelter and work, where their children, who are running wild because of the unsettled life and lack of proper care, will be able to go to school, where the family will be able to settle its problems and the men will find jobs.

But the same vain hopes attract other people as well, and the Joads see thousands and thousands of families leaving their homes and setting off, they know not where, in search of shelter and work. And having reached their promised land of California, lush with vines and peach trees, they find injustice in the most obvious, visible forms—fields surrounded by barbed wire, landowners driving around in armoured cars with a fleet of bodyguards, brutal sheriffs and armed deputies, property owning sharks, who offer them and other unemployed a pittance for their work, strikes and blacklegging.

True to life, Steinbeck shows how the Joad family, once strong and closely-knit by its communal labour and traditions, disintegrates because it cannot withstand the devastating onslaught of external social forces. But at the same time he shows how anger at the injustice which surrounds them grows and matures in their hearts. They bravely resist this injustice, retaining the moral basis of their natures, distinguishing good from evil, honesty from dishonesty and justice from injustice, with the unfailing sense of working people. Misfortune and adversity has not destroyed their feelings of brotherhood, solidarity, compassion for the sufferings of others, and the ability to help other people. Steinbeck portrays large, generalised, to a certain extent symbolic, characters, typifying in them the features of working people, and assessing things from their point of view.

This constitutes both the great merit and the weakness of his realism, a weakness which is found in other critical realists as well. The very circumstances of their lives force the Joads to reflect on the reasons for their misery, on the causes of social injustice. They are ready to fight against it. The father, the head of the Joad family, gets as far as concluding that everything must be changed because it is impossible to go on the way things are. But for the Joads social injustice is something abstract, a faceless force—a Bank, Trust, or Joint-stock company. They do not know how to fight against these abstractions. They cannot grasp the total, coherent picture of social causes and effects because they are ready to fight against individual shortcomings in society, but not against the whole social set-up. This is also the position of the author.

The property owners try to frighten and confuse the Joads and others like them with cock-and-bull stories about the intrigues and plots of the "Reds", but the Joads are not afraid of them: they simply do not yet know and are not allowed to know exactly what these "Reds" want. But they do feel the urge to unite with other people in the defence of their rights. The collective feeling has difficulty in breaking through to their hearts, but eventually it does, and this feeling and the high moral fortitude of these working people are a proof that capitalism has not succeeded entirely in corrupting and stupefying the masses of the people, and that in their midst the grapes of wrath are ripening against the property owning world and the social injustice which it engenders.

The critical realist writers, while reflecting the objective difficulties of bringing the masses of the people, ordinary people, to a higher social awareness, at the same time were aware that in the midst of the people forces were maturing capable of resisting imperialist reaction, forces for which the question of the nature of social action was inseparable from the struggle against the injustice prevailing in the bourgeois world.

The study of this process had an important influence on the critical realist method, helping it to overcome the crisis of historicism and enabling its writers to understand and grasp more fully the essence of the contradictions rending society. The study of this process encouraged the critical realists to reassess many, sometimes fundamental, values of bourgeois society, forced them to re-examine the question of the individual's social duty, his attitude to social struggle, and broadened the scale and significance of the conflicts on which their works were based.

From destitution, the tedium of provincial life, ignorance and daily encounters with human cruelty, Salka Valka, the daughter of an illiterate woman totally crushed by poverty, in Halldór Laxness' novel fights her way to independence, and firmly establishes herself in the world in which she is forced to live, fully aware of its vices, and able to withstand the onslaught of evil in its many forms, guided by a sense of justice and human dignity. From being an illiterate young girl who thought herself lucky to be hired on a daily basis for a mere pittance at the local rich man's fish factory, she becomes the secretary of the fishermen's trade union, boldly protecting her own and her comrades' interests and ready to resist anyone who threatens her liberty, her rights as an individual. Halldór Laxness has created the large-size, heroic character of a simple person who comes to recognise the historical aims of the working people and to understand the true position of the exploited masses in a property owning society. His narrative, rich in different shades, combining lyricism and irony, and rooted in the folk epic, his subtle social analysis, and his penetrating study of the social environment which forms the individual, enabled the writer to generalise the important processes taking place in the people's consciousness and inject a spirit of historical optimism, and faith in the moral strength of the people, into his gloomy picture of life seen and portrayed in all its authenticity.

Into the remote Icelandic village where Salka Valka lives and fights come the ideas of socialist revolution, albeit in a very impoverished and simplified form. Their propagandist, Arnaldur Björnsson, turns out to be an academic dreamer, who is fond of abstract ideas but not the people who are to be inspired and guided by these ideas. For this reason he suffers a defeat when he comes to grips with life and his preaching does not bear fruit. Salka Valka intuitively senses the truth of these ideas, but does not know how to put them into practice in real life where crafty tradesmen and wily politicians are pulling the wool over the eyes of the illiterate fishermen, poisoning their slumbering minds with high-sounding words about class co-operation, enslaving them economically, and preventing them from uniting in the defence of their interests. However, her healthy class sense arouses hatred in her for the power of the rich, and having begun her spiritual development Salka Valka does not stop half-way.

She is made of the same human material as the members of the Resistance who fought the nazis in the occupied countries of Western Europe.

The historical events which caused an upsurge in the anti-fascist movement, i.e., the civil war in Spain and the proximity of a new war, changed the spiritual climate in pre-war Europe and were reflected in critical realist literature. The question of the need for social action, for a correct historical choice, became the crucial one for critical realism in these decisive years, dominating all the other problems which came within its writers' field of vision. The contemplative world outlook common to many critical realists, their social scepticism, their view of the people as a sluggish mass, were destroyed by the logic of the anti-fascist struggle. The anti-fascist movement was most heterogeneous in its composition and, while helping the critical realists to think more historically, it also revived the illusions about the ability of bourgeois democracy to solve the social contradiction of the age. But the glaring nature of these contradictions, the reality and direct proximity of the fascist threat, the example of the social experiment of the USSR which inspired hope in people's minds and hearts, the implacable events of history transformed the consciousness of the critical realists, forcing them to try to find new solutions to social problems. This process of social activisation of critical realist literature affected all its exponents.

For a long time Romain Rolland defended the spiritual values created by democratic culture against the destructive influence of capitalist society. For many a year he defended man and human dignity from the pernicious influence of bourgeois ideology, exploding the myths invented by the bourgeoisie to defend their own interests. He sharply criticised the idea of nationalism, derided and exposed the intellectuals' illusions about the alleged freedom of thought and action in property owning society and the autonomy of art from social life and struggle. He perceived and showed the corruption of the politicians juggling with the slogans of decrepit, senile bourgeois democracy, for whom he felt undisguised contempt. He called the spiritual and political life of his society a market place where people, ideals, honour and conscience were traded, where art was false and where the artist's conscience was prostituted.

Rolland studied avidly the social experience of the land of the Soviets, defending it against the attacks of the enemies of socialism—the spiritual fathers of today's anti-communists. He sought tirelessly for historical truth, courageously discarding his own illusions and overcoming his own fallacies, for his path to truth was a hard and thorny one, and he did not conceal how difficult it was to break with the past, how complicated to find "a formula for transition" from one type of social thinking to another. His works, including the monumental *Jean-Christophe*, which defended man and humanity were for a long time characterised by the abstractedness of their social ideal, their preoccupation with man's inner world in which, as Rolland thought, changes would take place capable eventually of altering the world through making it more humane. This view led to his intense interest in Gandhiism and the principle of passive resistance. One might have expected these attitudes and ideas to set the tone for his second monumental novel *L'Ame Enchantée*, begun as far back as the twenties when the victors were reaping the rich harvest of victory purchased by the blood of the millions who fell on the battlefields of the First World War.

At first the character of Annette Rivière may seem a continuation of that of Jean-Christophe, i.e., a person who cherishes and defends the idea of the brotherhood of peoples, of humanity, and who rebels on her own against society. But having accompanied his heroine around the jungles of post-Versailles Europe, having grown and matured with her as he harked with an open heart to the mighty call of history, and gazed with eyes wide open at the light of truth, which sharpened, not blinded, his artistic sight; having seen and portrayed the decay of bourgeois society, the degeneration of its moral, political and ideological values, the corruption of the young in the stone debris of urban civilisation; having divined and described the secret machinations of the politicians hatching a new war, betraying the national interests of their peoples and unleashing the savage fascist curs on the masses who were defending their rights, Romain Rolland, like his heroine came to the conclusion that truth was now on the side of the new world which was building socialism in extremely difficult circumstances and opening up before mankind the true path to the future. *L'annonciatrice*, the final volume in the series *L'Ame Enchantée*, was the work of a writer who had already transcended the limits of critical realism and arrived at a new method—socialist realism.

This explains why the social criticism in this last volume, which crowns the whole work, is so clear and uncompromising, unclouded and intelligible, and the portrayal of the characters and their social positions so profound. Losing nothing of his skill, but rather enhancing it, Rolland creates the majestic figure of a mother, a woman, who has hope in the future and fights in the name of justice in the present. The novel, though full of inner tragedy, is imbued with a firm belief in life, in the creative forces of those who fight to give practical embodiment to the great social ideals of revolution.

Whereas at the beginning of her life's path Annette Rivière regarded the sacred feelings of love, motherhood and compassion as the highest values and gave them preference over social duty, now, when humanity is confronted with the need to defend itself against the fascist threat and blaze the true path to the future, these sacred feelings fuse with social duty into a single whole. The mother's spiritual evolution is also repeated by her son Marc.

His way to the truth about his times is more difficult, although he does not have to bear the material deprivation and moral torment which fell to the lot of Annette —an unmarried mother who cut herself off from her environment and material prosperity. But he has to fight a difficult battle with the idols and myths of the bourgeois consciousness, and overcome the spiritual temptations of individualism, the fear of dissolving, losing his personality in the group of fighters for the ideas of socialism. He has to get rid of the idealist view of revolution, which he saw as a single inspired outburst that will immediately solve all spiritual problems and social contradictions. He found a guide and counsellor in the person of Assia, who teaches him to understand that the revolution is not just an inspired outburst, but a lot of hard work to cleanse the new-born world of the debris, disease and errors of the old world, that it is hard, daily toil of millions advancing towards knowledge and culture, toil which demands patience and inspiration. Assia, who has been through the hard school of life and the civil war in Soviet Russia, teaches Marc to think realistically about people, not to pass abstract judgments on them, to see them not as generalisations, but as participants in the social struggle, defending concrete interests in it.

The spiritual experience of the October Revolution is assimilated by the heroes of *L'Ame Enchantée*, each in his own way, preparing them for conscious action. Marc is killed fighting the fascists, but the aim in life linking those who are blazing the trail to the future is not broken: this book, one of the finest accomplishments of twentieth century realism, contained a stern warning of the impending danger of fascism and a call to fight for freedom.

Without slackening his interest in the spiritual world of the individual or detracting from the study of the psychology of his characters, Rolland sets these characters in the mighty stream of time and examines man in his interaction with history, in their interdependence, thereby creating enlarged characters and generalising the essential forces of history in the figures of the main characters.

Through studying and analysing the state of his society, he reached the objective conclusion that it was bound to collapse and that the property owning order would be replaced by a socialist one. He regarded the struggle to establish justice in the world as man's highest duty.

A recognition of the need for joint struggle against social evil is also characteristic of the development of the heroes in Hemingway's works, written in the atmosphere of the gathering anti-fascist struggle and evincing clear anti-bourgeois tendencies. Social criticism in the novel *To Have and To Have Not* sprang from the realisation that the morality of the rich and the poor was diametrically opposed, that their social interests differed radically.

In order to portray the inner emptiness, moral corruption and blatant, egoistic cynicism of the rich, Hemingway uses condensed, satirical sketches of businessmen, wealthy ladies and their alcoholic husbands and lovers, people with cracked souls and dried-up hearts, whiling away their time on luxurious yachts in warm tropical seas. With merciless accuracy he reveals their innermost thoughts during sleepless nights when they are all alone and confronted by the meaninglessness of their existence. Using the moral criteria of the democratic consciousness, he created the satirical character of Richard Gordon, who prostitutes his talent in the service of bourgeois art, painting for the world of rich pleasure-seekers. Hemingway depicts with contempt the temptations of this world, which does not wish to know anything about what is happening in real life, where people are fighting and sweating to earn their daily bread. But in order to fight the world of the rich, the social order which makes possible the existence of parasitic classes feeding on other people's work, isolated individual effort is not enough, and it is by no means always applied in the right direction. Harry Morgan, a strong, brave man, whom Hemingway sets against the world of the rich, also lives by the savage laws of property owning society and, relying on himself alone, defending his private, personal interests alone, is inevitably and logically defeated in his fight against this society. Dying, he realises that a person can do nothing by himseľs. The father of the Joad family in Steinbeck's novel *The Grapes of Wrath* also came to the same conclusion. But this realisation could only become the initial and not the final stage in a person's development when he found an historically important aim in life. For the heroes of Hemingway's play *The Fifth Column* and novel *For Whom the Bell Tolls* this aim is the fight against fascism by the Spanish people, who were the first victims of fascist aggression.

Philip Rawlings, who works for the Republican security service makes his choice because he realises the danger of fascism to human freedom. He sees that one cannot remain neutral in the long and uncompromising struggle with social reaction that has begun, and therefore he rejects the temptations of the world of the rich and the opportunity of standing apart from the struggle. The play affirmed the idea of the need for people to join in the social struggle on the side of the forces defending freedom, human dignity and social progress. But Philip, although he sees participation in this struggle as his duty and risks his life continuously, does not identify himself fully with the social ideal which is to be confirmed as a result of the social struggle of our age. This was due to the inner contradiction in the author's development, typical of many other critical realist writers. Philip stoically accepts the need to join in the social struggle, and this stoic sense of duty distinguishes him from true revolutionaries who regard participation in the fight to reconstruct the world as a natural form of historical activity, however difficult it may be. The hero of the novel *For Whom the Bell Tolls*, Robert Jordan, also possesses stoic features.

The gloomy mood of *The Fifth Column* and this novel derives not only from the fact that the novel was written after the defeat of the Spanish Republic. It is also the result of the writer's social attitude. Although they recognise the need to join in the anti-fascist struggle and see this as their human duty, Hemingway's heroes do not think, in fact they try not to think, about the final aims of this struggle, namely, about what people should do after the defeat of fascism, how and on what basis social relations are to be built. They see before them only the immediate tasks dictated by the course of the struggle, and tackle these tasks bravely and honestly. But their reluctance to look ahead to the future gives them an aura of martyrdom.

Robert Jordan genuinely sympathises with the people, and Hemingway creates in the novel the monumental figure of the woman partisan Pilar who epitomises all that is best in the people—its bravery, commonsense, selflessness and great love of freedom. Robert trusts people like Pilar, which is only natural, but he is reserved with those who constitute the vanguard of the popular movement. He fights together with them against a common foe, but not for the same principles or the same ideals. Robert thinks that the aims of the Republican leaders and their political advisers and of the commanders of the international brigades do not correspond entirely to the aims pursued by him, a champion of the Lincolnian interpretation of democracy, a retrospective ideal, but one which he holds dear and in the name of which he lays down his life in the struggle against the enemy of freedom—fascism.

This inner discrepancy between the idea, upheld by Hemingway, of the Lincolnian type of democracy and the idea of socialism which was firmly established by the fighting people in the course of the Civil War, left its mark on his portrayal of the revolutionary camp, casting a somewhat false light on the revolutionaries depicted in the novel. Hemingway's constant feeling that Jordan was fighting for a hopeless ideal made Jordan a tragic character. But in spite of the writer's complex attitude to the historical situation portrayed in the novel, the need to fight is the dominant idea, which makes itself felt in both the reflections on death and the scenes showing the savage drama of the events and the people's heroism. The novel was essentially a call to resistance, as were the works of other critical realists who realised the need to defend humanism, culture and freedom by action.

In studying the phenomenon of fascism, the critical realists linked its emergence with the severe crisis in the capitalist system and hoped that the defeat of fascism would make for a better future for mankind which would be able to benefit from the terrible lessons of history. The crisis of the capitalist system was perceived by them in various aspects, not always in its directly social form. However their study and analysis of the manifestations of crisis invariably led them to social conclusions. Capitalism is, first and foremost, technical progress, declared the apologists of the property owning social system. Technical progress under capitalism means the enslavement and dehumanisation of man, the humanistically inclined critical realists replied. Immediately after the First World War Karel Čapek wrote his famous play *R.U.R.* (Rossum's Universal Robots), in which, anticipating, as it were, the fears expressed today in connection with the advance of cybernetics, he showed the human race being taken over by robots, the product of human genius.

Čapek endowed the robots with human features and qualities, while depriving them of human feelings, and the whole logic of the play was aimed at showing that by mechanising, unifying and standardising human beings, civilisation was bringing progress to a dead end, because it was replacing genuine human requirements and demands by false ones and destroying the humane feelings in man. Only the awakening feeling of love and compassion in robots, created entirely in man's image and likeness, prevents the thread of life from being broken forever, and the new Adam and Eve begin to create a new world on the ruins of the old one.

The writer's intense feeling for life enabled him to understand the important processes going on inside the capitalist system and to outline in the play, if not the means of solving the new conflicts—he was not in a condition to do that, because the contemplative nature of his humanistic views prevented him for a long time from turning to direct social action—at least the dangers presented by the one-sided, distorted technological progress in bourgeois society. In fact, many writers in our day who encounter phenomena characteristic of modern neo-capitalism and study the spiritual consequences of the one-sided development of "mass consumer society" are to a large extent developing the complex of ideas outlined in Čapek's play. Such is the case with Dürrenmatt in *Die Physiker*, for example, who draws attention to the danger to mankind of scientific discoveries used by the ruling class to suppress human freedom and creative thought, or with Max Frisch, who shows in his novel *Homo Faber* that the one-sided influence of technical progress dehumanises man, or with Max von der Grün, who in his novel *Irrlicht und Feuer* about West German working-class life describes the ways and means used by modern industry to turn the worker into a simple appendage to a machine with all the consequences that this implies—loss of individuality, of a conscious attitude towards life, and of class sense. But Čapek went further in his social analysis, showing that people who have been impoverished by bourgeois civilisation, restricted in their opportunities and desires, hardened by their struggle for existence, become easy prey for misanthropic ideology—national, chauvinist and fascist. The aggressive imperialist ideology prepared the spread of fascism by crushing and trampling on spiritual values, replacing them with a set of simplified ideas based on apologies for violence, national superiority, racial hatred, individualism and anti-communism. In his satirical utopian novel *War with the Newts* and the play *The White Disease* Čapek painted a gloomy picture, full of foreboding for the fate of mankind, about the growing fascist threat to the existence of human civilisation.

  Talking newts (it is easy to guess their historical prototypes from this broad image) who have mastered human technical skills, the art of using weapons, who are on the same intellectual level as people who read trashy and nationalistic newspapers full of jingoism, who have joined together in a disciplined army relying on a powerful industry run by trusts and cartels which they have set up in the World Ocean, who are led by a Führer that makes speeches which sound like fascist propaganda, who enjoy the support of arms dealers that supply them with weapons unbeknown to the rest of the population, who hire professional politicians to assist them—these talking newts invade the continents and lands destroying the human race. Using realistic allegory and grotesquely heightened characterisation, Čapek produced a satire on fascism, on the policy of compromise pursued on the eve of the Second World War by the bourgeois democrats in respect of fascist aggression. In *The White Disease* he also portrayed the tragedy and collapse of the hopes of the humanists, the champions of the democratic way of thinking, who were relying on preaching humane ideas to stop the spread of fascism. Doctor Galen, who possesses a secret cure for the white disease and who is torn to pieces by a crowd hysterical with nationalism, becomes a symbol of this way of thinking, which, as the writer was beginning to realise, lacked true effectiveness.

An open admission of the need for social action is found in Čapek's play *The Mother*, one of the finest works of modern critical realism. The inner drama and the atmosphere of foreboding, which pervade the play and give it its passion, reflected the tense historical conflicts and the anxiety prevailing in a world moving inexorably towards a devastating war. By depicting various people who sacrifice their lives in the name of action, as they understand it, Čapek not only criticises the philosophy of social neutrality. He himself believed for a long time that political action by no means always coincides with humanity since it inevitably implies the violation of someone's human rights: in acting, a person willy-nilly foists his own point of view, his own way of thinking, on another person. And in the play the Mother, that eternal symbol of all-forgiving humanity, at first tries to keep her sons away from action, although each of them goes his own way ignoring his mother's behest. But the Mother, like all her fellow-countrymen, is faced with making a choice in the hour of greatest danger for the fate of her native land, its culture, history and future—the choice of submitting and perishing or of fighting the cruel enemy to the bitter end.

With tremendous power Čapek shows the Mother's inner struggle, her dialogue with the dead who rise to join the ranks of the living in that terrible hour, her conversation, full of pain and love, with her dead sons and husband, who urge her to make the supreme sacrifice, to perform the sacred duty uniting supreme humanity with supreme courage—the duty of defending freedom. The figure of the Mother handing a rifle to her sole surviving son and giving him her blessing to join in the sacred struggle against the invaders marked the finest point in Čapek's writing and showed that at this time of great historical tribulation the progressive, democratically inclined critical realists were on the side of the people fighting fascism.

The Second World War which, after the entry of the Soviet Union, became an anti-fascist war of liberation, inspired great hopes for social changes that would transform the old world, the property owning society, after the peoples' victory. But not all these hopes were to be realised. The weakening of the whole capitalist system which took place after the end of the war revitalised political reaction in the developed capitalist countries and forced the ruling classes to mobilise their spiritual and economic forces in order to prevent capitalism from weakening further.

The propertied classes began transforming the patently obsolete forms of bourgeois democracy, adapting it to the new historical conditions. Terrified of the spread of socialist ideas, they began the "cold war", whipping up a war psychosis and anti-communist hysteria, and restricting the already considerably reduced democratic freedoms under the cover of a great deal of noisy propaganda about the communist threat. Many factors in the post-war social development of major capitalist countries had an unfavourable effect on the evolution of critical realism. On the other hand, the great liberating ideals which had inspired the peoples to fight fascism on the front-lines and in the resistance movement, the historical changes reverberating throughout the world, the universal growth in the power of socialism which had formed a world system, exerted a direct influence on the consciousness of the critical realists and their creative method. The complex historical situation in the post-war world, the web of contradictions making it difficult for the democratic consciousness to understand the movement of historical progress, could not obscure for the critical realists the polarisation of the forces of reaction and progress, and the question of choosing a path became not less, but more acute than before.

The threat to man, his freedom and spiritual development from the imperialist reaction and the excessively grown power of monopoly capital seizing key positions in the state machine, the danger of an atomic war, a fascist revival, and the restriction of democratic freedoms which hinders the struggle of the masses for their rights, made the critical realists more acutely aware of the social responsibility of the writer and literature. Thomas Mann, whose voice rang out loudly in the days of war, a writer who defended social humanism with all the force of his heart and talent, who had advanced to the realisation that only socialism is capable of putting mankind on the path of true historical creativity by unfettering people's ability to create, in his novel *Doctor Faustus* makes a radical reassessment of the spiritual values produced by the art and philosophy which defended the property owning society with all its diseases and defects, represented as virtues.

The writer deliberately chose the Faust theme in order to show how the late-capitalist society—which is how, Mann refers to modern capitalism—perverts man's creative ability, for the new Faust, the hero of his novel, Adrian Leverkühn, a brilliant composer, defends and proclaims the destructive forces in history and art.

Whereas Goethe's Faust found his raison d'être in serving the good of mankind, and whereas his character portrayed the boldness of human thought striving to understand the reason for living, Mann's new Faust hates reason, knowledge and faith in Man. He, too, creates, but his creation is full of disbelief, mockery and scepticism. This disharmony reflects fully his broken soul and the disharmony of the world, of which it is the mirror. Leverkühn's work shows the generic features of modern bourgeois society—abstraction and deliberate primitivism, nervy expressionism and inner soullessness, aristocratic contempt for the masses, withdrawal into a narrow circle of philosophical ideas, inflamed egocentrism and gloomy pessimism, spiced with apocalyptic foreboding and presentiments of universal disaster. His characteristic penchant for paradoxes, for combining the uncombinable, is a reflection of the relativity of spiritual values in bourgeois society. All ideas of good and evil are mixed up in Leverkühn's soul. The coldness radiated by Leverkühn and his art, his hatred for lofty, noble human feelings, are the result of his organic kinship with social evil.

Mann introduces the motif of temptation by the devil, an integral part of the Faust theme, thereby revealing the problem of choosing between the true and false historical path in all its acuteness. He shows the form which satanism and the barbarism lurking behind it take in modern history, by putting into the mouth of Serenus Zeitblom, Leverkühn's modest friend and biographer, an account of concentration camps and the unparalleled atrocities perpetrated by the fascists. The devil, who appears to Leverkühn and is in fact a hypostasis of his own personality, tempts Adrian, trying to make him renounce the concepts of goodness and humanity for ever in the name of creation and art and surrender to barbarism which will eventually gain control of all people. Leverkühn has a free choice, for he knows that wholesome art *is* possible in the modern world, but only if the artist links his destiny with the people, who are capable of changing the existing social relations and doing away with social evil. But in his arrogance he rejects this possibility, thus betraying once and for all the idea of freedom, and robbing people of the hope of triumph of goodness and nobility.

In the figure of Leverkühn the writer was squaring accounts with the reactionary traditions of German culture and ideology, which paved the way for fascist ideology. But the figure of the new Faust extends far beyond the national framework, for in sketching the social environment in which Leverkühn lived and developed, the writer stresses the destructive role of aestheticism and decadence, which advocate relativity of moral criteria, which extol violence and instinct, treating reason with contempt and rejecting the cognitive capacity of art. By its whole vast ideological content Mann's novel called for the rejection of the false, dangerous ideas of the past and a reexamination of the concepts on which the edifice of reactionary ideology rested, and urged literature to join in historical activity in the name of social humanism. This settling of old scores with the past and reassessment of many aesthetic and ideological principles became a typical feature of the development of critical realism in the post-war period. It was an essential process, because until the illusions of the past had been overcome it was impossible to defend and fight for man in the present.

Lion Feuchtwanger also reassessed his spiritual experience, renouncing his former view of history as the tragic balance of the forces of reason and barbarism and coming to the conclusion that history develops by overcoming the resistance of unreason and barbarism and that humanity moves unswervingly and inexorably forward.

He no longer saw individual bearers of reason as the motive force of historical change, but the masses of the people and those champions of progress who, together with the people and expressing its ideals and aspirations, fight against injustice and reaction. Historical progress became the true hero of his works written in the post-war years. In his novels on the period of the French bourgeois revolution, Feuchtwanger studied the decline of the old society and sought to show that justice, which develops according to the laws of wise and good necessity, will eventually triumph on earth, overcoming all the obstacles so generously put in its way. He also depicted people who defended justice—Benjamin Franklin, Jean-Jacques Rousseau and Francisco Goya.

In the old carefree society, which thinks of nothing but court intrigues, frivolous pastimes and fashionable entertainments, closing its eyes to the ominous signs of its approaching downfall, Benjamin Franklin, the envoy to the French court of the insurgent English colonies in America, fights for democracy, well aware of the defects and weaknesses of this society and understanding the limits of his fellow-countrymen's love of freedom. He skilfully influences the course of events, steering them forward, and obtaining more results than Beaumarchais, who is carried away by the excitement of politics and goes from one daring plan to the next, keeping his head above water only thanks to the stamina which he inherited as a true son of the third estate.

Unlike Beaumarchais, Franklin is not a supporter of direct political action. He is closer to the spirit of the Encyclopaedia, that is, the spirit of education, the careful cultivation of humanity in man. The old idea of the incompatibility of the humanist principle and revolutionary action, in a very muted form since Franklin does not reject revolutionary action in principle, runs through Feuchtwanger's later novels, showing how strong liberal-democratic illusions still are in critical realism. And the figure of Rousseau—the spiritual father of the Jacobins, attracted the writer primarily because Rousseau fought against the cold rationalism of the Enlightenment, advocating the poetry of human feelings, their complexity, illogicality, capacity for compassion, their great educative role.

The Montagnards school adopted only the critical, destructive aspect of Rousseau's teaching, his fierce rejection of the inhumanity of civilisation and the inequality of the estates. Feuchtwanger recognises that the Jacobins were historically in the right, and gets as far as understanding that great changes can be brought about only by the masses, but his inner sympathy is for Rousseau, the author of *Emile*, the book which urged the moral education of man as a means of rebuilding society.

The complexity of Feuchtwanger's spiritual development is most clearly reflected in his novel about Goya which is sub-titled *The Hard Path to Knowledge*. The brilliant artist, who is portrayed by Feuchtwanger with great affection and care, stood alone against savage reaction, which was striving to nip every freedom-loving idea in the bud and to preserve the moribund power of the monarchy, church and inquisition. He gazed avidly at the face of monstrous, cruel and stupid violence and fought it with the strength of his art, producing true, unvarnished pictures of the world in which he lived and which he hated. Goya listened carefully to the advice of his friends—the Spanish radicals and free-thinkers, who supported the French revolution. He knew that there was truth in their words. But he went his own way, realising that the strength of art is in its commitment to the people. This idea was the highest peak of Feuchtwanger's spiritual development. His Goya believed that painting which conveys the truth is capable of changing the minds and hearts of one's fellow-men. It was possible that these changes would take place more slowly than his radical friends thought, but come about they would, because the content of his work fitted in with the inexorable movement of history.

In spite of all the inner doubts in Feuchtwanger's later works, they clearly contain an idea which is characteristic of critical realism and which connects the writer's novels about the past with the pressing, acute problems of contemporary history. Feuchtwanger began to regard the present period as a turning point. The vast, painful and difficult process of replacing the declining, property owning civilisation by new social relations has begun, and man cannot stand aside from this all-embracing process, without defining his attitude to it, to the opposing social forces, to the traditions and established practices and principles of a society which history has condemned.

This thought, by no means always a conscious one, runs through many of the works of modern critical realism.

In the final parts of his tetrology *La Famille Boussardel* Philippe Heriat portrays the decline of bourgeois family traditions, the polarisation of the forces in the bourgeois camp, the break-up of the unity of its class consciousness, and the collapse of the social foundations on which the bourgeois clans rested, united by common economic and political interests.

Whereas the most conservative section of the Boussardel family clings tightly to family traditions, to the social structure and order which is capable of preserving these traditions and protecting the financial interests of the Boussardels, and therefore secretly sympathises with the collaborators, seeing them as the mainstay of that order in the troubled days of the German occupation, Agnès who breaks with the Boussardel way of thinking manages to free herself from the suffocating authority of family traditions. (Agnès's conflict with her family is shown in the second part of the tetrology, the novel entitled *Les enfants gâtés*, written before the war.)

When national tragedy befalls France, Agnès decides to join the Resistance (the novel *Les grilles d'or).* This does not mean that she shares the ideals and aspirations which were maturing inside the resistance movement. But she is drawn towards the new social forces operating in the arena of history, and respects the people who have taken arms to defend freedom. The new social ideas with which Agnès has come into contact enable her to adopt a critical attitude towards the efforts to preserve economic and, consequently, political power, which the bourgeoisie make in the post-war period relying on American support.

In Heriat's cycle of novels—which are uneven from the literary point of view—one senses the attempt to reconsider, to reassess the recent past, to find in it the sources of the mistakes and errors which have to be paid for today. Altogether, modern critical realist writers frequently turn to the recent past, leafing through the pages over and over again, as it were, in order to learn a lesson from history.

Studying human destinies and the human personality in the context of and in connection with real historical events, critical realists show how people become aware of the treachery of the ruling classes, who collaborated with the fascist aggression and who were responsible for the suffering inflicted on the masses of the people. This idea of the responsibility of the ruling classes begins to penetrate the consciousness of the heroes of Armand Lanoux's novel *Le commandant Watrin*, a young intellectual called Lieutenant Subeyrac and an old personnel officer—Major Watrin. Taught by their bitter experience of the "strange war" and of POW camp, they begin to understand that it is essential to get rid not only of fascism which is their immediate enemy, but of that which engenders fascism. With tremendous difficulty, feeling their way in the dark, as the writer puts it, they advance towards a new understanding of the world. Formerly they had lived in a world of illusions, false ideas about politics and the motives behind human activity, illusions which prevented them from seeing society as it really is.

A reassessment of the past began to determine the social content of C. P. Snow's sequence of novels *Strangers and Brothers* in which he presents a broad, psychologically authentic picture of life in English society over the last thirty years. Snow studies and depicts various social strata in present-day England—its ruling classes, intellectuals, university dons, civil servants and petty bourgeoisie—showing the vacillating views of English intellectuals, the struggle of various ideological trends within the ruling classes, the emergence of hope of rebuilding society by the forces of bourgeois democracy, the gradual embracing by English intellectuals of modern, not

Fabian, socialism—views which, incidentally, are most confused and imprecise—and the awakening fear of the ruling classes for the fate of society as a whole.

Snow is critical of the social practices of the English ruling classes, because he realises that they support the forces of social reaction both inside and outside England. In his novels he shows how the best, most progressively inclined people begin to understand that they can no longer remain "on the other side", that is, in the camp of social reaction, and must look for new ways and means of solving the social conflicts in which our age abounds, for the path which bourgeois society has followed up to now is liable to plunge mankind into an atomic war. This idea was expressed most clearly in the novel *The New Men*, which describes how, after Hiroshima, atomic scientists realise their terrible responsibility before the rest of mankind. They begin to see it as their personal and civic duty to struggle against the atomic danger and social reaction which uses the atom bomb in the fight against freedom. Snow's novels, which do not always show a true and sufficiently profound understanding of the social contradictions in the modern world, nevertheless pose the question of man's responsibility for what is happening and the need for people to take part in solving the basic historical conflicts, to fight for social progress and human dignity against all forms of social reaction.

Returning to the past enabled the critical realists to depict the maturing of socialist and communist consciousness in the best representatives of the people. By studying this process, which formed the nucleus of the Resistance, they transcended the limits of the critical realist method. Thus Cesare Pavese in *Il compagno* portrays a man who becomes actively interested in social problems.

Pablo, the hero of *Il compagno*, who is at first preoccupied with the petty everyday affairs of the ordinary man in the street, could have continued to lead this empty life, dividing his time between drinking-bouts and brief liaisons, drifting through life like many of his fellows. However, certain happenings, which would not appear to be very remarkable, compel him to reflect upon human relationships. He sees how the shrewd businessman and entrepreneur Lubrani is flourishing and how the chase after the good things in life destroys his beloved Linda, he meets people who are dissatisfied with the world as it is and reads illegal literature which opens his eyes to a great deal. His spiritual and political development is completed after his meeting with an Italian Communist who fought in the Spanish Civil War. Now there is no going back for Pablo. He can only go forward, enriching his soul and mind with a new understanding of reality and human responsibility and becoming an ideological opponent of capitalism.

Pavese immersed his hero in the stream of ordinary life, the element of the everyday, and, although the narration in *Il compagno* is written in the first person and is basically a monologue by Pablo, his psychology and inner world are revealed through actions and assessments of the people whom he meets and with whom he forms various types of relationships—friendly or hostile. This type of artistic objectivism, in which the writer's moral attitude to what is described is perfectly clear, is typical not only of Pavese, but of other important Italian realists, such as Alberto Moravia.

The spirit of social protest which is awakening in Pablo must surely bring him into the ranks of the Resistance fighters, just as the spirit of struggle and social protest radiated by the Resistance itself had a great influence on the development of the realist method in Italian literature, in particular, on Italian neorealism, which was characterised by close attention to the everyday life of ordinary people, their daily needs and worries.

Neorealist writing, beginning with Elio Vittorini's novel *Uomini e no,* sharply, unambiguously and openly rejected and criticised the past, with the fascist dictatorship, the demagogy of the fascist ideologists and the sufferings of the people, with its rotten regime gilded over by semi-official art, art that was rhetorical, bombastic and false.

Equally unambiguously neorealism criticised the social reality of post-war Italy, where the ruling classes, having united the forces of the industrial monopolies, agrarian circles and the Catholic Church under the aegis of Anglo-

American capital, were pursuing an anti-popular policy, striving to weaken the growing influence of communist ideas on the consciousness of the masses and prevent the workers from uniting.

Therefore, in settling scores with the past, the Italian critical realists—Moravia, Calvino, Levi, Venturi, Cassola, Bassani, Montella, and others—were thinking about the present. They studied the contemporary life of the people carefully, depicting the important contradictions of social development and those processes which were influencing, either directly or indirectly, man's position in society. Their field of vision, their sphere of portrayal, included the complex, dynamic life of workers and fishermen, former soldiers in the Italian army, peasants and hired farm labourers, fighting against the power of the estate owners and the mafia, clerks, commercial travellers, trattoria owners, small businessmen, etc. They analysed the social conflicts influencing the lives of their heroes who defended democratic rights in class battles, in skirmishes with reaction and neofascism, and in strikes. At the same time they traced how new social sections of the population were drawn into social activity. They perceived the appearance of new forms of exploitation to which the bourgeoisie began to resort, and also the emergence of new methods of industrial production and their influence on people's psychology and social consciousness.

New themes invariably leave their mark on art, both on its form and content. Neorealism, in portraying postwar reality, stressed the documental nature, the authenticity of what was being depicted, and therefore neorealist works presented a kind of lyrical document of the times, preserving and conveying the personal experience of the author. The lyrical element in neorealist works supposed to compensate for the obvious insufficiency of psychological analysis, which was common to works created in accordance with the principles of neorealist poetics.

Psychological analysis gave way in them to the portrayal of situation. But the characterisation of the hero was socially very precise, for by preserving the documentary element, the proximity to real life, the neorealists, as is the case with realism in general, examined a man's personality as part of the stream of life and the social processes taking place in it.

Democratic in its nature and origin, the art of the neorealists showed a sincere love of man and defended human dignity. But frequently, alongside people who had fought in the Resistance, they chose for their hero the "little man" who bears his life's burden with courage and determination, but is incapable of changing his fate, which often dooms him to deprivations and adversity produced, and the neorealists stress this, by social causes. The hero is not always aware of his position and not always capable of rising to social action. He frequently tries to solve his problems as a *private person.* This is why the universal themes of love, death, parting, friendship, and family unity occupy such an important place in neorealist works.

Neorealism reflected only one definite stage in the spiritual development of literature and the people and was linked with the awakening of democratic hopes, the spreading of democratic consciousness in a country which had experienced both a fascist dictatorship and the struggle against fascism by the nation's best forces. But when the social situation changed, when the social contradictions of capitalism grew more acute, although this was concealed behind the façade of the economic rearmament of Italian capitalism, which was out to create the so-called "society of mass consumption", the limits of neorealist lyrical-documentary prose came to the fore and by no means all its aesthetic principles and devices were used or could be used by critical realism, which had gone over to an analysis and study of the new social processes and phenomena. The analytically objective prose of Moravia, who sees man as the product of social conditions with which he has complex, mainly antagonistic relationships, the fairy-tale, poetic fantasies of Calvino, and the ironic narrative art of Montella which has its roots in the Gogol tradition and is full of compassion for all the "little men" of the modern world, as well as the literary quests of other critical realists did not fit into the framework of neorealism.

But while departing from the principles of neorealist poetics, Italian critical realism retains a constant interest in the social themes opened up by neorealism, and the spirit of criticism fostered by the Resistance and the subsequent struggle of the people for democratic rights and peace against the threat of a new war and against imperialist reaction.

At the same time, some critical realists, not only Italians, in returning to the period of the Resistance began to lay stress on the fact that the hopes and ideals of the Resistance have not been realised regarding it as a great historical misfortune. In portraying the tragic fates of members of the Resistance for whom modern bourgeois society closes all doors and whom it deprives of the rights which they won in open battle arms-in-hand, the critical realists condemn the modern bourgeoisie, which encourages or overlooks the activities of neofascist organisations and persecutes the members of the Resistance, the noble sons of the people.

Armand Lanoux in his novel *Le Rendez-vous de Bruges* showed how people who had fought in the maquis and remained true to the ideals of the Resistance could not find a place in the bourgeois world. The heroes of this novel, both Robert Drouin and the doctor Olivier Du Roy, are in headlong collision with the society in which they are compelled to live, and this rift runs through the whole of their being, affecting family feelings as well, for both of them continue to remain loyal to the moral and political criteria which they imbued in the years of the Resistance. Du Roy becomes a doctor at a mental hospital, and the figures of the patients symbolise the madness gaining an ever greater hold on the modern bourgeois world, where war and anti-communist psychoses and maniacal suspicion are being whipped up and people with different beliefs are persecuted. Pierre de Lescure showed how the ideals of the Resistance are being betrayed in his novel *La saison des consciences*, by creating the character of the spiritually degraded writer Conscience, who was once a member of the Resistance, but is now renouncing the past like a coward.

But much more serious for the fate of critical realism, for the moral and ethic criteria which guided its democratically inclined exponents, were the attempts to oppose the humanistic aspect of the Resistance to its revolutionary, active side, or at least to separate them, as in Carlo Cassola's novel *La ragazza di Bube,* in which a shade of moral guilt still attaches to Bube, a Resistance fighter who is now being victimised by bourgeois justice. This guilt is not absolved by the moral purity of Bube's initial motives, the moral fortitude of his bride Mara, a figure of considerable stature and content who embodies the positive aspects of the people's character. Such an approach to assessing the past testifies to the spiritual vacillations of the author, which reflected the confusion caused in the minds of his contemporaries by the complications of modern social reality. At the same time high social and ethical criteria of assessing reality enabled modern critical realists to record the turning of capitalist society to reaction, the strengthening of conservation tendencies in the social practices of the bourgeoisie and in the bourgeois consciousness, which gave rise to "witch-hunting", savage attacks on progressive ideas, the unleashing of anti-communism and racialism, and the support of neofascism. Lion Feuchtwanger's play *Wahn oder der Teufel in Boston* and Arthur Miller's *The Crucible* about the 17th-century trials of witches in Boston and Salem, studied and condemned the spiritual and political fanaticism which, in our time, has become fertile soil for ideological and political obscurantism, the controlling of people's minds, the suppression of personal freedom, and the rebirth of fascism. Graham Greene's satirical novels *The Quiet American* and *Our Man in Havana* exposed the corrupt, inhuman, insane logic of the instigators of the "cold war" who carried out their evil deeds blustering loudly about defending the sacred principles of Democracy, which in practice meant undeclared wars, napalm bombing of peaceful towns and villages, crushing popular movements, supporting reactionary and dictatorial regimes, conspiratorial activity, "cloak and dagger" politics, sabotage, terrorist acts, bribery and blackmail. By showing the perfidious behind-the-scenes activity of the "quiet American" Pyle, convinced of the superiority of the American way of life, and by describing the peripeteia of the cruel secret war as seen by Wormold, an ordinary person who never had anything to do with politics before, Graham Greene poses the problem of choice, a fundamental one for critical realism: "...sooner or later one has to take sides. If one is to remain human".

Remaining human means, first and foremost, fighting against all types and forms of social reaction. For the humanistically inclined West German writers one of the most important themes now is exposure of the "indeterminate past", namely, the struggle against nazi in the FRG. Wolfgang Koeppen's novels *Tauben im Gras, Das Treibhaus* and *Der Tod in Rom* show the collapse in West Germany of democratic illusions, of the hopes for a genuine democratic rebirth of a country which suffered military defeat, but did not have a resistance movement of the same scale and importance as in European countries occupied by nazi Germany.

In the country of the "economic miracle" the commanding heights are again being occupied by people like the SS General Judejahn *(Der Tod in Rom)* for whom nothing in the past is forgotten or renounced. Koeppen is a typical example of the cowardly compromising West German politicians, who conceal behind profuse talk of democracy their capitulation to the forces of reaction and revanchism, rearing their ugly heads in West Germany. Turning to the lessons of the past, Heinrich Böll in the novels *Wo warst Du, Adam?*, *Und sagte kein einziges Wort* and *Haus ohne Hüter* and in his short stories showed that the defeat of Hitler's army in the last war and the historical collapse of German militarism were inevitable. In his early works he portrayed the ordinary German soldier as both the bearer of evil and its victim. The essence and meaning of the war were not properly revealed yet—he saw it as an evil which destroys the souls of people dressed in soldier's uniform and turns them into murderers. Böll, however, avoided the tendency which was present, for example, in Hans Werner Richter's novel *Die Geschlagenen* or in Hans Helmut Kirst's trilogy *08/15* which criticised fascism and the Gestapo, military drilling, and the stupefying atmosphere of the barracks, but not the ordinary soldier. Richter shows how the soldiers in Hitler's army who were defeated in Italy and put into American prisoner-of-war camps fought against the fascists who had established their authority secretly in the camp, but he also shows how the soldiers in Hitler's army nobly did their duty on the battlefields. It never occurred either to Richter or to Kirst to wonder whether this duty indeed consisted in fighting to the last bullet and not in turning their bayonets against the fascists.

Böll is aware of this question and shows that ordinary soldiers also bear responsibility for the crimes of fascism, because they took part in the mass murder of people and were not only victims of the war. He traces the direct and indirect influence of the war on the popular consciousness, the collapse of family and marital relationships, the spiritual impoverishment of the younger generation which grew up to the wailing of air-raid warnings, received its education on the black market, and witnessed the moral corruption of the adults, the naked exposure of human relations and the unleashing of human egoism. Böll depicts the rebirth of revanchist forces striving to turn the clock back and reimpose on the German people an aggressive nationalist and militarist ideology. He leads the readers to the realisation of the need to struggle against political reaction. He considers, as did Günther Weisenborn (in his novel *Der Verfolger*), that the best way of fighting the rebirth of revanchism, neo-nazi ideology and militarism is to activise the progressive elements in society. Consequently he does not urge his heroes, as did Ulrich Becher, for example, in his novel *Kurz nach 4* or Alfred Andersch in the novel *Die Rote*, mete out personal vengeance on fascists whose conscience is burdened with bestial crimes. By satisfying their feeling of personal hatred, the heroes of these novels did nothing to help the struggle against fascism. Concentration on this type of individual struggle reflected the writers' lack of faith in the possibility of society withstanding the neo-fascist danger.

In fighting the "indeterminate past", the West German critical realists showed that with opportunist West German bourgeois democracy closing its eyes to the past of nazi criminals, the latter easily escape from responsibility, adjusting themselves to the new political conditions. Thus

Paul Verlaine Sondermann takes on the guise of a convinced democrat, in Paul Schallück's novel *Engelbert Reineke*, which shows how the neo-fascist spirit is penetrating West German schools. In this novel the writer seeks to combat the attempts by the reaction to seduce and poison West German youth with only slightly refurbished neo-nazi ideas. Thomas Valentin deals with the same subject in his novel *Die Unberatenen*.

The field of vision of the critical realists began to include the various aspects of the so-called "economic miracle", a satirical picture of which was given by Richter in his novel *Linus Fleck oder der Verlust der Würde*, where the writer showed fairly consistently and convincingly that there is not, nor ever has been, any real democracy in West Germany, that all talk about democracy and calls to follow its path were so much veneer concealing the avaricious machinations of the capitalists.

The economic boom produced unscrupulous businessmen, the founders and creators of huge enterprises and fortunes, such as Siegrid Merck who, with the help of the Americans, becomes the owner of a cinema network and the head of a film company, carrying on the profitable business of corrupting the people's minds by supplying pro-war films.

The hero of the novel, Linus Fleck, an unprincipled scoundrel, is also out to get rich, and his career enables the writer to show the corruptness of cheap journalism, cinema and other branches of the cultural industry. However Richter's novel, like Dieter Lattmann's *Ein Mann mit Familie*, contains only a partial criticism of the bourgeois system. The same can also be said of Günther Grass' *Hundejahre*, a satire which aims at studying and depicting the basic problems in German life over the last thirty years. The novel does not contain a synthetic analysis of reality, because Grass has not succeeded in discovering the initial causes of the main historical events—the causes of the emergence of fascism and the war which brought Germany to national catastrophe. Broader social criticism is to be found in Böll's later novels *Billiard um halb zehn* and *Ansichten eines Clowns*, in which many aspects of life in Bonn Germany, the intrigues of political and church reaction, uniting and cementing the bourgeois camp, are criticised, ridiculed and morally condemned. Hans Schnier, a professional clown and the son of a rich Rhenish factory-owner, breaks with his family and at the same time severs all spiritual ties with bourgeois society, in which he feels an outcast and an alien. He makes his choice and finds himself outside the society. But where and with whom this lonely seeker for the truth will end up is a more difficult question to answer, because Böll, like the other West German critical realists lacks a positive social programme. Their programmes either boil down to supporting Social Democratic ideology, as in the case of Günther Grass and Richter, or take the form of ethical criticism of capitalism from the abstract humanistic viewpoint. This blurred social ideal, characteristic of many modern critical realist writers, weakens their criticism of reality. This is borne out, in particular, by the work of the "angry young men" who in their time launched a bitter attack on individual aspects of modern English life.

Jimmy Dixon, a young university postgraduate student, the hero of Kingsley Amis' *Lucky Jim*, who embarks on life with hopes of realising his abilities, however modest they may be, comes up against the extreme mediocrity and monotony of the existence to which he is doomed and rebels against it. But all that Jimmy's rebellion consists of is ridiculing and poking fun at this environment, and self-mockery. Criticism also runs through the novels of John Wain. However, while ridiculing the spiritual bankruptcy of the modern bourgeoisie, despising its intellectual poverty and showing the absence of any prospect of a meaningful, creative life for their heroes, the "angry young men" had nothing to oppose to the society which they hated, except their own anger which, however, did not encourage them to take conscious social action.

The most scathing attack on bourgeois England was delivered by Jimmy Porter, the hero of John Osborne's play *Look Back in Anger.* His unnatural cynicism, his sharp, sarcastic invective against the conservative thinking of the bourgeois conceals a thirst for a meaningful life, instead of which he is doomed to a dull, humdrum existence, quarrels with his silly and submissive wife, full of middle-class prejudices, all-consuming discontent and dissatisfaction with himself and his own anger.

Jimmy Porter possesses nothing except his anger and does not know what can be built on the ruins of the social edifice which he longs to destroy.

The absence of any constructive social ideas in the "angry young men" impoverished their art and weakened the criticism in their works, which became a noteworthy episode, but only an episode, in the development of modern critical realism.

It must be said, however, that in its search for a true historical perspective modern critical realism in the highly developed capitalist countries is encountering a number of objective difficulties produced by structural changes in capitalism itself and the fact that the class contradictions in bourgeois society are beginning to appear in different forms than in the recent past and do not invariably and immediately reveal themselves as the expression of the basic contradiction of capitalism, that between the social nature of production and the private method of appropriation.

"Reality today is more abstract than in the past," said the well-known Italian writer Guido Piovene in his speech at a Leningrad symposium on the novel.

The scientific and technological revolution taking place in the world today, the tremendous development of industry accelerated by advances in automation and cybernetics and by economic programming has brought about changes in the sphere of production, the creation of new forms and types of mass consumption and the spread of new and more effective means of communication. The transformation of bourgeois democracy, the significant increase in the number of social organisations—trade-union, religious, cultural and so on—by creating the illusion of spreading democratic freedoms, has a most serious effect on the democratic consciousness and, as a rule, disorientates it, by instilling illusory hopes of solving social problems.

The progressive fusion of monopoly capital and the state, of the monopoly machine with the state machine, makes it possible to conceal both the exploitative nature of the bourgeois state and the intensification of direct and indirect exploitation of the working people by the monopolies. The concessions that the monopolies have been compelled to make to the workers have raised the average level of personal consumption which in turn was bound to affect their class consciousness. At the same time, in order to maintain the level of consumption reached, the workers have to carry on strike action, which is assuming ever greater proportions and acuteness. Protest also spreads against the dehumanisation of man by modern capitalism and modern production methods, which deprive man of an active role in labour and reduce him to the level of an accessory to a machine or system of machines. The masses are becoming increasingly alarmed about the fate of the world, seeing the aggressiveness of ruling anti-socialist circles and the growing threat of war.

Modern literature and art are faced with a complex reality, fraught with terrible cataclysms and convulsions. It can be understood, analysed and reflected really deeply only by an art which remains true to realism as its creative method. The non-realist trends in modern art are incapable of coping with this task.

Critical realism, which is continuing to develop and enrich its aesthetic properties in the modern age, has reflected and generalised the social processes which affirm the fundamental fact of modern history—the replacement of one social formation by another based on socialist principles. In portraying the life of modern society and analysing the relationship of the individual and society in the new historical situation, critical realism has shown that the conditions for liquidating alienation and its consequences are now maturing in society. In this respect critical realism is acting as the ally of socialist realism. The accomplishments of critical realism are based on the analysis, artistic study and understanding of reality, on the portrayal of man in concrete connections with the social environment in which he lives and acts.

Modern realism makes extensive use of the various means of artistic expression—montage, inner monologue, both direct and indirect, time shifts in the narrative, flashbacks breaking into the action, parallel subject lines within the main plot, and symbolic characterisation. Alongside these relatively new means and devices of narrative art, the realist tradition of the nineteenth century continues to develop, with a consistently chronological movement of the plot and a comprehensive description of the characters, scene of action, circumstances and environment.

All these various literary devices and means fit perfectly well into the aesthetics of realism if they contribute to the artistic comprehension of the world. For realism begins at the point when the movement of the plot and the development of the characters are the fruit of the writer's study of reality, of the relationship of the individual with society and of the social life of people in its genuine contradictions.

Realist literature—and this constitutes its greatness, the guarantee of its development, and its shining future—has shown man's progress along the paths of history, his realisation of his own role as the maker of history, as its demiurge, as an active principle of intellectual and social progress.

Man in the greatness of his deeds and sufferings, in the fullness and complexity of his spiritual manifestations, his possibilities, his will to create—this is the true subject of realist literature. Man liberating himself from the fetters of captivity, injustice, and exploitation, to achieve real freedom—this is the hero to whom the future belongs.